THE FIRST NAIPAUL WORLD EPICS

ABOUT THE SERIES

V. S. Naipaul is one of the most compelling writers of the twentieth and early twenty-first centuries. From the publication of his first book in 1957 to the last in 2010, his works have provoked a vast quantity of contradictory critical literature that raises the writer to the status of an enigma and produces a critical quagmire that few neophytes can easily navigate. This series intends to make navigation easier by generating and collecting the most pertinent essays representative of the dominant trends in the critical literature and providing overviews of each. Each of the first set of books will focus on Naipaul's oeuvre in sets of seven in the chronological order of their publication. Additional single-author volumes on major issues and ideas illuminated in Naipaul's writing will complement the essay collections. In this way, the series aims to make the enigmatic qualities readable and allow for an appreciation of the relevance and pertinence of V. S. Naipaul's oeuvre to burning contemporary issues.

THE FIRST NAIPAUL WORLD EPICS

From The Mystic Masseur *to* An Area of Darkness *and Beyond*

Edited by

J. Vijay Maharaj

B L O O M S B U R Y

NEW DELHI • LONDON • OXFORD • NEW YORK • SYDNEY

BLOOMSBURY INDIA
Bloomsbury Publishing India Pvt. Ltd
Second Floor, LSC Building No. 4, DDA Complex, Pocket C – 6 & 7,
Vasant Kunj, New Delhi, 110070

BLOOMSBURY, BLOOMSBURY ACADEMIC INDIA and the Diana logo
are trademarks of Bloomsbury Publishing Plc

First published in India 2021
This edition published 2021

Bloomsbury Academic
An imprint of Bloomsbury Publishing Plc

ISBN: HB: 978-93-90358-34-2; eBook: 978-93-90358-50-2
2 4 6 8 10 9 7 5 3 1

Typeset in Manipal Technologies Limited
Printed and bound in India by Replika Press Pvt. Ltd.

CONTENTS

EDITOR'S PREFACE

V. S. Naipaul's writing is embroiled in critical traditions that began in 1957 with the publication of his first novel, which continue to this day. In this series, we seek to disentangle some of the strands of the criticism in so far as the limits of each singular monograph will allow. The process begins by calling for and collecting recent samples of the paradigmatic critical literature on each of his works into single volumes. The first volume is self-explanatorily entitled *The First Naipaul World Epics: From The Mystic Masseur to An Area of Darkness and Beyond*. The series editor looks forward to receiving proposals for the subsequent three volumes that do a similar job of pulling together representative strands of the critical literature on seven books. In tandem with these four books, proposals for other monographs that engage thematically or otherwise with Naipaul's oeuvre as a whole are invited.

ACKNOWLEDGEMENTS

Needless to say, this book, like any other, would not exist without the support and encouragement of a great many people. Among those to whom it is indebted, I must first single out Mr Chandra Sekhar of Bloomsbury India. Until I came to know Mr Sekhar, I had relegated the idea of an inspiring motivational book editor to the regions of urban legend. I was so sure such a person did not exist. Mr Sekhar proved me wrong and his support and encouragement have been invaluable to the publication of this first book in the intended series of books on the compelling enigma of V. S. Naipaul.

Secondly, I wish to express my deepest gratitude to all the contributors to the volume for their interest in the work and their patience in waiting to be told whether their work could finally be accommodated or not. I, therefore, must thank not only those whose works have been included but more particularly those whose essays could not be, despite the fact that they were very fine essays and stories. Indeed, I hope that in the ongoing development of the series, these contributors will consider re-submitting their work for inclusion in subsequent volumes.

I must also gratefully acknowledge the many journals which unhesitatingly gave us permission for republication and to the authors as well, who sought and received permission and then reworked their essays to bring them up to date for publication in this book. Thanks are due to the management of the following journals: *Journal of Romanian Literary Studies* (2015), *Tout Moun: A Caribbean Cultural Studies Journal* (2019), *The Arts Journal* (2018), *Anthurium: A Caribbean Studies Journal* (2005), *JNT: Journal of Narrative Theory* (2016), *Twentieth-Century Literature* (2010); *Journal des Africanistes* (2010); *International Journal of Applied Linguistics & English Literature* (2014), *Modern Fiction Studies* (1984), *Literator* (2014) *Modern Language Quarterly* (2012) and *Sabaragamuwa University* Journal, vol. 14, no. 1, May 2015. Deepest thanks also to Professor Gordon Rohlehr personally for allowing his seminal essay which has been published in many collections to be republished here and to Ian Randle for permission to republish chapter three of Dr Bhoe Tewarie's book *V. S. Naipaul Revisited: Ethnicity, Marginality and the Triumph of Individual Will* (2007).

Finally, four important sources of support must be acknowledged. Firstly, the Campus Research and Publication Fund of the University of the West Indies St Augustine (UWI StA) must be recognised, with deep gratitude for the foresight of the then director, Professor Patricia

Mohammed. Professor Mohammed also kindly agreed to serve on the advisory board of the linesoflifenaipaul.com project out of which this book has emerged. The contributors to the volume who also serve on the board, Dr Weiwei Xu and Professor Sanjay Krishnan, must also be singled out for their encouraging support of the project and the book.

Deepest thanks must also be given to Dr Bhoe Tewarie who contributed his own work and pictures from his personal collection and film projects for the covers of the books in the series. He must be thanked too for agreeing to allow one of his films to be hosted on the project site and for always being ready with an encouraging email and attendance at our various events because of his appreciation for the value of the work of the Naipaul family—globally, regionally and nationally. Last, but by no means least, heartfelt thanks are due to the members of the non-governmental organisation (NGO) Friends of Mr Biswas and, in particular, to Chairman Professor Emeritus Kenneth Ramchand. The work of the organisation, including the promotion of local literature and preservation of local literary accomplishments, informs the Naipaul series as well as the linesoflifenaipaul website.

Of course, it goes without saying that without the support of my own family, nothing I do would be possible at all and I literally have no words to express the thanks that are their due.

Introduction

V. S. NAIPAUL'S WRITING: A CASE OF LITERATURE UNDOUBTEDLY TRANSFORMING OUR LIVES

J. Vijay Maharaj

Most people know the name regardless of the form in which it is iterated: Sir Vidia, Vido, Vidiadhar Surajprasad Naipaul or more often V. S. Naipaul, even if they have not read anything written by him. The name has indeed acquired mythic proportions and it connotes, to use Jessica A. Sequeira's term, "a literary institution" (*Harvard Crimson*). Along with him, the places about which he wrote—a vast swathe of global territory—have been similarly magnified. The books that achieved these phenomena can now be considered world epics along Virgilian and Homeric lines, albeit ones which began appearing on shelves only in 1957.

Over almost sixty years, between 1957 and his death in 2018, he produced over thirty. They brought him numerous awards, including the Booker, a knighthood and the Nobel Prize for Literature. Each book was unique. Everyone was related to the other. All had an impact on people everywhere from all walks of life but more so on a range of contemporary workers in the fine arts. One of the outcomes is an immense body of formal and informal critical and appreciative literature on the man and his work and, as a consequence, a body of insightful literature on the world in which we live today.

As the selection of essays in this book amply demonstrates, this material is indeed proof that many aspects of Naipaul's works have now achieved the status of hyper-interpretability and omni-significance. By this, I mean that, often, depending on who is reading, the work can elicit an extremely wide range of reflections. The work may be, and often is, read in relation to Naipaul's personal life or, in a closely related manner, it may be read through the lens of psychoanalysis. It can be read for sociocultural or alternatively anthropological truths, or it can be condemned as pandering to imperial dreams. The iteration of opposite ends of a continuum on any given perspective or theoretical approach can itself amount to a book-length list. Moreover, in the Caribbean where people are not too willing to suspend disbelief and demand an often not quite definable authenticity, multiple interpretations are even more common with some preferring to look into the omni-significance of his representations, which, as the *Oxford English Dictionary* defines it, still connotes universal meaning.

When he died on 11 August 2018, expressions of grief and reflections on his life also provided abundant evidence of omni-significance. In Trinidad and Tobago, the land of his birth, along with similar expressions in daily news forums, two memorials were held through the efforts of the NGO, Friends of Mr Biswas. The first, at the University of the West Indies St Augustine (UWI StA), called "Celebrating His Life, Mourning His Passing", was held on his birthday, 17 August 2018. The second, primarily for family and an act of love by his niece Shalini Aleong, the daughter of his older sister Kamla, was held the next day at the eponymous house of *A House for Mr Biswas* which is managed by Friends of Mr Biswas. This was hosted by the chairman of Friends of Mr Biswas, Professor Emeritus UWI StA Kenneth Ramchand.

Following these first memorials, a project, supported by the Campus Research and Publication Unit at UWI StA, then directed by Professor Patricia Mohammed, was started to collate the memorial material and to generate rethinking and revisioning of the work done by the man as well as that about his work written by the many who have been influenced by his thought. The base of the project is a digital platform, www.linesoflifenaipaul.com. This book, the first in a V. S. Naipaul series to be published by Bloomsbury India, is one of the by-products of the digital collation project. It seemed to be demanded by the volume of critical thought produced just recently, mainly in the twenty-first century, which is yet to be experienced collectively. In the first instance from 2020 to 2022, a simple quartet, comprising work on seven of his works in chronological order in each volume, is envisaged. The quartets to follow will adopt more sophisticated approaches based on the insights provided by the first four.

This book on the first seven—*The Mystic Masseur* (1957), *The Suffrage of Elvira* (1958), *Miguel Street* (1959), *A House for Mr Biswas* (1961), *The Middle Passage* (1962), *Mr Stone and the Knights Companion* (1963) and *An Area of Darkness* (1964)—published in the eight-year period between 1957 and 1964, begins the series. In order to develop a sense of the widespread interest in and the ongoing relevance of Naipaul's writing, essays produced in a wide range of journals have been selected and placed next to each other to demonstrate the breadth of disparate insight each text can elicit. Two academic essays on each of these books comprise the bulk of the volume.

However, essays sparked by *An Area of Darkness* open and close the book. The book is, in fact, sort of prefaced by a single brief evocative essay. It is called "V. S. Naipaul and Swachh Bharat..." a version of which was written first on a blog by Gollamudi Radha Krishna Murty. The collection deliberately selects this non-literary professional heartfelt tribute to Naipaul from the popular wide-ranging Indian website, Boloji.com, with which to begin. This essay responds to a statement made by the Prime Minister of India by remembering that Naipaul had remarked more than fifty years before on what the Prime Minister was attempting to address in 2018. This resonates with a persistent recognition over the course of the project of a singular but thus far largely unremarked element of affect that impacts readers of Naipaul's work. At the oddest moments, one recollects what he has said or says what he has said sometimes without even recollecting that he said it first. The memory of the writing becomes almost embodied, one might say. Thus, if Naipaul as a writer recalls for us Michel Foucault's statement that "One writes in order to become other than what one is", then, as readers, we would have to assert contra Foucault that the author is not dead because, in reading him, we also become other than what we were (*Primo Levi* 7).

This effect was indeed the main guide on the process of essay selection and a broad geographically dispersed wealth of essays has been gathered to demonstrate it. The generative, expansive acknowledgement of this affective quality of the writing is the anticipated cumulative outcome of this kind of repetition across the series as a whole. This is because consideration of Naipaul's work seems to lead readers into speculating on their own circumstances and the formation of their own intellectual perspectives and attitudinal positions. This, quite often, involves confronting some disconcerting truth about how the reader's own cherished outlook is shattered by the glimpses into Naipaul's imagination and his more provocative views or how Naipaul's perspective is apropos to current concerns. The writing, in other words, haunts the reader until some rapprochement is achieved, some enlightenment is achieved about the dynamics of the world in which we live and our place in it. We are, in other words, in the territory of the unconscious in the Naipaulian reading experience far more than we are with many other writers.

Murty's writing is a wonderful illustration of this and seemed most suitable, therefore, to begin the book. He makes no bones about the essay being written "in memory of Sir Vidiadhar Surajprasad Naipaul, a Nobel Laureate ... who, as an astute observer of the human condition, having written thirty-odd books that indeed caused many storms in readers' minds, died peacefully in bed on 11 August 2018 in England". While the memorial tone is, therefore, strongest in the essay, it also provokes recognition of Naipaul's immense impact on the Indian subcontinent and his lifelong continuing engagement with Indian issues, which is an important indication of this aspect of Naipaul's work that will be picked up in the second volume in the series.

Like this first essay, the last essay in this book, *The First Naipaul World Epics*, is also not only attentive to the text itself but also to Naipaul and his relationship to India and issues of religious faith and conversion. This is indeed the point from which the second volume will begin also because *An Area of Darkness* is often analysed in tandem with the three books which have come to be known collectively as the Indian trilogy and they will be the focus of attention in the next. In this first book, however, the final essay by Robert Balfour already gestures in this direction as it also makes references to many other books to demonstrate Naipaul's engagement with the idea and impact of religious faith and the potential of his work for developing critical insight on the issue. This essay and the two that precede it, in fact, step out of the two-essay per text pattern and point in the direction of the kind of critical work that the project hopes to spearhead after the first quartet is completed. The last three essays, including the second to last two by the Sri Lankan scholar Mahesh Hapugoda and postcolonial studies scholar Sanjay Krishnan, are indeed representative of the "beyond" of the book's title.

The Mystic Masseur has the honour of being the first Naipaul novel to be published. It was also the first and only one to be made into a film. Chapter 2, "Merchant-Ivory's *The Mystic Masseur*: When Caribbean Literature meets Filmi Dreams" by J. Vijay Maharaj, one of the five Caribbean scholars whose work is included in this eighteen-chapter volume, examines *The Mystic Masseur* in relation to the film of the same name in order to argue that the film erases many of those aspects of the novel so readily apparent to Roxana Elena Donçu who analyses the text alone in the following chapter.

As Maharaj notes, "The film, *The Mystic Masseur*, was released in 2001 with the DVD version becoming available the next year, forty-five years after the bookish character first entered readers' consciousness. Off set, the combined formidable talents of V. S. Naipaul, Ruth Prawer Jhabvala, Caryl Phillips, Ismail Merchant and James Ivory, among many others, went into the production of the film." Nonetheless, the film has troubled many and this essay identifies some of the problems of aesthetic recognition posed by the film in the history of its making as well as in the many texts involved in the translation of novel to film and in subsequent reproductions of the novel.

Chapter 3, "V. S. Naipaul's *The Mystic Masseur*: Defining Failure and Success for the Colonial Subject", is written by Roxana Elena Donçu. Donçu notes that *The Mystic Masseur* is the story of Ganesh

Ramsumair's journey from the margin to the centre, from colonial Trinidad to the imperial metropolis of London. The particulars of Ganesh's local and later metropolitan success are inscribed into the larger picture of a colonial society and its maladies. She argues that Ganesh's rise to prominence is premised on the bastardisation of both Hindu and Western cultural capital.

She asserts that yet still what at a superficial level appears in *The Mystic Masseur* as achievement is eventually revealed as a deeper failure. Instead of fighting, for example, for equal access to education or championing the rights of the subaltern, Ganesh proves to be a supporter of the status quo. Donçu argues, to paraphrase her lightly, that Ganesh uses opportunities only to further his own interests, and never takes a wider view on issues of social injustice. Through Ganesh's character and the story of his meteoric rise to power, Donçu notes that the novel satirises the limited social and political understanding of colonial society and directs a powerful critique at the effects of economic imperialism. Due to what Naipaul represents as a lack of authentic cultural traditions and real values, Trinidadian society appears as artificial, half-made and, thus, incapable of fostering and promoting excellence. This is familiar territory. But Donçu does not end there. She reflects further that the scenario Naipaul paints in this book is evident in contemporary Eastern Europe! The essay, therefore, provokes a new reading of an old favourite, *The Mystic Masseur.*

The next chapter picks up on this point Donçu makes as it moves on to Naipaul's second novel *The Suffrage of Elvira*. Chapter 4, "*The Suffrage of Elvira*: A Study of Politics in Pre-Independence Trinidad", is written by Bhoe Tewarie, another Caribbean scholar and former Principal of UWI StA as well as a well-known politician in Trinidad and Tobago. Tewarie insightfully brings that background to bear on his analysis of the political realities and problems in Trinidad and Tobago from the 1950s that Naipaul represented to our contemporary moment now. Tewarie states,

> *The Suffrage of Elvira* is Naipaul's second published novel. It concerns a contractor-politician, Surujpat Harbans, who is blackmailed by a political broker into paying out hard cash for his political support. As the campaign intensifies, more and more people ask for their payoff. The constituency or community of Elvira is a virtual hornet's nest of pettiness, intrigue, and guile, and when the election comes to Elvira every hornet, so to speak, is unleashed in the service of the new god, "Democracy", which the election comes to symbolise. In his portrayal of Ganesh Ramsumair in *The Mystic Masseur*, Naipaul displays some ambivalence and, in the end, in spite of Ganesh's faults,

> it is difficult to regard him as a totally contemptible character. There is no such ambivalence about Surujpat Harbans in *The Suffrage of Elvira.*

This unique turning point in Trinidad and Tobago's sociocultural and political history captured by this novel is also the point of interest for Kenneth Ramchand who is another Caribbeanist and Professor Emeritus of UWI StA and one of the most important contributors to the development of the study of Caribbean Literature and the field of literatures in English in general.

Ramchand's first essay, Chapter 5 in this book, is titled "Elvira, You Is a Bitch". Ramchand begins his essay with the assertion, "*The Suffrage of Elvira* is comically alive and politically relevant even after the age of sixty in 2018." He goes on to discuss the real-life incidents that impacted on the creation of this novel to prove the point and concludes: "You can read the whole of *The Suffrage of Elvira* as a sign portending the irresponsible and unimaginative political practices that have been destroying our country since independence. But the artist imposes no thesis. There is no thesis."

Chapters 6 to 8 are focused mainly on *Miguel Street.* Chapter 6 written by Italian scholar, Mariacristina Petillo, examines the difficulties of translating Naipaul's Creole work into another language and thus opens up a topic that continues to confront Caribbean literature, including many books by Naipaul. That problem is how to become visible and audible to a global audience given what Caribbean theorist Édouard Glissant has called the opacity of Caribbean subjectivity, history and culture. Her essay thus makes an invaluable contribution to this volume which raises a great many contemporary questions and concerns evoked by Naipaul's work but which, as a consequence, raises far fewer issues of language in Naipaul's writing.

Chapter 7, written by another Caribbeanist, Paula Morgan, professor at UWI StA, recognises the calypso-carnival aesthetic of Naipaul's work and is entitled: "With a Tassa Blending: Calypso and Cultural Identity in Indo-Caribbean Fiction". In this, Morgan follows Gordon Rohlehr, John Thieme and other Caribbean and Naipaul scholars who have analysed Naipaul's utilisation of the carnivalesque and the calypso. However, the essay is unique in that it offers us a sense of the place of this aesthetic, which is not normally associated with them, in the writing of the descendants of the Indian indentured labourers to Trinidad and Tobago and distinguishes between its gendered application. Morgan argues in fact that

> calypso with carnival as its encompassing ritual context originated in Afro-Caribbean resistance and cultural affirmation in the face

> of Eurocentric denigration and repression. Despite the fact that it has been a creative vehicle of African towards Indian diatribe and racial stereotyping, it emerges in Indo–Caribbean literary expression as emblematic of the possibility of raising a common voice against Eurocentric hegemonic discourses and asserting shared cultural belonging and national pride.

This is precisely, one can argue, the form that it takes in many of Naipaul's work and it is certainly most evident in *Miguel Street* as well as in the work of Samuel Selvon and the Indo–Caribbean women's work which Morgan also explores in this essay.

Chapter 8, "Elitist versus Vernacular Cosmopolitanism in Naipaul's *Miguel Street*", is written by Weiwei Xu, who is currently completing a book on Caribbean literature. Xu says that through his series of character profiles, Naipaul presents the microcosm of a colonial world. The major thematic concern of *Miguel Street* is not to depict natural eccentrics but to convey the social reality of Trinidad as an impoverished colonial society without any opportunity for a full life, forcing people to wear the mask of eccentricity. She uses Homi Bhabha's concept of vernacular cosmopolitanism to demonstrate the attractiveness of Naipaul's depiction and contrasts this with his superior tone that has long annoyed many scholars, including, most famously, George Lamming.

She concludes, "Naipaul's mockery of his characters' doomed efforts to escape from disillusionment and poverty is devoid of empathy and painfully condescending." Therefore, despite the beauty and subtly evocative representations of life on the street, this book, she concludes, jars on the reader's sensibility. Xu establishes indisputably, however, that Naipaul himself became aware as a mature writer of his own coloniality, what he calls his hysteria, in these early representations. For us as readers, the essay evokes the concern that whereas many nations taken into independence by men like Naipaul have continued to construct the national subject and the institutions and development plans for this subject on the basis of the idea that only "literacy by education can allow one a place in the larger discursive field of an articulated history … [and] a colonial subject cannot prosper unless he seeks the trappings and cultural privileges of elite cosmopolitanism", Naipaul moved beyond this subjectivity. This is something from which we can all learn much.

Chapter 9 is called "The Language of Advertising and the Novel: Naipaul's *A House for Mr Biswas*" and is written by Yi-Ping Ong who has recently published a book, *The Art of Being*, with Harvard University Press. This book has a decidedly metaphysical slant and the scholarly predilection it reveals is also apparent in the essay included in this volume. Ong's essay suggests that in Naipaul's work, modernity in Trinidad does indeed turn out to be, as Naipaul puts it in *The Middle Passage*,

> the extreme susceptibility of people who are unsure of themselves and, having no taste or style of their own, are eager for instruction. In England and America there are magazines for such groups; in Trinidad instruction is provided by advertising agencies, which have been welcomed by the people not only for this reason but also because the advertising agency is itself a modern thing. (47)

In this essay, she looks at the parallels between advertising and novel writing and reveals a keen understanding of the sociocultural and psychological handicaps of people in postcolonial settings who struggle to assert individuality against the crushing shaping forces emanating from the insubstantial imagery of the advertising industry.

Ong's words remind us of the powerful insights into our contemporary condition that *A House for Mr Biswas* never fails to evoke, a fact that was evident from the earliest critical responses, the most perceptive of which is included here in the following chapter. Chapter 10 is written by UWI StA Professor Emeritus Gordon Rohlehr and is entitled "Character and Rebellion in *A House for Mr Biswas* by V. S. Naipaul". The essay needs no further introduction since it is probably the most cited essay in any subsequent study of this novel and on Naipaul's work in general and may well have helped to make Naipaul "the literary institution" he was to become. Rohlehr's work has indeed been seminal not only in this regard but in the directions Caribbean Cultural Studies in general have grown and to which Naipaul's work adds such an important component.

Most Naipaul readers will recall that immediately after the success of *A House for Mr Biswas*, Naipaul was invited by the soon-to-be first prime minister of an independent Trinidad and Tobago, Dr Eric Eustace Williams, to undertake the travel and study that resulted in the very controversial—*The Middle Passage*. Despite its dark history of controversy, as many of the previous chapters reveal, this first work of creative non-fiction by Naipaul continues to inspire many academic reconsiderations of the discernments it contains. The following chapters illustrate the point further.

Chapter 11, "The Implications of Transtextuality in V. S. Naipaul's *The Middle Passage: The Caribbean Revisited*", is written by Zuzana Klímová Kršková. This essay troubles the confinement of Naipaul's work to the terms set out by fellow Caribbean writers and followed by Edward Said to thereafter inform subsequent postcolonial approaches to the text, most notably in Rob Nixon's early work.[1] But this and the following essay juxtaposed side by side demonstrate why making trouble is necessary.

In fact, Kršková argues:

> V. S. Naipaul had to face severe criticism from postcolonial scholars like Edward Said and local writers like Derek Walcott for his equivocal points of view. He was reproached for his attitudes towards the former British Empire and his alleged denial of his own community. To explore Naipaul's ambivalent standpoint, it is necessary to consider the role and obligations (if any) of the writer within a wider multicultural community. Naipaul refuses to retreat into the seeming stability of nationalism. Instead, he sticks to his personal views no matter how pessimistic or controversial they are. His highly emotional and daring account of the world is first and foremost a personal perception, ignoring social expectations of either side of the postcolonial world. Looking more thoroughly and in a wider textual and historical context on his transtextual references in *The Middle Passage*, we can see this work as a valuable contribution to postcolonial literature which goes beyond the restricted point of view of either the formerly colonised or the colonising.

These are very important points that few other scholars have dared to make. This does not include Chapter 12, "Did V. S. Naipaul Hate Trinidad?", which is another brilliant contribution to the volume by Ramchand. Through a roving examination of Naipaul's writings, Ramchand argues that Naipaul actually wrote out of a love for the island of his birth—to help it achieve the self-knowledge that would set it free. How he makes the point in relation to *The Middle Passage* is most interesting.

The following chapter serves as something of a mid-point summary of views since it analyses the major problems critics have had with Naipaul's treatment of history and the historylessness of Caribbean

---

1 Interestingly, from a Caribbean perspective, one can view Rob Nixon's work as having performed a work of metaphorically lynching Naipaul's writing as bearing witness for the prosecution. Nixon subsequently moved his attention entirely away from the type of work in which Naipaul engaged. Nixon thus performed a somewhat dramatic enactment of the type of privilege which can turn its back on the social and political problems of the developing world at any time it so desires after having used it for its own selfish interest that Naipaul wrote about on so many occasions.

peoples or, more specifically, the people of Trinidad and Tobago. In Chapter 13, Aaron Eastley argues:

> Matching the vehemence and prodigious output of the author himself, the debate surrounding Naipaul has been intense and multifaceted, and its prolonged fervour highlights the need for additional studies that carefully ground their analysis in historical particularities. This is where an event like the 1946 Trinidad general election becomes of extraordinary interest: as an indicator, however partial or narrowly focused, of how Naipaul's representations—both fictional and journalistic—compare with lived experience insofar as it can be reconstructed from formal histories and, more especially, from historically contemporaneous sources such as newspaper articles, interviews, diaries and government documents.

Eastley's essay is deeply indebted to the seminal work of postcolonial studies scholar Said as evident, for example, when he notes that "because Naipaul introduces coherent interpretive paradigms from the authoritative subject position of a societal insider, and because most of his readers are not in a position to bring any significant degree of parallel local knowledge to bear on his representations of places like the West Indies, his perspectives have attained a level of influence seldom achieved by modern literary discourse". This essay set against the backdrop of Chapters 1 to 11 deliberately creates a momentary pause for reconsidering Naipaul's writing and the unresolved problems it has caused for some critics.

After *The Middle Passage* and perhaps more so after the critical literature of the type in the previous chapter it generated began coming in, Naipaul turned his attention away from the Caribbean and to England for the first time. Chapter 14 which looks at this is also by Weiwei Xu. It is named "Colonial Fantasy Shattered, Cosmopolitan Dream Broken: V. S. Naipaul's *Mr Stone and the Knights Companion*". In this essay, Xu argues that Naipaul's depiction of the dull London life in *Mr Stone and the Knights Companion* challenges the metropolitan-centrism of cosmopolitanism.

Criticising the self-consciousness and insularity of English people, Naipaul illustrates the point that the multiplication of cultural contacts and exchanges facilitated in the metropolis does not necessarily mean that the metropolitan locals exposed to it are predisposed towards cosmopolitan openness. Xu's essay demonstrates how this novel provides insight into the allure and danger of cosmopolitanism because consumption of various cultural products and luxurious stylisation of metropolitan life are superficially understood as signals of access and openness to differences, while xenophobia towards immigrants lurks under the consumer orientation.

"Naipaul's English Fable: *Mr Stone and the Knights Companion*" by John Thieme is Chapter 15. Like the chapter by Rohlehr, this essay has now acquired classic status as evident in its citation by Xu in the previous chapter. The essay looks at the novel *Mr Stone and the Knights Companion* as one that addresses the fundamental existential problem of growing old and reveals the novel as a very significant one in the Naipaul oeuvre. It also serves as a significant corrective to many of the negative assumptions about the novel that were once prevalent. In this essay, Thieme makes a very useful comparison between the novel and T. S. Eliot's works, specifically "The Burial of the Dead" section of *The Waste Land* which is also about decadence, demise and dissolution. The connection is not surprising since Naipaul himself alludes to T. S. Eliot by stressing on "those who doubt the coming of the Spring" (*Mr Stone and the Knights Companion* 20).

Naipaul writes:

> In these dark damp days it is hard for us, daily pacing city pavements, to believe that winter is on the wane, that the days steadily lengthen. Below the frozen earth, however, and in the stripped black trees, life goes on. A trip to London's countryside where the winter-dun wrapping of buds conceals all the season's muted preparation will assure those who doubt the coming of Spring. Those who doubt the coming of the Spring: the words magnified and gave a focus to his uneasiness. They recalled a moment—then, memory and fear quickening, he saw that they recalled several moments, which had multiplied during the last year—of unease, unsettlement. (*Mr Stone and the Knights Companion* 20)

This existential crisis has of course been the one that has driven Naipaul's philosophising in much of his fiction and creative non-fiction and in this novel, it is foregrounded as Thieme rightly points out. This chapter by Thieme is essentially, however, the last of the duplicate analyses of each of Naipaul's first six works undertaken in this first book in the series.

The last three chapters reveal more sharply a common motivation in most of the critical literature gathered together in this volume and in Naipaul's readers' continuing interest in his works. Vijay Mishra expresses it best in his acknowledgement of what he calls Naipaul's shadows on his own writing, thinking and being (Mishra 123–126). Amitav Ghosh similarly claims that Naipaul's writing "has become so intimate a part of my experience that I cannot be certain where my memory ends and where Naipaul's narrative begins", although he confesses that:

> I almost always disagreed with [Naipaul's views and opinions]: some because they were founded on truths that were too painful to acknowledge; some because they were misanthropic or objectionable; and some because they came uncomfortably close to being racist.... Yet he was writing of matters that no one else thought worth noticing; he had found words to excavate new dimensions of experience. (Ghosh, "Naipaul and the Nobel 2001")

This reaction exists moreover because Naipaul's work so often helps scholars to study "the social transformation process called decolonisation", which is what Chapter 16 entitled "Failures in Decolonisation and the Return to the Past: Reading V. S. Naipaul" written by Mahesh Hapugoda aims to do. Like so much of the critical literature on Naipaul, Hapugoda's seeks "to interpret and contextualise selected works by V. S. Naipaul which depict the failures of the process". The essay reminds us, as Sanjay Krishnan remarks, that "many of the themes that Naipaul was among the first to explore, from ethnic violence and civil war to the self-destructive impact of religious fundamentalism, have become central questions of the global twenty-first century". However, Hapugoda is particularly concerned with what Samir Amin calls "retrogressive nostalgia" in previously colonised nations which attempts to "return to historical and traditional ideologies to address today's and tomorrow's problems, which ultimately results in nothing but violent totalitarianism" since such a return is impossible.

Similarly, Chapter 17, named "V. S. Naipaul and Historical Derangement", and written by one of the new generation of Naipaul scholars, Sanjay Krishnan, makes a point that is critically important and demanding of urgent attention still—now and for the foreseeable future. Krishnan writes:

> Naipaul's premise is that subjects in the periphery are shaped by complex pasts that they are not well placed to comprehend. For historical reasons, peripheral societies lack the institutions and social practices required for an adequate grasp of modernity's profoundly disruptive effects. The globalising forms of colonialism and capitalism diverted the social trajectories of the peasant formations of the precapitalist world. Such groups found themselves enslaved, displaced, indentured or colonised—in short, violently inducted into modern institutions of production and exchange. These peoples adapted to their new historical circumstances—some even thrived, materially speaking—but they could not reclaim or assert control

> over their disrupted social trajectories. The institutions and norms of their societies were deranged by modernity.

Finally, Chapter 18, by Robert Balfour, entitled, "Amongst the Unbelievable: Rage, Faith and Reason in Selected Writings by V. S. Naipaul", focuses on the representation of faith as conveyed by Naipaul in the course of four travelogues. Drawing on historical scholarship pertaining to Islamic societies in transition and comparing this to a selection of the literary-critical reception that Naipaul's writing about Islam has evoked, Balfour argues for a revision of the literary readings of Naipaul's travelogues. His premise is that the author's subject positioning influences both a self-critical as well as a more compassionate perspective on the relationship between faith and political transition in developing societies.

Together and individually, the essays collected in this book reveal that there can be absolutely no doubt about one thing—that those who are moved by Naipaul's work are prepared to put in a great deal of labour into articulating what moves them so. The essays are indeed all intended to be read independently. No attempt has been made to impose a requirement for thematic or theoretical connection between different chapters. This was deliberate because as Gillian Dooley reminds us:

> Although Naipaul's biography is that of a practically quintessential "postcolonial" writer, countless critics have shown, by attempting to fit him into this mold, how inadequate such a theoretical and political approach is to an appreciation of his work. Understanding Naipaul is a matter of empathizing, not theorizing, looking subjectively, as he does, rather than objectively, as many of his critics claim to do. (Dooley 3)

Collectively, however, the essays are certainly meant to develop the idea that literature has power to transform our lives and to exemplify the value of continued attention to Naipaul's work towards this end.

This entire book, and perhaps all the books in the series that will follow suit, is thus a hybrid entity—a kind of cross between a festschrift and a reader. The series hopes in this way to achieve for Naipaul something of what has been done for the work of other Caribbean intellectuals such as C. L. R. James of the generation before Naipaul's or Stuart Hall who belongs to Naipaul's own. These writers have all done so very much to introduce the terms of the debates of the anti-colonial struggle and decolonising process that occupy our attention still. Of James, Naipaul said many memorable things, one of which is apropos and goes as follows:

> Mr. James' career is of particular interest. Our backgrounds were dissimilar. His was Negro, Puritan, fearful of lower-class contamination; mine was Hindu, restricted, enclosed. But we have ended speaking the same language; and though England is not perhaps the country we thought it was, we have both charmed ourselves away from Trinidad. "For the inner self," as Mr. James writes, "the die was cast." (*The Overcrowded Barracoon and Other Stories* 22–23)

Despite the roll of the die for people like these men and so many of the rest of us, the intellectual and attitudinal models they have left us are worthy of our intense attention. This volume is the first contribution to this task taken on by the series, towards which many others will follow into the beyond. It also, therefore, goes beyond the work undertaken by other recent critical anthologies, such as *V. S. Naipaul: An Anthology of 21st Century Criticism*, and is part of a series and a long-term project aimed at achieving a comprehensive grasp of Naipaul and as a consequence of the pre-history of our present moment.

The work thus aims to participate in the process of transforming our lives positively and is intended for the lay reader and for undergraduates in general, although it also seeks to provide a launching pad for postgraduate scholarship on decolonisation and transformation in Naipaul's oeuvre. To borrow the words of Rohlehr, the "revolution of self-perception … grows increasingly more complex and multi-faceted.… It challenges conventional notions of history and is part of a vast world-wide movement to relocate the submerged cultures of the devastated in the kingdom of human and humane achievement."[2] Naipaul's work is a critical aspect of the revolution and the series will demonstrate how so.

Works Cited

Chaubey, Ajay K. *V. S. Naipaul: An Anthology of 21st Century Criticism*. Atlantic, 2015.

Dooley, Gillian. *V. S. Naipaul, Man and Writer*. 2006, Ebook University of South Carolina Press, 2017, muse.jhu.edu/book/49730. Accessed 28 November 2020.

---

2 See Gordon Rohlehr, "Articulating a Caribbean Aesthetic: The Revolution in Self-Perception", in *My Strangled City and Other Essays* (Port-of-Spain: Longman, 1992), 1–16, quoted in Jennifer Rahim, "Issues and Developments in Caribbean Literary Theory and Criticism", *Research Methods in Caribbean Literary and Discourse Culture*, ed. Barbara Lalla, Nicole Roberts, Elizabeth Walcott-Hackshaw and Valerie Youssef, 15–40, p. 15.

Ghosh, Amitav. "Naipaul and the Nobel." 2001, a mitavghosh.com/essays/naipaul.html. Accessed 28 November 2020.

Harrowitz, Nancy A. *Primo Levi and the Identity of a Survivor*. University of Toronto Press, 2016.

Krishnan, Sanjay. *V. S. Naipaul's Journeys: From Periphery to Center*. Columbia University Press, 2020.

Mishra, Vijay. "Lives in Halves: A Homage to Vidiadhar Naipaul." 2001. https://core.ac.uk/reader/11243780. Accessed 28 November 2020.

Naipaul, V. S. *Mr Stone and the Knights Companion*. Penguin, 1973.

———. *The Overcrowded Barracoon and Other Stories*. Andre Deutsch, 1972.

Rahim, Jennifer. "Issues and Developments in Caribbean Literary Theory and Criticism." *Research Methods in Caribbean Literary and Discourse Culture*, edited by Barbara Lalla, Nicole Roberts, Elizabeth Walcott-Hackshaw, and Valerie Youssef, 2013. pp. 15–40.

Rohlehr, Gordon. *My Strangled City and Other Essays*. Longman, 1992.

Sequeira, Jessica A. "One More for the Road". *Harvard Crimson*, 27 October 2010. www.thecrimson.com › 2010/10/27 › naipaul-africa-book-naipauls. Accessed 28 November 2020.

Chapter 1

V. S. NAIPAUL AND SWACHH BHARAT...

Gollamudi Radha Krishna Murty[1]

> In memory of Sir Vidiadhar Surajprasad Naipaul, a Nobel Laureate in Literature of Indian descent, who, as an astute observer of the human condition, having written thirty-odd books that indeed caused many storms in readers' minds, died peacefully in bed on 11 August 2018 in England.

Today, as I was flipping through the morning newspapers, there came a message in the name of our Prime Minister stating, "*Aaiye swachha Bharat kaa nirman kare,* 15th September *se swachhtaa hi seva se juden*" (Let's strive to create a Swachh Bharat). It at once reminded me that I have over-delayed paying my tributes to one of the twentieth century's most admired and contentious storytellers, V. S. Naipaul, who died at his home in London, aged eighty-five. And hence the following lines....

Naipaul was the grandson of a Brahman from the Banaras region who went to Trinidad in the nineteenth century as an indentured labourer. He was born in Chaguanas, Trinidad, in 1932 and later his family moved to the island's capital, Port-of-Spain. He claims this shift transformed him from a child who knew almost nothing, nothing beyond what he picked up in his grandmother's house, into an acute observer of the life of the street—the outside world. No wonder if Port-of-Spain then became the setting for his *Miguel Street*—a collection of stories that won him the Somerset Maugham Award in 1959. Much has been written about this book which establishes it as one of the most important produced in the twentieth century.

In 1950, after winning a government scholarship, Naipaul went to study at Oxford. Later, after Oxford, it is at BBC World Service where he analysed West Indian Literature that he found his footing as a writer. His breakthrough as a writer came with his first published

1 An earlier version of this article was published in the *Global Analyst Magazine* for which Gollamudi Radha Krishna Murty writes. See https://www.boloji.com/writers/6196/gollamudi

novel, *The Mystic Masseur*, in 1957. In it, he presented a dialogic intercourse between two cultures: conservative Indian culture and European liberal capitalist culture. This novel, therefore, treats the reader to an authentic history through stories of the powerless people of a Trinidad ghetto. It is through caricature and irony that he presents the aspirations, energy, vulgarities, inconsistencies and corruption of characters who belong to a rapidly changing society in which there are few stable values.

Ganesh Ramsumair, the protagonist of the novel, is presented as a bundle of all the controversies of the colonial society as he, oscillating between traditional Indian values and the lure of modern consumer capitalism, rises from a teacher to a masseur, from a masseur to a mystic, from a mystic to an MLC (Member of the Legislative Council) quite spectacularly. As the novel comes to an end, this struggling Pandit Ganesh Ramsumair becomes G. Ramsay Muir—a complete transformation into a colonial puppet who even defends British colonial rule. Interestingly, while narrating these two cultures, their institutions, processes and products, Naipaul can never be said to be siding wholly with either the Trinidadian Indian or the European ways of life.

Drawing upon his real experiences among Indians in Trinidad, Naipaul went on to write all of his earlier novels—*The Suffrage of Elvira* (1958), *Miguel Street* (1959) and *A House for Mr Biswas* (1961)—in which he narrates the struggle of charlatans, braggarts and dreamers to eke out a life with social respectability in their new worlds of settlement. However, it is his fourth novel, *A House for Mr* Biswas—a treatise on the pangs of exiles—that won him major recognition. Drawing from the experiences of his father, Naipaul narrated the struggle of the protagonist of the novel, Mohan Biswas, a Trinidadian Indian, to free himself from the predicaments of family, custom and religion.

Being the son of a poor labourer and having lived as a guest in one inhospitable house after another following his father's death and his marriage into a powerful family, Biswas vows to get a job on his own. And he vows to get his own house too. And, finally, by journeying through a variety of jobs, from sign painter to journalist, Biswas acquires a house of his own, which, in his view, is the signpost of his independence. But under the stress of getting the house repaired and the burden of repaying the debt, he suffers a heart attack and dies soon afterwards. Nonetheless, he leaves a house behind for sheltering his family for generations to come, and subsequently the literature of Trinidad and Tobago. Naipaul, while narrating the struggle of Biswas for dignity and independence, successfully explored the themes of family, poverty and the impact of colonialism on the economy of the vanquished colonial world from a postcolonial perspective.

The novel has succeeded in making an entry into *Time* magazine's 100 best English-language novels from 1923 to 2005 as a result of all of this.

Moving back and forth from Trinidad to other areas of the world, Naipaul used other national settings in his subsequent novels—*In a Free State* (1971), *Guerrillas* (1975), *A Bend in the River* (1979) and *A Way in the World* (1994)—but continued to explore the relationship between violence, contingency and politics and the emerging personal and collective alienation experienced by the victims in the new milieux emerging out of the struggle between native and Western-colonial heritages. *In a Free State* (1971), a novella with two supporting narratives, each set in different countries, which won him Britain's Booker Prize, was hailed by Neel Mukherjee as a "remarkable, clear-eyed, truthful and brutal meditation on exile and displacement".[2]

He accomplished this task by resorting to two techniques: in "One Out of Many", he resorted to first-person narratives through the voice of Santosh, an Indian servant in Washington and, in "Tell Me Who to Kill", it is the poor Trinidadian Indian who narrates the story in London; but in "In a Free State", he adopts a third-person narrative perspective to tell about a long car journey undertaken by two English persons, Bobby and Linda, across an unnamed African country.

In his other novels, such as *The Enigma of Arrival* (1987), *A Way in the World* (1994) or *Half a Life* (2001), he examined carefully his own inner demands and analysed even his deceptions through the protagonists. In fact, some critics consider *The Enigma of Arrival*, written eight years after his previous publication, as his masterpiece because of its structure as a long meditation on a work by the surrealist painter Giorgio de Chirico. In this novel, the narrator, who is perhaps no other than Naipaul himself with his own melancholy sense of rootlessness, takes many journeys, starting from colonial Trinidad, both imaginary and real, to the English countryside to become a writer. Interestingly, the narrator-migrator, choosing to inhabit a pastoral England, invents the earth below his feet and in the process feels as though the new piece of land has given him a second chance, a new life, richer and fuller than any he had had anywhere else, in which he can practise his writer's trade. However, later, in the second part of the book, the narrator, under the spell of sickness, observing the world around him from the perspective of an outsider, perhaps more as an anthropologist, describes in a sad, melancholic tone the collapse of an old coloniser.

---

2 See https://www.theparisreview.org/blog/2018/02/20/rereading-v-s-naipauls-free-state/ and https://books.wwnorton.com/books/ReadingGuidesDetail.aspx?ID=4294998368&CID=4294997518&tid=3288&tcid=

It is his non-fiction works that are large-sized narratives of his travels to different countries over different periods of time—*The Middle Passage: Five Societies in the West Indies* (1963), *An Area of Darkness* (1964), *India: A Wounded Civilization* (1976), *Among the Believers* (1981), *India: A Million Mutinies Now* (1990) and *Beyond Belief* (1998)—that attracted for him immense critical hostility and anger, particularly from the postcolonial world. But first things first: let us examine what he wrote under these titles.

At the time of publishing his first book on India, *An Area of Darkness*—a chronicle of his first visit to his ancestral homeland—India was indeed passing through darkness; it was just limping back from the humiliation inflicted by Chinese aggression. Owing to the widespread drought and the resulting shortage of food grains, we were then living off the American wheat supplied under the PL480 programme. And it was this despairing and hungry India that confounded him when he landed at the Bombay airport. Naipaul's declared state of mind as a result was: "I am profoundly Indian in my feeling, profoundly Indian in my sensibility … but not in my observation" (C. D. Narasimhaiah, *The Function of Criticism in India* 117). He recognised, however, that from his observatory, "from the railway train and from the dusty roads, India appeared to require only pity. It was an easy emotion, and perhaps the Indians were right: it was compassion like mine, so strenuously maintained, that denied humanity to many" (*Area of Darkness* 263).

At the very outset of this travelogue as he landed at the Bombay airport, he encountered the bitterest experience: despite having a permit for the two bottles of liquor that he had brought with him, they were confiscated by custom authorities who declared that a "transport permit" was needed. In search of this increasingly elusive item, he had to run from office to office, table to table facing every official behaving either indifferently or arrogantly. This was his first introduction to the real place with which he had identified in his imagination throughout his life. Thereafter, it was the all-pervading poverty and squalor that gave him a rude shock. He wrote: "I had seen the starved child defecating at the road side while the mangy dog waited to eat the excrement" (*Area of Darkness* 45). What was more distressing to him was that it was not only a village scene. Such habits could be seen on the slopes of Himalayas, at the bus-stand of Madras and on the beaches of Goa. It was to be seen everywhere. He went on penning:

> Indians defecate everywhere. They defecate, mostly, beside the railway tracks. But they also defecate on the beaches; they defecate on the hills; they defecate on the streets; they never look for cover …

> the peasant, Muslim or Hindu, suffers from claustrophobia if he has to use an enclosed latrine. (*Area of Darkness* 210)

In the same vein, he loathed the corruption prevailing in the country and was pained to note that no shame comes to those corrupt people; instead, a lot of social prestige and status is bestowed on such unscrupulous officials:

> It is estimated that in Kashmir, as in the rest of India, one-third of development funds drains away in corruption and the exchanging of gifts. No disgrace attaches to this. The Kashmir tailor spoke with envious admiration of his patwari friend, a surveyor and type of records-keeper, who in one day might collect as much as a hundred rupees; a lorry-driver had a similar admiration for a traffic inspector he knew who received monthly protection money from various lorry-drivers. (*Area of Darkness* 92)

He thus concluded that corruption had become deep-rooted in the Indian system of government and society and was as invisible as the habit of public defecation. And now, however sore we may feel about these observations, can we deny the fact that the same system of defecating is prevailing in the country even after about fifty years since Naipaul's visit? And even after seventy years of independence, can we not admit that the malady of corruption is haunting us, albeit with more ferocity? These are the questions that Naipaul's works force on us still and which made me remember him when I heard the Prime Minister's call for Swachh Bharat.

By the time he wrote his second India book, *India: A Wounded Civilization* (1976), the nation was passing through the pangs of the Emergency declared by Indira Gandhi. And, of course, poverty was relentless, while corruption mounted up in all walks of life. While the leaders were twittering about socialist slogans, the countryside presented a grim scenario of undernourished children. And visiting India for the second time but under such testing times, Naipaul continued to be disappointed by India. Reacting to the institutional collapse under the Emergency imposed by Mrs Gandhi, he pronounced: "The dismantled institutions—of law, press and Parliament—cannot simply be put together again" (*India: A Wounded Civilization* 98).

Speaking about Indian civilisation as a "wounded civilization"—decayed and dying—Naipaul states:

> No civilization was so little equipped to cope with the outside world; no country was so easily raided and plundered, and learned so little from its disasters. Five hundred years after the Arab conquest of

> Sind, Muslim rule was established in Delhi as the rule of foreigners, people apart, and foreign rule—Muslim for the five hundred years, British for the last 150—ended in Delhi only in 1947.

He pessimistically concludes his book with the statement: "The crisis of India is not only political or economic. The larger crisis is of a wounded civilization that has at last become aware of its inadequacies and is without the intellectual means to move ahead" (*India: A Wounded Civilization* 102).

No wonder if such comments attracted outrage from Indian readers: "He seems to me to write for the same reason that many ossified academics publish; else they must perish," said C. D. Narasimhaiah ("Naipaul's Indian Experience Again" 99). Nevertheless, one may have to admit that what Naipaul wrote about India is not wholly untrue, for India did suffer under the yoke of foreign rule for many centuries and responded by withdrawing into itself and as a result suffers from self-deception (*India: A Wounded Civilization* 102).

In his final book on the trilogy of India, *India: A Million Mutinies Now*, Naipaul appeared to have mellowed down. Or, perhaps by the 1990s, India was on the cusp of evolving into a nation, a promise in the emergence, perhaps! Although he witnessed a new generation of intellectuals crying in hoarse empty words, he could see that India was somehow managing to survive, and indeed evolving: "Independence had come to India like a kind of revolution; now there were many revolutions within that revolution.... All over India scores of particularities that had been frozen by foreign rule, or by poverty or lack of opportunity or abjectness had begun to flow again" (*India: A Million Mutinies Now* 19). What others might see as unrest, Naipaul saw as an awakening.

It is obvious that such a probing and the resultant writing about India in what some saw as disparaging ways brought a barrage of protests from the intellectuals of India. Some critics accused him of "look [ing] at India through Western kaleidoscope which takes myriad unreal shapes when aimed at lighted areas". They questioned him: "Why use the Western criteria in determining India to be an area of light or darkness?" ("India: Theirs and Mine" 143). Even such a reputed Indian critic as C. D. Narasimhaiah in "V. S. Naipaul: A Case of Bizarre Reputation" observed: "I must confess I was disturbed when someone spoke of the possibility of a Nobel Prize for Naipaul. I asked myself if the world's most prestigious award was instituted to honor someone who has injected so much poison into the world's body politic and seems to gloat over it?" (117).

Amidst such widespread resentment among the Indian intelligentsia about what Naipaul wrote about India, it is equally essential to note other comments. For example, there is what William Walsh said about Naipaul's journey to India: "Naipaul's return to India is as much as a research into himself as into another country. He is crawling on sensitive naked feet through the tunnels of his own self" (63). Equally, is it not right to say that even after seventy years of Independence, we are still struggling to cope with the long-buried disruptive peculiarities of religion, region, caste, clan, subalterns, a chasm between the Centre and states that has grown beyond the political sense of winning elections, etc. and the resultant strife in building a new India, in redefining the very sense of our economic independence? Indeed, because, ironically, the present government's call for Swachh Bharat—a call for "Clean India"—comes seventy years after we began what Nehru called our tryst with destiny which very much vindicates Naipaul's writings.

His other non-fictional writings such as *Among the Believers* and *Beyond Belief* attracted similar criticism. Writing these two big books on his Islamic excursions through Iran, Pakistan, Malaysia and Indonesia, Naipaul, approaching his subject from a secular perspective and perhaps going against the grain of cultural and intellectual relativism, made deliberately sharp and cutting remarks. As he had said to Michiko Kakutani:

> Certain subjects are so holy that it becomes an act of virtue to lie ... never say "bush people," never say "backward country," never say "boring people," never say "uneducated." But turn away from what is disagreeable and what happens in the end is that you encourage the chaps there to start lying about themselves too. So, they lie because it's what is expected of them. Soon everyone begins to lie. (C15)

Intent on not lying, in the section on Indonesia, for example, he said, "Islam sanctified rage—rage about the faith, political rage: one could be like the other. And more than once on this journey I had met sensitive men who were ready to contemplate great convulsions" (*Among the Believers* 230). In the book, *Beyond Belief*, he observed: "The cruelty of Islamic fundamentalism is that it allows only to one people—the Arabs, the original people of the prophet—a past, and sacred places, pilgrimages and earth reverences.... It is the most uncompromising kind of imperialism" (*Beyond Belief* 72). Reacting to his writings, Edward Said said that while Naipaul, in the West, is "considered a master novelist and an important witness to the disintegration and hypocrisy of the third world, in the postcolonial world he's a marked man as a purveyor of stereotypes and disgust for the world that produced him—though that doesn't exclude people thinking he's a gifted writer" (45).

Naipaul, in his long career of almost half a century, trusting his intuition, wrote about colonialism and decolonisation, exile and the struggles of people in the developing world to acquire political and moral freedom, causing many a storm in the minds of his readers. And the extent of success that he achieved can be gauged from what Nan Doerksen said: "Perhaps where Naipaul's genius lies is in his ability to take an existing literary genre, or idea, and bend it to his own peculiar vision, finally creating something that is definitively his own as Shakespeare did" (107). All this accomplishment finally won him the Nobel Prize in literature in 2001 for his revelations about suppressed histories.

Let me now stop here by paying my tributes to Sir Naipaul, our own *philosophe* who transformed rage into precision and allowed events to speak out of their own inherent irony, for readers everywhere to react in whatever fashion they want. As one writer said of him, "There is perhaps no significant contemporary writer whose work has been shaped as profoundly by his cultural background and who, in learning to write about it, has made its disorienting strangeness as intelligible" (*Naipaul's Strangers* 1). Many others agree. Sanjay Krishnan, for example, said: "The continued appeal of Naipaul's work to readers across the world lies in the way he modeled a style of peripheral reflection that people from quite different histories could recognize or identify with and, consequently, draw upon to reflect upon their own pasts" (19–20).

Works Cited

"A Conversation between Neel Mukherjee and Hanya Yanagihara on *A State of Freedom*". *Norton Reading Group Guide*, https://books.wwnorton.com/books/ReadingGuidesDetail.aspx?ID=4294998368&CID=4294997518&tid=3288&tcid. Accessed 26 April 2019.

Barnouw, Dagmar. *Naipaul's Strangers*. Indiana University Press, 2003.

Doerksen, Nan. *In a Free State* and *Nausea*, *World Literature Written in English*, vol. 20, issue 1, 1981, pp. 105–113.

Kakutani, Michiko. "Naipaul Reviews His Past from Afar." *New York Times*, 1 Dec. 1980, C15.

Krishnan, Sanjay. *V. S. Naipaul's Journeys: From Periphery to Center*. Columbia University Press, 2020.

Masih, I. K. "India: Theirs and Mine: V. S. Naipaul's *An Area of Darkness*." *The Commonwealth Review*, Vol. IX, no. l, 1977–1998, p 143.

Naipaul. V. S. *An Area of Darkness*. André Deutsch Limited, 1964.

———. *India: A Wounded Civilization*. André Deutsch Limited, 1977.

———. *India: A Million Mutinies Now*. Heinemann, 1990.

———. *Among the Believers: An Islamic Journey*. Knopf Doubleday, 2011.

———. *Beyond Belief: Islamic Excursions among the Converted Peoples*. Vintage, 1998.

Narasimhaiah, C. D. "V. S. Naipaul: A Case of Bizarre Reputation." *The Function of Criticism in India: Essays in Indian Response to Literature*, Central Institute of Indian Languages, 1986, p. 117.

———. "Naipaul's Indian Experience Again", *Contemporary Indian Fiction in English*, ed., Ayyappa Panikar, Kerala University Press, 1981, p 99

Said, Edward. "Intellectuals in the Post-colonial World." *Salmagundi*, no. 70/71, 1986, pp. 44–64.

Walsh, William. *V. S. Naipaul*. Oliver & Boyd, 1973.

Chapter 2

MERCHANT-IVORY'S *THE MYSTIC MASSEUR*: WHEN CARIBBEAN LITERATURE MEETS FILMI DREAMS[1]

J. Vijay Maharaj

....at a time when masseurs were ten a penny in Trinidad.

—*The Mystic Masseur* 1

The coinage of Trinidad is no longer measured in pennies, but masseurs still proliferate. Singling out and making representative, which are definitive characteristics of V. S. Naipaul's style, are evident in the careful penny selection and development of the character Ganesh in his first published novel, *The Mystic Masseur* (1957). This is how the crafting of the novel begins: "Later he was to be famous and honoured throughout the South Caribbean; he was to be a hero of the people and, after that, a British representative at Lake Success. But when I first met him, he was still a struggling masseur" (1).

In an ironic reversal of the lone flower technique through which Ngũgĩ wa Thiong'o discusses this aspect of Naipaul's creative process, however, the masseur of this first novel, *The Mystic Masseur*, has proliferated as well as ramified over the years, often bearing but an oblique resemblance to the one first released into the world in 1957. One is hard-pressed to say unequivocally, therefore, that the Ganesh character, who is sufficiently renowned as to have made it into the *Chambers Dictionary of Literary Characters*, is the same one that readers first met in 1957. This essay explores some of the problems of aesthetic recognition involved in this turn of events and the politics of these problems inherent to the production of some of the versions of *The Mystic Masseur* available for consumption today, among which the most important is the adaptation of the novel in the Merchant-Ivory film, *The Mystic Masseur,* on which this chapter focuses.

1 This paper was first published with the title, "The Politics and Aesthetics of Recognition: A Case of Too Many Mystic Masseurs?" in *Tout Moun: A Caribbean Cultural Studies Journal*, Vol. 5, No. 1, March 2019.

THE EVERYDAY POLITICS OF "MINENESS" AND BEYOND

The film, *The Mystic Masseur*, was released in 2001 with the DVD version becoming available the next year, forty-five years after the bookish character first entered readers' consciousness. Off set, the combined formidable talents of V. S. Naipaul, Ruth Prawer Jhabvala, Caryl Phillips, Ismail Merchant and James Ivory, among many others, went into the production of the film. If, as a Caribbean film expert, Jean Antoine-Dunne says, "Filmmaking, perhaps more than any other art form, complicates the question of national or regional affiliation," then in this instance, the complications of affiliation or lack thereof are immense indeed ("Sound and Vision" 95). If according to Christian Lara, five characteristics are essential for a film to be considered Caribbean—"the director should be from the Caribbean, the subject matter should be a Caribbean story, the lead actor/actress should be from the Caribbean, Creole should be used, the production unit should be Caribbean"—then this film would definitely not be considered Caribbean ("Sound and Vision" 95).

Indeed, one of the more prominent aspects of this non-Caribbeanness in the film would be the "accented speech of the diegetic characters", which certainly required a little more attention than that which another film scholar, Hamid Naficy, calls for in *Accented Cinema*. Apart from this, however, it may be necessary to view the film in terms such as those established by Naficy, who says that "if the dominant cinema is considered universal and without accent, the films that diasporic and exilic subjects make are accented … the accent emanates not so much from the accented speech of the diegetic characters as from the displacement of the filmmakers and their artisanal production modes" (4). This, of course, raises its own issues with regard to negotiations between the dominant and the displaced. For example, in the case of this film, as one pre-launch article put it, we must bear in mind that the film was "a bargain-basement production, even by Merchant-Ivory's own cost-conscious standards [and on set, a clearly stunt] cocoa tree drops its solid fruit like grenades over the set and some stunt cockerels are tethered to the roof to add local colour" ("Waiting for Vidia…").

Caribbean viewers are quite familiar with stunts pulled by many and are not generally averse to pulling some themselves but these and other aspects of the film were troublesome nonetheless.[2] Beyond all

---

2 See David Tindall, "Trouble in Paradise", *The Guardian*, https://www.theguardian.com/film/2001/mar/23/classics.culture. Accessed 28 November 2020.

expectations would be a convenient way to express my own reactions, if beyond is understood in Homi Bhabha's terms as comprising, in the first instance, "a sense of disorientation, a disturbance of direction, in the 'beyond': an exploratory, restless movement caught so well in the French rendition of the words *au-delà*—here and there, on all sides, *fort/da*, hither and thither, back and forth" (1). Because, certainly, as I concluded by and by, the disorientation was not due to academically overtrained eyes, a matter I ascertained by screening the film with a variety of audiences in private and professional settings: among family, friends and students. (I didn't run the experiment with postgraduates whose eyes I feared maybe too much like my own). In every setting, the film evoked a similar quizzical response.

Responses to the screening of the film at the sixtieth-anniversary celebration of the novel's publication in 2017 echoed my own and those I had heard and felt before and revealed something of the difficult-to-articulate trouble involved. The sixtieth-anniversary observance was held as a joint venture between the National Library and Information System of Trinidad and Tobago and the non-governmental organisation, Friends of Mr Biswas, which was established with a two-pronged goal: the first, to nurture at least a few of the talents of the many present-day Biswases who still walk among Caribbean populations and, the second, for the first purpose of taking charge of the titular house immortalised in Naipaul's novel *A House for Mr Biswas*, purchased by the Government of the Republic of Trinidad and Tobago when it was put up for sale on the open market. Sixteen years after its release, the film screening was a precursor to a round table the next day on local views of the adaptation.

On 10 November 2017, Dara Healy wrote an article following the screening, entitled "Whose Mystic Masseur?" in the *Newsday*, a Trinidad and Tobago daily newspaper, in which she recorded and continued some of what the round table set out to achieve. She notes that "the general feeling [was] that the film missed many of the cultural nuances of TT [Trinidad and Tobago] that make the book so poignant". The point is echoed in a bit of Earl Lovelace's novel *Is Just a Movie* in which the distress associated with the loss of cultural nuance in the local experience of playing at shooting and the American filmic parallel is recounted. Among Caribbean children at play, Lovelace writes:

> There is a certain give-and-take, reasonableness, like in a fiction, rooted in the idea that life gives everybody a chance, that leaves everybody satisfied, whether you are the one shot or the one doing the shooting. The shooter must miss a few times, since it is quite fatal

> when he connects. But here, in this movie, the fellars who shooting, they not missing at all. The only people who they missing is the fellars from the States: the stars. (26)

Both Healy's and Lovelace's complaints are encompassed in the idea of "mineness", which, as Lovelace revealed in a class discussion on 25 March 2019, is based on what someone told him about his/her experiences on a local film set for a foreign movie—quite possibly the one in question in this essay. Healy meanwhile observes, "The goal [of the film] was not to present a story about this country to its people, which is the fundamental point of indigenous literature. Rather it was to create a film based on the book of a renowned author and Nobel laureate, and market it for commercial gain."

Such concerns are by no means confined to the Caribbean. Jennifer Jeffers, for example, has aired similar concerns about the Americanisation of British culture to meet "American middle-class expectation" (112). And, she argues further, "capitalist Hollywood is now the only global model" for adaptation (206). Her study is also concerned about Merchant-Ivory productions, in this case, *Remains of the Day* (1993). Her conclusion regarding that film is, "America has arrived and England is receding" (75). Merchant-Ivory Productions have also been queried in terms of complicity with cultural imperialism. Dan Venning, for example, explores their early 1965 film *Shakespeare Wallah* to determine "whether the film engages in genuine, postcolonial intercultural exchange, by which I mean respectful balancing of cultures in the encounter and challenging Western hegemony, or is a work that, using Shakespeare as a tool, perpetuates cultural imperialism, serving colonialist ideology although produced in a postcolonial era" (150).

Be that as it may, we are here concerned with Caribbean feelings of "mineness". Julian Hannich has explored fears about transgressions of readers' feelings of "mineness" in film adaptations. He conceptualises the idea of mine via Keith Oatley's description of the reader-text relationship: "The best metaphor for our relationship with a fictional story is friendship. Friends affect us. They change us. And just as we are careful whom we choose as friends ... so we are careful what we read and what literary characters, or what narrators, we become mentally involved with" (101). The narrators and characters that we do "become involved with" become ours and, for casual Caribbean readers as well as Caribbean literary and cultural critics, mineness develops in relation to aesthetic recognition, a sense of the rightness of the representation of ourselves and acceptance, to use Healy's words, that the creative artist was attempting "to present a story about this country to its people".

This is never a straightforward matter. The isles, to appropriate a very familiar line, are always full of noises and these stories we consider mine are not always simple or pretty ones as the story of Ganesh in the novel, *The Mystic Masseur*, reveals. But, just like the rest of the work written by Naipaul as well the man himself, they are important to Caribbean people because they have changed us and possess the potential to continue to do so in revealing us to ourselves.

Noises of the Isles: About Nothing, Mineness or Aesthetic Recognition and Complicated Relationships

In her examination of the unsavoury in Ganesh's story, eminent Caribbean literary and linguistic scholar and creative writer, Barbara Lalla, rightly has the following to say about *The Mystic Masseur*:

> [It] is about lack of signification. Observations of what are presented as curious facts lead to absence of information, cryptic utterances beneath which gape meaninglessness, rituals of lost significance, fake honors and letters behind the name that attest to nothing, titles like teacher or Lord that lack authenticity, directives like RSVP that "don't mean nothing but is nice to have," all "pretty wordings" empty of any signification beyond their niceness. ("Signifying Nothing")

This tango with nothing is a prevalent characteristic of a Caribbean aesthetic and lifestyle. Indeed, for many who live in the Caribbean, Lalla's articulations of these issues in the novel would be considered succinct expressions of their everyday realities. Phillips wrote the screenplay for the Merchant-Ivory film company's adaptation of The *Mystic Masseur*. It became the first node for the adaptation and Phillips himself must have recognised the problems of "nothingness". This is copiously evident. For example, down to the fidelity the script displays in giving the character Ramlogan the question, "But tell me, what is this 'RSVP'?" Film script Ganesh is then allowed to repeat his answer in the novel: "It don't mean nothing but it nice to have it." This fidelity is perhaps not surprising since Phillips has much in common with Naipaul, including the interesting equivalents in their ways of self-identification and feelings of homelessness. Abigail Ward remarks, for example, that Phillips "once requested that his ashes be scattered at his 'Atlantic home'—point in the Atlantic Ocean between the Africa of his ancestors, the England of his childhood, and North America, where he now lives" (629). Like many other well-known Caribbean writers, these two have stared at the void of nothing quite intently.

So has Derek Walcott. Echoing fellow artist, writer, literary scholar and void-gazer, Garth St Omer, in *Nor Any Country*, Walcott recreates the contrapuntal dance like this in "Homecoming: Anse La Raye", a poem dedicated to St Omer:

> You give them nothing.
> Their curses melt in air.
> The black cliffs scowl,
> the ocean sucks its teeth,
> like that dugout canoe
> a drifting petal fallen in a cup,
> with nothing but its image,
> you sway, reflecting nothing.
> (*The Poetry of Derek Walcott 1948–2013* p. 99)

In precarious spaces between nothing and everything in which quotidian Caribbean lives are lived, "with nothing but … image[s]", captured so exquisitely in this novel, the film will almost automatically be approached as "mine" because it is related to my "friends"—the novel's recognisably Trinidadian narrator and characters who are attempting to deal with the condition of living with a sensibility of plenitude albeit in the midst of a void. Both ends of the spectrum are equally ideologically loaded and partisanship can sometimes arise. Sometimes the response is linked to simple preferences such as that for optimism or pessimism. As filmographer Richard Fung reflectively explains:

> One of the things that I find difficult to see with Trinidad is that you're stuck with so many inherited lenses. The lens of tourism, for example, that Trinidadians see themselves in. And I'm always struck when I'm there, and people say, "We live in a paradise", and at the same time, they're locking their gates and, you know, worrying if they can go out late at night and stuff like that. The lens of the paradise, the lens of the natural disaster, all those kinds of third-world lenses are there, and I find it very hard to see Trinidad as fresh and to frame it in ways that are somehow new. ("Kitchen Table" 126)

As Fung's remarks indicate, the creative impulse to see beyond inherited and constructed lenses is powerful indeed. When the impulse succeeds, the creative output is widely embraced as mine.

Apparently, sensitive to the ideological terrain of mineness, the day after Naipaul was awarded the Nobel Prize, a trained eye would have been able to recognise the care that went into the article Phillips wrote for *The Guardian*. In it, he reflects on Caribbean celebrations of the award and his earlier discussions with Walcott, the other Caribbean Nobel Laureate in literature, after they had viewed the film *The Mystic Masseur* together, about the possibility of Naipaul being the next laureate. This tête-à-tête would of course have been related to Walcott's own long-standing "love affair with film", to use Antoine-Dunne's term. But Phillips does not go into this. The article is about Naipaul and he asserts that Naipaul, in implicit contrast to Walcott, "is a writer whose hostility towards the Caribbean has been well documented.... One would imagine that such barbs would earn Naipaul only contempt and rejection from the people and the region ... but to my own cost I have discovered that this is not the case."

In saying as much, Phillips recalls old critical contestations that were at their hottest in the late 1960s and 1970s in the Caribbean and linger on still. In her revisitation to the quarrels, Alison Donnell reminds us that

> [w]hat shape critical agendas should take and what ideological bearings they might follow became ... a matter of serious contestation. What we commonly remember of this moment are the internal political and intellectual disputes among differently but equally committed critics that energized and mobilized critical debates for decades to come. (76)

Bridget Brereton speaks of debates like these in the context of "culture wars" and in light of their history as Donnell's remarks show, Phillips' explanation that "the people of the Caribbean, not only those of Trinidad, celebrated because the self-contempt that Naipaul feels is part of their own colonial legacy" makes sense. But while his assertion gives some insight into Caribbean responses to Naipaul, whether or not they were also imbricated in wider global trends such as that indicated in Naipaul's biography should also be considered.

In *The World Is What It Is: The Authorized Biography of V. S. Naipaul*, Patrick French ends his very first paragraph with the following conclusion based on his observation of events following the award of the Nobel Prize: "At this point in British history, when the sensational and immediate mattered above all else and fame was becoming more important than the achievements that might give rise to fame, Naipaul's half-century of work as a writer seemed less significant than his reputation for causing offence" (1). Clearly, therefore, as this brief recap of the reception of the book, film and man hopefully specifies, any analysis of Naipaul's work and work related to that work must take into account a dense discursive thicket in which the work will un/consciously be caught.

The sense of mineness or aesthetic recognition with which a Caribbean reader might approach the work is, therefore, of course, not solely or experientially immediately related to Caribbean colonial legacies or defense against them or on feelings of kinship. It is also about the relationship between the reader and text which would be idiosyncratically linked to such legacies and feelings depending on how one is positioned in relation to them. On the most basic and important level, as Hannich argues by drawing on the work of Winfried Fluck, aesthetic recognition would occur because

> [w]hen readers effectively co-create the aesthetic object, they do so in very personal ways; during the act of reading they transfer parts of their own interiority onto the book. Yet seeing an adaptation on the screen means being confronted with another concretization of the novel. When this concretization corresponds to and thus confirms the reader's own concretization, this process can imply an aesthetic recognition: an intersubjective acknowledgment of what the reader has conjured up mentally while reading. (427)

Herein may lie the crux of the reception of the film since the co-creation that results in mineness of the aesthetic objects that Naipaul has proffered to us has always been mired in myriad adjustments for "concretisation" and "intersubjective acknowledgement". Revealing something of Phillips's position in this regard, according to Bénèdicte Ledent, "that Phillips accepted the offer readily may have come as a surprise, if not a shock, to critics and scholars of Caribbean literature, for the younger writer is not exactly known as a Naipaul fan" (155–156). Despite the similarities noted above, Ledent asserts that "their visions of the world and of literature are as widely apart as can be" and she supports the point with a quote from Phillips who says that his and Naipaul's "outlook on most things, literary and otherwise, differs quite radically" (156).

Ledent argues further that

> in Phillips's decision was also the hope of seeing Caribbean life at last represented for an international audience as something else than "an exotic backdrop for stories of people whose lives are not invested in the region" (Caryl Phillips, *The Mystic Masseur: Essays and Excerpts from the Screenplay* 6). This film could therefore hopefully contribute to changing people's uninformed view of that part of the world as characterized exclusively by beaches, carnival and Calypso, a preoccupation that also underlies many of Phillips's artistic undertakings. (157)

These would no doubt sound like wonderful intentions to many, hence the possibility of expressing them in the first place. They are also nonetheless entrenched firmly in those early concerns that drove the critical debates about authenticity and misrepresentation, and the statement implies that Naipaul participated in the practice of faulty representation which Phillips set out to put aright.

Sharing something of Naipaul's background, just like Phillips, but because my parents were born in Trinidad in parallel circumstances somewhat later than Naipaul, and I have lived my whole life here, I have myself co-created Naipaul's work in myriad ways to accommodate its representations of the Caribbean. For example, I have not been overly thrilled by his lampooning of Ganesh's reverence for books because, although I certainly do not measure books like the novel's characters, I trace Ganesh's and other characters' love of books in myself, among diverse groups of friends and all members of a long-lived family. The family members include those who were ex-indentured as well as those who are four generations removed from India and staunch members of a Creole class, in which there is a similar reverence for books. But the adaptation to film of the novel for which I had had to make such adjustments has demanded far greater adjustments that do not yield a perspective like Ledent's. Instead, they lead me to ask of the adaptation, perhaps like the fictional Beharry: Why? The answer that comes to mind immediately is imbricated in the loss in the film of Naipaul the calypsonian with his carnivalesque and créolité that Gilberto M. Blasini describes as "the configuration and constant reinvention—the imaging and imagining—of transnational cultural communities emerging from or historically connected to the Caribbean" (70).

It is worthwhile in the circumstances, therefore, to pause a moment and consider how Ledent's statement positions carnival and calypso in a Caribbean aesthetic and this is best achieved by way of contrast. Bernadine Evaristo's praise for Lovelace's *Is Just a Movie* in *The Guardian*, reproduced in blurbs of praise in the peri-text of the novel, provides a convenient and necessary difference. She says: "And when things become too difficult, there is always the spirit of Carnival that presides over their lives: recuperative, cathartic, communal, celebratory." Here calypso and carnival, like the carnivalesque in any of its meanings, are rightly seen as possessing immense value for the people of the Caribbean rather than as part of their stereotypical party-animal image, which underwrites Ledent's expression.

In what follows, therefore, I examine créolité and the carnivalesque in Naipaul's writing in relation to the film script and the film. This is to identify how the script reconstructed the novel, as well as the relations among the two written texts and their conversion to vision, sound and moving images, bearing in mind, of course, that in the final analysis, no one can be sure precisely who called the shots that resulted in the final aesthetic object we experienced as the film. Given situations of cultural war, to use Brereton's term, these are necessary investigations. Lisa Lowe, albeit in a different context, explains that such situations arise "where the political terrain can neither resolve nor suppress inequality, [and] it erupts in culture. Because culture is the contemporary repository of memory, of history, it is through culture, rather than government, that alternative forms of subjectivity, collectivity, and public life are imagined" (22). It is thus useful to identify how some of the shots were called.

Calling the Shots for a Bollywood-Style Recreation: Character Conflation and Other Metaphorical Collapses

The easiest place to begin to look for where the shots are called is in the script. The first thing that stands out is that Ganesh becomes "Mr Ransumair"—a title without meaning that impacts the reader with greater violence than the various encodings of meaninglessness and nothingness in the novel. The script thus reproduces the naming problem that has been an aspect of colonial rule across the globe as Nelson Rolihlahla Mandela lamented.[3] The Ramsumair in the novel, on the one hand, carries layers of signification that are yet to be spelt out fully in any work of criticism. The misspelling, on the other hand, has been reproduced by those who commented on the film.[4]

The choice of Partap, a character who is quite violently despised by Ganesh and who appears very late in the novel in Chapter 9, "Press Pundit", as the narrator, is the second shot called by Phillips. The construction of a narrator so significantly different from the one in the novel seems a strange move to say the least, given the extreme importance of narrators in Naipaul's writing. Partap of the script translates smoothly to screen although the casting of Phillip's Partap character provides another beyond moment. The film opens with an apparently white man, looking puzzled, wearing a long coat and carrying an umbrella, waiting in a definitely non-Caribbean location on a train. It takes some adjustment to think of him in terms of the novel or the film script Partap. The soundtrack that accompanies the train is

3 See the effort to redress the pain he suffered in not being addressed by his correct name at https://www.nelsonmandela.org/content/page/names. Accessed 28 November 2020.

4 See for example Kevin M. Williams "Indian `Masseur' has mystic touch", *Chicago Tribune,* 17 May 2002. https://www.chicagotribune.com/news/ct-xpm-2002-05-17-0205170003-story.html. Accessed 6 April 2019.

composed by Zakir Hussain and Richard Robbins and emphasises the opening scene's foreign location. The opening credits roll against the camera's movement towards and over the top of the rusting hulk of the smoking train and last for almost two minutes. The credits declare a twenty-first-century Bollywood Indian *pardesi* or diaspora production in its roll call of starring actors and actresses.

Most of the actors were well known at the time and some went on to star in quintessential American blockbusters with Om Puri continuing to epitomise the rude, funny, illiterate immigrant, which he first manifests in the character of Ramlogan, right up to his death in 2017. Jimi Mistry, who can easily pass for white and does as the trench-coated Partap in the opening shot, had acted previously as Om Puri's son and continues to play a variety of roles on stage and in film. Ayesha Dharkar would glitter later in *Bombay Dreams* and has become one of the many faces of the *desi-pardesi* girl so prominent in Indian cinema that speaks to and for the diaspora. The others are even bigger names now. The accents from the very beginning produced by these characters as well as the visual images distance the Caribbean viewer. Only two Caribbean names are included in the opening credits—Grace Maharaj and Albert Laveau—and as we view the roles they play in the film, perplexity grows.

Once one becomes familiar with the name Partap being given to the unexpected narrator, the fact that this first scene collapses the epilogue and the first chapter into one can be viewed as part of the anticipated condensation necessary for a script that must provide only words spoken, with a minimum of description of place, time, mood and other directives permitted to the scriptwriter. This complacency about Partap remains until he becomes not just the narrator but replaces the non-Indian boy who is followed by the black cloud in the novel, which is a real manifestation of the psychological trauma of witnessing his brother's death. The brother was crushed to death as he was running an errand the mother had given to the boy. The way this occasion is jarring is similar to that elicited in many of the next scenes. These complex issues play havoc with aesthetic recognition.

This happens, for example, with the third shot, similarly called by Phillips, which is as interesting as those already mentioned. The Slugline or Scene Heading specifies: "2. FLASHBACK. 1943. EXT. HEADMASTER'S OFFICE—DAY. The HEADMASTER, a heavy-set, bald, black man, is sitting behind a desk" (3). The casting team eventually fitted Laveau to this role and the description in the script is annulled. But the relation of the description in the script to the one in the novel is worth considering further. In the depiction of the headmaster in the novel, we see an early example of one kind of singling out that became a pivotal part of Naipaul's "lone flower" style seen often enough throughout his oeuvre in depictions of big men in small places and small men in big spaces. What Phillips condenses to "heavy-set" in the script is transmitted in the novel through Naipaul's positioning of a big man in a small room full of children which serves as his office and classroom simultaneously. The image that Naipaul evokes is of a colonial school in which the disciplinary method of flogging that the headmaster dispenses to maintain stillness and quiet in the room causes him to expend energy incommensurate to that he attempts to control in the children. It is a potent illustration of colonial educational ineptitudes. The disappearance of the classroom in the movie turns the subsequent dialogue in the script and the film into a singularity of unabashed racial conflict rather than a reproduction of the multiplicities of class, race, gender and ethnicity that Naipaul illustrates in the text.

In addition, in the novel, we meet Ganesh at the beginning of World War II, in 1939, as an already-established author. This allows us to pinpoint the setting of his story reasonably accurately as that period after the end of indentureship and the visit of the Moyne Commission which led to people of Indian origin perceiving themselves in a certain way through a variety of deliberate efforts to do so, which has hardly abated to this day. These efforts and their motivations are some of the things the novel allows us to consider. The pieces of the novel not incorporated into the script or reformulated for the film are mainly from this chapter, Chapter 2, "Pupil and Teacher", in which these issues are first signified.

In a few swift lines at the very beginning of this chapter, Naipaul recalls indentureship and how it ended for many, with the acceptance in one way or another of an unusable five acres of land that required a great deal of creativity and innovation if it were to yield anything at all. But the background of indentureship and its triumphant end, the emerging into Caribbean life out of indentureship and into becoming colonial, driven by the desire for social mobility which is signified in the rural to urban movement, are all obliterated in the script and the film. In the novel, Ganesh is introduced as a graduate of Queen's Royal College but what is even more important are the circumstances under which he goes there, the reasons he does so and their effects on him. The elimination of this part of the novel is an appropriation of the novel for different purposes entirely and this fact may well have been flagged in the opening credits with the line "from a novel by V. S. Naipaul" rather than "based on a novel by V. S. Naipaul" in the script. "From" is the more accurate signifier borne out in the rest of the movie, most prominently visible in the recasting of the Mrs Cooper of the novel.

Phillips seems to be attempting to reproduce the créolité of the novel in maintaining a similar fidelity to the novel's characterisation as he did with the headmaster by making her Partap's mother. In the novel and film script, Mrs Cooper is depicted as the quintessentially urban Creole figure who helps and guides the inept Indo–Caribbean newcomer. The film, however, casts Grace Maharaj in a role in which she almost exactly reproduced the character she played in the 1974 movie *Bim* whose Caribbean credentials were called into question for far fewer reasons and in far less complex ways than attempted here. The trouble with the role in *The Mystic Masseur* is that her Mrs Cooper is an undecidable cross between a Creole belle and the Indo–Trinidadian mother of Partap. Sometimes the two distinct positions lead to the thought that maybe she is playing a double role. More important, however, is the erasure of the class structure of Trinidad and Tobago and how it manifested in the pre-independence period imbricated in race, gender and ethnicity which inhere in Naipaul's depiction of the headmaster and Mrs Cooper.

Although much more can be said in this vein, the last change that occurred in the adaptation of the book considered here is the use made of the symbol of the book which comprises a strange journey through an archetypal Caribbean Mi-Jean and stereotypical Western depictions of the Indian guru. The image on the DVD cover says it best. A generic guru sits on a stack of books with another stack in front of him as a desk on which the opened book from which he is reading rests. The man and his two stacks are positioned as though floating on blue water, possibly Caribbean waters, but definitely tropical waters since both banks are lined with coconut palm trees. The open book recalls the magic texts of every old-world civilisation around which a seemingly unending flow of movies has been emerging. The cover promises the film's location in the genre.

Among the three texts, novel, film script and film, books play an even more powerful role. The movie opens with Ganesh's awe over the books in Oxford University's library and then moves in scene two, to the library behind the headmaster in his office—"The HEADMASTER, a heavy-set, bald, black man, is sitting behind a desk. He looks at a young GANESH, in his early thirties. The air is being slowly turned over by an old ceiling fan. The office is book-lined, and the windows propped open with sticks" (2). From there, we become engulfed in Ganesh's desire to become a part of that world of books. His predecessor is without a doubt the second son, Mi-Jean of Walcott's *Ti-Jean and His Brothers*. By a series of subtle shifts, Ganesh in V. S. Naipaul's *The Mystic Masseur* thus merges seamlessly with other fictional characters, such as Shri Ganesha of W. Somerset Maugham's *The Razor's Edge* who is also in a *Dictionary of Literary Characters* in which he is described as: "Benign, holy man whose teachings include the idea that wisdom is the means to freedom; at his Ashrama Larry Darrell experiences a strange mystical illumination that gives him a profound sense of inner peace" (724). The film may also have generated the new covers for more recent publications of *The Mystic Masseur* which are all very Bollywood Indian images for the typically Caribbean figure of the 1957 Ganesh, including one of a bansuri-playing boy in dhoti and kurta. This is surely a great pity.

To Aim beyond Mere Proliferation: Some Lagniappe Thoughts

These many differences that occurred in the process of adaptation, which are but a mere few among the many in the three texts and their peri-texts, can be subsumed under one major difference. The most useful term for identification of that difference may be neo-racialisation. The first manifestation of this inheres in how the narrator is reconstructed. The reconstructions after this are legion. One may consider, therefore, that the novel was re-scripted in terms of diaspora and out of the original framework of nationalism within which the novel was constructed.

As Stuart Hall has taught us so well, all discourses of the diaspora are identitarian discourses created within racist national spaces from which many who long to belong are excluded. Naipaul's representation of the offspring of the Indian indentured is, therefore, often read within the terms of an Indian diaspora in the Caribbean. Arguably, however, Naipaul was writing in the late 1950s out of a nationalist sensibility rather than actively trying to create an Indian identity, and within that framework, Ganesh was depicted as trying to fit into a Trinidadian Creole mould represented in the figures of Mrs Cooper as well as the Headmaster. The Indian identity that Ganesh ends up with is a result of the sheer need to survive and is no more or less real than the Member of the Legislative Council or Member of the British Empire ones that he also earned for himself. Ganesh's recreation as solely Indian positioned in antagonism to a solely African world can thus be seen as counter-intuitive if not deliberately provocative. There are also pronounced differences with regard to the engendering of the characters as well as in how class is depicted differently in the three texts.

For those who may be unaware, it may thus be useful to point out that *The Mystic Masseur* was not the first book Naipaul wrote. *The Mystic Masseur* was Naipaul's first published novel and an attempt to produce something less episodic than his first written work, *Miguel Street*, which has remained in most readers' minds, a collection of short stories, despite Kenneth Ramchand's call for recognition of the Caribbean novelist as a short-story writer in disguise. Like the writers of whom he speaks, Ramchand somewhat hyperbolically claims in his 1997 essay "The West Indian Short Story", "There are no West Indian novelists, only short story writers in disguise; no West Indian novels, only fabrications taking their shape and structure from the transfigurated short stories they contain" (22). Most of the features and techniques of *Miguel Street* are reproduced in *The Mystic Masseur* although the setting includes the rural which was placed as distant background in *Miguel Street*. The calypsonian techniques that most find vividly evident in *Miguel Street* are also present in this book, which thus certainly fits Ramchand's perspective of the Caribbean writer.

As Paula Morgan reminds us: "The calypso has been traditionally regarded as the lash of the small man who deploys picong and wit for boastful self-assertion and for sustained counter discourse with the hegemonic worldview, in the protected arena of the performance space" (1).[5] The space of his writing became that arena for Naipaul in which he created so many delightful characters by "lift[ing] the petty events out of their specific confines and mak[ing] them representative experiences.... The smallness of *Miguel Street* through which a stranger could drive and dismiss as a slum" could as easily be that of Fuente Grove. And as in *Miguel Street*, it "is alleviated by the notoriety of the calypso which projects the community's mundane dramas onto the national and international stage and thereby amplifies its tragedies. In the process it lends significance and import to all", as Morgan puts it.

The depiction of the narrator's mother is a case in point. The traits given to her are paradigmatic of the Indo–Trinidadian urban lower class of the time, who Naipaul unfailingly depicted with the calypsonian's verve. The following brief scene in which she is shown in interaction with her son is illuminating:

> My mother distrusted doctors and never took me to one. I am not blaming her for this because in those days people went by preference to the unqualified masseur or the quack dentist.
>
> "I know the sort of doctors it have in Trinidad," my mother used to say. "They think nothing of killing two three people before breakfast."
>
> This wasn't as bad as it sounds: in Trinidad the midday meal is called breakfast. (*The Mystic Masseur* 1)

---

5 See Chapter 7 later in this volume, "With a Tassa Blending: Calypso and Cultural Identity in Indo–Caribbean Fiction" by Paula Morgan.

The scene is subtly comedic in ways that may escape those unfamiliar with cultural traits such as the extreme skepticism regarding figures of authority that both mother and son display. It is a characteristic that Naipaul endows on many, including the taxi-driver: "Our taxi-driver shouted, 'Ai!'" When Beharry anticipates the question that follows the shout, the taxi-driver responds with a typical brand of exasperated sarcasm to say: "Nah. We come all the way from Port-of-Spain just for the scenery" (*The Mystic Masseur* 1). This feature of Naipaul's writing seems to be untranslatable into film because there is nothing to approximate it in the film that carries the name of the novel. Instead, we have quaint images of polite postmen and the barest hint of sarcasm from Bissoon, the bookseller, which is negated by the quiet demeanour of David Sammy who is cast in this role. The diagnosis and perceptive representation of cultural features and social issues that we have come to associate with Caribbean literature were entirely eroded by the loss of the calypsonian and the créolité of the carnivalesque which comprise the prominent structures of this literature.

The centenary year of Indian cinema was commemorated in 2013. When it began in 1913, Indian indentureship in the Caribbean was still in effect. On the other hand, when indentureship began in 1838, Indian cinema was not yet much of a dream, even though interest in photography and image-making technologies was high and may have promised its coming. How the Indian diaspora is positioned in relation to the development of Indian cinema is a good question and one that is as yet not explored, although much has been said about developments in Indian cinema and the emergence of an Indian diaspora. This essay thus signals problems in the appropriation of Indian cinema for accented purposes. It illustrates also the caution required when Indian/diaspora/accented cinema does try to speak to and for the diaspora and in future work an attempt will be made to join in the discussion of the problems of Indian/diaspora cinema in shaping the lives of those in the Caribbean diaspora.

At present, it must suffice to state the obvious with Viranjini Munasinghe: "Ethnic stereotypes are pervasive in contemporary Trinidad." Given this state of affairs, her warning is pertinent and urgent: "When cultural attributes are perceived as natural and innate, it becomes imperative to understand the productive context for the emergence of such ethnic ideologies" (140). It is even more imperative to unveil such ethnic ideologies and to help to develop an understanding of the context of their emergence. Naipaul's work has done a great deal to do precisely that for the people of the Caribbean particularly those in Trinidad and Tobago. The film, on the other hand, unreflectively reproduces those ideologies and positions the Trinidadian characters in the diasporic framework of accented cinema, to use Naficy's term, that flattens them beyond the point of caricature. The beyond that we seek, however, is of a different sort.

As Bhabha reminds us, our efforts can only "embody … [the] restless and revisionary energy [of that beyond] if they transform the present into an expanded and excentric site of experience and empowerment" (4). Such a "beyond" is critically important in Naipaulian studies since Naipaul, like so many of those who inherited a colonised world, crossed vast terrains of space and time to try to understand the vulnerabilities of old worlds that facilitated a colonial world order and the problems posed by this order for individual self-actualisation and fulfillment. Naipaul adopted techniques of the calypsonian in order to do this and his performances of créolité in the process are inspirational early forays. The film that was generated from his first novel betrayed this and atavistically regressed to the ethnic ideologies that existed even before the arrival of the indentured labourers in the Caribbean. The critical vigilance such an outcome demands cannot be overstated.

Works cited

Antoine-Dunne, Jean. *Derek Walcott's Love Affair with Film*. Peepal Tree Press, 2017.

———. "Sound and Vision in the Caribbean Imaginary." *The Journal of West Indian Literature,* vol. 18 no2, 2010, pp. 95–116.

———. *Time and Space in Their Indissoluble Connection: Towards an Audio-Visual Caribbean Aesthetic*. Rodopi, 2004.

———. "Time to Break down the Cages." *Caribbean Studies*, vol. 36, issue 1, 2008, pp. 236–240.

———. "Visions and Revisions: Film/in(g) the Caribbean." *Caribbean Quarterly*, special issue of *Visions and Revisions: Film/in(g) the Caribbean*, vol. 61, issue 2–3, 2015, pp. 1–6.

Besson, Gerard, and Caryl Phillips. *The Mystic Masseur: Essays and Excerpts from the Screenplay*. Paria Publishing, 2001.

Blasini, Gilberto M. "Caribbean Cinematic Créolité." *Black Camera: An International Film Journal*, vol. 1, No. 1, 2009, pp. 70–90.

Bhabha, Homi. *The Location of Culture*. Routledge, 1994.

Brereton, Bridget. "Contesting the Past: Narratives of Trinidad and Tobago History." *New West Indian Guide / Nieuwe West-Indische Gids*, vol. 81, No. 3–4, 2007, pp. 169–196.

Donnell, Alison. "All Friends Now?: Critical Conversations, West Indian Literature, and the 'Quarrel with History.'" *Small Axe*, vol. 16, No. 2, No. 38, 2012, pp. 75–85.

Fluck, Winfried. "Playing Indian: Aesthetic Experience, Recognition, Identity." *Romance with America? Essays on Culture, Literature, and American Studies*, edited by Laura Bieger and Johannes Voelz, Universitätsverlag Winter, 2009, pp. 433–452.

French, Patrick, *The World is What It is: The Authorized Biography of V. S. Naipaul*. Alfred A. Knopf, 2008.

Gosine, Andil. "Kitchen Table Talk: Richard Fung and Ian Harnarine in Conversation." *Small Axe*, vol. 21, No. 2, No. 53, 2017, pp. 123–134.

Griffith, Glynne. *The BBC and the Development of Anglophone Caribbean Literature, 1943–1958*. Palgrave Macmillan, 2016.

Healy, Dara. "Whose Mystic Masseur?." *Newsday*, 17 November 2017. https://newsday.co.tt/2017/11/10/whose-mystic-masseur/ Accessed 6 April 2019.

Jeffers, Jennifer M. *Britain Colonized: Hollywood's Appropriation of British Literature*. Palgrave Macmillan, 2006.

Lalla, Barbara. "Signifying Nothing: Writing About Not Writing in *The Mystic Masseur*." *Anthurium: A Caribbean Studies Journal*, vol. 5, issue 2, article 6, 2007. http://scholarlyrepository.miami.edu/anthurium/vol5/iss2/6. Accessed 6 April 2019.

Ledent, Bénèdicte. "The Same, Yet Different: Caryl Phillips's Screen Adaptation of V. S. Naipaul's *The Mystic Masseur*." *V. S. Naipaul: A World in Tension*, edited by Judith Misrahi-Barak, Universite de Montpellier, 2004, pp. 155–169.

Lovelace, Earl. *Is Just a Movie*. 2011. Haymarket Books, 2012.

Lowe, Lisa. *Immigrant Acts: On Asian American Cultural Politics*. Duke UP, 1996.

Mc Govern, Una. "Ganesh" *Chambers Dictionary of Literary Characters*. Chambers Harrap, 2004.

Munasinghe, Viranjini. "Foretelling Ethnicity in Trinidad: The Post-emancipation 'Labor Problem.'" *Clio / Anthropos: Exploring the Boundaries between History and Anthropology*, edited by Andrew Willford and Eric Tagliacozzo, Stanford UP, 2009, pp. 139–186.

Naficy, Hamid. *An Accented Cinema: Exilic and Diasporic Filmmaking*. Princeton UP, 2001.

Naipaul, V. S. *The Mystic Masseur*. 1957 (renewed 1985). First Vintage International Edition, 2002.

Oatley, Keith. *Such Stuff as Dreams: The Psychology of Fiction*. Wiley-Blackwell, 2011.

Paddington, Bruce, and Keith Q. Warner. "The Emergence of Caribbean Feature Films." *Black Camera: An International Film Journal*, vol. 1, No. 1, 2009, pp. 91–108.

Phillips, Caryl. "Reluctant Hero." *The Guardian*, Friday, 12 October 2001. https://www.theguardian.com/books/2001/oct/12/fiction.vsnaipaul Accessed 23 March 2019.

Ramchand, Kenneth. "The West Indian Short Story." *Journal of Caribbean Literatures* Vol. 1, No. 1 (Spring 1997): pp. 21–33. https://www.jstor.org/stable/40986061 Accessed March 26, 2019.

"Shakalaka Baby." *Bombay Dreams*. Performance by Ayesha Dharkar, produced by Andrew Lloyd Webber and Shekhar Kapur, composed by A. R. Rahman, directed by Steven Pimlott, Apollo Victoria Theater, London. 2002, https://www" https://www.youtube.com/watch?v=rPdBCxXRPw4 Accessed 6 April 2019.

Sollars, Michael D. "Ganesha." *Dictionary of Literary Characters*, Facts On File, 2011, p 724.

The Guru. Directed by Daisy von Scherler Mayer, produced by Shekhar Kapur, MCA/Universal, United Kingdom, 2002, 94 min.

The Mystic Masseur. Directed by Ismail Merchant, produced by James Ivory, ThinkFilm, India/Trinidad and Tobago, 2002, 117 min.

Venning, Dan. "Cultural Imperialism and Intercultural Encounter in Merchant Ivory's *Shakespeare Wallah*." *Asian Theatre Journal*, vol. 28, No. 1, Spring 2011, pp. 149–167.

"Waiting for Vidia…" *The Guardian*, https://www.theguardian.com/film/2001/apr/15/features Accessed 6 April 2019.

Walcott, Derek. "Homecoming: Anse La Raye". *The Poetry of Derek Walcott 1948-2013*. Ed Glyn Maxwell. Farrar, Strauss, Giroux, 2014. p 99.

Ward, Abigail. "An Interview with Caryl Phillips." *Contemporary Literature*, vol. 53, No. 4, Winter 2012, pp. 628–645.

Wa Thiong'o, Ngũgĩ. "V. S. Naipaul, his Kenyan-born wife, me and lone flower at the dinner table." *Daily Nation*, 19 August 2018, https://www.nation.co.ke/news/V—S—Naipaul—his-Kenyan-born-wife—me-and-a-lone-flower/1056-4718690-754pr7/index.html. Accessed 6 April 2019.

Williams, Kevin M. "Indian 'Masseur' has mystic touch." *Chicago Tribune*, 17 May 2002, https://www.chicagotribune.com/news/ct-xpm-2002-05-17-0205170003-story.html. Accessed 6 April 2019.

Chapter 3

V. S. NAIPAUL'S *THE MYSTIC MASSEUR*: DEFINING FAILURE AND SUCCESS FOR THE COLONIAL SUBJECT[1]

Roxana Elena Doncu

> "Is my only vice," Ganesh said. "Only vice. I don't smoke. I don't drink. But I must have my books."
>
> —*The Mystic Masseur* 5

The Mystic Masseur is built on the tension between the protagonist's understanding of his life journey as a success and the subversion of that definition by the events of the plot, which reveal Ganesh's failures. If we were to deconstruct the idea of divine providence put forward by Ganesh in his autobiography, it would appear to consist in the convergence of several factors responsible for what Ganesh terms his success. Naipaul writes:

> In his autobiography, *The Years of Guilt*, Ganesh attributes his success (he asks to be pardoned for using the word) to God. The autobiography shows that he believed strongly in predestination; and the circumstances which conspired to elevate him seem indeed to be providential. If he had been born ten years earlier it is unlikely, if you take into account the Trinidad Indian's attitude to education at that time, that his father would have sent him to the Queen's Royal College.... If he had been born ten years later his father would have sent him to America or Canada or England to get a profession—the Indian attitude to education had changed so completely—and Ganesh might have become an unsuccessful lawyer or a dangerous doctor.... He was served even by his enemies. Without Narayan's attacks Ganesh would never have taken up politics and he might have remained a mystic. With unfortunate results. Ganesh found

1 A version of this chapter was first published in the *Journal of Romanian Literary Studies*, Issue no. 6, 2015.

> himself a mystic when Trinidad was crying out for one. That time is now past.... Providence indeed seems to have guided Ganesh. Just as it told him when to take up mysticism, so it told him when to give it up. (193–194)

In a similar fashion to his divine namesake and protector, the elephant-headed god Ganesh who is the lord of success and the god of education and knowledge, prudence and wisdom in Hindu mythology, the worldly Ganesh also seems to be born at an auspicious hour—on the cusp of important historical shifts. Colonialism is on its last legs. Towards the end of World War II, an exhausted Great Britain went through a deep power crisis, with liberating effects for the colonies. As imperial authority became shakier every moment, the colonies were given a freer hand in political and administrative matters. For educated colonials like Ganesh, this proved to be a golden opportunity. *The Mystic Masseur* discloses Naipaul's concern that a long history of colonial exploitation and the segregation inherent to manufactured societies like the one in Trinidad would be an impediment to the progress and new freedom made possible by the historical circumstances.

What these circumstances allow is the rise to power of ambitious mediocrities like Ganesh. His success would have been impossible in the conditions before the war, when colonial administration was still powerful, or, ten years later, when the confusion engendered by this historical catastrophe was over, democracy and capitalism firmly established, and the need for mystics was a thing of the past. The most important historical event of the period is the first election featuring universal adult suffrage, held on 1 July 1946. This was a momentous change in the history of Trinidad. Voting on a limited scale had been introduced only a couple of decades before, in 1925, and the universal adult suffrage expanded the electorate from a couple of thousands to almost three hundred thousand, including the previously disenfranchised non-whites and women.

It is no coincidence, therefore, that "nineteen forty-six was the turning point of Ganesh's career" (8). Yet, Ganesh's upward social mobility cannot be explained exclusively by recourse to the turbulent war period and the shifts it brought about in the world distribution of power. It is made possible by these circumstances, the lack of which would have foreclosed Ganesh's every chance of success, but, at the same time, it is the result of personal choice and competent strategies. In a study of V. S. Naipaul, Fawzia Mustafa notes that *The Mystic Masseur* is "the chronicle of Ganesh's success as a flawed and misguided achievement within a political and social milieu that cannot as yet read itself as the tangled amalgam of badly translated texts" (46). This observation, rooted in the analysis of colonial Trinidad, would seem to imply that Ganesh's political achievement is no more than an accident attributable to fortune and circumstance. The novel's comic form reinforces this kind of reading, with its emphasis on the humorous effects of mistaken interpretations, mistranslations, linguistic and cultural quid pro quo.

As Susan Bassnett and Harish Trivedi note in the introduction to *Post-Colonial Translation: Theory and Practice*, there is a close relationship between colonisation and translation: colonies are regarded as translated copies of originals "located elsewhere on the map" (5). While it may be true that Ganesh's success is to a great extent the consequence of the general cultural incompetence of colonial society (this cultural and political incompetence is the very target of Naipaul's satire), it soon becomes obvious that Ganesh is able to turn this cultural incompetence to his own advantage and exploit the ignorance, superstition and gullibility of others. Mustafa seems to make a similar point when she notices that Ganesh reads different situations with "considerable sophistication" (47).

Ganesh's principal strategy is to trade on his cultural and religious capital. He is able to do that as he is among the first generation of Trinidadian Indians to receive formal education at a college in Port-of-Spain. However, the profitable exploitation of cultural capital becomes a viable strategy under the double circumstance of a general lack of formal education among Indians and their desire and respect for it. Had Ganesh been born among the former black slaves, who may have been less inclined to appreciate formal education because of its association with the rule of the white elite, the situation would have been different. Recently returned to his village after his father's death, Ganesh shares his life projects with his aunt, The Great Belcher. Hearing that he is about to take up massaging people, she is the first to suggest a different path to him: "It sound good. But a man like you should be doing something else. Bookwork, man" (47). She voices the collective insecurity in her justification of books as necessary for a sense of identity lacking in colonial Trinidad:

> "People go want to buy that sort of book?"
>
> "Is exactly what Trinidad want, boy. Take all the Indians in the towns. They ain't have any pundit or anything near them, you know. How they go know what to do and what not to do, when and not when? They just have to guess." (47)

Writing books in Trinidad means not only providing guidance for lost sheep—as a business that responds to a specific market demand (of spiritual guidance), it is also a lucrative activity: "It have money in books, you know. I suppose the man who write the Macdonald Farmer's Almanac just peeling money. Why you don't try your hand at something like the Napoleon Book of Fate?[2] I just feel you could do that sort of thing good" (47).

Popular opinion in colonial Trinidad relegates books, knowledge and writing to the domain of the magic and the occult. Ganesh's use of writing to impress and earn the respect of others often intermingles with his shrewd appraisal of the power that superstition exerts on the uneducated average Hindu. Thus, when Ramlogan goes to his house after the wedding to insult him and proffer threatening remarks, Ganesh asks Leela to bring him the copy-book from the bedroom and then writes down Ramlogan's words in it. This makes Leela suspicious; her suspicion changes into firm certitude when Ganesh takes Ramlogan's picture: she is sure that her father is going to be the victim of obeah.[3] As a dutiful daughter, she informs Ramlogan of Ganesh's intention, and the aggressor instantly turns into a terrified victim: "Oh, God! What I do to your husband to make him prosecute me in this way? What he going to do with the picture?" (*The Mystic Masseur* 51).

Ganesh thus speculates on the cultural and religious capital he possesses and exploits the superstition and gullibility of others that are less educated. The widespread appeal of superstition and black magic in Trinidad is explained by the fact that they offer people immediate gratification and provide a rough means of dealing with the complexity of their world in the absence of real knowledge. The roots of Ganesh's failure lie in his refusal to acknowledge the injustice at the root of this situation. Instead of fighting for equal access to education or championing the rights of the subaltern, he is often a stark supporter of the status quo.

Ganesh uses opportunities only to further his own interest and never takes a wider view on issues of social injustice. This is all too evident in his treatment of Leela. Though a modern educated man, his family life begins with the beating of his wife, a common practice among Trinidadians. Bridget Brereton argues, furthermore, that due to

2 Napoleon's *Book of Fate* (anonymous writer) was allegedly found by Napoleon and translated by a German scholar. It is an oraculum that describes various methods of divining the future and was very popular among superstitious Hindus who replaced the customary visit to the astrologer with a consultation of the book.

3 Sorcery of West African origin, similar to voodoo practices, which are popular throughout the Caribbean.

the scarcity of women among indentured labourers, domestic violence increased among Trinidad Indians

> in a situation where women were scarce, the possession of a wife was an important symbol of status and masculinity ... a crucial element in the husband's self-esteem, which he could ill afford to lose. Traditionally, the Indian husband was expected to keep his wife in subjection ... the shame of failure was wiped out by "the cleansing violence of self-righteousness". (182–183)

Wife beating is such a common practice that it is ironically described as a rite of passage to adulthood and Ganesh's initiation into manhood:

> It was their first beating, a formal affair done without anger on Ganesh's part or resentment on Leela's; and although it formed no part of the marriage ceremony itself, it meant much to both of them. It meant that they had grown up and become independent. Ganesh had become a man; Leela a wife as privileged as any other big woman. Now she too would have tales to tell of her husband's beatings; and when she went home she would be able to look sad and sullen as every woman should. (49)

And yet, in addition to his cultural and religious capital, it is to Leela that Ganesh owes a large part of his success. The miserable interlude of "The Trials" (the fifth chapter that recounts Ganesh's struggles in Fuente Grove) ends when Leela decides to leave Ganesh in an attempt to persuade him to write his first book. Although The Great Belcher had kept her promise and given Ganesh all the Sanskrit books his uncle possessed, he kept postponing the actual writing of the book, concentrating on making notes and ordering them in differently coloured notebooks. Ganesh's first book is a compilation entitled *101 Questions and Answers on the Hindu Religion*, written with the express purpose of getting Leela back and impressing Beharry, his neighbour and friend from Fuente Grove.

Going to Ramlogan with the book, Ganesh earns from his father-in-law both the title of author and that of "Ganesh the Radical". Ramlogan's attitude changes dramatically at hearing that he has "an author" in the family: "Come inside, man, sahib. Why you pretending that you is a stranger and standing up outside? Come in, sahib, come in, sit down in your old place in the hammock. Oh, sahib, is a real honour. I too too proud of you" (*The Mystic Masseur* 88). Ramlogan's deferential attitude is symbolic of the mechanism of public reaction in Trinidad, where social and political life is mainly organised around the related concepts of pride, honour and self-esteem. Furthermore, due to the close connection between books and magic, being an author is regarded by Ramlogan and others as possessing a kind of mystical aura that reflects positively on everybody around.

Magic symbols, as James G. Frazer claimed, work according to two major principles: the principle of similarity and the principle of contagion. The law of similarity means that an effect will resemble its cause, and the law of contagion extends the negative or positive attributes of things in space and time through physical contact. The kissing (or touching) of saints' relics in Christian Orthodox religion is an example of contagion: the sacredness of the saint's body extends to the one who touches (kisses) his holy relics. Similarity functions when an icon (an image/representation) stands for God/saints in receiving believers' prayers. In the novel, by contagion, books are not perceived as the independent production of a single individual. Instead, due to their function as carriers of occult knowledge, they spread their auratic rays over the whole community. That is what earns Ganesh the respect of relatives and neighbours and also contributes to the poor sales of his book.

The salesman tells him the book sold badly because it "is the sort of book you go have hell even giving away because people go think you want to work some sign of magic on them" (100). Ganesh's success as a mystic owes much both to his knowledge of Hinduism and local magic practices (obeah) and to the encouragement of The Great Belcher. His aunt and Leela join forces to convince Ganesh that he has "the Power". Beharry writes an advertisement for "pundit Ganesh", but Ganesh himself, dissatisfied with the pundit title, nails "a signboard on the mango tree: Ganesh, Mystic" (110). Ganesh's preference for "mystic" (a word that alludes to initiation into religious mysteries, occult forces, etc.) instead of "pundit" (an Indian scholar, an expert in Hindu law and philosophy) shows his awareness of the power of superstition and his eagerness to capitalise on that. Appearances are not neglected either; Ganesh gives up wearing trousers and shirts and dons the traditional dhoti[4] and white turban.

Ganesh's fame as a mystic begins after he manages "to cure" a boy who thought he was followed by a black cloud. Ganesh finds out from his parents that the boy started having hallucinations after his brother's death. The parents had gone to the Christian priests as well, and they were told that the boy had to pay for his sins. The reader is thus given to understand that the boy's hallucination was part of a guilt complex—knowledge that is not available to the average uneducated Trinidadian.

4 A rectangular piece of cloth, wrapped around the legs and knotted at the waist.

Ganesh puts up an impressive performance in front of the boy, pretending to see the black cloud, fight it and dispel it—an exorcism inspired from the practice of obeah. The success of his performance is augmented by the Niggergram—the local word used for rumours spread by the ignorant and superstitious black population about events in the community:

> There was no report of this incident in the newspapers, yet within two weeks all Trinidad knew about Ganesh and his Powers. The news went about on the local grapevine, the Niggergram, an efficient, almost clairvoyant, news service. As the Niggergram noised the news abroad, the number of Ganesh's successes were magnified, and his Powers became Olympian. (125)

Ganesh's mystic career, although rooted firmly in popular belief and superstition, is propelled by his "intelligence and sympathy" (128) and his love of learning. Intelligence and sympathy refer to his ability to "read" people and circumstances and exploit them in his favour. The books which surround him kindle respect and reinforce his authority: "You never felt that he was a fake and you couldn't deny his literacy or learning—not with all those books" (128). His mysticism also reflects the cultural hybridity of the island in embracing all religious traditions:

> He was no bigot. He took as much interest in Christianity and Islam as in Hinduism. In the shrine, the old bedroom, he had pictures of Mary and Jesus next to Krishna and Vishnu; a crescent and star represented iconoclastic Islam. "All the same God," he said. Christians liked him, Muslims liked him, and Hindus, willing as ever to risk prayers to new gods, didn't object. (128)

This universalism is not depicted, however, as an effect of the pluralism and tolerance of Hindu religion but as the consequence of an emerging capitalist frame of mind, for which nothing should be discarded as long as it brings profit. Ganesh's financial flair is again at work. He realises that, in a poor society like the one in Trinidad, it is generosity rather than strict fees that can earn him a practice: "But more than his powers, learning, or tolerance, people liked his charity. He had no fixed fee and accepted whatever was given him" (128). He finds alternative ways of making money: by reprinting his book, "the first best-seller in the history of Trinidad publishing" (140). He also acts with considerable shrewdness when he discovers that Ramlogan had been making money off his back by establishing a taxi service to drive Trinidadians to the mystic's residence. Ganesh blackmails Ramlogan into selling him the taxis and this prompts Ramlogan to look for revenge and inform

Narayan about the whole affair. The war with Narayan, as I have shown previously, is again a stepping stone for Ganesh, launching his career as a politician. Another incident that testifies to Ganesh's use of cultural symbols to further his own interests is his self-promotion with the aid of the written word in the war with Narayan.

Ganesh's second book is called *The Guide to Trinidad*. Here, Ganesh proves his ability to master the Western double code of dressing up business interests as multicultural rhetoric. In the guise of an innocent booklet introducing foreign visitors to the multiracial Trinidad, it contains hidden publicity for Ganesh's mystic practice:

> The book spoke about the romance of Trinidad's many races. In a chapter called The East in the West the readers were told that they would be shocked to find ... in a village called Fuente Grove, a genuine Hindu temple which looked as if it had been bodily transported from India. The Fuente Grove Hindu temple was considered well worth a visit, for spiritual and artistic reasons. (147)

The Guide to Trinidad is also a cunning attempt to destroy the credibility of his rival. Pretending to take an objective look at Trinidad's mass media, Ganesh's book does its best to cast a shadow on Narayan's paper: "The anonymous author of The Guide was enthusiastic about the island's modernity.... But he deplored the absence of any influential weekly or monthly paper, and he warned foreign advertisers to be wary of the mushroom monthlies which claimed to be organs of certain sections of the community" (147).

If being an author served his interests in the Hindu community when writing his first book, Ganesh is conversely aware of the benefits of anonymity when launching an "objective" book to an international audience. He learns about the practice of foreign publishing houses of sending away free catalogues from Beharry. Yet, though acquainted with the practice, Beharry is completely unaware of its meaning and intention, and watches in bewilderment how Ganesh "sent free copies of The Guide to all the American Army camps in Trinidad.... He also sent copies to export agencies and advertising agencies in America and Canada which dealt with Trinidad" (147).

Education gives Ganesh an understanding of practices and meanings unavailable to the average person. His knowledge of Western ways and awareness of local cultural practices enable him to make the best of both worlds and carve a personal space for success and recognition. Fawzia Mustafa argues that Ganesh's ascension is "emblematic of the rise of the first generation of colonial entrepreneurs who unethically capitalized on the political opportunities the era offered" (45). What she implies by "unethically capitalized" is that Ganesh, who although to a large extent is able to "read" people and circumstances correctly and act on that knowledge, is nevertheless limited in his agency by personal interest.

In terms of the Kantian and continental philosophical tradition, Ganesh does not act freely because he does not act morally. For Kant, freedom is a consequence of the ethical act, which presupposes a universal law: one should act only in such a way that would constitute a universally accepted law. Acting out of personal interest is not a moral, and, thus, not a free act. Another important distinction is made by David Detmer in his analysis of Sartre's *Being and Nothingness*, between practical (limited) and ontological (absolute) freedom (60–61). Insofar as Ganesh is not able to dictate the terms of his success, he does not have ontological freedom (the freedom of choosing for oneself how one should act). Ganesh has only practical freedom, which is the capability to achieve what one desires.

Ganesh acts only when his interests are at stake. As a politician, he fails to represent adequately the interests of the black people who had elected him. Yet, circumstances act again in his favour, and he is awarded an MBE by the British authorities who were too far away to be in touch with the political realities in Trinidad. There is also a deeper criticism embedded in the irony. The implication is that, in colonial countries like Trinidad, political elites will fail to represent people's interests because politicians are mere imperial stooges (a criticism that foreshadows *The Mimic Men*). Thus, what at a superficial level appears as achievement is revealed as a deeper failure.

Ganesh's successful strategies are premised on the bastardisation of Hindu and Western cultural capital. This bastardisation and the mistranslation of values become possible against the backdrop of colonial manufactured societies, which lack a powerful tradition. The cultural fields in colonial societies are incapable of preserving their autonomy and establishing a firm basis for political debate. The cultural and religious hybridity that characterise Trinidad Indians is perceived as negative effects of the lack of Hindu cultural autonomy. The displaced Hindu spirituality loses its capacity to act as an integrative cultural system ordering people's lives and is consequently invaded by the modern capitalist spirit.

The result is a formal Hindu culture whose meanings are supplied by capitalist practices. It is important to note that while Naipaul seems to decry the lack of authentic traditions in colonial societies, he takes an ironic stand towards the recuperation of authentic precolonial traditions. His argument in *The Middle Passage*, for example, is that the precolonial past has been erased with the genocide of the indigenous population and the languages spoken in the Caribbean were borrowed from the imperial masters. As colonial societies are incapable of nurturing strong and authentic values, they pave the road forward for opportunists like Ganesh, conversant both with formal Hindu custom and capitalist practice. They are emblematic of the period right before independence and they constitute, more or less, that class of locally born colonials for whom Macaulay's infamous 1835 Minute to Parliament advocated the creation: "A class of interpreters between us and the millions whom we govern—a class of persons Indian in blood and colour, but English in tastes, opinions, in morals and in intellect" (Ashcroft 140). The result of such mimicry, however, is not the subversion of the colonial order as Ashcroft claims but the creation of a class of opportunist "picaroons" like Ganesh (141). In *The Middle Passage*, Naipaul compares the opportunist politicians of the 1946 elections to "the sixteenth century picaroon of Spanish literature, [who] survives and triumphs by his wits in a place where it is felt that all imminence is arrived at by crookedness" (72).

For some readers like me, a Romanian reader, characters like Ganesh appear strangely familiar, and there is a feeling of "family resemblance" between the early postcolonial Trinidad and the panorama of Romanian society sketched by I. L. Caragiale in his plays and short stories—the same opportunism, double-standard morality and hybrid practices, the result of the meeting of two worlds, one dying and the other not yet born: the traditional, Balkan–Ottoman practices grafted onto incipient capitalism. Like Caragiale, a conservative who repeatedly offended the liberals by revealing the discourse of modernisation to be just empty mimicry of the West, Naipaul proved a very unwelcome voice in postcolonial literature, with his implication that colonials conversant both with their culture and the coloniser's culture will develop a double-standard morality that will serve only their own interests. He later had to face this accusation himself from critics like Selwyn Cudjoe, Rob Nixon and even Edward Said. For early postcolonial literature, therefore, the ambivalence of hybridity and mimicry is not necessarily positive. For a start, cultural hybridity indicates the degree to which traditional Hindu customs become corrupted by the emergent American capitalist culture. Furthermore, while it empowers educated individuals like Ganesh to accede to high positions, it also serves as an instrument for the oppression of the illiterate masses.

Ganesh's from-rags-to-riches Cinderella story is illustrative of both the shortcomings and mediocrity of Trinidadian colonial society and the opportunities for change offered by the turbulent war period. Through Ganesh's character and the story of his meteoric rise to power, the novel satirises the limited social and political understanding of colonial society, launching a powerful critique on the effects of economic imperialism. Due to the lack of authentic cultural traditions and real values, Trinidadian society appears as manufactured and artificial—or half-made—and is thus incapable of encouraging, fostering and promoting excellence. A society lacking in adequate standards becomes the competing field for mock personalities like Ganesh and his political rival Narayan. Their success is primarily the conjoined effect of the flawed social structure of Trinidad and the volatile circumstances of World War II. At the same time, the novel becomes, in reverse, the mirror of Naipaul's own journey of literary discovery from the colony to the heart of empire and then back home again. Together with *Miguel Street*, *The Mystic Masseur* testifies to the emergence of the writer's own voice after overcoming the intellectual colonialism that had kept him tied to the cultural heritage of the Empire.

Works Cited

Ashcroft, Bill. *Key Concepts in Postcolonial Studies*. Routledge, 1998.

Bassnett, Susan, and Harish Trivedi, eds. *Post-colonial Translation: Theory & Practice*. Routledge, 1999.

Brereton, Bridget. *Race Relations in Colonial Trinidad 1870–1900*. Cambridge UP, 1979.

Detmer, David. *Freedom As a Value: A Critique of the Ethical Theory of Jean-Paul Sartre*. Columbia UP, 1980.

Frazer, James G. *The Golden Bough*. Macmillan, 1922

Mustafa, Fawzia. *V. S. Naipaul*. Cambridge UP, 1995.

V.S. Naipaul. *The Middle Passage*. Andre Deutsch, 1962.

———. *The Mystic Masseur*. Picador, 2002.

Chapter 4

THE SUFFRAGE OF ELVIRA: A STUDY OF POLITICS IN PRE-INDEPENDENCE TRINIDAD[1]

Bhoe Tewarie

V. S. Naipaul's first four book-length works, including *A House for Mr Biswas*, generally regarded as a masterpiece of twentieth-century fiction, are all set in pre-independence Trinidad and Tobago. However, although these early works possess elements of local colour and to some extent are period pieces, all of these early works have resonance beyond their time and location and are not without relevance to contemporary society.

The Suffrage of Elvira is Naipaul's second published novel. It concerns a contractor-politician, Surujpat Harbans, who is blackmailed by a political broker into paying out hard cash for his political support. As the campaign intensifies, more and more people ask for their pay-off. The constituency or community of Elvira is a virtual hornet's nest of pettiness, intrigue and guile, and, when the election comes to Elvira, every hornet, so to speak, is unleashed in the service of the new god—"democracy"—which the election comes to symbolise. Harbans wins the election, but his constituents are disappointed in his attitude following the victory. He turns up at a prize-distribution ceremony one week after his victory, arriving in a suit, driving a new Jaguar, seeming very aloof and uninterested in the personal problems of the villagers, who respond by setting his Jaguar on fire. The insurance company replaces the car, but the representative for Elvira never returns to his constituency.

Naipaul's approach in this novel, as in *The Mystic Masseur*, is satirical, and his intention is comic. *The Suffrage of Elvira* does not paint a healthy picture of colonial Trinidad, nor is it a flattering depiction of the colonial politicians who emerge in this new era of democracy. In *The Mystic Masseur*, the first elections are a novelty and the villagers

1 A version of this chapter has been published as Chapter 3 in Bhoendradatt Tewarie, *V. S. Naipaul Revisited: Ethnicity, Marginality and the Triumph of Individual Will*. Ian Randle Publishers, 2007.

support Ganesh Ramsumair, simply because they know him to be a good man. By the time of the second elections in Elvira, the democracy which in *The Mystic Masseur* seems like a joke turns into an outright farce. Beyond the farce, however, the tragic undertones are strong. In a 1979 review of Naipaul's *A Bend in the River*, Irving Howe, in "A Dark Vision", in the *New York Times Book Review* (13 May 1975), writes that

> Naipaul offers no intimations of hope or signals of perspective. It may be that the reality he grapples with allows him nothing but grimness of voice. There is a complicated literary-moral problem here that cannot be solved in a few sentences, if solved at all. A novelist has to be faithful to what he sees, and few see as well as Naipaul; yet one may wonder whether, in some final reckoning, a serious writer can simply allow the wretchedness of his depicted scene to become the limit of his vision. (37)

But if Naipaul's vision of politics in Third World societies in his later works is dark and brutal, as Howe and other critics have claimed, then that sombre vision can definitely be traced back to his two earliest published novels. In just four years, after one election under adult suffrage, corruption and cynicism have swiftly become firmly entrenched in Elvira. In his portrayal of Ganesh Ramsumair in *The Mystic Masseur*, Naipaul displays some ambivalence, and, in the end, in spite of Ganesh's faults, it is difficult to regard him as a totally contemptible character. There is no such ambivalence about Surujpat Harbans in *The Suffrage of Elvira*. He is portrayed as a contemptible, irresponsible politician, pure and simple, who seeks to exploit the possibilities for economic gain through the prize of political office. Harbans does not even live in Elvira, but in Port-of-Spain, and everyone knows that his only interest in politics comes from the lucrative road contracts that will become available once he becomes a political representative.

Interestingly, in his recent book on Naipaul, the following remarks by Sanjay Krishnan suggest further that V. S. Naipaul was aware of class distinctions within a few miles of each other in Port-of-Spain:

> The contrast between *Miguel Street* and *The Suffrage of Elvira* is striking in several respects. The stories in *Miguel Street* are distinguished by their quiet pathos. Although humorous, the underlying mood is melancholy and sympathetic. The narrator is drawn to stories of individuals whose aspirations for a better life are informed by their longing for creative self-expression rather than wealth or power. Their often fragile psychological state is treated with gentle irony. The characters in *Suffrage*, by contrast,

> appear devoid of inner lives and are exclusively motivated by a desire for material gain. Dress and mannerisms are described in great detail, whereas introspection is largely absent. The narrator's amorality reflects the superficial and briskly vulgar traits of the inhabitants of Elvira. In an interesting reversal, the country people of Elvira are mostly cynical and materialistic, whereas the city folks of *Miguel Street* are often described as idealistic. (56)

Naipaul's view of Trinidad society is certainly harsh. But in *Miguel Street* and *The Mystic Masseur*, while amorality is not condoned, there is a kind of tacit acceptance implicit in the tone of both works (tolerance, if you will). In *The Suffrage of Elvira*, society is shown to be more emphatically cynical, selfish and crassly materialistic. Yet, Naipaul does not simply place the blame at the doorstep of Elvira's citizens alone. He recognises the complicity of the colonial office, with its cynical involvement in this business of democracy which is being exported and transferred to colonies around the world. During the election campaign in Elvira, Naipaul writes: "A long grey van pulled up. It belonged to the Trinidad Film Board who were shooting scenes for a colonial office Documentary Film about political progress in the colonies, the script of which was to be written, poetically, in London by a minor British poet" (180).

After the Elvira election, the observer-narrator tells us: "It was a fantastically high poll; more than eighty-three percent. The fact was noted with approval in the official reports" (188). What is implicit is Naipaul's point that democracy demands more than just a high poll at elections. In a multi-ethnic community, such as the one described in *The Suffrage of Elvira*, true democracy should mean nothing less than effective representation for all segments of the population, a result that would only be achieved if valid institutional arrangements constituted part of a coherent vision for the whole society so that, in the long run, the integrity of the whole will always be greater than the sum of its parts.

In this context, elections would be merely one aspect of a set of long and complex social and political processes that are required to take place if real democracy is to exist. In the society portrayed in *The Suffrage of Elvira*, the necessary democratic prerequisites to elections are entirely missing. When Naipaul writes: "And so democracy took root in Elvira", he is being heavily ironic; democracy can only be perverted in such an ill-prepared community (192). And who is responsible for this state of affairs, if the colonial office has been in charge for one hundred years prior to the elections? That is one of the unarticulated questions that *The Suffrage of Elvira* poses.

In this sense, *The Suffrage of Elvira* is not merely about democracy in pre-independence Trinidad; it is also about the mishandling of the colonial encounter and the inadequacy of the colonial heritage in preparing colonial societies to manage self-governance and development and to adequately meet the challenges of effective participation in the modern world. What passes for democracy is the mere celebration of symbols: the concern with rituals and forms.

Much irony is levelled at the British, who seem to believe that they have passed on a valuable legacy to Elvira and to Trinidad. *The Suffrage of Elvira* demonstrates, with humour and pathos, that democracy will not work in Elvira as it was intended to. The real legacy handed down by the British is not democracy alone; it is instead the way of life of the plantation, with its support systems, slavery and indenture, with its legacy of human degradation, economic destitution, ethnic division and polarisation, and not to mention an obsession with the humiliation of others. This other legacy of the colonial encounter lurks in the silent background throughout the novel as the farce of the main plot unfolds.

The lack of a sense of community that is demonstrated in *The Suffrage of Elvira* has its roots in the colonial plantation legacy for which the British were responsible. Naipaul's *The Loss of El Dorado* makes clear that the causes of the contemporary dislocation with which he deals are rooted in colonial history. The charge of non-creation is, therefore, made against the colonists, not the colonised. It is no accident that Naipaul's *Loss of El Dorado* ends in 1813, two decades before slavery was abolished. It is clear that Naipaul feels that the pattern of human relations and the accompanying depravity of human endeavour were already established at that time. As Margaret Nightingale has written in "V. S. Naipaul as Historian Combatting Chaos":

> Naipaul's history of Trinidad concentrates on the period during which patterns of colonial behavior were established, tracing it to the origins of modern sterility, lack of creativity, racial stratification, roguery and self-denigration he has recorded in the Middle Passage in his journalism and his fiction. (240)

It is debatable whether Surujpat Harbans is the protagonist of this novel. The real protagonist seems to be adult suffrage itself. Everything seems to proceed from the fact of the coming elections, and, subsequently, the consequences after the elections, which act as a catalyst for releasing personal ambitions, only some of which are realised. The short epilogue makes clear that though there are winners as well as losers, the world of

Elvira is turned upside-down because of the elections as the worst traits of Elvira citizens of all dimensions manifest themselves.

Miguel Street had depicted a multi-ethnic, ragged band of street people, the urban underclass, some of whom were marginal Indians. *The Mystic Masseur* portrayed the countryside, where Hinduism survived relatively intact and the notion of an Indian community could be regarded as a reality. When adult suffrage comes to Trinidad, as it does in *The Mystic Masseur*, Ganesh Ramsumair, living in an all-Indian, dominantly Hindu environment, emerges as a Hindu leader who wins a seat in the Legislative Council through support from a largely ethnic community. Because Naipaul focuses largely on the Hindu community in *The Mystic Masseur*, inter-ethnic rivalries do not emerge and inter-religious differences are not explored. Indeed, the political infighting in *The Mystic Masseur* is a rather insular affair involving three Hindus: Ganesh, Narayan and Indarsingh.

In *The Suffrage of Elvira*, however, the themes of religious differences and inter-ethnic rivalry come to the fore in what is portrayed as the backward community of Elvira, whose residents consist of Hindus, Muslims, Spanish–Negroes and Negroes. (These are Naipaul's descriptions of the people. *The Suffrage of Elvira* was published in 1958). Life in Elvira must not have been very different from life in Four Ways or Fuente Grove or even Miguel Street (communities identified in Naipaul's other works). A dull routine appears to be the norm. The elections, however, transform Elvira overnight by unleashing the monster of ethnic division and polarisation. As the teacher, Francis, a character in the novel says: "Elvira was a good and friendly place before this universal suffrage nonsense" (85). In his opinion, "Election bringing out all sort of prejudice to the surface" (120).

Indeed, quite often prejudice approaches an explosive pitch. As Krishnan observes:

> [T]here are scenes in *The Suffrage of Elvira* where the anger and mutual incomprehension that make this one of Naipaul's funniest novels also threaten to result in physical violence. A hostile exchange ensues between Mr. Cuffy and Mahadeo when an ailing black man unexpectedly dies under the latter's watch. Mr. Cuffy suspects foul play on the part of the Indians on Harbans's inept campaign team, who had gambled that pretending to minister to the needs of a sick black man would win some black votes. Unfortunately for the team, the man in question was more ill than they realized, and Mr. Cuffy angrily alleges that the Indians working for Harbans's election campaign were not negligent so much as witch doctors using their traditional "obeah" to kill black people. (57)

The fortunes of Harbans, therefore, bounce up and down, depending on the degree of ethnic shifts in the election. He tries to unite the Hindus and Muslims against people of African descent because his opponent is an African, but the situation turns out to be much more complex than he imagines. Harbans approaches Baksh, the self-appointed Muslim leader, with a prepared speech: "In this modern world everybody is one. Don't make no difference who you is or what you is. You is a Muslim, I a Hindu. Tell me, that matter?" The wily Baksh, who has his own plans to profit from the elections, replies, "Depending" (17).

The election campaign in Elvira turns out to be a kind of free-for-all guerrilla warfare. Ethnic power brokers make personal deals with the candidate in return for the votes of their respective ethnic blocks. In a situation in which there is no cohesive vision and, therefore, no campaign issues, everyone ends up fighting his own little war or championing his little cause. Harbans, the candidate, seeks lucrative road contracts. The Muslim leader, Baksh, finding himself in a pivotal position with the 1,000 Muslim votes that he controls, seizes the opportunity to get as much money as he can from the candidate. Chittaranjan, the goldsmith who controls the Hindu as well as Spanish votes, sees the elections as an opportunity for finalising marriage arrangements between his daughter Nalini and Harbans' son. Foam is interested in securing a van and a loudspeaker system to establish his own business after the elections. Lorkhoor uses the campaign as a means of securing enough money to escape to Port-of-Spain with the woman he loves and embark on a career as a journalist. Everyone is aware that selfish motives predominate. When candidate Harbans expresses dismay at the money and materials that are being demanded of him, Foam, his campaign manager, consoles him: "Don't worry Mr. Harbans.... When we put you in the Leg. Co. you going to make it back" (20). It is taken for granted by all that society operates on the basis of corruption and that corruption is acceptable.

Against the guerrilla-like individualism of people like Baksh, Naipaul juxtaposes a general atmosphere of cultural confusion, religious syncretism, superstition and ignorance, reflecting a backward but easygoing and tolerant society. This is how the situation in Elvira is described:

> Things were crazily mixed up in Elvira. Everybody, Hindus, Muslims and Christians, owned a bible; the Hindus and Muslims looking on it, if anything, with greater awe. Hindus and Muslims celebrated Christmas and Easter. The Spaniards and some of the Negroes celebrated the Hindu festival of lights.... Everybody celebrated the Muslim festival of Hosein. In fact, when Elvira was done with religious festivals, there were few straight days left. (66)

It is paradoxical that in a society of such religious, cultural and ethnic diversity, with so much tolerance and acceptance, ethnic polarisation and division would nevertheless become a major factor in the election. It is also important to note what is taking place within each of the ethnic communities. The leader of the Hindus is not Pundit Dhaniram, who is portrayed as a buffoon and mischief-maker, but Chittaranjan, the goldsmith and moneylender. The leader of the Muslims is not the orthodox Haq, but the alcohol-consuming Baksh, a man of reputed wealth. The leader of the African community is not the teacher Francis, but Mr Cuffy, an idle shoemaker who calls his shop "The United African Self-Help Pioneer Society". The Spanish have no leader and so, in the novel, the Jehovah's Witnesses from the United States almost succeed in neutralising them politically.

There is also a clear generational conflict. The world opens up for the younger generation in a way that it never could for their elders. Elvira's youth wish to make a break with traditional ways. Nelly wishes to attend the London Polytechnic, which she eventually does. Pundit Dhaniram's son abandons his young wife and his parents and goes off to London. His wife, in turn, abandons the role of a traditional daughter-in-law and runs off to Port-of-Spain with Lorkhoor. Lorkhoor escapes from Elvira by getting a break in journalism. Even before the election campaign is over, Foam asserts his independence from his father.

Ethnic assertion in the realm of politics may suggest communal and ethnic solidarity, but, in fact, the reality is family and communal disintegration. Materialistic values are replacing religious and spiritual ones because those charged with spiritual responsibilities fail to live up to their responsibility and the outside world of possibility has a strong pulling effect on the ambitious and enterprising. The election is merely one symbol of the modern world. As Western ways encroach more and more, as ambitions and aspirations are released, the old world of traditional customs finds it increasingly difficult to survive. The narrator indicates this trend in a telling comment on Mahadeo:

> Mahadeo was a devout Hindu. He did his puja every morning and evening ... all the ritual, the arti and the bell-ringing and conch blowing ... seemed in the most discouraging way to have nothing to do with what went on in Elvira. (164)

Mahadeo's story is one of spiritual dislocation and it is debatable whether he will ever find his way again. So *The Suffrage of Elvira* is also about the clash between the old world and the new world, the tension between the traditional and the modern and the gap in sensibility between the politically ambitious and those who seek individual achievement and personal fulfilment.

In this novel, ethnic chauvinism and communal division are clearly a hindrance to progressive political development. If the ethnic division is to be taken for granted in the election, then each group merely serves as a pawn in the bargaining because the leader bargains on his own behalf rather than on behalf of the group. Also, if ethnicity is what determines the result of the election, how can there be any other issue in the campaign, since there is neither need nor opportunity to raise issues that would appeal to a broad constituency? The election can be won simply by manipulating ethnic blocks.

Ethnic chauvinism in politics, therefore, is portrayed as a national intellectual failure. Because no cohesive vision of the society exists and none is articulated—and because politicians too busy with personal gain are unable to project a vision of the future of the society—politicians and voters lean on quick and easy answers that in the long run are in nobody's interest. Neither politicians nor citizens see themselves as part of a larger nation; there is no common purpose around which people are able to rally. Lacking a sense of common purpose and lacking a sense of wholeness as a community, the citizens of Elvira fall back on tribal loyalties. It should not for a moment be thought that this situation is peculiar to Trinidad. Harriet Blodgett, in "Beyond Trinidad", has written that one could "change a few incidental details and what goes on in Elvira could just as well be set in, say, any of the boroughs of New York" (392).

The Suffrage of Elvira is a novel set in pre-independence Trinidad; it speaks to the pre-independence condition of most ex-colonial societies. Though a comic novel, it nevertheless gives us an early insight into Naipaul's darker dimension, which becomes more prominent in his later works. In fact, Lloyd Best, Naipaul's contemporary, as Krishnan remarks

> called *The Suffrage of Elvira* "the most important of Naipaul's novels." … [in which Naipaul] "founded a whole new school of empirical political science" by revealing "how the society worked, as distinct from how people thought it ought to work. In those days, that was almost impossible with the colonial film on your eyes. People couldn't tell perception from reality, and he was absolutely lucid as to how the political system actually worked, and how people actually behaved." (58)

Contemporary readers may thus ask themselves after reading *The Suffrage of Elvira* whether there have been any significant changes in post-independence politics in former colonial territories and whether Naipaul's early insight into the ill-preparedness of ex-colonial societies to rise to the challenge of self-governance was misguided or not. Later works, such as *In a Free State*, *Guerrillas* and *A Bend in the River*, are even harsher on the political realities in the ex-colonies.

WORKS CITED

Blodgett, Harriet. "Beyond Trinidad: Five Novels by V. S. Naipaul." *South Atlantic Quarterly*, vol. 73, 1974, pp. 388–403.

Howe, Irving. "A Dark Vision." *New York Times Book Review*, 13 May 1975.

Krishnan, Sanjay. *V. S. Naipaul's Journeys: From Periphery to Center*. Columbia University Press, 2020.

Naipaul, V. S. *The Suffrage of Elvira*. Penguin, 1978.

Nightingale, Margaret. "V. S. Naipaul as Historian: Combating Chaos." *Southern Review: Literary and Interdisciplinary Essays*, vol. 13.3, 1980, pp. 239–250.

Chapter 5

ELVIRA, YOU IS A BITCH[1]

Kenneth Ramchand

> That afternoon Mr Surujpat Harbans nearly killed the two white women and the black bitch.
>
> —*The Suffrage of Elvira* 1

The Suffrage of Elvira is comically alive and politically relevant even after sixty-something plus years on our library shelves. It is, as Jeff Hush mentions, informed by Naipaul's wish to shock the reader into realisation about the complexity of the mundane. Hush remarks:

> When V. S. Naipaul was a toddler growing up in Trinidad, his grandmother sold marijuana. Only old people bought it, for, during the early 1930s in Trinidad, only the elderly, whose energies were depleted and for whom life had become boring, desired to smoke hemp. Naipaul told this story to his students at Wesleyan University in 1978 because he wanted to shock; he wanted us to see that "History" is layered—each layer hides the past as much as it reveals it. (89)

The layers of history in Naipaul's work are many. The novel, *The Suffrage of Elvira*, was published in April 1958, two years after Naipaul's first return visit to Trinidad in 1956. His uncle Simboonath Capildeo was a candidate for the People's Democratic Party, the PDP, which was considered the "Indian" party. During his visit, Naipaul experienced the campaigning for the election that was to initiate thirty unbroken years of control by the other political party, the People's National Movement, the PNM. The good things that happened during this period have been recognised, but the malformations that set in have not been corrected and may never be able to be corrected. As Lloyd Best remarks, for example, in this regard, "The hardware of our Constitution may sound

1 This chapter was first published in *The Arts Journal*, vol. 11, No. 1–2, 2018, pp. 29–32.

like Westminster but the software of our political culture makes a government and politics of its own kind" (21).

The racial tensions in the software that Naipaul saw in 1956 may have contributed to his fears for the fate of the Indian population, and his sense of the communal terrors independence might bring. *The Mimic Men* (1967) and *Guerrillas* (1975) are both books written after some time had passed and after further grounding visits to the island had been made, which reveal Naipaul's composition style as one that we can call distress confronted in tranquility.

The mind has its own ways of working and, even before the tranquility, he had seen enough. It came to Naipaul during those disturbing weeks that he should write a novel about a rural election. He chose to build the story around the 1950 general elections. He invented a fictional constituency called Elvira in the remote county of Naparoni, and he provided a voters' list. Elvira has 8,000 registered voters: 4,000 Hindus, 1,000 Muslims, 2,000 Africans and 1,000 Spanish cocoa-panyols. The new voters have no idea what the vote means or what to do with it except to sell it to the highest bidder or surrender it to a broker.

The invented constituency used to be a grand cocoa estate and is named after the plantation owner's wife Elvira who had had a baby by an African worker and buried it in the foundation at the time the cocoa house was being built. All Elvirans are afraid to encounter the baby ghost of the cocoa house when darkness falls. But not of course as much as they fear the obeah dog that crawls the high street like a gunslinger at high noon: "But the dog. What about the dog? Where was that going to stall him?" (62) Naipaul gave to Elvira a geographical setting that is recognisably in Caroni, around Couva, Gran Couva and Tortuga. It is an "innocent" landscape already being exploited for lumber and quarrying. One of the finest views of Trinidad is seen (and can still be seen from Tortuga) from the top of Elvira Hill:

> Below, the jungly hills and valleys of the Central Range. Beyond, to the South, the sugarcane fields, the silver tanks of the oil refinery at Point-a-Pierre, and the pink and white houses of San Fernando; to the west, the shining rice fields and swamps of Caroni, and the Gulf of Paria; the Caroni Savannah to the north, and the settlements at the foot of the Northern Range. (11)

To candidate Harbans and the large-scale operators whose lethal coming Naipaul's novel anticipates, it is "a lot of bush" for lumber and plenty rock and dirt for quarrying. In the 1950 elections, the general area in which Elvira is located, is divided into Caroni North (won by Mitra Sinanan) and Caroni South (won by Ranjit Kumar). All the island's constituencies had been adjusted to make sure that each of them would have around 12,000 voters. There were eighteen elected seats for which 141 business-minded candidates offered themselves. Of the 90 Independents, six were returned; of those with nominal affiliations twelve won places. The Butler party won six, the Trinidad Labour Party (TLP) won two and the Caribbean Socialist Party (CSP) won two. The moderate Political Progress Group (PPG) also won two seats.

Before and after the election, there was talk about an alliance of the radical groups but all the party candidates were individualists to whom the so-called party affiliations were relationships of convenience, with people shifting around to suit their personal interests. The Elections and Boundaries Commission did not bother to list any of the candidates as belonging to a political party. Some of the campaigners complained that the only sure thing you could count on to influence voters was personal influence and bribes.

Elvira knows nothing about the political parties and does not know the names of the political figures of the time, but it shared in the reliance on personal influence and bribery to get votes. If the native politicians in the Legislative Council of 1950 could have brought themselves to unite, they would have been a potent majority in the Legislative Council and could have held a majority in the Executive Council. They would not have been able to take charge since the new constitution left the governor with the absolute power to curb their enthusiasm. But that was not a good reason to refuse to unite.

In the novel, the political candidate, Harbans, has his home in Port-of-Spain and Chittaranjan has a lawyer brother in the city. And Elvirans can refer to Hitler or call another "Nazi spy", but the constituency is quite closed in upon itself. The national and political issues aired in Port-of-Spain and other "developed" areas do not figure in *The Suffrage of Elvira*. There is nothing of political parties or coalitions. But in *The Suffrage of Elvira*, you can see the beginnings of what is to be the power of the party, the beginning of the time when the individuality of the candidate does not matter, a time when, as one prime minister would gloat, any crapaud the party puts up will win the seat.

At one point, Harbans's campaign committee finds that the whining candidate (mounting expenses, negotiating with tricky voters and demanding allies) gets in their way, and they want him to go back home to Port-of-Spain and leave them to do what has to be done to win the election. Among the Indians, the day of the village headman and the religious leader is passing: the modern time of the loudspeaker and the motorcade, the platform and the heckling crowd, the backroom boys, the bread and the circuses is establishing itself.

Naipaul started to write the novel at the end of 1956 and finished it in 1957. As a social scientist, he sets it down as he picked it up. For instance, none of the campaigners in Elvira targets the female vote. The assumption of the time and the assumption in the novel is that the wife votes as her husband does. But there are signs of the coming thing: there are three women in the book who speak up for themselves and rebel against male control. The deserted "doolahin" works resentfully as an unpaid servant in the house of her father-in-law. (The marriage was a set-up. Dhaniram knew that "the boy" was going away to further his studies, and a servant was needed.) The duped "doolahin" breaks tradition and elopes with Lorkhoor, the broadcaster; the teenager Nelly Chittaranjan refuses an arranged marriage and gets to attend The Regent Street Polytechnic in London where she goes to all the dances; and the stressed-out Mrs Baksh (who reveres Pundit Ganesh Ramsumair of *The Mystic Masseur*) rules the backsliding Baksh household with a heavy hand and a withering tongue. She sees the family being destroyed by the new dispensation:

> Is your fault, Baksh. Is this election sweetness that sweeten you up so? And now you seeing how sour it turning. You having people throwing all sorta magic and obeah in my house, you have all my sons lying to my face, and you have my biggest son talking to me like if I is he daughter. Is your fault, Baksh. This election business done turning sour, I tell you. (34)

In *The Suffrage of Elvira*, Naipaul disciplines himself to paint an accurate picture of how his characters behave and interact in society. No more. No less. The mirror that is held up to society shows the influences of personal ambition, greed, poverty, race, religion, superstition and language limbo. The registers of Trinidad English used by the characters slide into one another, from rural Indian dialect right through to the grandiloquent utterances of Lorkhoor and Foam vying to be the finest English speaker in the County of Naparoni. Here is Foam, ostensibly mocking Lorkhoor's spiel but copying him: "People of Elvira, this is the voice of Foreman Baksh, popularly known to all and sundry as Foam, asking you—not begging you or imploring you or beseeching you or entreating you—but asking you and telling you to vote for the honourable and ever popular candidate, Mr Pat Harbans" (35).

The influencing factors overlap and work at different times in different ways, with the proportions and dominant combinations constantly shifting. Just as they did at that confusing time, and as they do now:

> Things were crazily mixed up in Elvira. Everybody, Hindus, Muslims and Christians owned the Bible, the Hindus and Muslims looking

> on it, if anything with greater awe. Hindus and Muslims celebrated Christmas. The Spaniards and some of the Negroes celebrated the Hindu festival of lights. Someone had told them that Lakshmi the goddess of prosperity was being honoured; they placed small earthen lamps on their money-boxes and waited as they said for the money to breed. Everybody celebrated the Muslim festival of Hosein. In fact, when Elvira was done with religious festivals, there were few straight days left. (54)

The scientific observations contained in *The Suffrage of Elvira* contradict many of our analysts who see race as the defining factor in Trinidad politics. The novel recognises the influence of race and registers that it is the mindless fallback position. However, it casts doubt on the promotion of race as the exclusive and dominant active factor. It exposes the discontinuity between our culture and the systems and institutions that we imitatingly work and cavalierly bend to suit our partisan purposes. The humour and comedy of the work thrive on these and other incongruities.

This is why Lloyd Best described *The Suffrage of Elvira* as the exemplary work of an artist and scientist. As Best puts it:

> It is in its remarkable powers of observation and scrutiny, now his trademark, that lies Naipaul's appeal. The novelist was 18, it was the second election on the basis of adult suffrage [represented in *The Suffrage of Elvira*]. First time round, in 1946 he was 14. But he discerned that the T&T public had not yet "seen the possibilities". His theme is familiar: government from above with little politics from below. Elections were then, and are still largely now, mostly business opportunity. Make money by any means. This is society not lawless but with no concept of law or responsibility. Were not our peoples transplanted only to lose old tradition while finding new tradition almost impossible to create? Is the problem not identity? Is it not the terror of being, with little reference to time or to place? It is precisely Naipaul's point that we suffer a mis-match between culture and institutions. (20)

How Naipaul helps the reader to see what Best observes is important. The Prologue of *The Suffrage of Elvira* begins with a host of signs like "Awake", "We are Witnesses" and "Harbans Transport Service". It contains portents or apparitions—two white women travelling through Elvira; a black bitch crossing the path of Harbans's Dodge and the truck stalls not once, but twice. You can read the whole of *The Suffrage of Elvira* as a sign portending the irresponsible and unimaginative political practices that have been destroying our country since independence.

But the artist imposes no thesis. There is no thesis. The elements are just found floating around in the not-yet-awakened Elvira.

From Naipaul, this is not a surprising position. He asserts after all that "Revolutions—understood as the complete overturning of a society—are a philosophical absurdity. How can men remake themselves totally unlike themselves?" (Hush 92). Showing people who they are becomes, therefore, one of Naipaul's most important tasks and he does this with great clarity in *The Suffrage of Elvira*. For example, when democracy comes to Elvira, Mrs Baksh, the wife of the Muslim leader, is afraid of what catastrophe the free-for-all might bring into the society: "Nobody ain't listening to me, everybody just washing their foot and jumping in this democracy business. But I promise you, for all the sweet it being sweet, it is going to end damn sour." Mrs Baksh says this so often that it becomes a motif in the novel.

Near the end, the function at which the committee is to receive a case of whisky for "winning" the election is disrupted by the voting crowd's protest that it is they who deserve the reward and it is an insult to ask them to come and witness the committee receiving an award:

> Look at these poor people! They come from all over the place. You think a man go put on his clothes, take up his good good self and walk from Cordoba to Elvira in the night-time with all this dew falling, just to see committee get a case of whisky? (146)

Chaos ensues. The point of the argument shifts from whisk to religion and like a pack of dogs everybody takes turns attacking everybody else. In the babel,

> Rampiari's husband switched his attack to Baksh. Baksh was attacking Harbans. Foam was being attacked by innumerable anonymous people. Mahadeo was being attacked by people whose illness he had spurned. Haq was poking questions directly under Harbans's nose. Harbans's was saying "Ooh, ooh" and trying to pacify everybody. (151)

Naipaul works in certain Biblical allusions devastatingly. The Jehovah Witnesses in the novel preach that "politiçs ain't divine" and an old Cordobon pronounces the name of Nimrod (without fully understanding the allusions to the Biblical figure who invented politics and imposed a destructive Stateism that set itself up as above family, personal relationships, community, country and God). The Presbyterian-educated Hindu pandit Dhaniram slaps his thighs and parrots the catchword "Armageddon" with reference to the bacchanal in Elvira.

Naipaul rounds off the novel with a witty balance sheet of who gains what and who loses what in the election raffle.

But the real climax comprises claims of victimhood and betrayal and the subsequent babel of protest and violence—the violent action of the mob against the organisers and the elected representative now clothed in jacket and tie and sporting a shiny Jaguar motor car. The mob pushes Harbans to see Jordan, the Elviran villager, who sets out to test the thesis on everyone's behalf that, now that the elections are over, the free medical attention will no longer be available. Jordan claims to have had a stroke. The villagers support the claim and point to the number of dependents the man has but even while they are doing this, revenge is taken on the candidate and his Jaguar is burnt. The story ends on a note of typical postcolonial violence against privilege and the lack of participatory democracy. Not far away are the explosions of 1970 and 1990, and the sense of doom and danger that many people still feel today.

Hush says that Naipaul asked the students at Wesleyan just before his departure in May 1979:

> Ask yourself whether the people around you are being made to question or examine themselves. whether, at a place like Wesleyan, they are merely inducted into the ways of their tribe, and not made to look beyond or inside their tribal limitations. The young people at the university, [the] ones you try to talk to, are really like old men. Their minds closed, by television discussions, by newspapers, by their successes. (90)

The questions remain pertinent to students everywhere, especially in the Caribbean, and to the list of things that close their minds, we can now add many others from social media. While this remains so, the problems of suffrage in places like Elvira will remain pressing and real. After all, as Tony Deyal reminds us, *The Suffrage of Elvira* is an instance of "life imitating and outdoing art while, in the context of today's politics and political leaders, validating it" (25).

Works Cited

Best, Lloyd. "Scientist as Well as Artist." *Caribbean Quarterly*, special issue of *V.S. Naipaul: Nobel Laureate for Literature, 2001 Call and Response*, vol. 48, no. 2–3, 2002, pp. 19–21.

Deyal, Tony. "Naipaul: Greatness and Ungraciousness." *Caribbean Quarterly*, special issue of June–September, vol. 48, no. 2–3, 2002, pp. 25–26.

Hush, Jeff. "Trailed by the Black Dog." *Ploughshares*, special issue of *What's a Story*, vol. 12, no. 1–2, 1986, pp. 89–98.

Mann, Harveen Sachdeva. "Variations on the Theme of Mimicry: Naipaul's *The Mystic Masseur* and *The Suffrage of Elvira*." *Modern Fiction Studies*, special issue of Autumn, vol. 30, no. 3, 1984, pp. 467–485.

Naipaul, V. S. "The Suffrage of Elvira." *The Nightwatchman's Occurrence Book and other Comic Inventions*. 1958. Vintage, 2002.

Chapter 6

THE TRINIDADIAN CALYPSO AS ORAL HERITAGE: LINGUISTIC AND CULTURAL ISSUES IN THE ITALIAN TRANSLATION OF V. S. NAIPAUL'S *MIGUEL STREET*[1]

Mariacristina Petillo

> *Tutte le mattine, appena alzato, Cappello si sedeva sulla balaustra della veranda dietro casa sua e gridava: Come va, Bogart?. Bogart! si! rigirava! nel! letto! e! borbottava! a! voce! così! bassa! che! non! lo! sentiva! nessuno:! Come! va,! Cappello?.*
>
> —*Miguel Street* (Arnoldo Mondadori Editore 1991, 12)

Calypsos as Epitome of African Orality in the Caribbean

Due to complex and often traumatic historical processes, the Caribbean region has emerged as a space of hybridity and creolisation, cross-cultural encounter and interracial coexistence. The Caribbean is a highly syncretic place in which the heterogeneous and scattered genesis of its population has brought together people of different origins: native Caribs and Amerindians, Africans and Indians, Europeans, Chinese and Middle-Eastern minorities. Nevertheless, in spite of this ethnic and cultural plurality, the African presence informs the core of the region and gives shape to its innermost identity.

Since the majority of Caribbean people have African ancestry, the survivals of West African linguistic, cultural, artistic and religious elements are still evident across the Caribbean. As the key feature of most African societies was a "traditionally limited use of literacy" (Warner-Lewis 117), it is not surprising that "verbal traditions were among the few but highly significant possessions brought to the Americas by the enslaved survivors of transatlantic crossings" (Warner-Lewis 117).

1 "The Trinidadian Calypso as Oral Heritage: Linguistic and Cultural Issues in the Italian Translation of V. S. Naipaul's *Miguel Street*" was originally published in *Journal des Africanistes*, vol. 80 issue 1–2, pp. 205–215.

Today, the weight of this African legacy in the West Indies emerges more substantially in some forms of Creole-based orature, including both poetry and music, which are deeply influenced by African oral traditions.

This is, for example, the singular artistic experience of the Barbadian oral poet Bruce St John (1923–1995), who wrote and performed his poetry in the so-called Bajan speech, a Creole resulting from the fusion of Standard English and other West African languages. More interestingly, he used a call-and-response structure inherited from African song and this antiphonal technique drew his poems closer to a "performative oral mode" (Savory 728); the oral nature of his poetry is even more emphasised on the printed page, with the words arranged in two columns, in order to visually display the vocal interweaving of different speakers.

In the musical field too, the calypso represents a significant aspect of this cultural continuum between Africa and the New World, because the origins of this peculiar musical genre are in the early oral forms of expression introduced to the plantation fields by the enslaved Africans; in their songs, folktales, religious chants, ritual practices. Undoubtedly, calypsos belong to the many-faceted field of Caribbean orature, where the influences of the African diaspora have been more enduring. Thus, calypsos can be considered as an African-derived form of folklore, which expresses a distinctive African sensibility in the mingling of music, dance and orality.

Although it is not so easy to reconstruct the exact history of the term itself and of the genre as a whole (Crowley 57–66), calypso seems to be the synthesis of different cultural echoes, among which the African contribution is the most strongly recognisable and incisive. Like other forms of African expression, calypsos have an extempore nature and are based on musical and textual improvisation, although nowadays calypso competitions are less spontaneous events than they were in the past, to such an extent that true extempore performances are really rare today.[2] In addition to these improvisational features, Crowley argues that calypsos descended from the African tradition of satiric songs; moreover, even after formal emancipation from slavery, this musical genre continued to be perceived as a means of artistic resistance to exploitation and oppression. Consequently, its texts are satirical and wittily allusive in content, conversational and informal in tone. They are always ready in recording the historical and political

2 For further information on the "calypso war" and "picong", see Warner, Chapter 1, pp. 11–15.

changes which constitute the calypsonians' raw material. Calypsonians are always eager to express bitter criticism of society and actively engage in the complex process of moulding a Caribbean national identity.

Other scholars claim that calypso is an interesting example of a crossover form, whose origins are deeply rooted in the West African musical tradition of the praise and blame song, based on a counterpoint between individual and community, as in all forms of "total expression" where the oral tradition "demands not only the griot but the audience to complete the community: the noise and sounds that the maker makes are responded to by the audience and are returned to him" (Brathwaite, *History of the Voice* 18–19). More specifically, Gordon Rohlehr traces the source of the political Trinidadian calypso to this kind of antiphonal African songs, which often exercised a function of social control: it is now fully acknowledged that criticism of political leaders or complaints about other reasons of unrest, turbulence and instability were only possible within the restricted area of orature, through oral songs and stories. Rohlehr states:

> African music often served the purpose of social control, and the roots of the political calypso in Trinidad probably lie in the African custom of permitting criticism of one's leaders at specific times, in particular contexts, and through the media of song and story. The leaders of society recognized the value of such satirical songs in which the ordinary person was given the privilege of unburdening his mind while the impact of his protest was neutralized by the controlled context in which criticism was possible. (2)

Similar to its ancient ancestor, the Trinidadian calypso inherited this privileged position too and successfully acted, according to Jennifer Rahim, as a "barometer of social consciousness, an expression of collective identity, and a vehicle for anti-establishment critique". Thus, calypsonians are allowed to display a boastful alternative to the hegemonic set of current values, protected as they are by the safe boundaries of the performance space during the "calypso season" once a year or by the fictitious constraints in a narrative framework, as happens in Naipaul's third novel, *Miguel Street*, where a remarkably high number of quotations from real calypsos resounds throughout the pages, focusing especially on such issues as gender, wife-beating, ethnicity and politics.

In *Miguel Street,* calypso emerges as a prevailing stylistic feature of the narration, conveying and constantly reshaping the social, cultural and sexual identities of the Caribbean people in Port-of-Spain represented in the stories. Naipaul's aim in his use of the calypso seems to be to provide a philosophical framework to the seventeen chapters of his work, thus, offering a sort of unifying ironic counterpoint to a novel which is more similar, perhaps, to a collection of short stories, all sharing the same characters and the same nameless boy narrator.

Moreover, Naipaul depicts how calypsos reflected and contributed to the redefinitions of Trinidadian society during World War II and in the post-war period, when unexpected changes deeply affected the lower strata of Port-of-Spain's population, including increased migration of Indians from rural places to towns. This resulted in the process of acculturation for younger generations often because of the American military occupation which induced Indian women to offer sex as an easy commodity in exchange for the Yankee dollar. Ultimately, calypsos prove useful to humorously show and mercilessly amplify the domestic dramas of everyday life in the degraded suburbs of Port-of-Spain, where people vainly strive for a heroic stature they are unable to attain because they are doomed by social structures to failure and frustration, misfortune and vulnerability, disillusionment and alienation.

Since calypsos are a most authentic expression of West Indian popular culture, "born of the folk and intrinsically tied to the folk" (Warner 151), and since, as Paula Morgan puts it, they really have "the power to convey the Trinidadian 'spirit' and worldview in the way that few other cultural practices can", it is no wonder that they are created, sung and performed in what Edward Kamau Brathwaite labels as "nation language", which is "the kind of English spoken by the people who were brought to the Caribbean, not the official English now, but the language of slaves and labourers, the servants who were brought in by the conquistadors" (Brathwaite *History of the Voice* 5–6). Very interestingly, this scholar stresses the need to investigate language structures through music. Thus, nation language, whose best feature is its orality, is also characterised by a deep connection between "native musical structures and the native language. That music is, in fact, the surest threshold to the language which comes out of it" (Brathwaite *History of the Voice* 16).

TRANSLATING CALYPSOS INTO ITALIAN: AN OVERVIEW

Due to their linguistic and geographical specificity, calypsos symbolise a perfect example of cultural specificity and rootedness which may cause some serious difficulties during the translation process. In other words, calypsos are a culture-bound artistic form of expression and, as such, they exist almost on the verge of untranslatability. On this point, Naipaul himself claims in *The Middle Passage* that "calypso is a purely local form. No song composed outside Trinidad is a calypso. The calypso deals with local incidents, local attitudes, and it does so in a local language. The pure calypso, the best calypso, is incomprehensible to the outsider" (66).

Therefore, any translator must be keenly aware of the linguistic problems that he/she may have to face when transposing calypsos into another language. Naipaul's novel was translated into Italian by the experienced translator Marcella Dallatorre in 1991, who, therefore, found herself with an immense task.[3] The Italian translation of *Miguel Street* shows that a twofold difficulty arises: firstly, the translator needs to decide how to reproduce the colloquial liveliness of the Creole language used for calypsos and, secondly, how to translate into Italian the manifold cultural data that all those popular ditties convey. It is important to state, therefore, that it is not our intention to criticise Dallatorre's translation; instead, the goal is to highlight those linguistic and cultural features which offer resistance to the translation process in order to point out how translating Caribbean forms of orature inevitably implies a considerable amount of semantic and stylistic loss in any target language.

One of the most interesting features of Naipaul's novel is the striking contrast between the faultless standard English spoken by the boy narrator and the Creole language always used by the residents of the street of the same title. As in all popular cultures, those people rely heavily on orality as the most direct instrument of daily communication; hence, the importance of long dialogues and the obsessive quotations from calypsos. In this oral context, the continuous singing of calypsos also means the desire to turn the petty events of their lives into representative experiences, "proverbial expression of private situations", which, thereby, acquire a sort of universal and anecdotal value (Hendry and Watson 196). In *Miguel Street*, calypsos epitomise both the importance of orality in spreading shared social and cultural values and a functional communicative fusion among words, music and orality.

Consequently, an "ideal" translation should be able to reproduce the double linguistic channel of the novel—the code-switching

---

3 Naipaul's novel was translated into Italian by the experienced translator Marcella Dallatorre in 1991, under the imprint of Mondadori Editore. Since then, no other attempt has been made to provide a second translation; hence, Dallatorre's version is the only translation of *Miguel Street* still circulating in Italy. Therefore, all Italian references in the paper are from V. S. Naipaul, *Miguel Street*, Milano, A. Mondadori, 1991.

between Standard English and Trinidadian Creole—in order to fully respect Naipaul's artistic intentions and to lay emphasis on the popular culture with which his characters are imbued. Special attention should also be addressed to the translation of the textual quotations from calypsonians, whose presence is extremely telling of the oral nature of the characters' culture. Thus, since calypsos represent the highest achievement of West Indian orality, they could be properly translated into Italian by resorting to the rich linguistic resources of a spoken register in the target language.

A close examination of the calypso fragments translated into Italian shows, however, that an almost unavoidable loss affects the rhyme pattern because all the rhymed couplets in the source text have no corresponding rhyme in the target language. For example, in the calypso sung by Lord Caresser, the two lines "Is love, love, love, alone / That cause King Edward to leave the throne" are translated as "L'amore, l'amore, solo l'amore / Ha fatto perdere il trono a re Edoardo" (Naipaul, *Miguel Street* 126). Apart from the rhymed couplet "alone / throne" which is not replaced by any similar effect in the Italian version, the remarkable musicality of Lord Caresser's lines with the repeated alliteration of the liquid sound "i" cannot be reproduced in the target text. In addition, in Lord Invader's calypso, the intensely musical and rhythmic lines "I was living with my decent and contented wife / Until the soldiers came and broke up my life" are deeply modified in their rhyme and verse structure because the two source lines are graphically arranged in three lines in the translation, with no rhyme possibilities being explored: "*Avevo una moglie brava e soddisfatta / Poi vennero i militari / A rovinarmi la vita*" (168).

Another interesting example is The Mighty Sparrow's calypso blatantly claiming the necessity for men to beat their wives in order to be loved eternally. The first two lines quoted in *Miguel Street* are made up of monosyllabic words that sound extremely musical in the English version: "Every now and then just knock them down / Every now and then just throw them down." Obviously, it is impossible to reproduce the prosodie structure of the source text in a language that privileges the polysyllabic constructions instead. Therefore, the Italian translation chooses to preserve the semantic aspects of the original text, rather than trying to imitate its poetic features: "*Ogni tanto suonagliele / Ogni tanto dalle una bella battuta*" (104).

What is most striking here is the loss of a symmetrical repetition in the translated version, whereas, in the original calypso, there is a perfect parallelism between the two lines, which differ only in the verbs "knock [and] throw". The other stylistic difference consists in the contrast between a chiefly monosyllabic source language versus a high number of trisyllabic words (such as "*battuta*", "*livido*", "*ginocchio*") and a line ending with a word stressed on the fourth-last syllable ("*suonagliele*"). However, although the Italian translation is far from the fluent rhythm of the English text, there is a lexical gain which allows the retrieval of at least the oral and informal tone of the original calypso. This result is made possible through the use of the verb "*suonarle*", which is a familiar and colloquial expression for the act of beating someone, and instead of the more formal "*percuotere*", "*picchiare*" and "*colpire*."

Some other examples of a similar strategy refer to the calypsos "All day and all night Miss Mary Ann" by The Roaring Lion and "Matilda" by King Radio, where a subtle shift of linguistic register partly compensates for the loss of the Creole-language liveliness. In the first calypso, the line "Down by the river-side she taking man" has been translated as "*Se la spassa col suo uomo dalle parti del fiume*" (152); in the second example, the lines "Matilda, you thief my money / And gone Venezuela" has become "*Ti sei arraffata i miei soldi / E sei andata in Venezuela*" (191). In this context, both "*spassarsela*" and "*arraffare*" can be perceived by Italian readers as an apt choice because these verbs are mainly used in an informal register and seem to vividly embody Trinidadian people's attitude to life.

But in other calypso quotations, the Italian translator was not able to reproduce the colloquial tone of some Creole expressions and simply omitted them. This is what happens in the calypso about Popo, whose first line "A certain carpenter feller went to Arima" has been translated as "*Un certo falegname ando ad Arima*" (29). The target text is a literal translation into a perfect standard Italian, with no dialectal or oral inflections, whereas, the source text is characterised by the anti-formal jocular word "feller". Such forms and expressions survive in folktales, proverbs, sayings and calypsos of course. Their deliberate misspelling is an attempt to represent in a realistic way the folk speech and pronunciation of West Indian people. Linguistically speaking, "feller". is an example of eye-dialect, that is, the use of an incorrect spelling to convey the effect of a dialectal or uneducated speaker. Thus, its omission in the Italian version is not a painless loss, since the non-standard spelling of the word in the calypso is a linguistic marker that highlights the importance of orality for Miguel Street inhabitants.

Translating calypsos into another language is not an easy task, since both linguistic and cultural difficulties can intervene to frustrate the translator's efforts. This assumption is well demonstrated by the Italian rendering of Duke's calypso "Man centipede bad. / Woman centipede more than bad", literally translated as "*L'uomo centipede è un male. / La donna centipede è peggio*" (118). The awkward result reveals that the translator must have ignored the metaphorical usage of the word "centipede" in the Trinidadian context where, according to Richard Allsopp, a centipede is a "woman given to brawling and fighting; a foul-mouthed prostitute ... perhaps by reference to the vicious sting of the original crawling myriapod". The word "centipede" is a culture-specific term that has a double meaning in the Caribbean region.

The Italian translation grasps only the denotative meaning and misses the metaphorical one which is essential for a true comprehension of the calypso quotation. Instead of portraying the image of a contemptible and rowdy woman, "centipede" is unnaturally translated as "*centipede*", which seems to be a sort of caique of the original, probably relying on its auditory resemblance to the word commonly used by Italian people to describe a centipede, "*centopiedi*". Obviously enough, the Italian reader has been deprived not only of a smooth and aesthetically pleasing translation but also of the derogatory force of this culture-bound expression, with all the chain of connotations it raises.

Ultimately, the analysis of Naipaul's early novel translated into Italian reveals that the two linguistic levels of the source text—the continual shifting from standard English to Creole language—are not so well differentiated; instead, the target text is characterised by a consistent levelling-down of the linguistic markers expressing orality to such an extent that there is little difference between the narrator's formal language and the characters' more colloquial speech. For example, the calypso quotations taken into account show that all the interjections have been constantly omitted in the target text; as a result, the Italian translation sounds somewhat detached from the frankness and informality of the original texts.

This is what happens in The Mighty Terror's calypso "Chinese children calling me Daddy", where the line "Oh God, somebody putting milk in my coffee" has become "*Qualcuno deve avermi messo del latte nel caffè!*" (119), with the total loss of the original emphasis. Also, in Lord Invader's calypso "I living with my Yankee soldier", the exclamation "The Yankee dollar, oh!" has been turned into a verb phrase "*Arrivano i dollari yankee!*" (168), with no interjection in the target text.

Although the directness and expressive immediacy of the Creole language are almost untranslatable in any other language, the oral and popular culture it conveys ought to be highlighted in any translation but this has not happened in the Italian version. Similarly, the translation of calypsos could have better underlined the linguistic and cultural spontaneity of the Trinidadian world, especially if it is true that the "calypso medium and message certainly acts as a fragment of national culture on many Caribbean islands, turning calypsonians into culture brokers who use their expressive and evocative performance tools to leave behind an oral heritage" (Hendry and Watson 196–197).

Works cited

Alleyne, Mervyn. C. "The linguistic continuity of Africa in the Caribbean." *Black Academy Review*. vol. 1, issue 4, pp. 3–16.

Allsopp, Richard. *Dictionary of Caribbean English Usage*, new edition. U of the West Indies P, 2003.

Boyce-Davies, Carole. "The Africa Theme in Contemporary Calypso in the Caribbean." *Neohelicon*, vol. 16, issue 2, 1989, pp. 265–291.

Brathwaite, Edward Kamau. "The African Presence in Caribbean Literature." *Daedalus*. vol. 103, issue 2, 1974, pp. 73–109.

———. *History of the Voice: The Development of Nation Language in Anglophone Caribbean Poetry*. New Beacon Books, 1984.

Collins, John. *African Pop Roots: The Inside Rhythms of Africa*. W. Foulsham, 1985.

———. *West African Pop Roots*. Temple UP, 1992.

Constance, Zeno Obi. *Tassa, Chutney and Soca: The East Indian Contribution to the Calypso*. Jordan's Printing, 1991.

Cowley, John. *Carnival, Canboulay and Calypso: Traditions in the Making*. Cambridge UP, 1996.

Crowley, Daniel J. "Toward a definition of Calypso." *Ethnomusicology*, vol. 3, issue 2, 1959, pp. 57–66.

Dash, J. Michael. "Postcolonial Caribbean Identities." *The Cambridge History of African and Caribbean Literature*, edited by Fabiola Irele, and Simon Gikandi, Cambridge UP, 2004, pp. 785–796.

Dudley, Shannon. *Carnival Music in Trinidad: Experiencing Music, Expressing Culture*. Oxford UP, 2004.

Fondazione, Adkins Chiti, editor. *Calypso as an Instrument of Social Justice: Contributions from the Conference Held in Sao Paolo, Brazil, 2004*. Editore Colombo, 2007.

Gunner, Elizabeth. "Africa and Orality." *The Cambridge History of African and Caribbean Literature*, edited by Fabiola Irele, and Simon Gikandi, Cambridge UP, 2004, pp. 1–18.

Hendry, Joy, and Conrad W. Watson, editors. *An Anthropology of Indirect Communication*, Routledge, 2001.

Hill, Donald R. *Calypso Calaloo: Early Carnival Music in Trinidad*. UP of Florida, 1993.

Hill, Errol. *The Trinidad Carnival: Mandate for a National Theatre*. New Beacon Books, 1997.

Irele, Fabiola, and Simon Gikandi, editors. *The Cambridge History of African and Caribbean Literature*. Cambridge UP, 2004.

Liverpool, Hollis. *From the Horse's Mouth: Stories of the History and Development of the Calypso from the 1920s to 1970s*. Juba Publications, 2003.

———. *Rituals of Power and Rebellion: The Carnival Tradition in Trinidad & Tobago, 1763–1962*. Research Associates School Times Publications, 2001.

Morgan, Paula. "With a Tassa Blending: Calypso and Cultural Identity in Indo-Caribbean Fiction." *Anthurium: A Caribbean Studies Journal*, vol. 3, issue 2, 2005.

Naipaul, V.S. *Miguel Street*, Italian trans. by Marcella Dallatorre, Arnoldo Mondadori Editore, 1991.

———. *The Middle Passage. Impressions of Five Colonial Societies*. Picador, 2001.

———. *Miguel Street* Picador, 2001.

Nurse, Keith. "Globalization and Trinidad Carnival: Diaspora, Hybridity and Identity in Global Culture." *Cultural Studies*, vol. 13, issue 4, 1999, pp. 661–690.

Petillo, Mariacristina. "Problemi traduttivi in Miguel Street di V.S. Naipaul." *Traduzione letteraria e oltre / Literary translation and beyond*, edited by Rosella Mallardi, Peter Lang, 2008. pp. 231–252.

Pouchet Paquet, S., and Stephen Stuempfle, editors. *Calypso and the Caribbean Literary Imagination: A Special Issue*, special issue of *Anthurium: A Caribbean Studies Journal*, vol. 3, issue 2, 2005.

Rahim, Jennifer. "(Not) Knowing the Difference: Calypso Overseas and the Sound of Belonging in Selected Narratives of Migration." *Anthurium: A Caribbean Studies Journal*, vol. 3, issue 2, 2005.

Reddock, Rhoda E., editor. *Interrogating Caribbean Masculinities: Theoretical and Empirical Analyses*. U of the West Indies P, 2004.

Regis, Louis. *The Political Calypso: True Opposition in Trinidad and Tobago, 1962–1987*. UP of Florida, 1999.

Rohlehr, Gordon. *Calypso and Society in Pre-independence Trinidad*. Lexicon, 1990.

———. *A Scuffling of Islands: Essays on Calypso*. Lexicon, 2004.

———. "I Lawa: Masculinity in Trinidad and Tobago Calypso." *Interrogating Caribbean Masculinities: Theoretical and Empirical Analyses*, edited by Rhoda Reddock, U of the West Indies P, 2004, pp. 326–403.

Savory, Elaine. "Anglophone Caribbean Literature." *The Cambridge History of African and Caribbean Literature*, edited by Fabiola Irele, and Simon Gikandi, Cambridge UP, 2004, pp. 711–758.

Scher, Peter W. *Carnival and the Formation of a Caribbean Transnation*. UP of Florida, 2003.

Thieme, John. "Calypso Allusions in Naipaul's *Miguel Street*." *Kunapipi*, vol. 3, issue 2, 1981, pp. 18–33.

Van Dam, Theodore. "The influence of the West African songs of derision on the New World." *African Music*, vol. I, 1954, pp. 53–56.

Warner, Keith Q. "Creole languages and national identity in the Caribbean." *CIA Journal*, vol. XX, issue 3, 1977, pp. 319–332.

———. *The Trinidad Calypso: A Study of the Calypso as Oral Literature*. Heinemann, 1982.

———. "Carnival and the folk origins of West Indian drama." *The Cambridge History of African and Caribbean Literature*, edited by Fabiola Irele, and Simon Gikandi, Cambridge UP, 2004, pp. 137–152.

Warner-Lewis, Maureen. "The Oral Tradition in the African Diaspora." *The Cambridge History of African and Caribbean Literature*, edited by Fabiola Irele, and Simon Gikandi, Cambridge UP, 2004, pp. 117–136.

Chapter 7

WITH A TASSA BLENDING: CALYPSO AND CULTURAL IDENTITY IN INDO-CARIBBEAN FICTION[1]

Paula Morgan

> It is only in the Calypso that the Trinidadian touches reality.
>
> —*The Middle Passage*

Calypso occupies a privileged position in the Trinidadian cultural imagination. Given its enormous popularity within the island, regional and diasporic populations, calypso retains strong associations with home and with "the Trini mentality". Indeed, calypso, along with carnival, is often cited as possessing the power to convey the Trinidadian "spirit" and worldview in the way that few other cultural practices can. Associated with lower-strata Afro–Trinidadian cultural identity, calypso is a hybrid form, the origin of which has been the subject of much contestation and debate.[2] A peculiar creation of the Afro–Caribbean urban folk, the calypso has been traditionally regarded as the lash of the small man who deploys picong and wit for boastful self-assertion and for sustained counter-discourse with the hegemonic worldview, in the protected arena of the performance space. Drawing from the African tradition of the praise and blame song, calypsonians have, by dint of struggle, created and maintained a relatively permissive platform for stinging, incisive humour, cutting

1 A version of this chapter was first published in *Anthurium: A Caribbean Studies Journal*, vol. 3, issue 2, article 10, 2005.

2 The origins of calypso have variously been traced to the West African praise-blame songs which utilised litany or call and response forms. See Gordon Rohlehr, *Calypso and Society*, J. D. Elder, "Evolution of the Traditional Calypso of Trinidad and Tobago"; and Errol Hill, *The Trinidad Carnival.*

criticism and for simultaneously airing and masking fear and antipathy through verbal power play and excess.[3]

Over time, calypso has drawn from and fertilised myriad crossover music forms and has risen to prominence in the contemporary commoditisation and globalisation of local sound. In terms of its content and significance as a cultural practice, this shape-shifting nation-music occupies pivotal interface with literary and other textual discourses on gender, ethnicity and nation. Contextualising a reading of the calypso in Indo–Trinidadian literature against a broader framework of gender and ethnic identity politics, this chapter examines a range of symbolic associations, which attend the calypso as pointers to evolving gender constructions and as metaphors for cultural hybridity. It argues that the calypso with its cohesive links with Afro–Creole cultural assertion and identity also functions predominantly as an ambivalent trope for freedom and belonging for Indo–Trinidadian writers and protagonists.

Scholars have carefully documented the process by which a shared history of enforced labour through slavery and indentureship—with common legacies of anomie, institutionalised poverties, social and cultural dislocation, loss of ancestral heritages and traumatic gender relations—has been transmuted into interethnic hostility and rivalry.[4] The tenuous nature of the nation state in the resultant, fragile, island societies is reflected in the contestation over markers of rootedness and belonging. Citing calypso and carnival as the manifestation of both "the theatres and metaphors through which Trinidad's social history is encoded and enacted", cultural critic Gordon Rohlehr argues in "Calypso Reinvents Itself":

> The Trinidad experience has involved an intense expenditure of energy in a process of continuous indigenization, enacted on ground stolen from the terribly reduced though not totally erased Amerindian presence, committed to create out of this teaming

3 Rohlehr states: "African music often served the purpose of social control, and the roots of the political calypso in Trinidad probably lie in the African custom of permitting criticism of one's leaders at specific times, in particular contexts, and through the media of song and story. The leaders of society recognized the value of such satirical songs in which the ordinary person was given the privilege of unburdening his mind while the impact of his protest was neutralized by the controlled context in with criticism was possible" (Rohlehr, *Calypso and Society* 2).

4 See Brinsley Samaroo, "Two Abolitions: African Slavery and East Indian Indentureship"; and Kusha Haraksingh, "Control and Resistance among Indian Workers."

> welter of ethnicities, a restless and according to V. S. Naipaul, "half-formed" society, sufficiently flexible to accommodate the paradox of homogeneity and difference, of one heart and yet multiple heartbeats; a jarring, jamming Carnivalesque collusion and clashing counter point of rhythms. (374)

Trinidadian discourses of cultural belonging have deployed tropes of hybridity and emblems of nationhood drawn from a range of icons. Seeking fluid and varied locations on a complex matrix of inclusions and exclusions, Indo–Trinidadians have for the most part rejected notions of an essentialising "creole" social fabric to which their Indianness adds an "exotic" flair. Nationalist discourses continue to revolve around questions such as: should the steel pan, the percussion instrument created by the Afro–Trinidadian urban folk in the 1930s, be emblematic of national creativity? Every Trinidadian and Tobagonian would recall, in fact, that the Trinidad and Tobago High Court had to adjudicate a motion that questioned the legality of the State's institution of the Trinity Cross as the highest national award in a multireligious society, given the symbol's associations with Christianity. The contestations continue from decade to decade and even generation to generation, with unsullied freshness and fervour.

Calypso is another such icon. With its attendant culture of competition and performance, it is a barometer of public opinion, a reflector of collective identity and a manifestation of the construction of individual and communal identity through performance. Its seasonal projection onto the national stage hinges on a strong, obtrusive, visual presence by performers who are identified by characteristic costumes that project lavish stage personas. What would a Shadow, Black Stalin, the soca artiste Ronnie Mackintosh or the Chutney Soca Queen Drupatee Ramgoonai be without their trademark garments? In the performance, there is an increasing propensity to incorporate mime and play-acting. Each of these elements adds to the texts to be decoded, thus, pushing the signification beyond the semiotic and verbal to incorporate the mimetic, dramatic and performative.

This process becomes all the more contentious within the multiethnic environment. In 2003, for example, Denyse "Saucy Wow" Belfon, famed for her dizzying pelvic gyrations, crossed boundaries when she constructed the Indo–Trinidadian male as sexually desirable. Hitherto, the Indian male had been constructed in calypso, and arguably by virtue of selective representation and erasure in the mass media advertising industry, as weak, small-bodied and feminised. Conservative elements within the Indo–Trinidadian community took issue with her other boundary-crossing action—the use of a sari for her performance. They contended that she was, thereby, defiling the sacred garment.

In terms of its verbal dimension, the calypso is one facet of a diverse oral tradition, which has been used by all ethnic groups to express racial antipathy—a deep-rooted self-derision and contempt for the other through music and childhood rhyming songs. Indeed, the intraracial and interracial diatribes are an extension of the self-contempt and reductive laughter which Caribbean folk art forms, reflecting a historical legacy of ethnic denigration and disempowerment through naming, democratically employ within the ethnic group and towards other ethnicities. Rohlehr recalls the rhymes of his Guyanese childhood through which children expressed the hostilities of their elders and of their societies in verses, which groups of Indian and African children would hurl at each other.[5] He argues that these cancerous racial stereotypes are inculcated from childhood and, hence, are all the more

---

5 The Indo–Guyanese children would tease:

> "Black man salla pound massalla
> Who is yuh daddy
> Coolie is yuh daddy."
>
> The Afro–Guyanese children would tease:
> "Coolie water rice
> pork and spice
> get some cow dung
> to make it nice."
>
> And both groups would intone variously:
> "Nigger/coolie is a nation
> very botheration
> Go to police station."

Reflecting on the stereotype of Indian husbands as jealous, vengeful wife-beaters, the Afro–Guyanese children interpreted the message of the tassa drums which heralded the Hindu wedding procession thus:

> "Bum bum bum
> Ra taa taa taa
> Lil lil gyal me going to marry to yuh
> And if yuh take another man
> Ah going to cut off yuh neck."

—Unpublished interview with Gordon Rohlehr.
UWI, St Augustine, February 2005.

insidious and resistant to erasure. Reflecting this history of latent and manifest racial antipathy, calypso provides the most effective medium for race and gender stereotyping and for satirising the other. Shalini Puri comments that the "them and us" constructions, which continue to dominate Trinidad's discourses of cultural nationalism until today, posits notions of racially distinct ethnic parties who exist in racial antipathy and, to a large extent, in culturally specific spheres with a minimum of admixture. Puri contends:

> [R]acialization of politics in post-colonial Trinidad, the persistence and active redeployment of colonial stereotypes, and the importance of stereotype in the popular national art form, Calypso, result in a public discourse in which racial stereotypes are unusually prominent. What these stereotypes produce for contemporary dominant nationalist discourse is the fiction of a seamless and monolithic racial community with common interests, pitted against another seamless and monolithic racial community with common interests. (Puri 240)

Indo–Trinidadian cultural identity has been savagely satirised in calypso through a mockery of mannerism, food, religious ceremonies and other cultural traditions. Conversely, there are the calypsos that offer rhapsodies about the sexual desirability and beauty of Indian women. Invariably, this genre of calypso thinly disguises male–male competition with a primary focus on phallic boasting about the amazing capability of the Afro–Caribbean male for conquest within and across ethnic lines. Let the implicature of phallic inadequacy fall where it may.[6] This tendency surfaces also in literary discourse. George Lamming, in his address entitled "Language and the Politics of Ethnicity" delivered at the Cultural Studies Conference in Trinidad, in January 2004, commented on literary representations of African–Indian relations:

> There are numerous examples in our literature of hostility between individuals which derive from these toxic sources of power that manipulate the original neutral difference between characters—the innocent malice for example of Masie directed at Philomen in James's *Minty Alley*; the censoring of Pariag's inclusion and participation

6 Klass, in his study of an Indian village that he names Amity, notes the assumption of overwhelming sensuality of the young Indian girl which needed to be strictly policed to avoid the disgrace of pregnancy out of marriage and, even more so, vulnerability to the excessive phallic prowess which was the boast of Afro–Caribbean populations as represented through the calypsonian.

> by the yard in Lovelace's *The Dragon Can't Dance*. The strategy of ensuring allegiance by dramatizing the menace of the Indian was most effectively used by the old colonial power and it has often been called into service by both African and Indian political leadership in the new independent countries. It has been a major obstacle to the realization of an authentic, civic nationalism that will embrace and recreolise all ethnic types in Caribbean society.

Through the analysis of Indo–Trinidadian literary examples, I argue that the calypso in its broader discursive associations with ethnic dissociation and stereotyping functions as a trope of hybridity and belonging which, nevertheless, is constructed differently depending on the gender of the writer.

The earliest mention of calypso in Indo–Caribbean fiction is in Seepersad Naipaul's *Gurudeva and other Tales* (1943).[7] Seepersad Naipaul alludes to women, even those from conservative Indian homes, who took advantage of the American presence in Trinidad to enter into transactional sexual relations with the prosperous soldiers. The brief allusion is telling. While her parents are fretting about Daisy Seetohal's late nights and frequent absences, the latter laces her ablutions and denial of misbehaviour with snatches of the calypso "Rum and Coca Cola", signifying that she is in fact "working for the Yankee dollar".[8]

A generation later, V. S. Naipaul refines his father's allusion to calypso to point out the complex and diverse social movements in *Miguel Street* (1959). Calypsos offer a running unifying commentary on its vignettes, which are also united through expanded character development from story to story, temporal progression and a shared narrator for whom keen observation of the complex social history of the *Miguel Street* residents is inextricable from his coming-of-age process. In the final segment, the youthful narrator equates walking into his future with walking into his own shadow: "I left them all and walked briskly towards

---

7 V. S. Naipaul dates the first publication of *Gurudeva and Other Indian Tales* as 1943, in his Foreword to the André Duetsch edition in 1976. No date is recorded in the original publication.

8 The original lyrics to "Rum and Coca Cola" were composed and sung by Lord Invader (Rupert Grant) in Trinidad in 1943. This calypso was subsequently recorded by The Andrews Sisters with Vic Schoen and His Orchestra, 18 October 1944. Credits for the words and music were given to Morey Amsterdam (words) and Jeri Sullavan (music) and Paul Baron (music). The dispute over ownership was settled in court in Invader's favour.

the aeroplane, not looking back, looking only at my shadow before me, a dancing dwarf on the tarmac" (222). The novel is both a celebration of vivacity and coping strategies of a people doomed ultimately to fail, and a lament at an inevitable creeping loss, disillusionment and the passing of a world of innocence. In V. S. Naipaul's *The Middle Passage* (1962), whose perceiving eye and voice combines those of the journalist, the traveller/adventurer and social commentator, Naipaul ties the peculiar dynamic which characterises Trinidad society to the calypso:

> The Land of the Calypso is not a copy-writer's phrase. It is one side of the truth, and it was this gaiety, so inexplicable to the tourist who sees the shacks of Shanty Town and corbeaux patrolling the modern highway, and inexplicable to me who had remembered it as the land of failures, which now, on my return, assaulted me. (58)

Published in 1959, nine years after Naipaul migrated to England, *Miguel Street* unfolds against the backdrop of World War II (1939–1945) and the American military occupation of Trinidad.

This period also coincided with increased urban–rural migration of Indians in Trinidad and the heightened pace and visibility of the acculturation process. This is the 1940s to 1950s during which calypsonians vented their resentment at the intrusion of Indo–Trinidadians into the urban space. In this period, The Mighty Terror sang "Grinding Masalla" (1947), "Indian Women with Creole Names" and "Indian Politicians" (1950), all of which thinly masked fear at the intrusion and enhanced competition.[9]

Significantly though, this is not the focus of Naipaul's *Miguel Street* where calypsos provide an underlying philosophical frame for the narratives. The text mentions no fewer than ten of them: "The More They Try to Do Me Bad" (1938) by Lord Caresser (Rufus Callender) (82); "The Burning of the Treasury" (91); "Cuff Dem Down" (n.d.) by The Mighty Sparrow (Slinger Francisco) which both The Roaring Lion (Hubert De Leon) and Lord Beginner (Egbert Moore) claimed to have invented (111); "Chinese Children Calling Me Daddy" (1950) by

9 These are not the earliest calypsos focusing on the Indian presence. Rohlehr notes: "Consciousness of the East Indian presence would begin to emerge in the twenties, and by the thirties calypsos such as Executioner's 'My Indian Girl Love', Lion's 'Bhago Pholouri', and 'Ara Da Da', Tiger's 'Gi Rita Ram Gi' and King Iere's 'Madras Wedding' would be sung" (*Calypso and Society* 40–41). No recording information is available for the calypsos "Grinding Masalla" (1947), "Indian Women with Creole Names" (1950) and "Indian Politicians" (1950).

The Mighty Terror (127); "Is Love Love Love Alone" (1937) by Lord Caresser (136); "All Day All Night Miss Mary Ann" (1954) by The Roaring Lion (166); "Working for the Yankee Dollar" (1943) by Lord Invader (185); "The Soldiers Came and Broke up My Life" (1944) by Lord Invader (196); "I Living with My Yankee Soldier" by Lord Invader (197); "Matilda" (1953) by King Radio and popularised by the famous American entertainer of Jamaican parentage—Harry Belafonte (210).

Miguel Street deals with the issue of what it means to be a "man among we men". Its characters—some of whom are transient—grapple with turbulent gender and family relations. The calypso forms an ironic counterpoint to the feverish machinations of a small world in which persons seek in vain for heroic stature but are dogged by failure and frustration. The frustrated artiste exemplified in the Carpenter Popo does not work gainfully, preferring to strive to create the elusive "thing without a name" (*Miguel Street*, "The Thing Without a Name" 17–25). The calypso becomes an ambivalent symbol of low culture creativity for the failed artist Black Wordsworth, who strives to write "the greatest poem in the world" but sheepishly confesses that he makes his annual income by singing calypsos during the calypso season (*Miguel Street* 63). *Miguel Street* also represents frustrated careerists like the aspiring doctor turned Scavenger Cart driver in "His Chosen Calling" (*Miguel Street* 36–43), and the mechanical genius Mr Bhakcu who is more skilled at deconstruction than construction (*Miguel Street*, "The Mechanical Genius" 147–154). Moreover, in this world of men among men, an inordinate number meet misfortune and frustration in their pursuit of love.

Threaded throughout the narratives, the calypsos, the majority of which deal with the debacle of violent male–female relations, variously amplify and undercut the action. Although the narrator is proud to affirm that *Miguel Street* is a cut above the barrack-yard environment, the eruptive violence in male–female relations does not reflect this differentiation. The scripts are varied but with a common thread. There is the failure of one party or the other to meet expectations; the escape of the aggrieved party from the disappointing relationship, and the attempt to win the loved one back with the help of violence, often eliciting the intervention of the law. The calypso serves to analyse and magnify the domestic dramas. It lifts the petty events out of their specific confines and makes them representative experiences. When Popo beats his wife's lover, the incident becomes the basis for the road march "Emelda",[10] which the popular all-female American vocalists,

10 I have not been able to trace a calypso on this topic named "Emelda". John Thieme in *The Web of Tradition: Uses of Allusions in V. S. Naipaul's Fictions*

The Andrews Sisters, subsequently recorded for an American company.[11] The smallness of Miguel Street though, which a stranger could drive and dismiss as a slum, is alleviated by the notoriety of the calypso which projects the community's mundane dramas onto the national and international stage and, thereby, amplifies its tragedies. In the process, it lends significance and import to all. The narrator declares: "It was a great thing for the street" (22).

Naipaul also deploys reversals or spins on popular calypsos, providing an alternative take on the popular lore. "The Maternal Instinct" alludes to the infamous calypso-expounding wife-beating which popularises the assumption that "women and them like a good dose of blows": "Black up their eyes and bruise up their knee / And then they love you eternally" (111). This ironically named narrative reverses the male beater/female beaten paradigm by presenting a female abuser. This woman, who is said to love her children, regularly deals them murderous verbal abuse. The lover, Nathaniel, who is physically abused also, suffers from an ego-retrieving need to project the fabrication that he is the beater and not the beaten. Laura is reminiscent of the matador woman, that is, the woman who provides clothes, food and lodging for her "sweet man" in exchange for his sexual favours and exclusive attention.

Equipped with both physical and verbal ascendancy, she follows through on her beatings with a verbal emasculation suggestive of the African–American tradition of the dirty dozens—the male-dominated verbal power play that is a safer substitute for physical violence. In a public verbal game of one-upmanship, she emerges the victor by stripping him naked: "Yes, Nathaniel, is you I talking to, you with your bottom like two stale bread in your pants" (113). Yet, the abusive

---

indicates the same and surmises that it may be an invention on Naipaul's part (Thieme 205). This calypso is not to be confused with Young Killer's "Emelda's Nightmare" (1959), which is about Emelda's night-long attack on the persona's "little finger" and his inability to find a police man to rescue him.

11 The Andrews Sisters were an extremely popular all-female trio who maintained their impact on the entertainment industry for about thirty years. According to their official website, they sold over 90 million records, recorded approximately 700 songs and earned nine gold records. Their energy, virtuosity and harmony helped to brighten a dark period in American history. The Andrews Sisters popularised the calypso "Rum and Coca Cola". http://www.cmgww.com/music/andrews/about/bio3.html. Accessed December 2020.

matador woman is eventually stumped not by her own childbearing potential but by the prospect of the generational continuity of her impoverished lifestyle. She faces the likelihood that her daughter may follow her pattern of bearing eight children for seven men. In a bizarre double reversal, Laura's abuse of her pregnant daughter would have been indicative of love; her terrible silence seems a form of rejection of the girl who eventually resorts to suicide. Naipaul zeroes in here on a cultural tradition that habitually greets tragedy with laughter that becomes both a palliative and a substitute for more explosive and dangerous forms of expression.

A similar reversal is deployed in the short story "Is Love Love Love Alone", which is named after Lord Caresser's calypso about Edward VIII who forsook the British throne to marry a commoner and divorcee. This statement on the ennobling power of love to transcend class barriers is the counterpoint to the story of a woman who leaves a sanitised, professional husband and luxurious lifestyle for a Miguel Street slum-dwelling and an unkempt, drunken, abusive lover. The community disciplines the abuser with a severe beating, not because wife-beating is unacceptable, but because his practices are sufficiently extreme to transgress even their boundaries. Arguably too, because the couple is unmarried, the violence does not securely remain under the category of "husband and wife business" as may be the case in George's pink house.

Between the 1940s and 1950s, lower-strata gender relations in Trinidad were dealt a harsh blow with the intrusion of American soldiers during the World War II. The chagrin was great among calypsonians who found that prosperous American soldiers had muscled in on their turf. This move, which coincided with Indian rural–urban acculturation, crossed ethnic barriers so that Indian women became complicit in sex as a commodity exchange, which left their former partners out in the cold. Culturally conservative Indians and Afro-Creole calypsonians agreed on the destructive power of cultural assimilation. In "Indian People with Creole Names" by Mighty Killer, the calypsonian decries a shift in naming conventions as evidence of an Indian takeover of naming, privilege, occupation and cultural identity. The stripping away of markers of cultural distinctiveness is seen as a threat which drives the calypsonian to seek to protect his name, status and wealth from impending "trouble":

> Now what's wrong with these Indian people,
> as though their intention is for trouble?
> Long ago you meet an Indian boy by the road
> with his capra waiting to tote your load,

> but I notice there ain't no Indian again
> since the women and them taking Creole names.
> Long ago was Sumitra, Ramaleela, Ramaliwa
> But now is Jean and Dinah and Dorothy etc. etc. etc.

More explicitly, the calypso notes admixture in terms of hitherto taboo aggression, food and intimate relations:

> Long age you hadn't a chance
> To meet an Indian Girl in a dance
> But nowadays it is big confusion
> Big fighting in the road for their Yankee man
> And see them in the market they ain't making joke
> Pushing down nigger people to buy de poke.

The naming to which Mighty Killer refers in "Indian People with Creole Names" is indicative not simply of a shift in cultural identification but a muscling in on the transactional sex turf. The calypso cleverly links anglicised naming with prostitution when Killer attributes to the Indian working girls, the names of Sparrow's prostitutes (Jean and Dinah) whom the latter threatens with sexual revenge in the wake of the Yankees' departure. This dubious form of women's work attracts the censure of the licentious and libidinous calypsonian turned moraliser, the better to document the process of degeneration. As indicated by Rohlehr:

> The American presence undermined the traditional saga boy pose of the Calypsonian who had presented the woman as an easily exploitable and expendable commodity. With American soldiers there to provide both mother and daughter with a "better price," the woman had become a sort of professional who no longer needed her parasitical saga boy. (*Calypso and Society* 365)

The Yankee soldier with his almighty dollar was instrumental in the unmasking of the Trinidadian male whose phallic boasting and control over a series of women disguised his fear of commitment. *Miguel Street* makes fictional allusions to this in "Edward's Wife" in which the protagonist's pale, sickly woman leaves him for an American soldier. This is related even more directly to the issue of potency because Edward, the longing and the fearful, claims that he is constrained to marry the woman because she is pregnant with a baby that never materialises. His impotence is exposed when his wife leaves him and conceives by an American soldier lover. In this instance, life imitates the calypso, which amplifies, explains and rationalises life. As it often is in reality, the narrator creates a seamless weave between the grim facts of characters that are grappling with crises and the scripted fictionalised lives of characters of calypso. Hence, Popo's actions make him the subject of a calypso which becomes the road march, while, in "Until the Soldier Came", Lord Invader sings the calypso first, and subsequently Edward's wife mouths the calypsonian's scripted words. When he begs her to come back to him, she responds: "Invader, I change my mind / I living with my Yankee soldier." This was exactly what happened to Edward (*Miguel Street* 197).

Despite the community's willingness to blame the wife and embrace the cuckolded husband, Edward—Hat's brother—takes himself and his shame away from *Miguel Street*. In terms of the construction of a national community, the *Miguel Street* dwellers live side by side for the most part, blissfully ignorant of markers of ethnic divisiveness. The construction of ethnicity surfaces here in relation to whiteness which in this grim scenario becomes ugly because of ugly actions: "Hat said … 'You see what a dirty thing a white skin does be sometimes.' And in truth he had a nasty skin. It was yellow and pink and white with brown and black spots. The skin above his left eye had the raw pink look of scalded flesh" (137).

In the *Miguel Street* world, there is no contestation over national identity. Hat, subtly signalling his potency, is a surrogate father to children of all ethnicities whom he proudly instructs in the intricacies of the national game—cricket. And calypso is the common repository into which all characters dip variously for reference points. Indeed, the calypso is also indicative of patriotism and the good life. Morgan, the pyrotechnist turned arsonist, sings: "The more they try to do me bad / Is the better I live in Trinidad" (*Miguel Street* 82).

Calypso in *Miguel Street* becomes a unifying force in its promotion of patriotism and its construction of the nation as a shared homeland. Its barbs and balms are applied in an egalitarian manner to all ethnicities and classes. As a marker of communal identity and affirmation, it functions as an indigenous boundary marker. Naipaul comments in *The Middle Passage*:

> It is only in the Calypso that the Trinidadian touches reality. The Calypso is a purely local form. No song composed outside Trinidad is a Calypso. The Calypso deals with local incidents, local attitudes and it does so in a local language. The pure Calypso, the best Calypso, is incomprehensible to the outsider. Wit and verbal conceits are fundamental; without them no song, however good the music, however well sung, can be judged a Calypso. (75–76)

In *The Middle Passage*, Naipaul insists on the indigeneity of the calypso and its inability to travel as exemplary of its rootedness and its power to bind Trinidadians to locality, communal perspectives and worldviews. Yet, it is precisely as rooted, ethnic music that it travels so very well.

The tension between calypso as a culturally and geographically rooted form and its ability to reinvent itself on foreign terrain is explored in Selvon's short story collection, *Ways of Sunlight*. In "Basement Lullaby", the inability of the musicians to get the melody of the new calypso right is associated with their growing alienation and dissociation within a hostile environment in which they live half-lives, submerged in underground burrows. The alienation operates on several levels. They are divorced from the natural environment of both Trinidad and London. They seem to be suffering a lack of exposure to the energising, life-giving sun. And access to the sun is a tall order with smog blocking out its feeble rays on the streets of London. The quality of their calypso performances is suffering because they are playing before non-discerning English audiences. The calypso symbolises here a cultural rootedness and an inner well-being which they are losing hold of, and, therefore, they find themselves producing discordant, jangling music.

In Selvon's "Calypso in London", the art form is deployed as a contradictory marker of Trinidadian distinctiveness and the translocation of Anansi-style coping strategies within the metropolitan scenario. Trapped within the harsh wintry environment, bereft of employment and the support of extended community, Mangohead, the Vincentian, hones his skills as a hustler seeking to sell his lyrics to the composer Hotboy for quick money. The flash-in-the-pan creativity becomes an alternative to soul-destroying, burdensome, manual work. Its financial reward is swiftly dissipated on basic necessities. More significantly, the story unveils the impulses that impact cultural production. This creation on foreign soil needs to be both distinctly Trinidadian and acutely relevant to the broader metropolitan framework, in this case, the Suez Canal issue. The composition must satisfy opposing impulses—a parochial backward glance to Trinidad and its homegrown foci, rhythms and roots and the outward-oriented global appeal, which was always a facet of the traditional calypso, but becomes even more vital to its success in the new terrain.

The Trinidadians as the "authentic" owners of the cultural form are proprietary and defensive: Hotboy, the composer, berates Mangohead as a Vincentian who should leave Trinidad calypso alone, while Rahamut, the "legitimate" arbiter of the calypso's worth, berates his enthusiastic English assistant: "Why you don't shut you mouth? What you English people know about calypso" (129). Yet it is clear, even to the displaced Trinidadians, that the calypso must speak both to nationals abroad thirsty for connections to home and the growing circle of foreign consumers. To accomplish the second goal, the calypso must move away from a thematic focus on the specificities of individuals' lived experience. The brief story is a telling commentary on how calypso travels and the impact of forces that shape cultural production on calypso as a commodity with increasing global appeal.

In Naipaul's and Selvon's fictions of the 1950s and 1960s, the calypso is reflective of shared experiences of poverty, social adversity, individual and communal disempowerment and of adversarial gender relations. As Indo–Trinidadian writers who adopted calypso for their thematic and stylistic emphases, they resisted the propensity to use this nation song to signify ethnic dissociation. Instead, the calypso as literary emblem was associated with belonging, rootedness, homecoming and the formation of a common front in relation to external global events such as war, American army occupation and its paradoxical impact on the social conditions of Trinidadian life.

As already indicated, the construction of the Indian woman within this male-dominated, lower-strata, Afro–Caribbean art form became a pivotal element of interracial tension and contestation. The early literary expressions of Naipaul and Selvon did not follow this mould. Their location on the ever-shifting continuum of discourses in relation to nationalism in Trinidad saw muted possibilities for an emerging Creole cultural aesthetic. Even for a writer of Naipaul's persistent pessimism, denigration and self-exclusion, the calypso with its vigour, inventiveness and ebullience signalled a bewildering rootedness and potential in the face of all evidence to the contrary.

Selvon's perspectives in *Ways of Sunlight* were qualified in his 1979 Opening Address to the India in the Caribbean Conference, when he called for an end to ethnic antipathy and divisiveness. He is particularly critical of Caribbean islanders in the metropolis whose diseased sense of national belonging was susceptible to a shape-shifting fluidity which readily wrapped itself around political expediency: "With no tradition, no national pride, no patriotism, lacking values but full of calypso and carnival and what happening boy, it was as easy as kissing hand to deny their birthright" (18). And in relation to the Caribbean island dweller, he comments, "[In] spite of the cultural growth in these islands since the last war, we are still being identified on a level which does not seem to rise above cricket, calypso, steelband and limbo" (19–20).

Issuing a call for unity, Selvon cites Black Stalin's "Caribbean Unity" (more popularly known as "The Caribbean Man") as a grassroots expression of the dream of Caribbean unity, which "transcends the parochial and becomes regional rather than insular" (22). The calypso's function as reflector and shaper of mass perspectives demonstrates the potential for significant ideological intervention. Ironically such is the state of racial tension that this very calypso generated intense and sustained public dialogue much of which was focused on its racist character in its supposed exclusive identification of the Afro–Caribbean as "the" Caribbean man.[12]

The second part of this chapter demonstrates that calypso and other predominantly Afro–Caribbean cultural forms play a divergent role for Indo–Trinidadian women writers. Indo–Trinidadian women, reflecting their secluded positions within the home, their traditional silencing and later access to education, came to creative expression later than both Indo–Trinidadian men and Afro–Trinidadian women. The post-independence period gave Indian women free primary education, access to jobs in the public service and the private sector. This was accompanied by intensified urban migration and a shift to more nuclear-type families. These women writers' deployment of calypso and carnival as emblematic of Afro-Creole society can be located variously on a continuum.

The younger Indo–Caribbean women writers strike out for a more transgressive representation of their position in relation to a broader, multi-ethnic social order. Calypso and carnival are evoked as tropes of intentional hybridity, signifying a different way to be Indian and female within a Trinidadian context. The difference between the portrayal Naipaul and Selvon explored earlier and that of the younger women, Joy Mahabir and Rajandaye Ramkisson-Chen, is reflective of the nuances of Robert Young's differentiation between unconscious and intentional hybridity: the gap between "unconscious processes of hybrid mixture or creolization and a conscious and politically motivated concern with the deliberate disruption of homogeneity" (Young 120).

The intentional hybridity finds the fullest expression in Ramkissoon-Chen's "When the Hindu Woman Sings Calypso", which was inspired by Drupatee Ramgoonai, the Queen of Chutney Soca. The Chutney tradition, which came to Trinidad with indentured Indians and survived in pockets in villages, represented resistance to a colonial hegemonic order which sought to nullify and demonise Hindu culture. Chutney was derived from the rural folk song and dance tradition associated with the Matikor ritual, that is, the exclusively female space in which women frankly instructed the bride-to-be on sexual matters through song, dance and ribald humour. Brinda Mehta, in *Diasporic (Dis)locations*, associates "wining" with the birthing contractions of

---

12 For a detailed study of the media debates surrounding "The Caribbean Man", see Ramesh Deosaran, "The 'Caribbean' Man: A Study of the Psychology of Perception and the Media."

the body as it breaks free from itself and releases new life (98). This female-dominated space, Kanhai suggests in *Matikor*, served to affirm the sensuality of Hindu women but it may also have been the site of surreptitious female-to-female caresses under the guise of preparing the bride for her most important traditional role. Until today, Chutney runs afoul of Brahminical notions of purity and seclusion as ideal behaviours for Hindu women. According to Mehta, "[T]he political dimensions of Chutney are located in women's contestations of class distinctions.… The suggestive movements of Chutney dancing are a public demonstration of women's efforts to defy normative codes of Hindu patriarchal morality …" (98).

By the time Chutney reached the national stage in the 1980s, some of its elements had previously been appropriated by the calypso. The acknowledgement of the Indian presence in terms of lyrics as well as musical instruments was evident from about the 1970s onwards:

> This new style of music included the Indian instruments of the tassa, dholak & sitar. It also incorporated the more Calypso flavor of the steel pan and synthesizer and even the electric guitar. The lyrics were also mostly sung in West Indian creole with maybe the exception of only a few Hindi words. However, by far the most significant change in this new style was the fact that it was almost solidly dominated by Afro West Indians during its early days. Songs such as Baron's "Raja Rani", Mighty Trini's "Curry Tabanca", Sugar Aloe's "Roti & Dhalpourie" & Sparrow's "Marajin" dominated the Indian Soca scene from 1980–1987. (Saywack)

The impact of this was to push Chutney far more decisively and centrally onto the national stage. Many of these songs were about the sexual attractiveness of the Indian woman to the calypso persona. Given the systematic effort to construct this persona as a sexual predator bent on the rake and scrape type intertribal penetrations or revenge through miscegenation, it is understandable that the conservative Indian elements in the society were not pleased with this appropriation of Indian cultural forms.[13]

13 For obvious reasons, the thought of Afro–Trinidadian male and East Indian female sexual relations was disturbing for most East Indians. Saywack notes that Sparrow's "Marajin", where he describes his love interest for a pandit's (Hindu priest) wife, was banned in Guyana for several years, after a huge outcry from the Hindu community in that country. Puri mentions the outrage that greeted the nani songs. This term, which means grandmother on the mother's side, is in Trinidad also a vulgar name for vagina. It, therefore,

Predictably the emergence of Hindu female Chutney artists on the public stage occasioned a veritable outbreak of male censure and censorship. Ramkisson-Chen pens a poetic intervention in the dialogue in "When the Hindu woman Sings Calypso", based on the career of Drupatee Ramgoonai, who emerged out of the rural village of Penal in South Trinidad via the Afro–Trinidadian male-dominated Calypso state to enjoy international fame at a period when few Indian men were willing to make their presence felt in this location. To appropriate this space was to violate numerous deeply intense taboos. Her intrusion can be contextualised by Rosanne Kanhai's statement on the traditional Bhowjee, the term applied to "old fashioned" Indian ladies who had had arranged marriages and who stayed "at home to take care of the children and do housework" (Kanhai 3):

> Indeed the figure of the traditional Bhowjee, humming at the masala stone is familiar to the Indo–Caribbean landscape.... She hums under her breath because breaking into song is bolder than her life of repression and rigorous domesticity allows.... A hardworking woman is likely to be docile and virtuous, and Bhowjee's skill in grinding masala is proof of her chastity and morality; she symbolizes all that is wholesome and proper in the Indo–Caribbean community. Expressions of playfulness or waywardness are curbed, and creativity is channelled into household chores. The masala stone receives her complaints, reflections, longings, griefs, joys.... The massala stone sings. (Kanhai 209–210)

The "Bhowjee" in Drupatee Ramgoonai's initial composition "Pepper, Pepper" brought into the public arena the hardships endured by young East Indian women in the marriage relationship. It posed a simple strategy for taking revenge by putting excessive quantities of pepper in the husband's food.

Swift and strong censure was levelled against Drupatee Ramgoonai for her transgressive act: "No Indian woman has any right to sing Calypso" and "Indian women have been a disgrace to Hinduism" were cries from the fraternity (Constance 51). Mahabir Maharaj, writing in the *Sandesh* paper, added: "[F]or an Indian girl to throw away her high upbringing and culture to mix with vulgar music, sex and alcohol in

---

lends itself to the double entendre so well that it became the subject of the popular Crazy's "Nani Wine", Scrunter's "Nanny" and Becket's "Nanny Revival". The uproar was great when Drupatee Ragoonai sang the Chutney Soca song "Lick Down Me Nani", thereby, disrupting the "idealization of a desexualized Indian grandmother" (Puri 257–262).

carnival tents tells me that something is radically wrong with her psyche. Drupatee Ramgoonai has chosen to worship the gods of sex, wine and easy money" (Constance 51). Drupatee's defiance of patriarchal dictates has been made more visible by her dramatic success since she made history as not only the first female Chutney Soca artist to hit the national stage but also the first Indo–Trinidadian to successfully cross over into the Soca charts and to have a number one hit.

Rajandaye Ramkisoon-Chen's poem, "When the Hindu Woman Sings Calypso", traces the journey of her protagonist from the rural peasant environment and the female-only matikor prenuptial ritual to the national calypso stage. The old restrictions and symbols of the enclosure are reconstituted with radically divergent meaning. Progress in the form of electric light and glaring stage light replace the gloaming, moonlight and lamplight. The poem unfolds:

> Strings of rhinestone now
> "Purdah" her forehead
> Hair frizzled to a "Buss-up-shot"
> The long tresses of
> A long tradition
> Seared in the electricity
> Of the mike's cord length. (50)

Within the broadened social framework, purdah—the tradition of sex segregation, which functioned traditionally to restrict women to the domestic space—has been radically reinterpreted. The only purdah enclosures that the persona entertains are the ones that enhance her glamour and sensuality. Her clothing reflects her selective incorporation of her Eastern ancestry. Significantly, it is not the traditional Hindu female's sari but trousers that reflect the wealth and opulence of the rich Moghul's garb. Her long hair, emblematic of traditional beauty and that most telling ethnic marker within the Caribbean framework, is "frizzled" into a "buss up shot" (a flour and butter roti whose flakes resemble a torn shirt). This uneasy metaphor signifies linguistic, culinary and phenotypical fusions that have been enthusiastically embraced by all members of Trinidadian society.

The frizzling of the hair is suggestive of the admixture—a douglarisation (read bastardisation)—of hair quality and culture. Her disruptive and transfiguring location calls the world, even the natural world, to come and see. The sleeping "fowl cocks" of the villages are replaced by the silenced night insects who stop their churrings to pay obeisance to the Chutney artiste's resounding voice. Her act includes a signifier of the brotherhood of the boat or ocean crossing—the limbo—which has traditionally been emblematic of the burial and re-emergence of slaves who survived the middle passage to arise to a new life in a new land:

Her midriff's bare
Looped white with pearls
Her body sinuous
With the dance of muscle
She stoops as for a "limbo" number
Head held backwards from the rod-fire
Leaves of flame
Play on her bodice. (51)

Ultimately, the poem is about the power of border crossing and the potential and release that can be afforded by hybridity. Her music remains rooted in the oral tradition of the matikor, but it reinterprets traditional socially restrictive conditions.

Even more so than Ramkisson-Chen, Joy Mahabir evokes associations between Indian female sensuality and Afro–Caribbean cultural expressions. In "Fire and Steel", Mahabir explores potentiality and ambivalence in relation to the pan as a symbol of spontaneous cultural fusion:

Steel bursting into song
Sticks clenched in sweating hands
...
I remember only intense union
freeing uplifting minutes of living
and after I forget. (45)

The passionate sensuality offers momentarily the possibility of a near orgasmic union, but this is swiftly supplanted by a deliberate forgetting of the process and of the possibility. The protagonist is condemned subsequently to an amnesiac existence, conveyed as lacking, or existing in happenings I forget (45).[14] The transitory intense nature of the

14 The full text of "Fire and Steel" reads:
I remember only
One night
Nights of fever and beating
Brought us to his place
Voices, stilled passion

possibility begs the question of how to sustain or crystallise the potential and the enrichment; how to cause the minute of heightened living to be sustained, to endure, to remain and not to be relegated to oblivion.

Persistent images of bodily heat, of fever and passion are translated into energy that, in turn, fuels the beating of the pan and internal compulsion that produces sweating hands. In contrast to this transitional ecstatic moment is the absence and lack that endures. The persona sets up a tension between the brevity of the remembering which is entrenched by frequent repetitions: "I remember only one night … one moment … intense union" (45). This is counterbalanced by the persistence of the forgetting. Yet, the narrative inscription of the experience disputes the dominance of the forgetting and privileges the fire and the steel and it is this which the reader remembers. This formulation recalls Lamming's poignant statement of the power of such remembering as the tongue probes the space left by an extraction and intensifies the memory of loss all the more (*In the Castle of my Skin* 279). Highly sexualised orgasmic pulsation becomes the barely veiled metaphor for creative awakening and cultural hybridity. Why is the persona of "Fire and Steel" constrained to forget the orgasmic moment? Amnesia is indicated because of the potentiality of the ecstatic moment to give way to a lifetime of communal dissociation and disconnectedness. Not to forget may be to court disaster.

In conclusion, "With a Tassa Blending" argues that calypso with the carnival as its encompassing ritual context originated in Afro–Caribbean resistance and cultural affirmation in the face of Eurocentric denigration and repression. Despite the fact that it has been a creative vehicle of African towards Indian diatribe and racial stereotyping, it emerges in Indo–Caribbean literary expression as emblematic of the possibility of raising a common voice against Eurocentric hegemonic discourses and

---

Movement in anticipation
I remember only
One moment:
Steel bursting into sound
Sticks clenched in sweating hands
Now lacking, existing,
In happenings I forget.
I remember only:
Intense union
Freeing, uplifting
Minutes of living
And after, I forget. (Creation Fire 45)

asserting shared cultural belonging and national pride. It is not at all surprising that the explosive, spiritual energies of calypso and carnival should fuse with the eruptive, reproductive energies of the matikor folk ritual to usher Chutney and Chutney Soca unto the national stage. The musical and literary allusions and blendings reveal both the impulse towards intragroup competitions and communalism and the inevitably of its fusions, all of which proceed simultaneously in the Trinidadian project of feverish hybridisation which Rohlehr describes in "Calypso Reinvents Itself" as "a jarring, jamming carnivalesque collusion and clashing counter point of rhythms" (374). These rich energised fusions now coexist comfortably on a public stage.

Indo–Trinidadian women writers like Ramkisson-Chen and her real-life model Drupatee Ramgoonai have moved beyond the confines of a deliberate forgetting and an oblique testimony of erased ecstasy. For Indo–Trinidadian writers, calypso has always signalled a belonging to the multi-ethnic social order. For the earlier male writers, it signifies an unintentional hybridity. For the younger female writers, it signifies an intentional trope and a liberationist aesthetic associated with sensuality and sexual autonomy. Notwithstanding legal contestation among conservative Indian elements in the society in respect to national symbols and emblems, today's Bhowjee has laid claim to a densely textured, inclusive narrative of intentional hybridity and "she sings and 'winds' / To calypso and 'pan' / With a 'tassa' blending" (Ramkisson-Chen 51).

Works Cited

Becket. "Nanny Revival." Fresh. CD Cocoa Records ABC-F-00110, 1993.

Constance, Zeno Obi. *Tassa, Chutney and Soca: The East Indian Contribution to the Calypso*. Jordan's Printing Service, 1991.

Crazy. "Nani Wine." Nani Wine. LP Trinity Records TR 001, 1989.

Dabydeen, David, and Brinsley Samaroo. *India in the Caribbean*. Hansib Publishing Ltd., 1987.

Deosaran, Ramesh. "The 'Caribbean' Man: A Study of the Psychology of Perception and the Media." *India in the Caribbean*, edited by Dabydeen and Samaroo, Hansib Publishing Ltd., 1987. pp. 81–118.

Elder, J. D. "Evolution of the Traditional Calypso of Trinidad and Tobago: A Socio-Historical Analysis of Song Change." Diss., University of Pennsylvania, 1996.

Espinet, Ramabai. *Creation Fire: A CAFRA Anthology of Caribbean Women's Poetry*. Sister Vision, 1990.

Haraksingh, Kusha. "Control and Resistance among Indian Workers: A Study of Labour on the Sugar Plantations of Trinidad 1875–1917." *India in the*

Caribbean, edited by Dadydeen and Samaroo, Hansib Publishing Ltd., 1987. pp. 61–80.

Hill, Errol. *The Trinidad Carnival: Mandate for a National Theatre*. University of Texas Press, 1992.

Kanhai, Rosanne. *Matikor: The Politics of Identity for Indo–Caribbean Women*. UWI School of Continuing Studies Press, 1999.

Lamming, George. *In the Castle of my Skin*. Longman, 1970.

———. "Language and the Politics of Ethnicity." Address delivered at the Cultural Studies Conference Cross Culturalism and the Caribbean Canon. The University of the West Indies, Trinidad, West Indies. January 13–17, 2004.

Mahabir, Joy. "Fire and Steel." *Creation Fire*, edited by Ramabai Espinet. p 45.

Mehta, Brinda. *Diasporic (Dis) Locations: Indo–Caribbean Women Writers Negotiate the Kala Pani*. The University of the West Indies Press, 2004.

Morgan, Paula. "East / West Indian / Woman / Other: At the Crossroads of Gender and Ethnicity." *Ma Comere: Journal of the Association of Caribbean Women Writers and Scholars*, vol. 3, 2000, pp. 109–122.

Naipaul, Seepersad. *Gurudeva and Other Indian Tales*. n.d. André Deutsch, 1976.

Naipaul, V. S. *Miguel Street*. 1959. Heinemann Caribbean Writers Series, 1974.

———. *The Middle Passage: Impressions of Five Societies, British, French and Dutch in the West Indies*. 1962. Penguin, 1969.

———. Foreword. *Gurudeva and Other Indian Tales* by Seepersad Naipaul. André Deutsch, 1976.

Puri, Shalini. "Race, Rape, and Representation: Indo–Caribbean Women and Cultural Nationalism." *Matikor: The Politics of Identity for Indo-Caribbean Women*, edited by Rosanne Kanhai. UWI School of Continuing Studies Press, 1999. pp. 238–282.

Ramgoonai, Drupatee. "Pepper, Pepper." Pepper. EP Kash Productions SP 2001, 1989.

———. "The Car Lick Down Me Nani." Down in Sando. CD Multitone Records DMVI 1335, 1995.

Ramkissoon-Chen, Rajandaye. "When the Indian Woman Sings Calypso." *Creation Fire*, edited by Ramabai Espinet. p 50.

Rohlehr, Gordon. *Calypso and Society in Pre-Independence Trinidad*. Lexicon, 1990.

———. "Calypso Reinvents Itself." *The Scuffling of Islands*. Lexicon Publishing, 2004, pp. 374–449.

Samaroo, Brinsley. "Two Abolitions: African Slavery and East Indian Indentureship." *India in the Caribbean*, edited by Dabydeen and Samaroo. Hansib Publishing Ltd., 1987. pp. 43–60.

Saywack, Rajendra. "From Caroni Gyal to Calcutta Woman—A History of East Indian Chutney Music in the Caribbean." Black & Puerto Rican Studies Department. Thomas Hunter College, December 1999. http://www.saxakali.com/caribbean/Hemchandra1.html. Accessed March 2020.

Scrunter. "Nanny." Nanny / John Dick. 12" 2Guys SCR-002, 1986.

Selvon, Sam. "Calypso in London." *Ways of Sunlight*. 1957. Macgibbon & Kee, 1961, pp. 125–131.

———. "Basement Lullaby." *Ways of Sunlight*. 1957. Macgibbon & Kee, 1961, pp. 175–180.

———. "Three into One Can't Go—East Indian, Trinidadian, West Indian." Opening Address to East Indians in the Caribbean Conference, University of the West Indies, Trinidad, *India in the Caribbean*, edited by Dabydeen and Samaroo, Hansib Publishing Ltd., 1987. pp. 13–24.

Sparrow, Mighty. "Marajhin." Sweeter Than Ever. LP with 12, Charlie's JAF 1005, 982. The Official Web Site of The Andrews Sisters. http://www.cmgww.com/music/andrews/about/bio3.htm. Accessed December 2005.

Young, Robert. "Hybridity in Post-Colonial Studies." *Post-Colonial Studies: The Key Concepts*, edited by Ashcroft Griffith and Tiffin, Routledge, 1998, pp. 118–121.

Chapter 8

ELITIST VERSUS VERNACULAR COSMOPOLITANISM IN NAIPAUL'S *MIGUEL STREET*[1]

Weiwei Xu

> I don't know if you remember the year the film *Casablanca* was made. That was the year when Bogart's fame spread like fire through Port-of-Spain and hundreds of young men began adopting the hardboiled Bogartian attitude.
>
> —*Miguel Street* 1

V. S. Naipaul began his career in the 1950s as a comic writer with four novels set in Trinidad—*The Mystic Masseur* (1957), *The Suffrage of Elvira* (1958), *Miguel Street* (1959) and *A House for Mr Biswas* (1961). Written from the viewpoint of a young writer describing the social circumstances in which he grew up, the novels are clever, funny and accomplished, as well as original in their technique and vision. These early social comedies of Naipaul are poker-faced, instilled with strong streaks of irony and satire. The comic effects arise not so much from events and incidents as from characters and dialogue. The eccentric way that people behave and speak is one example. There is, in Naipaul's amused or satiric manner, contempt, even brutality. He consciously presents a situation of absurdity, ignorance, knavery, self-interest and superstition as the farcical reality in Trinidad of the 1930s and 1940s. What underlies this partial representation is his mockery of the all-consuming poverty of Trinidad, its concomitant conservatism, narrowness, passivity and lack of authenticity.

George Lamming has stoutly questioned this authorial implication. Commenting on Naipaul's first three novels, Lamming states in *The Pleasures of Exile*:

---

1 This chapter was first published in *JNT: Journal of Narrative Theory*, vol. 46.3, Fall 2016, 287–311. The research for it was supported by the Fundamental Research Funds for the Central Universities No. SWU1509173.

> His books can't move beyond a castrated satire.... When such a writer is a colonial, ashamed of his cultural background and striving like mad to prove himself through promotion to the peaks of a "superior" culture whose values are gravely in doubt, then satire, like the charge of philistinism, is for me nothing more than a refuge. (225)

From Lamming's point of view, satire precludes sympathy and allows Naipaul to berate Trinidad from a stance of superiority, which Lamming interprets as a position of complete detachment. His charge is that the cultural values and societal norms by which Naipaul measures the distortions in Trinidadian society are basically Eurocentric.

In a 1971 interview with Ian Hamilton, Naipaul admitted to having been "a thorough colonial" when he first arrived in England. He reflected on his "complete colonial attitude" at that time: a kind of existentialist impotence, a condition in which he felt powerless to exercise freedom of choice (14). This idea of a colonial background providing security for a colonial subject deprived of choice sets up an important basis for the reader to form a picture of Naipaul's early cultural and political orientation as well to the right of the Trinidadian norm; it points the way to a staunch conservatism founded on an acceptance of the status quo.

A colonial subject when he began writing, Naipaul seems to have been unable to fulfil his later, more mature, conception of the writer's duty: "The artist who, for political or humanitarian reasons, seeks only to record abandons half his responsibility. He becomes a participant; he becomes anonymous. He does not impose a vision on the world" ("The Documentary Heresy" 24). Andrew Gurr reads this statement as Naipaul's rejection of his first four novels (87). Later, in a 1995 interview, Naipaul further confessed that

> the early comedy was really hysteria, the hysteria of someone who was worried about his place as a writer and his place in the world. When one is really stressed one makes a lot of jokes. You can make jokes all the time. That's not healthy. The profounder comedy comes from greater security. (Niven 6)

This might be Naipaul's most candid verdict on his colonial hangover: in these early novels, he mockingly distorted scenes of Trinidadian life from a Eurocentric or Western perspective.

Drawing on Homi K. Bhabha's theory of vernacular cosmopolitanism, this chapter contends that Naipaul adopts a rather unique narrative technique of doubling in *Miguel Street* to depict two kinds of cosmopolitanism: vernacular versus elitist. Through the boy narrator, the novel, which presents the lived cosmopolitan experience arising at a local, micro level, can be read as a Trinidadian example of vernacular cosmopolitanism. However, through the adult narrator who used to be the boy narrator, Naipaul obliterates the cosmopolitan ethos of a hybrid community and reveals a longing for the status conferred by elitist cosmopolitanism in the Enlightenment intellectual tradition.

In the novel, after some initial jostling, vernacular cosmopolitanism, which points to the active practice of the subaltern individuals operating primarily alone, is rendered meaningless. On the other hand, elitist, top-down cosmopolitanism wins out with the support of a satisfactory culture, that is, a Western, or Westernised, culture based on individual responsibility and vocational ambition.[2] The satirical edge of *Miguel Street*, which insists that only literacy by education can allow one a place in the larger discursive field of an articulated history, reflects Naipaul's colonial mentality, which, in the context of the novel, implies his conviction that a colonial subject cannot prosper unless he seeks the trappings and cultural privileges of elite cosmopolitanism.

Elitist Cosmopolitanism versus Vernacular Cosmopolitanism

Modern European thought on cosmopolitanism achieved significant articulation during the Enlightenment. According to Thomas J. Schlereth, European cosmopolitanism in its Enlightenment version "has its origins in the international class which had been developing since … 'the great revival of letters in the Renaissance'" (xv). In the eighteenth century, the cosmopolitan ideal arose among artists, intellectuals and scholars who saw themselves belonging to a transnational "Republic of Letters"; common to its various streams was the belief that knowledge and above all science would offer humanity a shared basis for a positive future.

2 The closest that Naipaul came to expressing a vision of such a satisfactory culture is his talk "Our Universal Civilization", given at the Manhattan Institute of New York. There he says that Western civilisation, always in creative process, gave him "the prompting and the idea of the literary vocation" together with "the means to fulfil that prompting", and enabled him to "make that journey from the periphery to the centre" (506–507). In this universal civilisation, it is "necessary to be an individual and responsible", and "people developed vocations, and were stirred by ambition and achievement, and believed in perfectibility" (514–515).

For Lorraine Daston, this ideal of the Republic of Letters was essentially "an elite confraternity distinguished by merit in literature, scholarship, and science", promoted by intellectuals who enjoyed a new social status (374). As a state of mind, Enlightenment cosmopolitanism was largely symbolic. To some extent, it was a doctrine that only a rationalist intellectual could embrace. It lacked appeal to the ordinary people. The intellectual and aesthetic orientation in the European context has ever since been associated with cosmopolitanism.

The beginning of global travel and travel writing in the eighteenth century—Montesquieu's *Persian Letters* and Oliver Goldsmith's *The Citizen of the World*, for example—contributed to Enlightenment cosmopolitanism and its concern with knowledge, including knowledge of other cultures. Many of the major philosophers of the eighteenth and early nineteenth centuries who travelled extensively in Europe (such as Gottfried Wilhelm Leibniz) or visited the United States (such as Jacques Pierre Brissot) evoked the image of a world citizen and popularised cosmopolitanism as an ideal of cultural sophistication, physical mobility and high social status. Discussing this cosmopolitan ideal and the Grand Tour, institutionalised by upper-class Europeans who regarded travel as an educational rite of passage in the seventeeth and eighteenth centuries, Melissa Calaresu points out:

> Travel, as well as the reading of travel accounts, by the European elite, are often seen as having made an important contribution to the founding principles of enlightened thought, in particular, toleration, by having extended not only the perimeters of human knowledge but also by testing the moral certainties of an expanding world. (140)

Enlightenment culture placed increasing importance on the value of travel as an educational tool: physical mobility provided the cultural capital for developing cosmopolitanism. Schlereth thus defines Enlightenment cosmopolitanism as follows:

> First, it was an attitude of mind that attempted to transcend chauvinistic national loyalties or parochial prejudices in its intellectual interests and pursuits. In the ideal, the "cosmopolite," or "citizen of the world," sought to be identified by an interest in, a familiarity with, or appreciation of many parts and peoples of the world; he wished to be distinguished by a readiness to borrow from other lands or civilizations in the formation of his intellectual, cultural, and artistic patterns. Therefore, the typical Enlightenment cosmopolite aspired to be ... eclectic in his philosophical and scientific outlook, synergistic in his religious perspective, and international in his economic and political thought. (xi–xii)

On a theoretical plane, the Enlightenment cosmopolitan outlook enabled its believers to transcend the limits and limitations of the specific place and time that they inhabited. In stark contrast to the national subject who was presumably static, parochial and inevitably bored, the cosmopolitan subject lived in a state of delightful detachment. To be cosmopolitan was to be a worldly-wise, privileged social actor, distinguished by a command of resources (for example, higher educational level and income) that enhanced transnational mobility. Cosmopolitanism became a conscious choice of the upper and middle classes, a manifestation of the mentality of the mobile elite.

Even in contemporary discourses, Enlightenment remains the main point of reference when defining cosmopolitanism. As a result, discussions about cosmopolitanism tend towards elitism. Ulf Hannerz, for example, while proposing a set of useful distinctions between cosmopolitans, locals, transnationals and frequent travellers (usually occupational), lumps together the formative makers of diasporas (migrant-settlers, exiles and refugees) with tourists. He casts cosmopolitanism's "intellectual and aesthetic stance of openness toward divergent cultural experiences" as the property of upper- and middle-class individuals, who possess sufficient occupational and experiential competencies enabling them to appreciate varied cultures and to maneuver within new meaning systems" (239). This motif of the cosmopolitan as privileged, capital-laden and globally mobile has proved remarkably durable in cosmopolitan studies. As Bruce Robbins insightfully points out, "The word cosmopolitan immediately evokes the image of a privileged person: someone who can claim to be a 'citizen of the world' by virtue of independent means, high-tech tastes, and globetrotting mobility" (171).

However, in the last two decades, there has been a veritable explosion of new thoughts on cosmopolitanism within different disciplines (especially cultural studies, sociology and anthropology). Replacing the Eurocentric sovereignty of Western culture (or individual) with the convivial, hybrid culture (or subject) of postcoloniality, Bhabha coined the compelling term "vernacular cosmopolitanism" to theorise the ambivalence, negotiation and the in-between of cultural translation. In "Unsatisfied: Notes on Vernacular Cosmopolitanism", Bhabha defines vernacular cosmopolitanism as "a form of marginal or partial interpellation that opens up a space occupied by those who seek to establish an ethic of community" and singles out three features (43).

First, vernacular cosmopolitanism stops short of the transcendent human universal and provides an ethical entitlement to the sense of community. Second, it is conscious of the insufficiency of the self and the imperative of openness to the needs of others. Third, it finds in the victims of progress the best promise for ethical regeneration. Vernacular cosmopolitanism is "not simply to be in a dialogic relation with the native or the domestic", but "to be on the border, in between, introducing the global-cosmopolitan 'action at a distance' into the very grounds—now displaced— of the domestic" (48). Bhabha's vernacular cosmopolitanism is not an all-encompassing project dictated from above, but one, patchwork-like, emerging from "the ordinariness of the day to day" and "the intimacy of the indigenous" (44). It is both less universalising and more inclusive, as it rejects a too easy universalisation, and allows for the importance of the local and everyday interactions in small ways.

"Vernacular cosmopolitanism", Bhabha asserts, is "not a cosmopolitanism of the elite variety inspired by universalist patterns of humanist thought that run gloriously across cultures, establishing an enlightened unity" (139). Instead, it refers to the routine and rarely documented cultural encounters of diasporic life and signals undifferentiated elements of contemporary global culture. Most importantly, it brings to the fore a range of ignored or unnoticed cosmopolitan sensibilities and worldviews present in circumstances not typically considered cosmopolitan (for instance, rural communities and small cities rather than the metropolis). Bhabha's vernacular model focuses on forms of minoritisation derived from the experience of traditionally disempowered, marginalised people. It can be applied to indigenous people, labour migrants, refugees, diasporic and exilic people, who are exposed to cosmopolitan experiences through immigrant networks, and not from original access to centres or groups of power in their communities of origin.

In "Speaking of Postcoloniality, in the Continuous Present", Bhabha points out that the Western individual connotes a "self-fulfilling, plenitudinous personhood", whereas, the colonial subject is "a kind of split-subject" that inherently accommodates an imperial otherness (21). He calls this an instance of living-in-difference, in which the process of cultural negotiation and translation is a necessary mode of survival, for the experience of colonisation coerces its subjects to cultivate social identifications that are non-identical to their cultural selves. This ethic of survival in modernity reflects the spirit of cosmopolitanism for Bhabha. Therefore, the de-centred self, not the sovereign individual, becomes inherently cosmopolitan:

> The "decentering of the self " was the very condition of agency and imagination in these colonial and postcolonial conditions, and it becomes more than a theoretical axiom; it becomes a protean, everyday practice, a way of living with oneself and others while

> acknowledging the "partiality" of social identification; it becomes part of one's ethical being in the sense that such a "decentering" also informs the agency through which one executes a care of the self and a concern for the "other," in the late Foucauldian sense. (21)

Gaining its momentum from concrete history and material realities, colonial experiences in particular, Bhabha's theory posits a kind of cosmopolitanism from below. His inclusion of subaltern individuals, while broadening definitions of cosmopolitan subjects, compels us to reimagine the abstracted relation in actually existing geographical and human terms. In addition, by noting that immigrants with prior experience of colonial contact zones have always already been cosmopolitan, Bhabha gives those in the diaspora a leading edge in these experiences. Bhabha's underlying question of who counts as a cosmopolitan and what kind of movement constitutes cosmopolitan mobility challenges the accepted notion of elitist cosmopolitanism.

Vernacular cosmopolitanism is, to quote Pnina Werbner, "an oxymoron that joins contradictory notions of local specificity and universal enlightenment" (496). It avoids the elitist stance on the one hand and stresses the need to recognise multiple modalities of cosmopolitanism (especially the marginal ones) on the other hand. Re-conceptualised in a multicultural light, it is highly aware of the complexity and diversity of forms of human life, disrupting the absolute claims of the local and the enforced unity of an allegedly superior European culture. The major examples of such dialogic, imaginative ways of everyday cosmopolitanism are the actions of ordinary migrants and minorities, instead of the mobile elite whose identification is largely with Western ideals. The fact that ethnic, vernacular rootedness does not negate openness to cultural difference not only makes a reading of Naipaul's *Miguel Street* from the perspective of vernacular cosmopolitanism theoretically valid but also proves especially productive for both a new understanding of the novel and Naipaul's own conflicted cosmopolitanism.

Reading Miguel Street from the Perspective of Vernacular Cosmopolitanism

In contrast to Naipaul's later Trinidadian novels in which he addresses the isolation and marginalisation of the Indo–Trinidadian community, rendering the matter of ethnic division a central issue, in *Miguel Street*, he presents Trinidad's universally acclaimed cosmopolitan feature—its racial heterogeneity. In 1922, the Honorable E. F. L. Wood adumbrated Trinidad's mixed population: African, Chinese, East Indian, French Creole and Spanish. "With a population so constituted", Wood wrote, "Trinidad is exceptionally cosmopolitan" (23). Lamming, who worked in Port-of-Spain from 1946 to 1950, writes: "Trinidad is the most cosmopolitan of the islands. Chinese, Indians, Negroes, Portuguese—all native to this soil—are involved in constant interplay of local forces" ("A Trinidad Experience" 1657). Aisha Khan points out that Trinidad celebrates itself as a callaloo nation, a metaphor of its heterogeneity and diversity connoting "democratic political representation, racial and ethnic tolerance, and a cosmopolitan worldview" (12).

In Naipaul's novel, Miguel Street is the epitome of Port-of-Spain (the narrator finds about six Miguel Streets in the city) and a microcosm of Trinidad. It is peopled with intermixing races and nations (black, brown, white, mulatto, Chinese, Indian, Portuguese and Spanish) and is frequented by Americans. Since Bhabha's vernacular cosmopolitanism highlights new cultural and social configurations emblematic of the increased intermingling of people, the different forms of minoritisation experienced by the exilic, diasporic people who comprise the hybrid community of *Miguel Street* assume special importance. The inhabitants of *Miguel Street* consume multicultural products and services and interact with people from different origins. They buy groceries at Chinese shops and patronise the big café owned by a Portuguese. Eddoes, from a low Hindu caste, sweeps the street and takes away people's rubbish; a black calypso singer, B. Wordsworth, occasionally knocks on the door and two Grenadian islanders work as loaders for Bhakcu, a Brahmin. The boy narrator befriends black people like B. Wordsworth and Bolo, and Hat's brother Edward favours painting "a brown hand clasping a black one" among all possible subjects (141). They imply the possibility of belonging to more than one ethnic and cultural localism simultaneously.

According to the counter-elitist inclination of vernacular cosmopolitanism, which challenges popular accounts of cosmopolitans as invariably members of the elite, the poor people living in the hybridisation and creolisation of *Miguel Street* are "world citizens", because of their knowledge of and openness to otherness. Their cosmopolitan orientation and competence show that multiple modalities of cosmopolitanism develop at the peripheries, as vernacular cosmopolitanism allows such a possibility. According to Stuart Hall, the racial and cultural mixing marks the Caribbean as "by definition cosmopolitan", since "everybody who is there came from somewhere else" (351). Thus, the most distinctive trait of Caribbean culture is "creolisation, the cultural mix of different elements, which is a kind of 'cosmopolitanism at home'" (351).

Such a "true diasporic society", according to Hall, makes the Caribbean individual "sort-of a 'natural' cosmopolitan" (351). In Hall's understanding, which is closely aligned with Bhabha's vernacular cosmopolitanism, the experience of participating in a transnational and indigenous cultural community and partaking of specific cultural traditions that partially incorporate and transcend one another, means to engage in cosmopolitan relations. In *Miguel Street*, multiple cultural elements coexist, reciprocally impacting one another; people's lives are thus enriched by their experience of alternate cultures. Trinidad's big fêtes at the time include Races, Carnival, Discovery Day and the Indian Centenary.

The news at Piarco airport is broadcast in both Spanish and English, while people on Miguel Street speak Creole English with an American or British accent. They enjoy *wappee* (a card game), calypso and carnival immensely on the one hand, and are big fans of cricket (a quintessentially rural English game) and American popular culture (particularly film and music) on the other. A Chinese woman with the anglicised name "Mary" raises her children on chop suey, chow mein, chow-fan and "things with names like that" (82). The novel does not contrast the vernacular (the local traditions of the small place) and the cosmopolitan (the larger tradition of the broader space); instead, it shows them as constituting each other. Holding a live-and-let-live attitude, the inhabitants of Miguel Street accept, as ordinary, different kinds of otherness, including eccentricity, and neither expect nor respect assimilation:

> A stranger could drive through Miguel Street and just say "Slum!" because he could see no more. But we, who lived there, saw our street as a world, where everybody was quite different from everybody else. Man-man was mad; George was stupid; Big Foot was a bully; Hat was an adventurer; Popo was a philosopher; and Morgan was our comedian. (59)

This exemplifies Daniel Hiebert's understanding of cosmopolitanism as "a way of living based on an 'openness to all forms of otherness' adopted by people from different origins to render diversity ordinary" (212).

The cultural outreach that normalises difference in everyday life produces a public sphere of kindness and inclusion on Miguel Street in the novel, not unlike the "cosmopolitan neighbourliness" that Ayona Datta observes in the everyday life in a Delhi squatter settlement (747). The qualities of affection, compassion and humanity are never absent in the Delhi slum even during moments of crisis and communal violence. Similarly, in *Miguel Street*, the cultivation of a compassionate and inclusive neighbourhood sphere works to protect its inhabitants, especially those experiencing hardship. When Popo's wife elopes with another man, all the men in the street "began to gather in Popo's workshop, and they would talk about cricket and football and pictures—everything except women—just to try to cheer Popo up" (10–11); when Eddoes is trapped into raising a baby girl, obviously not his, all the men praise her as "good-looking", "sweet" and "nice," while "all the women, Mrs. Morgan, Mrs. Bhakcu, Laura, and my mother, helped to look after her" (99); and when Mrs Hereira (a white woman who leaves her almost perfect husband) is beaten by her lover, she always runs to her neighbour (the boy narrator's mother) to seek solace (103–106).

A. C. Derrick is surely correct in observing that "as a whole, the series of sketches in this book evidences a human warmth and a vitality that are hardly to be found anywhere else in Naipaul's work" (195). More importantly, generosity, humaneness and warmth are extended beyond the community:

> Three beggars called punctually every day at the hospitable houses in Miguel Street. At about ten an Indian came in his dhoti and white jacket, and we poured a tin of rice into the sack he carried on his back. At twelve an old woman smoking a clay pipe came and she got a cent. At two a blind man led by a boy called for his penny. (40)

Poor themselves, people on Miguel Street are willing to show their kindness to strangers and help the poorer as their capacity allows. The word "we" implies that the boy narrator is not simply an observer but an active participant.

Indeed, the boy's formative years are spent within the cosmopolitan neighbourliness of Miguel Street. After his father's death, his mother picks him up from Chaguanas, a small town south of Port-of-Spain, to live with her in Miguel Street. Unlike the adolescent Ganesh from *The Mystic Masseur* who feels ill at ease and unhappy in Port-of-Spain because his Indian country dress and manner are always mocked, the boy narrator instantly falls in love with Miguel Street and never feels out of place there.[3] From the very start, he is eager to interact with people

3 The boy narrator's curiosity and warmth towards Miguel Street is identical to Naipaul's own feeling about his childhood street life in Port-of-Spain, which he recalls in "Prologue to an Autobiography": "After the shut-in compound life of the house in Chaguanas, I liked living on a city street. I liked looking at other people, other families. I liked the way things looked" (69).

of different racial and cultural backgrounds, and the street responds to him with all-embracing inclusiveness.

Popo's wife often takes him into the kitchen of the big house where she works as a cook and gives him a lot of nice things to eat; B. Wordsworth invites him to eat mangoes and comforts him after he is beaten by his mother; Laura, who raises eight children on her own, gives him fruit and dessert whenever she has them; whenever he offers his opinion on mechanical problems, the "mechanical genius" Bhakcu listens; even the cynic Bolo is willing to cut his hair. For the boy narrator, Miguel Street is like an extended family, in which he loves everybody and is loved in return. Treated with generosity and kindness, he learns to develop sympathy for other people at an early age. For instance, he displays heartfelt concern when the "really big and really black" Big Foot is beaten by a self-boasting "champion" of the Royal Air Force; realising how deeply Big Foot is hurt, the boy narrator does not join in the crowd's jeering and laughter (49).

Naipaul's Use of Double Narration and Denial of Vernacular Cosmopolitanism

It is through the narrator's vision that the cosmopolitan neighbourliness of Miguel Street is revealed on the one hand, and perversely denied on the other. In *Miguel Street*, Naipaul follows the model of the Bildungsroman in using a double narrator—a boy as the hero/focaliser and a young man, who was once the boy, as the storyteller. The novel opens when the narrator remembers being a newcomer in the street and ends when he leaves for a university in London at about eighteen. The young man looks back upon his childhood and recalls every happening, yet the first-person focalising voice for all the stories is that of the boy. In the words of Gérard Genette, explaining internal focalisation, "the [narrative] focus coincides with a character, who then becomes the fictive 'subject' of all the perceptions, including those that concern himself as object" (74). According to William F. Edmiston, internal focalisation is the vantage point from which a first-person narrator presents his or her story:

> The narrator can place the focus in his experiencing self, a participant inside the story, and allow the latter to focalize characters and events just as he perceived them at the time of the events. The focalization is delegated to the experiencing self, and the narrating self remains silent, provides no correction, and with-holds all subsequent knowledge ("I believed," "I was convinced," etc.). Spatially, the

> subject's vision is limited to proximal objects, those found in his immediate environment.... We can say that the experiencing self is the focalizer when a narrative statement contains nothing more than what he could have perceived or known at the moment of the event. (739)

In *Miguel Street*, the boy reports the events with the enthusiasm and naïve involvement of a child living among characters whose environment and aspirations he shares. In the first sketch, the young man returns to his childhood and relates the story with the naïve wonder and forsaken innocence of the boy, for whom the play-acting Bogart is a veritable hero, though, in fact, as the boy is to discover, Bogart is merely a bigamist.[4] Reality is refracted and enlarged through the immature vision of the curious, enthusiastic and innocent boy; it is the way how he observes the world at the moment of the event.

The narrative fluctuates now and then between the naïve vision of the boy and the mature voice of the young man. Suddenly, hearing Mrs Morgan's sharp shout at night, the boy immediately runs to Morgan's house, but it sounds like the voice of the adult narrator, who has furthered his study in London and "travelled in many countries since" (69), that is commenting on his younger self—"I never slept in pyjamas. I wasn't in that class" (66). The mature man's judgement and critique complicate the boy's naïve childhood perspective. Through most of the novel, readers are invited to see things through the boy narrator's eyes and follow his lead in accepting the cosmopolitan neighbourliness of *Miguel Street*.

Nevertheless, in the last sketch, the insider perspective of the boy suddenly turns on itself. When his mother rebukes him for his wild

4 Naipaul narrates the true story of the real Bogart in "Prologue to an Autobiography", written over twenty years after *Miguel Street*. The character in *Miguel Street* is modelled on a real man connected with Naipaul's mother's family. Unlike his fictional doppelgänger who pretends to be a tailor, the real Bogart is an actual tailor. While the real Bogart migrates to Venezuela, Naipaul, as he confesses, "had cruelly made him a bigamist" (79). Moreover, Naipaul chooses not to relate the stories of two of Bogart's real-life brothers in his novel: one of them became a teacher, the other a well-known cricketer (56). This omission serves the purpose of criticising Trinidad, "a place where the stories were never stories of success but of failure: brilliant men, scholarship winners, who had died young, gone mad, or taken to drink; cricketers of promise whose careers had been ruined by disagreements with the authorities" (*The Middle Passage* 35), and exemplifies Naipaul's intentionally distorted representation of Trinidad in *Miguel Street*.

dissolute ways, he enunciates his own, new-found view of Trinidad: "Is not my fault really. Is just Trinidad. What else anyone can do here except drink?" (171). The change in the boy's attitude from wondering relish to disillusionment is complete here, and the young man now emerges as the real narrator. This is an example of what Dorrit Cohn calls "dissonant self-narration"—"a lucid narrator turning back on a past self steeped in ignorance, confusion, and delusion" (145).

In *Miguel Street*, the young man is a dissonant narrator who views his younger self retrospectively, distancing himself from the past. The time of reflection is the present, not the past; so the dominant consciousness belongs to the young man rather than the boy. This echoes Edmiston's statement that "in a first-person narrative, the perceptual point of view is that of the younger self, while the conceptual or ideological point of view belongs to the narrator" (737). The boy narrator in *Miguel Street*, then, is simply a narratorial device, while the real narrator speaks from beyond the end of the novel, conveying its author's "implicit cultural critique", which is "evident only in retrospect" (Gupta 5).

Certainly, from the mature perspective of the adult narrator, which surfaces incrementally in the course of the novel, *Miguel Street* is "entrapment in a condition of cultural vacuum" (Gupta 5). It is peopled with derelicts, drop-outs, petty criminals, prostitutes and rum addicts. Most of them are eccentric, half-crazed and doomed. The men beat their children and wives violently while promiscuity haunts the women living in a macho man's world. The nearest parallels to such a condensation of eccentrics are Sherwood Anderson's *Winesburg* and John Steinbeck's *Cannery Row*. Naipaul's *Miguel Street* is an updated Dickensian world rife with comic energy. But if the early Dickens was at least hopeful or optimistic, Naipaul is not. All the stories of the eccentrics in *Miguel Street* are of personal failures—death, imprisonment, madness, violence.

The pattern of the novel reveals fleetingly but carefully the inevitable movement from aspirations to disappointments, from laughter to tears. This is not to say that the street is devoid of individuals with genuine yearnings. But their yearnings are sadly out of tune with their environment. Popo, who busies himself with making "the thing without a name", ends up producing nothing and steals the furnishings for his house (14); Elias, a serious student who aspires to be a doctor, fails to pass most examinations and ends up driving the scavenging cart (31); and B. Wordsworth, who claims to be writing "the greatest poem in the world", manages to write only one short line (45). In *Miguel Street*, nothing is made, no artwork is finished, no business succeeds, no love or marriage lasts. The entrapment is so complete that even the desire to achieve something appears meaningless. It is no wonder that driving the scavenging cart holds unrivalled glamour for the street boys.

Yet the novel does not hold the characters themselves responsible. Through his series of character profiles, Naipaul presents the microcosm of a colonial world. The major thematic concern of *Miguel Street* is not to depict natural eccentrics but to convey the social reality of Trinidad as an impoverished colonial society without any opportunity for a full life, forcing people to wear the mask of eccentricity. In *The Middle Passage*, Naipaul defines eccentricity as "the expression of one's own personality, unhampered by fear of ridicule or the discipline of a class" (74). In *Miguel Street*, eccentricity may be a stylish matter of mystifying the past and imitating a popular movie star like Bogart, publicly displaying an assumed character like Big Foot, showing off the mistaken notion of masculinity like Morgan or obsessing over cleanliness like Eddoes. No matter what, it is "a way of defending against or escaping from a milieu that does not satisfy their desires for meaningful work and identity" (Weiss 28).

In Naipaul's estimation, eccentricity is a mask for failure, the underdog's way of asserting identity and visibility in a hopeless environment. Bhabha, by contrast, reads in such eccentricities evidence of "ironic style, tolerance, a refusal to take the eminent at their own estimation", and "the cosmopolitan ethic that emerges from the colonized Trinidadian's embattled existence"; of course, Bhabha also reminds us that what he finds intriguing about Naipaul's novels is the way in which they are "capable of being read against the author's intention and ideology" (*The Location of Culture* xii–xiii). It is important to emphasise, nonetheless, that what Naipaul reiterates in *Miguel Street* are the typically derided aspects of Trinidad's picaroon society—"tolerance for every human activity and affection for every demonstration of wit and style" (*The Middle Passage* 74). In short, he intends to show how severely limiting the environment of a colonial society such as Trinidad's is. In his view, the individual cannot prosper in such a disappointing society; so their struggle (no matter in what form) is valueless, even ridiculous. This makes his satire cruel and unsympathetic.

Naipaul's cultural critique of Trinidad makes it possible for him to trivialise the evidence of the cosmopolitan neighbourliness of *Miguel Street*, a Trinidadian version of vernacular cosmopolitanism. In order to feel the cosmopolitan neighbourliness in the face of insuperable frustration, it is necessary to have something in common with other people. First, in Naipaul's characterisation of Trinidad, the distortion of accepted values is the norm and common ground means joint degradation. When Popo, abandoned by his wife, stops working, gets drunk and throws his temper around, he finally becomes "an accepted member" of the street (11). He is fully embraced when he goes to jail for stealing. The verdict of the street, voiced by Hat, is: "We was wrong about Popo. He is a man, like any of we" (11). Later, released from prison, Popo returns to Miguel Street "as a hero" (14).

Second, Naipaul draws attention to people's insuperable frustration rather than their sympathetic response to it. Even amidst the boisterous laughter, Naipaul never allows his readers to lose sight of the central tragedy in people's life for which he holds the society largely responsible. For example, through Laura, the most vivacious person in the street, the boy narrator realises that laughter is a mask of bravado that people wear to hide the bitter reality of their lives. Thus, in Naipaul's depiction, the cosmopolitan neighbourliness of Miguel Street is nothing more than mutual sympathy of fellow sufferers stranded in the same hopeless environment.

The question arises: what is cosmopolitanism in Trinidad really like in Naipaul's eyes? Or, put more sharply, does cosmopolitanism even exist in Trinidad? Naipaul's *The Middle Passage* suggests one answer:

> There is no set way in Trinidad of doing anything. Every house can be a folly. There is no set way of dressing or cooking or entertaining. Everyone can live with whoever he can get wherever he can afford. Ostracism is meaningless; the sanctions of any clique can be ignored. It is in this way, and not in the way of the travel brochure, that the Trinidadian is a cosmopolitan. He is adaptable; he is cynical; having no rigid social conventions of his own, he is amused by the conventions of others. (74)

Naipaul views Trinidad's heterogeneity, its most celebrated cosmopolitan feature, as a lack of a strong indigenous culture. In his eyes, Trinidad is an absurd society to which the people (mainly Africans and Indians) have been transplanted by force or persuasion, torn away from their home, its traditions and cultural authenticity and then forced to reinvent themselves on an almost daily basis. Trinidad's lack of indigenous culture makes for a chaotic world. The cultural confusion fragments the society, which in turn intensifies the identity crisis at the individual level. In Thomas Hylland Eriksen's words, Naipaul's early novels:

> sharply satirize what the author sees as Trinidadian cultural promiscuity; the "carnival mentality" which encourages people to mix, in noisy and boisterous ways, cultural stuff one has done nothing to deserve, and then creating an identity which consists

> of shiny surfaces without the slightest intimation of depth or inner consistency. (226)

Naipaul, in his early phase, does not share the perspective of vernacular cosmopolitanism, which starts from the premise of diversity and indicates the increasingly hybrid, post-multicultural and undifferentiated transformations as outcomes of diasporic cultural mixing and indeterminacy. Eriksen reminds us:

> Naipaul's scepticism towards contemporary celebrations of mixing and hybridity is obviously influenced by his own class experience as a boy from the periphery, whose highest aim in life consisted in being recognized by the metropolitans.... To Naipaul, celebrations of hybridity must seem ... a luxury to be afforded only by the leisured class. (225)

Naipaul's Yearning for Elitist Cosmopolitanism

As Naipaul depicts the dissolute chaos in which his Trinidadian characters show openness to otherness, he reveals the standard by which he judges which experiences and practices deserve to be called cosmopolitan and which do not. This standard turns out to be the elitist cosmopolitanism bound up with the European Enlightenment and associated with "urban sophistication, learning, privilege, high status, and a quasi-aristocratic intellectuality and aestheticism" (Marx 19). In his early novels, Naipaul always privileges what he calls "a feeling for lettering" and "ambitions connected with the printed word" ("Prologue to an Autobiography" 69).

As Peggy Nightingale points out, Man-man in Miguel Street is "the first of Naipaul's characters to take refuge in the written word" (19). Like Ganesh in *The Mystic Masseur*, who takes pleasure in the feel of the whole infrastructure of the writing and printing of books (ink, paper and typography), Man-man is "hypnotized by the word, particularly the written word" (32). He would spend a whole day writing a single word like "school" and "cricket" on the pavement. As Nightingale argues, "Shaping a word is for him an attempt to order experience, to give a form and with it meaning to institutions like school and cricket which are essential parts of experience in Trinidad" (19). If Man-man is a kind of failed writer, the narrator of *Miguel Street* is "the first of Naipaul's writer narrators, using writing as a way of exploring the sensibility of his society" (19–20).

Like Mr Biswas, the boy narrator begins his career as a sign-writer at an early age. Bogart, who pretends to make a living by tailoring, first pays him some money to write a sign—"TAILOR AND CUTTER/Suits made to Order/Popular and Competitive Prices" (2). This fancy for lettering is not purely fictional. In "Prologue to an Autobiography", Naipaul declares that it was his idea to paint a signboard for the real Bogart's shop. He recalls: "I thought it looked genuine, a real sign. I was amazed; it was the first sign-board I had ever done" (57). In *Miguel Street*, from this first venture, the boy narrator goes on to do another project for Popo. At first, Popo wants to announce himself as an architect, but he is not sure about the spelling of the word. The boy narrator manages to dissuade Popo and finishes the sign as "BUILDER AND CONTRACTOR/Carpenter/And Cabinet-Maker" (9). He proudly signs his name "as sign-writer" in the bottom right-hand corner (9).

The question that emerges is: how is writing, a certain form of literacy, linked with the boy narrator's intellectual and emotional detachment? The fact that he voluntarily leaves for London (the centre of the British Empire) to receive a college education with a Trinidadian government scholarship should be borne in mind. Looking back on the street that he has left behind for good, he uses standard English, in sharp contrast with the Creole English spoken by other characters, including his own boyhood self. Christian Mair observes:

> Sociolinguistically speaking, the distribution of "high" and "low" varieties in *Miguel Street* is the same as in society at large, and the narrator's mastery of the "high" variety, the literary standard, becomes an outward sign of his personal growth—away from the narrow provincial surroundings of his boyhood. (149)

Mair concludes: "In his attitudes and values, the narrator is clearly no longer part of the world he describes" (149).

Fawzia Mustafa emphasises that, in *Miguel Street*, standard English is presented as the domain of the educated and the powerful, and, therefore, foreign to the underclass world of the novel's other characters.

The standard English of the narrative interludes or transitions is constantly challenged by the dialect and distinct syntax of a more local Trinidadian English so that, eventually, as the narrator grows older, and his English becomes more standard, the level of his "education" becomes the measure of both his distance from the world of the street and the means whereby the street community is given its "coherence" (34).

In *Miguel Street*, the ability to read and write Standard English is an indicator of the narrator's high status—the reward of his elitist, Western education—which he employs to further distance and alienate himself from his native community. Naipaul casts his narrator's physical and ideological detachment from the world of *Miguel Street* as an achievement.

At the end of the novel, before his departure from home, the narrator kicks over the brass jar of milk set by his mother in the middle of the wide gateway. His mother cries: "I know I not going to ever see you in Miguel Street again" (175). Although the boy narrator seems not to believe in this kind of superstitious rite, he declares that he has known deep inside that he would be "destined to be gone for good" (175). Suman Gupta reads this announcement as one made by "the real narrator, who now appears clearly" in the last lines of *Miguel Street* because it exposes the view of "cultural displacement" that takes the boy away (6). The boy walks "briskly" towards the plane that takes him to England, "not looking back, looking only at my shadow before me, a dancing dwarf on the tarmac" (176).

Bruce King believes that the boy may already have a premonition of "a break with the past and facing an alien world without the support of family, friends and excuses" (25). Detachment, Naipaul implies, is an unavoidable but ultimately worthy sacrifice, since it guarantees access to a satisfactory culture and personal achievement. The adult narrator successfully proves this: he writes the book and becomes a "worldly-wise" traveller who "can contrast Miguel Street with other places he has travelled to" (Weiss 24). Regarding his intellectuality and transnational mobility, the adult narrator of *Miguel Street* becomes an elite cosmopolitan, the one with the capacity and resources necessary to travel and to absorb other cultures by individual actions.

Naipaul wrote *Miguel Street* when he had not yet begun his world travels. The image of the elite cosmopolitan evoked by his narrator epitomises his own personal yearning—a colonial-turning-to-cosmopolitan who has a perfect grasp of other cultures but can return to the First World anytime. For Naipaul, such self-fashioning as elite cosmopolitan, one with excessive knowledge of particular cultures and social conventions, paves the way for the production of texts and books. Naipaul, as he recalls in "Reading and Writing, a Personal Account", had early formed a "settled ambition" to be a writer (3). Drawn, in boyhood, to the world of books as a way of transcending his colonial society, Naipaul invented himself as a writer long before he had concrete evidence for his literary gifts. Listing the English literary works that he read when he was twelve, including Charles Dickens, Charles Kingsley, George Eliot, Joseph Conrad, Charles Lamb, Aldous Huxley,

J. R. Ackerley and Somerset Maugham, he explains: "I wished to be a writer. But together with the wish there had come the knowledge that the literature that had given me the wish came from another world, far away from our own" (5–6).

Naipaul's reading preference reflects what Belinda Edmondson calls "aspirational status": "What people read reflects not just who they are (in terms of socioeconomic status) but who they wish to be" (10). She echoes King's remark that "Naipaul when younger wanted to be a 'sophisticated' writer, a world traveller, like Somerset Maugham, writing about exotic foreign places and the shocking ways of the rich" (98). Naipaul himself notes that his awe for books, reading and intellectuals, apparent in even his earliest writing, fed his wish to be a writer, a wish he describes as "less a true ambition than a form of self-esteem, a dream of release, an idea of nobility" ("Reading and Writing" 12).

Naipaul regards the escape into the world of metropolitan letters as the only successful mode of becoming a legitimate, that is, elitist, cosmopolitan. Espousing the metropolitan ideological position, Naipaul seems unaware that "his translation from the Caribbean to the metropolis is among the posthumous benefits conferred by the old principle of Imperial Preference" (Miller 111–112). It is thus difficult for him to overcome the physical and ideological distance between the elite intellectuals and ordinary people (especially immigrants).

In *Miguel Street*, emigration (no matter whether legal or illegal, voluntary or involuntary) is a common and available means of escape in people's minds. When Bogart leaves the street for the first time, Hat's immediate reaction is that "he gone Venezuela" (3). After Morgan burns down his house with his fireworks, rumour goes that he ends up in either Venezuela or Colombia. The narrator remarks: "They said all sorts of things, but the people of Miguel Street were always romancers" (69), implying that emigration is no more than a fantasy by hopeless people of finding a new life elsewhere. Yet, even emigration to another Third World country fails sometimes. Bolo, deceived again and again by Trinidadian newspapers, makes a secret plan to go to Venezuela, but the smuggler, who takes his money, just circles around Trinidad and puts him down in a swamp a few miles from La Brea, claiming that they have reached Venezuela. Hat soothes Bolo: "Bolo, you don't know how lucky you is. Some of these people woulda kill you and throw you overboard, man. They say they don't like getting into trouble with the Venezuelan police. Is illegal going over to Venezuela, you know" (137). Naipaul's mockery of his characters' doomed efforts to escape from disillusionment and poverty is devoid of empathy and painfully condescending.

Conclusion

Whereas elitist cosmopolitanism may well be a Western project and projection, vernacular cosmopolitanism points to active practice for it encompasses subaltern subjectivities. Reading *Miguel Street* from the perspective of vernacular cosmopolitanism demonstrates that there are varieties of cosmopolitanism present besides those promulgated in the West. The openness to the agency and cultural expression of others in the hybrid community of Miguel Street is one equivalent form of cosmopolitan practices that has developed at the peripheries.

Yet Naipaul himself does not share or celebrate vernacular cosmopolitanism. In his novel, he adopts a double narrator who ends up disengaging from Miguel Street in order to unravel the worthlessness of cosmopolitan lifestyles, behaviours and interactions on the individual level in a disappointing colonial society. In Naipaul's early consideration, elitist cosmopolitanism is a two-way street. On the one hand, only the elite intellectuals of the Anglo–American artistic coterie can access and hold a cosmopolitan worldview; on the other hand, elitist cosmopolitanism, ordering the principle of action and participation of individuals from above, gives perfection to both individuals and the progress of society. This is a reinstatement of the all too familiar structure of privilege from the Enlightenment. Naipaul's longing for elitist cosmopolitanism as a managerial design or a project, in which everyone is readily categorised and defined, reflects his colonial mentality.

A frequent critique of elite cosmopolitans is that they share a common educational background, and, thus, carry a heavy cultural baggage of similar prejudices. Naipaul, who received a colonial education that has long been recognised as a vital institution of colonial power in upholding the traditional values and visions of the mother country, is such an enlightened subject. This explains why his identification and perspective in *Miguel Street* are largely Eurocentric, and his judgement of Miguel Street, Port-of-Spain and Trinidad in relation to English culture is prejudicial. In his preoccupation with elitist cosmopolitanism, he panders to Eurocentric sensibilities and tastes and upholds the desirability of assimilating into a unified, homogenising culture. Only later, after more than ten years' actual lived experience in London, did Naipaul begin to question elitist cosmopolitanism. In *Mr Stone and the Knights Companion* (1963) and *The Mimic Men* (1967), Naipaul disputes his earlier fantasy of elite world citizenship and exposes the damaging effect of the colonial education that supplies such a fantasy.

Works Cited

Bhabha, Homi K. *The Location of Culture*. Routledge, 2004.

———. "Unsatisfied: Notes on Vernacular Cosmopolitanism." *Postcolonial Discourses: An Anthology*, edited by Gregory Castle, Blackwell, 2001, pp. 38–52.

———. "The Vernacular Cosmopolitan." *Voices of the Crossing: The Impact of Britain on Writers from Asia, the Caribbean and Africa*, edited by Ferdinand Dennis and Naseem Khan, Serpent's Tail, 2000, pp. 133–142.

Bhabha, Homi, and John Comaroff. "Speaking of Postcoloniality, in the Continuous Present: A Conversation." *Relocating Postcolonialism*, edited by David Theo Goldberg, and Ato Quayson, Blackwell, 2002, pp. 15–46.

Calaresu, Melissa. "Looking for Virgil's Tomb: The End of the Grand Tour and the Cosmopolitan Ideal in Europe." *Voyages and Visions: Towards a Cultural History of Travel*, edited by Jas Elsner and Joan-Pau Rubies, Reaktion Books, 1999, pp. 138–161.

Cohn, Dorrit. *Transparent Minds: Narrative Modes for Presenting Consciousness in Fiction*. Princeton UP, 1978.

Daston, Lorraine. "The Ideal and Reality of the Republic of Letters in the Enlightenment." *Science in Context*, vol. 4, issue 2, 1991, pp. 367–386.

Datta, Ayona. "'Mongrel City': Cosmopolitan Neighbourliness in a Delhi Squatter Settlement." *Antipode*, vol. 44, issue 3, 2012, pp. 745–763.

Derrick, A. C. "Naipaul's Technique as a Novelist." *Critical Perspectives on V. S. Naipaul*, edited by Robert D. Hamner, Three Continents Press, 1977, pp. 194–206.

Edmiston, William F. "Focalization and the First-Person Narrator: A Revision of the Theory." *Poetics Today*, vol. 10, issue 4, 1989, pp. 729–744.

Edmondson, Belinda. *Caribbean Middlebrow: Leisure Culture and the Middle Class*. Cornell UP, 2009.

Eriksen, Thomas Hylland. "Creolization and Creativity." *Global Networks*, vol. 3, issue 3, 2003, pp. 223–237.

Genette, Gérard. *Narrative Discourse Revisited*, translated by Jane E. Lewin, Cornell UP, 1988.

Gupta, Suman. *V. S. Naipaul*. Northcote House, 1999.

Gurr, Andrew. *Writers in Exile: The Identity of Home in Modern Literature*. The Harvester Press, 1981.

Hall, Stuart, and Pnina Werbner. "Cosmopolitanism, Globalisation and Diaspora: Stuart Hall in Conversation with Pnina Werbner, March 2006." *Anthropology and the New Cosmopolitanism: Rooted, Feminist and Vernacular Perspectives*, edited by Pnina Werbner, Berg, 2008, pp. 345–360.

Hamilton, Ian. "Without a Place: V. S. Naipaul in Conversation with Ian Hamilton." *Conversations with V. S. Naipaul*, edited by Feroza F. Jussawalla, UP of Mississippi, 1997. pp. 14–21.

Hannerz, Ulf. "Cosmopolitans and Locals in World Culture." *Theory, Culture & Society* 7, SAGE Social Science Collections, 1990, pp. 237–251.

Hiebert, Daniel. "Cosmopolitanism at the Local Level: The Development of Transnational Neighbourhoods." *Conceiving Cosmopolitanism: Theory, Context, and Practice*, edited by Steven Vertovec, and Robin Cohen, Oxford UP, 2002. pp. 209–223.

Khan, Aisha. *Callaloo Nation: Metaphors of Race and Religious Identity among South Asians in Trinidad*. Duke UP, 2004.

King, Bruce. *V. S. Naipaul*. 1993. Palgrave Macmillan, 2003.

Lamming, George. *The Pleasures of Exile*. Michael Joseph, 1960.

———. "A Trinidad Experience." *Time and Tide* 5 October 1961: p 1657.

Mair, Christian. "Naipaul's *Miguel Street* and Selvon's *Lonely Londoners*—Two Approaches to the Use of Caribbean Creole in Fiction." *The Journal of Commonwealth Literature*, vol. 24, issue 1, 1989, pp. 138–154.

Marx, Leo. "Neglecting History." *The Boston Review*, vol. 19, issue 5, 1994, pp. 19–20.

Miller, Karl. "V. S. Naipaul and the New Order." *Critical Perspectives on V. S. Naipaul*, edited by Robert D. Hamner, Three Continents Press, 1977.

Mustafa, Fawzia. *V. S. Naipaul*. Cambridge UP, 1995.

Naipaul, V. S. *A House for Mr Biswas*. Everyman's Library, 1995.

———. *Miguel Street*. Heinemann Educational Publishers, 2000.

———. *Mr Stone and the Knights Companion*. Andre Deutsch, 1963.

———. "Our Universal Education." *The Writer and the World: Essays*, Picador, 2003, pp. 503–517.

———. "Prologue to an Autobiography." *Literary Occasions: Essays*. Picador, 2004, pp. 53–111.

———. "Reading and Writing, a Personal Account." *Literary Occasions: Essays*. Picador, 2004, pp. 3–31.

———. "The Documentary Heresy." *Critical Perspectives on V. S. Naipaul*, edited by Robert D. Hamner, Three Continents Press, 1977, pp. 23–25.

———. *The Middle Passage: The Caribbean Revisited*. Vintage Books, 2002.

———. *The Mimic Men*. Picador, 2002.

———. *The Mystic Masseur*. Picador, 2001.

———. *The Suffrage of Elvira*. Penguin Books, 1969.

Nightingale, Peggy. *Journey through Darkness: The Writing of V. S. Naipaul*. University of Queensland Press, 1987.

Niven, Alastair. "V. S. Naipaul Talks to Alastair Niven." *Wasafiri*, vol. 10, issue 21, 1995, pp. 5–6.

Robbins, Bruce. "Comparative Cosmopolitanism." *Social Text*, vol. 31, issue 32, 1992, pp. 169–186.

Schlereth, Thomas J. *The Cosmopolitan Ideal in Enlightenment Thought: Its Form and Function in the Ideas of Franklin, Hume and Voltaire, 1694–1970*. U of Notre Dame P, 1977.

Thieme, John. "Calypso Allusions in Naipaul's *Miguel Street*." *Kunapipi*, vol. 3, issue 2, 1981, pp. 18–33.

Weiss, Timothy F. *On the Margins: The Art of Exile in V. S. Naipaul*. U of Massachusetts P, 1992.

Werbner, Pnina. "Vernacular Cosmopolitanism." *Theory, Culture & Society*, vol. 23, issue 2–3, 2006, pp. 496–498. SAGE Social Science Collections.

Wood, Edward Frederick Lindley. *West Indies: Report by the Honourable E. F. L. Wood on His Visit to the West Indies and British Guiana, December 1921–February 1922*. His Majesty's Stationery Office, 1922.

Chapter 9

THE LANGUAGE OF ADVERTISING AND THE NOVEL: NAIPAUL'S *A HOUSE FOR MR BISWAS*[1]

Yi-Ping Ong

> Modernity in Trinidad, then, turns out to be the extreme susceptibility of people who are unsure of themselves and, having no taste or style of their own, are eager for instruction. In England and America there are magazines for such groups; in Trinidad instruction is now provided by advertising agencies, which have been welcomed by the people not only for this reason but also because the advertising agency is itself a modern thing.
>
> —*The Middle Passage* 47

Naipaul's acerbic reflections in *The Middle Passage* link advertising agencies to three things: modernity, derivative modes of taste and instruction. Given that Naipaul's account assumes a somewhat distorted view of the history of colonial and postcolonial advertising, why should it warrant further scrutiny?[2] Objections to the broader

1 "The Language of Advertising and the Novel: Naipaul's *A House for Mr Biswas*" was originally published in *Twentieth-Century Literature*, vol. 56, issue 4, pp. 462–492. Republished by permission of the copyright holder, and the present publisher, Duke University Press www.dukeupress.edu.

2 In *The Middle Passage*, Naipaul claims to remember a time that preceded this imitative phase of "modernity", a "time when Trinidad had no agencies and the nearest we got to copywriting was Limacol's 'The Freshness of a Breeze in a Bottle' and Mr Fernandes's 'If you don't drink rum that is your business; if you do drink rum that is our business'" (47–48). His narrative of advertising on the island thus neglects to mention the rise of the modern advertising agency in Britain at least five decades prior to this period, as if it had little or no influence upon the copywriting to which he nostalgically alludes. Furthermore, the distinction between products such as "Limacol" and "Mr Fernandes's ... rum" and the "American things" that the people of

historical perspective evinced in *The Middle Passage* are by now familiar, and I shall not rehearse them here.[3] Instead, I wish to focus on a relatively neglected feature of Naipaul's remarks: in linking the rise of advertising in Trinidad to modernity and to a people who, "having no taste or style of their own, are eager for instruction", these statements imply a striking connection between advertising and the genre of the novel. This connection, in turn, illuminates the thematic and formal significance of the language of advertising in several of Naipaul's novels. *Guerrillas* opens with a slew of ads, from "the side wall of a concrete house ... painted over with an advertisement" (3) to the "signs for Thrushcross Grange", each bearing "the name of the firm that had put the sign up": "local bottlers of Coca-Cola", "Amai (the American bauxite company)", "a number of airlines" and "many stores in the city" (4). The narrator of *The Mimic Men* bemoans the

---

Trinidad supposedly favour as a result of modern advertising is unclear (47–48). Limacol was invented by Johnny "Limacol" Adamson, a managing director at Bookers-British Drug House: a subsidiary firm of the British company Bookers Brothers McConnell and Company Limited, whose dominance of British Guiana was the reason why "some Guyanese wryly called their country Bookers' Guiana instead of British Guiana" (Alexander 329). Its chairman, Sir Alfred Sherlock, was "like his chief lieutenant in British Guiana, F. J. Seaford ... wedded to old notions of colonial peoples. They were both most uncomfortable with ideas of reform on the plantations" (Seecharan 90–91). "Mr Fernandes" of "Mr Fernandes's ... rum" was a Portuguese immigrant who came to Trinidad from Madeira, whose son inherited the business from him and eventually went on to hold the largest stocks of aging rum in the Caribbean.

3 Leela Gandhi describes Naipaul's "gaze upon his former homeland" in *The Middle Passage* as "mediated, without qualification, through the condemnatory imperial prose of former Victorian travelers to the region" (128); similarly, Fawzia Mustafa characterises Naipaul's method in *The Middle Passage* as an act of "profound historical repression", arguing that "without acknowledging the class differentiation of the groups he chooses to compare, or the agency of colonialism's programmatic subordination and denigration of subject peoples, he engages in the practice of blaming slavery's victims rather than its perpetrators" (80). These assessments reveal how Naipaul's distorted views of colonial and postcolonial history continue to puzzle even his most sympathetic critics, who, even if they find themselves in disagreement with Said's accusation of Naipaul as "a witness for the Western prosecution" (53), are still compelled to note what Baidik Bhattacharya has recently called his "perverse political agenda" (245–246).

commercialisation of his native island, noting that in "the recent tourist publicity for Isabella", boys who will dive for small change and even rotten fruit "are again presented as a feature" (60).

In particular, Naipaul's early work, *A House for Mr Biswas*, addresses the themes of modernity, instruction and derivative modes of taste by foregrounding the way that forms of advertising are implicated in the modern anxiety over self-definition. Mr Biswas—a painter of signs, a student in the "Ideal School of Journalism" and an avid consumer—must simultaneously make sense of his life in a highly commercialised world and attempt to break free from its illusory constructions. If the language of advertising creates a vivid, luxurious and appealing world of future promise, constructed around the importance of possessing the advertised object, then it is within the particular constraints and possibilities of this world that Mr Biswas must carry out his lifelong struggle for autonomy.

As theorists such as Ian Watt and Michael McKeon have demonstrated, the rise of the novel is closely linked to those aspects of modernity that Naipaul associates in *The Middle Passage* with the growth of advertising culture. The upheaval of various categories of social class identity, as well as the rising influence of booksellers upon the literary market, play powerful roles in shaping the evolution of the novel as a genre of mass appeal. The constitution of a "general reading public" by the expanding middle class establishes the market in place of the patron, and necessitates the growth of new institutions for the publicity and distribution of reading material (Heyck 25). Indeed, according to William B. Warner, the eighteenth-century novel is increasingly characterised by a "disrepute and illegitimacy that ... results from its close entanglement with the market", and "many of the vices attributed to these novels are also traits ascribed to the market: both breed imitation, incite desire, are oblivious to their moral effects and reach into every corner of the kingdom" (95). In the illicit relationship between the novel and the market, advertising performs the role of panderer: first, generating niche markets for diverse kinds of novels, and, second, enabling the formulation of desirable identities for potential readers qua consumers.[4]

The development of the novel as a popular literary genre is thus intimately intertwined with the rise of modern consumerism and commercialism, to such an extent that understanding the concurrent

4 For an account of how advertising led to increased audience fragmentation and the creation of niche markets in the nineteenth-century American literary market, see Sarah Wadsworth, "The Margins of the Marketplace" 193ff.

growth of modern advertising strategies considerably deepens our historical account of the rise of the novel. Recent studies of the relation between advertising and the novel have expanded the scope of analysis beyond the economic influence of advertising upon the selling and consumption of novels, exploring the impact of advertising culture upon historical conditions of novelistic writing and interpretation. Jennifer Wicke's *Advertising Fictions: Literature, Advertisement, and Social Reading* is among the earliest and most influential studies that aims to "set [advertising] in motion with the chief modern discourses", including the novel (11). Tracing the relation of advertising to literary practice, she argues that their "discursive rivalry and mutual interdependence" can shed light on the work of novelists such as Dickens, James and Joyce (173).

Subsequent analyses by Sharon Marcus, Garry Leonard, Emily Steinlight and Sara Thornton draw attention to the ways in which the cultural context of advertising transforms understandings of authorship, readership and subjectivity in the nineteenth century. Whereas Marcus's study of *Jane Eyre* focuses on advertising as a strategy for gaining professional—and, in Brontë's case, authorial—agency, Thornton and Steinlight examine how the juxtaposition of advertising text and novelistic text in Dickens's serialised novels inform modes of reading. In *Advertising and Commodity Culture in Joyce*, Leonard argues that the depictions of advertising in Joyce's novels reveal the extent to which "mass media in general, and advertisements in particular, frequently offer Joyce's characters ... a way to frame reality, to configure desire, and to fantasize about what is needed to complete the self" (17).

This study takes as its starting point Wicke's insight that "the interpenetration of advertising with the other social discourses, above all the literary" provides new critical approaches to the novel (170). However, whereas previous work addresses how advertising alters our perspective of the novel, I argue that Naipaul's *A House for Mr Biswas* engages with the formal qualities of advertising language and narrative to reveal how the novel can shape our understanding of advertising. By weaving the formal and rhetorical devices of advertising into a novelistic narrative, Naipaul generates mutual reflection between the genres of advertising and novel on multiple aesthetic, psychic and sociohistorical levels.

First, Naipaul draws upon the rhetorical and narrative forms of what Torben Vestergaard and Kim Schroder call the "sub-literary" genre of advertising, exposing an intricate interplay between the novel as a distinctively postcolonial commodity and the mass corporate influence of advertising language (9). Second, Naipaul employs what we might call a commercial narrative—a narrative centred around the acquisition of a product—to frame his protagonist's quest for autonomy, thereby, foregrounding the relation between dissatisfaction, desire and different forms of advertising.[5] Third, Naipaul's extended depictions of Mr Biswas's work as a sign-painter and as a failed writer address the ways in which both advertising and literary work inform his protagonist's relation to a world in which signs and their multiple significations are both created and consumed. Finally, Naipaul establishes deep tension between the reality depicted in advertising and the reality that lies beyond its illusory and romanticised constructions, thus, placing in sharp relief the relation between the style of advertising and the distinctive style of the novel: realism.

A close examination of how the language and forms of advertising are at work in *A House for Mr Biswas* will reveal that both the novel and its protagonist follow a similar progression with respect to their relation to advertising. At first, both appear to draw on forms of advertising, imitating its rhetoric and using its creative force in an instrumental manner to increase their appeal to an outside audience; in the end, however, both novel and protagonist subvert the typical narratives of advertising, rejecting the overblown fantasy of its vision in exchange for a more exacting and honest realism. Analysing Naipaul's depiction of the relation of advertising to the novel furthermore suggests the value of inverting a standard cultural studies approach in the interest of contextualising Naipaul's historical views on colonial and postcolonial advertising within his novelistic treatments of these themes. For, if cultural studies prompts us to probe the various historical inaccuracies in his diagnosis of the advertising agency in Trinidad, and to ask why the study of pronouncements by literary figures are still relevant in an age of global mass culture, inverting this question leads us to ask why and how the study of global commercial mass culture is relevant to a reading of Naipaul's literary work. To engage seriously with his critical claims about advertising in this context requires, I argue, more than a historical, sociological and economic approach to the relation between the forms of advertising and the novel; it requires a conception of how Naipaul uses both: forms of advertising to

5 As Escalas and Stern have shown, not all narratives used in commercials are "commercial narratives" in this narrow sense; advertisements use a wide variety of "different dramatic plots ... to evoke various types of feelings" in association with the product (171). For a more detailed account of the construction of narrative in advertising, see Escalas, "Advertising Narratives: What Are They and How Do They Work?"

construct a novelistic narrative and employs forms of novelistic narrative to reflect on the phenomena of advertising in modernity.

Advertising the Colonial Space

> The drive was lined with orange trees and gri-gri palms with slender white trunks, red berries and dark green leaves. The land itself was a wonder. The samaan trees had lianas so strong and supple that one could swing on them. All day the immortelle trees dropped their red and yellow bird-shaped flowers through which one could whistle like a bird. Cocoa trees grew in the shade of the immortelles, coffee in the shade of cocoa, and the hills were covered with tonka bean. Fruit trees, mango, orange, avocado pear, were so plentiful as to seem wild. And there were nutmeg trees, as well as cedar, poui, and the bois-canot which was so light yet so springy and strong it made you a better cricket bat than the willow ... the hills, the sweet springs and hidden waterfalls.
>
> —*A House for Mr Biswas* 376

The world of *A House for Mr Biswas* is crammed full of advertisements, slogans and signs: "Dodd's Kidney Pills Almanac", with its trumped-up stories of miracle cures (45); "the faded advertisement for Cydrax", hanging below Mr Biswas's stack of credit notes (164); the elaborately distinguished brands of rum—"Indian Maiden", "The White Cock", "Parakeet" (59)—which, despite their different label designs, all carry the same exact liquor; and many others. Not only do the words of actual commercials, slogans and ads litter the novel like colourful scraps torn from newspapers and the labels of store goods, but the novel itself explodes with passages that could almost be read as copy for a tourism brochure, presenting Trinidad as a proliferation of bright colours, tempting materials and paradisiacal beauty.

The description of the Shorthills estate, above, clearly utilises the formal characteristics of advertising language, as outlined in *The Cambridge Encyclopedia of the English Language*: Lexically, it tends to use words which are vivid (new, bright), concrete (soft, washable), positive (safe, extra) and unreserved (best, perfect). Grammatically, it is typically conversational and elliptical—and often, as a result, vague (a better deal [than what?]). It uses highly figurative expression (taste the sunshine in K-Y peaches), deviant graphology (Beanz Meanz Heinz) and strong sound effects, such as rhythm, alliteration and rhyme, especially in slogans . It can also make effective use of wordplay.[6] (388) Commercial in every sense of the word, the prose in this passage is marked by the prevalence of glossy, eye-catching colours ("orange", "white", "red", "dark green", "yellow"); the persistent use of alluring yet somewhat vague modifying adjectival phrases ("a wonder", "so strong and plentiful", "so springy and strong", "wild", "sweet", "hidden") and the abundance of goods that can be sold or used to produce commodities ("cocoa", "coffee", "tonka bean", "mango", "orange", "avocado pear", "nutmeg", "cedar", "poui", "bois-canot", "cricket bat").

Like Mr Biswas himself, this portrayal of the estate seems constrained by the need to be captivating to an audience with the money and means to convert raw resources into marketable goods.[7] Yet, within the context of the novel, the passage appears not as a direct description from the narrator's point of view, but as an account of the overblown depiction of the estate that the Tulsi sisters give to Shama—"Shama heard its glories listed again and again" (376). This vivid picture of heavenly beauty and abundance is thus evoked by the Tulsis in order to incite Shama's envy and desire, and to shame her for marrying a man who can only provide meagre, lowly lodgings. Mr Biswas immediately sees through this scheme and scoffs at their attempt to influence Shama: "'Horses?' Mr Biswas said. 'I bet when you go there all you find is one old monkey swinging from the liana on the samaan tree. I can't understand this craziness that possess your family'" (377). His mocking humour deflates their hyperbolic account, and the gap between his worldview and theirs becomes clear.

Nevertheless, Mr Biswas can no more cast off the vivid image created by this description of the Shorthills estate than he can disown his long-cherished dream of becoming a property owner, and the

6 A. R. Fathi draws a distinction between "informative language" in advertising, which is "marked by its former style" and "heavily depends on technical terms to inform the consumer", and "consumer language", which is "marked by a blend of glamorous and catchy expressions" such as "metaphors, analogy, imagery, idiom, slang, colloquialism and informality" (44). Although the boundary separating these two types of advertising language in practice is far from strict, we are primarily concerned with the latter in this analysis.

7 The language of commercial tourist brochures is also evident in the first section of the novel, "Pastoral", in which the tragedy of the death of Mr Biswas's father is set in an idyllic setting: "the sky was gold and smoke" (25), "the water shimmered like sequins" (29), "dew-wet leaf from the hibiscus shrub" (37) glistens in the morning light.

vision of the Tulsi sisters seems to merge fluidly with the sirenlike lure of his perpetual longing to possess a house of his own. Etymologically, advertisement is that which adverts or turns us towards something, that which gets our attention ("Advertisement"). Do such passages in the novel turn our attention towards their own vivid and lyrical use of language, or do they advert to an enchanting and exotic land, one in which we ourselves might—like Mr Biswas—desire to own property? Indeed, the language of this passage closely parallels a description of the pastoral beauty of Caribbean islands in another of Naipaul's novels, *The Mimic Men*, in which Singh, the novel's protagonist, dreams of "retirement [on] an old cocoa estate":

> There are freshwater springs that make miniature waterfalls over mossy rocks and then run clear and cold and shallow in their own channels of white sand. The floor of the cocoa woods is covered with broad brown-and-gold cocoa leaves; and between the cocoa trees, stunted, black-barked, as nervously branched as the oak, there are bright green coffee bushes with red berries; the whole sheltered by giant immortelle trees which at their due season lose all their leaves and set every hillside ablaze with bird-shaped flowers of yellow and orange which then, for days, float down on the woods. You hear the murmur and gurgle of streams everywhere.... The true cocoa, such as Montezuma and his court drank.... Cocoa and papaw and fried plantains, freshly baked bread and avocados; all served on a tablecloth of spotless white ... the clean napkin on the polished plate; the glassware catching some sparkle from the light filtered through the ferns. (39–40)

Focalised through first-person narration, this passage is set in the context of the narrator's own self-consciousness about "that dream of the run-down cocoa estate", "a dream of the past" that "came at a time when ... we had destroyed the past" (43). It is thus situated in a similarly ironic position to its counterpart in *A House for Mr Biswas*; Singh, as Bruce King notes, is "mocked by Naipaul for his desire to return to pre-natal wholeness" (80). The greater irony of the situation is that the formerly colonised Singh now dreams of becoming a colonialist on his own island, indulging, as Ian Strachan claims, in "the imperialist delusion: that the Caribbean was a paradise and was where all nature's riches presented themselves freely and without sweat or suffering" (169). The gap between the brilliant, colourful and idyllic world of the advertisement for colonial sites and the reality of the "sweat and suffering" of colonised labour is brought into focus by the overt use of the language of advertising. In *A House for Mr Biswas*, this gap parallels the divergence between the Tulsis' ostentatious social pretensions and the reality of Mr Biswas's protracted struggle for social respectability, as well as the inner conflict between his attempts to reject the Tulsis' values and his desire to beat them on their terms.

Formally, then, the use of advertising language in the novel adverts to a dual vision, emphasising the disparity between Mr Biswas's romantic images of himself and his life possibilities, and the thin and tenuous fabric of his actual life with all of its negativity, insecurity and deprivation. In contrast to these "vivid", "concrete", "positive" and "unreserved" descriptors of a world aspiring to an ideal state of plenitude and optimism, the reality of Mr Biswas's existence is dirty, mean, poor, dispiriting and constantly undercutting his attempts to rise above it. Yet the "conversational", "elliptical" and "highly figurative" elements that characterise the grammatical constructions of advertising language recall several key aspects of Mr Biswas's own preferred mode of language: his elaborate graphology, his wit and verbal playfulness and his predilection for vague schemes and formulas. His designation throughout the novel—even during childhood—as "Mr Biswas" suggests a brand name that must remain clear and never-changing; in actuality, however, Mr Biswas himself constantly feels the lack of the very stable and reliable qualities that such a branding is meant to suggest. As a sign-painter who is nevertheless vulnerable to false advertising schemes, Mr Biswas stands both inside and outside the world of advertising language. His ambivalent relation to advertising generates the constant tension driving the narrative development of the novel.

The novel begins with the appearance of commercial promise fulfilled, then moves backward to describe Mr Biswas's early encounters, through advertising, with an "intoxicating world" that leaves him in "despair of finding romance in his own dull green land" (74). Throughout Part One, Mr Biswas retains the conviction that there is value in believing in a certain imaginary world, giving himself over to the seductive possibility that choice and money will make life what it should be. As a colonised subject, however, Mr Biswas's relation to the dreams of effortless fulfillment and freedom evoked by advertising language is necessarily troubled by the facts of his life and its struggles.

In Part Two, the relation between Mr Biswas and the world of advertising undergoes a radical change. His arrival in Port-of-Spain precipitates his realisation that the perfect freedom and happiness he had dreamt of attaining through escape from his reality is, in fact, impossible. It is only after he realises the uselessness of fantasy and longing that he is able to grasp the actual power of a lie or half-truth, converting his earlier skill at sign-painting to an ironic statement that leads to his first real job and taste of autonomy. In contrast to the Prologue, the Epilogue is stripped bare of the lexical and grammatical characteristics of advertising; it presents a naked, unsentimental, almost journalistic account of Mr Biswas's debt, disease, loneliness and demise, an account as "unaccommodated" as his corpse (11). Although the gap between fantasy and reality exemplified in advertising language produces an energy that drives the plot; narrative resolution seems to require dismantling the powerful allure of this language.

Naipaul's use of advertising language in the novel thus reveals how the shadow genre of advertisement that floats upon the surface of the novel, colouring it with generic and forgettable junk material, illuminates the significance of the marginal, the "sub-literary", the misleading and the marketable in defining the colonised space that Mr Biswas inhabits and exposes the barriers that he must overcome in order to face the reality of his own situation. In calling advertising a "sub-literary" genre, we can think of it both as a form that appeals to mass consumption and taste through clichéd formulas and as a creative and rhetorically sophisticated form of representation that uses imagery, narrative and fictional characterisation to provoke various emotional and cognitive responses.

The difficulty for Mr Biswas in establishing his identity and place in the world of the novel arises from the ambiguous consequences of appropriating the language of advertising. Is it possible, the novel asks, to give voice to one's "own" dreams without allowing oneself to be manipulated and exploited by the desires of others? Learning to defy the appeal of language that speaks of a happiness and perfection existing only in fantasy, not in reality, is the task that Mr Biswas must face again and again in his encounters with various forms of advertising.

Narratives of Advertising

> Once upon a time there was a man who ... whatever you do for him, wasn't satisfied.
>
> —*A House for Mr Biswas* 363

The relation between advertising language and the evocation of the states of satiety and dissatisfaction is the subject of Jean Baudrillard's analysis of "the very real effectiveness of advertising" in *The System of Objects*:

> Neither its rhetoric nor even the informational aspect of its discourse has a decisive effect on the buyer. What the individual does respond

> to, on the other hand, is advertising's underlying leitmotiv of protection and gratification, the intimation that its solicitations and attempts to persuade are the sign ... that somewhere there is an agency ... which has taken upon itself to inform him of his own desires, and to foresee and rationalize these desires to his own satisfaction. (167)

Mr Biswas, persuaded to buy his house by a "scene as cosy and rich as something in an advertisement" (8), is perpetually attracted to the promise of "protection and gratification" because he is frustrated again and again in his attempts to fully satisfy his ideals and desires. There is a double sense in which Mr Biswas is never "satisfied". First, he is eaten away by regret, discontentment and bitterness; his stomach illness serves as a metaphor for the fact that he cannot derive adequate nutrition or a sense of fullness, no matter what he consumes. Second, Mr Biswas is perpetually thwarted by the difficult circumstances of his life from ever reaching personal fulfillment or realisation, even dying before he can witness the success his son achieves in a world that denied him the recognition he craved.

The language of advertising is closely intertwined with this dual dissatisfaction of Mr Biswas's life. First, advertising depends on its ability to arouse a feeling of lack in the person seeing it, a feeling that something is missing no matter what one already possesses in one's life. It justifies its own production by creating the desire for consumption, but this desire is diverted away from itself towards the object it promotes. Advertising requires for its efficacy the prolonged "feeling of freedom and urgency" (61) that lingers in Mr Biswas, even when he purchases and consumes "innumerable soft drinks and hard cakes"; like a person who has watched hours of commercials, he remains throughout much of the novel "tired, empty, miserable, yet still excited", in a continuous, overstimulated state of unfulfilled arousal.

Second, the paradox inherent in advertising language is that although it depicts a rich, luxurious and comfortable reality, it is often addressed to people who do not have access to such a reality. Advertising is the only literary and visually aesthetic material that one does not have to pay for in order to consume, but that other people pay one to consume and for which one might even pay in order not to consume; as a genre, its impact on its audience is thus overtly inflected by class difference.[8] Its constant presence in the novel serves not only as a constant reminder

---

8 In addition to the lexical and grammatical characteristics we have already discussed, the last sentence in this passage also displays what Geoffrey Leech has isolated as a typical tendency in copywriting: "non-linking co-ordination (parataxis and apposition) in preference to linking co-ordination" (143).

of the dissatisfaction and longings for satiety that define much of Mr Biswas's inner reality but also as a prominent marker of class. The "free copy of the paper" (5) that arrives at Mr Biswas's house every morning is only one of the many indicators that his poverty subjects him to continued exposure to the language of advertising.

Savi's cutting comment to Mr Biswas—"I hope the low minds of some people are satisfied" (343)—thus seems to be proleptically fulfilled by the way in which Mr Biswas understands his acquisition of a house of his own:

> What a change from those back yards, overrun with chickens and children, to the drawing room of the solicitor's clerk who, coatless, tieless, and in slippers, looked relaxed and comfortable in his morris chair, while the heavy red curtains, reflecting on the polished floor, made the scene as cosy and rich as something in an advertisement! (8)

Indeed, Mr Biswas's "low" background—the crowded, dirty, chaotic reality from which he seeks to escape—conditions his imagination of a "scene as cosy and rich as something in an advertisement". Its similarity to an advertisement consists in its being ordered, composed and marked by the absence ("coatless, tieless") of those accoutrements that characterise the necessities of the working world, showing only that which connotes leisure time, luxury and comfort.[9] The staged appearance of the "slippers", the "morris chair", "the heavy red curtains" and even the "solicitor's clerk" himself suggest a kind of artificial backdrop comprising only those clichéd elements necessary to bring to mind as quickly as possible a "cosy and rich" English home, a location as exotic and removed from Mr Biswas's actual life as the tropical beaches featured in British advertisements would be to the average Englishman.

The "polish" shining on the floors further implies that the absence of flaws or dirt is, for Mr Biswas, closely associated with the social and cultural "polish" that he has been ashamed of lacking his entire life. Moving into such a house is like the experience of moving from the "back yards", a space behind the scenes, to the glossy world displayed within the advertisement. Moreover, the cultural and racial significance of going

---

9 To call it a "genre" of a culture emphasises the way in which advertising, as Vestergaard and Schroder argue in *The Language of Advertising*, has its own aesthetic: "Not only does advertising help make products appear as aesthetically pleasing as possible, the advert becomes an aesthetic object in itself ... this aestheticization of the advertising message means that adverts can profitably be analysed by means of techniques normally applied to verbal and visual art; advertising is in fact a 'sub-literary' genre" (9).

from the brown dirt of the "back yards" to a culturally English façade—"the white-pointed brickwork of the front, the white woodwork and the frosted glass of doors and windows"—is made pointedly obvious (7).

From the homemade "tea and cakes" down to the display of "much affection" "between mother and son", the entire scene is the stuff of bourgeois ideality, appearing in sharp contrast to the actual "neglect" and "great poverty" that has characterised Mr Biswas's existence. The temptation of erasing this gap between desired fantasy and undesirable reality is what makes the illusion of the "advertisement" work so effectively on Mr Biswas: "And during his search for a house he had always assumed new and modern concrete houses, bright with paint, to be beyond him. So when he was faced with one which was accessible, with a solid, respectable, modern front, he was immediately dazzled" (7–8). What was "beyond him" now becomes "accessible"—the "solid, respectable, modern front" that will hide from view the shaky failures and sordid circumstances of his past.

This scene can furthermore be viewed as an advertisement within an advertisement, insofar as it is framed by a larger commercial narrative. *A House for Mr Biswas* begins with an event that would conventionally mark the terminal point of any consumer's contact with a successful advertisement: the purchase and ownership of the object depicted (here, a house), and the satisfaction of the desires aroused by that advertisement.[10] In starting with this endpoint, the novel reverses the expected structure of the consumer narrative, establishing in its place a narrative that traces the evolution of its protagonist from a naïve relation to signs and advertising to a realisation of their instrumental, illusory and ultimately unsatisfying nature. Possessing the money to make the fantasy into a reality ends the allure of the commercial; the

---

10 Commenting on a related passage at the end of the novel which recounts in greater detail the events leading up to Mr Biswas's purchase of this house (see pp. 540–42), Mustafa notes:

> Not only does this pivotal moment in the novel develop the resolution of the plot—a house for Mr Biswas—but as resolution, it also reveals the necessarily idealised nature of desire. Naipaul's tableau, "a picture of a house cosy in the rain, with a polished floor, and an old lady who baked cakes in the kitchen", could not be more emblematic of a commodified desire, even though the novel never really seems aware of its own implicit socialist critique. (223)

The earlier counterpart to this passage that is quoted above, however, very explicitly compares the scene in Mr Biswas's imagination to "an advertisement", suggesting that Naipaul deliberately calls attention to this precise aspect of Mr Biswas's desire.

act of buying ends the fiction. "The very day the house was bought they began to see flaws in it" (9). Yet Mr Biswas seems to persist in the idea that through his ownership of the house, he has succeeded in buying the dream presented to him in the advertisement:

> He had stepped ... into a welcoming world, a new, ready-made world. He could not quite believe that he had made that world. He could not see why he should have a place in it. And everything by which he was surrounded was examined and rediscovered, with pleasure, surprise, disbelief. Every relationship, every possession. (10)

If the possessions represent a kind of scrapbook history of his actual life—with its failures, its attempts to paint things over, its uselessness—the house represents the realisation of a lifelong aspiration.

> How terrible it would have been, at this time, to be without it: to have died among the Tulsis, amid the squalor of that large, disintegrating and indifferent family; to have left Shama and the children among them, in one room; worse, to have lived without even attempting to lay claim to one's portion of the earth; to have lived and died as one had been born, unnecessary and un-accommodated. (11)

Despite the temptation to be convinced by this commercial narrative into thinking that Mr Biswas's life ends here, however, the end of the commercial does not mark the end of the overall narrative of the novel. It is placed at the beginning of the novel because it only touches on the superficial, enchanting appearances of things; the real story of how Mr Biswas moves from a notion of reality governed by the language of advertisements to a recognition of the value in his actual life that has yet to be unfolded. Just as one might read the lettering on a label before actually drinking it, the language of advertisement used in the Prologue simply "mask [s]" the complex and, at times, bitterly pungent taste of Mr Biswas's real life (8).

Sign-Painting and Autonomy: The Parable of Colonial Self-Possession

> They didn't even pay me for the signs.
>
> —*A House for Mr Biswas* 94

If the main theme of the novel, as Naipaul himself claims in 1974, is the acquisition by a man of a house of his own, then one of the secondary themes is the way in which this material possession takes on the symbolic meaning of self-possession and autonomy for the novel's protagonist.[11] Modern consumerism is premised on the ideal of choice: in the idealised world of the advertisement, the modern consumer does not just own things, she owns the privilege of self-determination and self-expression through the exercise of choice. As Judith Williamson argues, "Advertising is part of a system which not only sells us things—it sells us 'choices:' or to be more precise, sells us the idea that we are 'free' to 'choose' between things. To nourish this 'freedom' advertising must, like other key ideological forms, cover its own tracks and assert that these choices are the result of personal taste" (396).

The use of particular myths and parables in advertising to appeal to the sociopolitical ideals of a particular place and time has been vividly illustrated by Roland Marchand's analysis of the various myths that dominated American advertising in the 1920s and 1930s (206–232). If what Marchand calls "The Parable of the Democracy of Goods" (222) encouraged people to understand their status as a citizen in a democracy in terms of their equal access to an advertised product ("anyone can buy it"), then we might call the myth at work in *A House for Mr Biswas* "The Parable of Colonial Self-Possession". The underlying myth or idea that seems most attractive to Mr Biswas is one that unites the idea of the accessibility of property possession with a notion of self-determination and autonomy: each man can own his own piece of land, each man can rule according to his own laws in the castle of his home. In a colonial context, the dispossession of the colonised reappears as a dream of self-possession.

This dream of self-possession remains, for the greater part of the novel, an empty fantasy. As a person who is easily captivated by idealised advertisements, Mr Biswas tries to overcome the sordid and undesirable aspects of his life by preserving a vision of how it could be otherwise; however, his tendency to be taken in by the lure of romantic possibilities leads him to be easily exploited again and again.[12]

---

11 In her study of the vocabulary of advertisement, Indubala Pandya notes that the most frequent verbs used in Indian Press advertising in English "denote one aspect or another of the relationship between the consumer and the product. The possession of a product, its acquisition or its conferment on somebody else are the areas of this relationship which are brought into prominence" (46–47).

12 When asked in a seminar at Fatima College in 1974 by Bruce Paddington what the "larger themes" of *A House for Mr Biswas* were, Naipaul replied: "I think that the theme was outlined very simply—the theme about a man getting a house" ("Extract of Seminar with V. S. Naipaul", Fatima College, 1974).

His repeated failure to recognise the distance between sign and signifier causes disappointment and even financial ruin. His role as a "sign-painter" thus suggests how Mr Biswas, as both a creator and spectator of advertisements, experiences through each position multiple aspects of the emptiness of signs (46).

Mr Biswas embarks on his early career as a sign-painter because he believes that it will allow him to achieve personal independence: "Give up sign-painting? And my independence? No, boy. My motto is: paddle your own canoe" (101). As a "sign-painter", an active designer of words in advertisements, he begins to discover the potential of signs both to enact rebellion and to provide a sort of free-standing aesthetic experience that grants him some relief from his day-to-day reality. The connection between sign-painting and autonomy is represented in an early scene in the novel in which Mr Biswas "discovered his gift for lettering":

> [Lai] ordered him to write I AM AN ASS on the blackboard. Mr. Biswas outlined stylish, contemptuous letters, and the class tittered approvingly. Lai, racing about the classroom, waving his tamarind rod for silence, brushed Mr. Biswas's elbow and a stroke was spoilt. Mr. Biswas turned this into an additional decoration which pleased him and impressed the class. It was too late for Lai to flog Mr. Biswas or order him to clean the blackboard. Angrily, he pushed him away, and Mr. Biswas went back to his desk, smiling, a hero. (46)

Turning an accident into a flourish, Mr Biswas transcends the forced humiliation of his situation; rebelling against the disciplinary order established by his teacher, he liberates the individual letters from their subordination to a self-incriminating phrase and makes them into distinctive and expressive symbols.[13] The episode recalls not only

---

In his 1983 "Foreword to *A House for Mr Biswas*", Naipaul recalls how his "original idea ... to tell the story of the life as the story of the acquiring of the simple possessions by which the man is surrounded at his death ... became the story of a man's search for a house and all that the possession of one's own house implies" (131).

13 In addition to the house which Mr Biswas buys despite having never examined it realistically for its flaws, the other key incident in which Mr Biswas is fooled by an advertisement (this one spoken) occurs at The Chase, when Moti, bearing the "badge of the rural literate", sucks "Paradise Plum[s]", asks to see the accounts that "hung above a faded advertisement for Cydrax", sells Mr Biswas the services of his friend Seebaran, and ends up cheating him and eventually ruining his business (162–164).

the attention-getting quality of advertisements but also the power of advertisements to evoke the allure of personal freedom. Later on, when Mr Biswas becomes more established as a sign-painter, his ability to become totally absorbed in this activity gives him a sense of distance and detachment from his actual circumstances:

> And yet there were moments when he could persuade himself that he lived in a land where romance was possible. When, for instance, he had to do a rush job and worked late into the night by the light of a gas lamp, excitement and the light transforming the hut; able then to forget that ordinary morning would come and the sign would hang over a cluttered little shop with its doors open on to a hot dusty road. (75)

The "excitement" and "transformation" of the "ordinary" that he seeks in the "intoxicating worlds" of foreign magazines is attained not through passive absorption in fantasies that negate his actual experience, but through a kind of artistic labour that empties his mind of its exhaustion and despair, freeing it from its usually "cluttered", "hot" and "dusty" existence (75).

Mr Biswas's career as a sign-painter is thus bracketed on both sides by a yearning for a certain kind of life: "he no longer simply lived. He had begun to wait, not only for love, but for the world to yield its sweetness and romance" (76); "he was going out into the world, to test it for its power to frighten. The past was counterfeit, a series of cheating accidents. Real life, and its especial sweetness, awaited; he was still beginning" (292). The juxtaposition of sign-painting and sweetness here suggests various interpretations of the importance of the emptiness of the sign in advertising: emptiness in the sense of the "empty calories" in sweets, and emptiness in the sense of lacking any essential meaning—arbitrary, thus, allowing new signs to be constantly created and manipulated in symbolic discourse.[14] In the first sense, the appeal by advertisements to a desire for something over and above one's current situation—something more rewarding, gratifying, pleasing and exciting, something that is, by its very definition, "no longer simply living" (76) but more than what mere reality has to offer—is what

14 The aesthetic attention with which Mr Biswas lavishes each individual letter suggests the evolution of lettering as an art form from ancient to modern times: "the Greeks and Romans regarded the letter as a work of art, and classical lettering reflects this strongly felt attitude"; "many modern designers have thought to modify the classic letters by adding some personal preference of proportion or curve" (Constantine and Jacobson 75–76).

imbues the language of advertisement with its somewhat hollow, sugary and even artificial register.

Of course, no one would be eager for a false life to yield its *mundane bitterness* and *disenchantment*. Yet, insofar as a portrayal of "the world" as completely desirable is highly romanticised, it deviates from the mixed and "accidental" nature of the actual world; it presents an ideality that seems to lack the substance of true experience. Interestingly enough, as the second sense of "emptiness" suggests, the ideal portrayal generated by advertising reflects less upon some underlying truth of life and more upon the presentation and interpretation of life through mediating symbols by people in different social contexts. A concrete example will clarify this second meaning.

The scene in which "Mr Biswas became a sign-writer" can be read as a miniature semiotic allegory on the emptiness of signs in the Saussurean sense of signifiers. Much in the same way that the sounds and graphic figures of an ordinary language acquire meaning because of how they are used by people in various contexts, the phrases proposed by Alex are not, for the most part, informative of what the café actually offers; they are proposed simply because they have been observed on actual signs, and are hence deemed appropriate due to the social context in which words painted on notices acquire a status as a "sign".

> "The modern thing is to have lots of words. All the shops in Port-of-Spain have signs with nothing but words. Tell him"....
>
> "Sweet drinks, cakes, and ice," Mr. Biswas said ....
>
> "Beware of the dog," Alec said.
>
> "I ain't got a dog."
>
> "Fresh fruits daily," Alec went on. "Stick no bills by order." .... "Trespassers will be prosecuted. Overseas visitors welcomed. If you don't see what you require please ask. Our assistants will be pleased to help you with your inquiries." (72)

The signs Alec suggests are all just copies of other signs: the irony of the situation is that Alec and Mr Biswas are actually making use of signs as signs to sell more signs. The very conventionality of the signs they recommend is used as an advertisement for the creation of more signs. Both signs in the sense of actual painted notices and signs in the sense of signifiers appear arbitrary.

It is not only the distinctive "sign-like" quality of these signs that is being advertised by Alex and Mr Biswas, but also their modernity. Over and above, the painting of hummingbirds around the words "THE HUMMING BIRD CA[FE]" (a mode of visual repetition which Alec calls "follow-fashion" (71), suggesting the way in which the pictures would literally follow and repeat the words), the proprietor is urged to consider "the modern thing ... [of] hav[ing] lots of words" (72).[15] This claim turns out not merely to be a cajoling advertisement for his advertisements, but also a claim about the history of advertising. As Sabine Gieszinger argues in *The History of Advertising Language*, "A typical feature of advertisements in the middle of the nineteenth century was their small number of words" (39), but "as at the end of the nineteenth century production grew rapidly and many products were launched, the advertised goods needed extensive explanation either because they were new on the market or because their singularity had to be emphasized" (41). The "modern thing ... [of] hav[ing] lots of words" (72) thus reflects the corresponding explosion of consumer options along the Main Road in Pagotes, where the proprietors are expected to constantly renew their signs to fit with the changing fashions that advertising conditions their consumers to expect.[16]

As Beasley, Danesi and Perron suggest in *Signs for Sale: An Outline of Semiotic Analysis for Advertisers and Marketers*, "The inbuilt ephemerality of advertising makes it possible to ensure that newness and faddishness can be reflected in the product through adaptive change in the style and content of ads and commercials" (12). The signs that Mr Biswas and Alec recommend are furthermore indicative of an attempt to affiliate themselves with a certain conception of modern progress through the adoption of English phrases. The official tone of "stick no

---

15 Phrases like "sweetness and romance" and "especial sweetness" are suited to the vagueness of advertising rhetoric, because the underlying notion of sweetness can be applied to any number of products or situations in ways that result in different and multiple connotations: a sweet friend, a sweet song, a sweet smell, sweet promise, etc.

16 Mildred Constantine and Egbert Jacobson describe the chaos of the modern landscape riddled with a proliferation of advertisements in "Sign Language, an art historical examination of the relation between architecture and lettering": "Whether on Peachtree Street in Atlanta, Market Street in San Francisco, Broadway in New York, Piccadilly in London, the Piazza del Duomo in Milan, or on Main Streets throughout the world, we are confronted with a vulgar and mistaken notion of free enterprise, expressed in the sign language of our time. We are assailed with a confusion of words, names and slogans in all sizes, in all forms, in all colors and shapes—a never-ceasing roar that moves, blinks, flashes warnings, pleads and cajoles, demands, reminds, but seldom instructs. In this cacaphonic bombardment, what do we look at? What do we see? Can anybody see in this impetuous, disorderly landscape of lettering?" (9)

bills by order" literally "stick[s]" out in contrast with the proprietor's grammatically incorrect sentence, "'I ain't got a dog.'" As David C. S. Li argues, "The global spread of English ... evident in multilingual adverts" has led some commentators to describe English as "the *lingua franca* of the marketplace", for "in non-English settings ... the use of English is often associated with prestige and power, symbolizing progress, modernity, and technological advancement" (433).[17] If the use of English in this context signals a cosmopolitan "modernity", however, it is not an unequivocal sign of "prestige and power".

Many of the phrases that Alec suggests appeal obsequiously to those with the money to purchase goods or services; they are not phrases that carry any special rhetorical or lyrical force, nor are they spoken from the position of the dominant class. The oddly constructed phrase "Overseas visitors welcomed" is a reminder that this use of the English language is largely a strategic adaptation by local businesses that must compete in an economy shaped by foreign tourism. As Alec instructs the proprietor in what modernity and modern advertising requires, he assumes the role that the narrator of *The Middle Passage* ascribes to the advertising agency in my epigraph:

> Modernity in Trinidad, then, turns out to be the extreme susceptibility of people who are unsure of themselves and, having no taste or style of their own, are eager for instruction ... in Trinidad instruction is now provided by advertising agencies, which have been welcomed by the people not only for this reason but also because the advertising agency is itself a modern thing. (47)

"Modern" signs with words thus turn out to be as "follow-fashion" as their predecessors, leading to hollow imitations whose independence from conventionality is highly conventional. Contra to Mr Biswas's hope, the creation of signs for advertisements does not lead to the freedom of a new life, a break from the repressive traditions of the Tulsi household. "It was satisfying work, but it came irregularly" (73). The trouble with sign-painting is that despite the temporary autonomy it grants Mr Biswas, it only reflects the essential arbitrariness of his existence without giving him the power to transcend it. Despite his talent at sign painting, he is never considered an artist. "Mr. Biswas couldn't draw" (71); his lettering skills are not perceived as original

17 Fairfid M. Caudle has also shown persuasively that "language [in international advertising] serves not only its expected function as information is communicated through written advertising copy; language is also employed in a symbolic manner to identify a brand's country of origin" (119).

artistic talent, but rather as a superficial embellishment on a system of other people's signs that does not result in any lasting meaning or value. He remains, for the most part, mired in the system of conventions that define his existence.

Even the signs that Mr Biswas takes the most pride in creating are ultimately turned against him, largely because he cannot control the context in which they will be interpreted. The first sign he paints at the Tulsis' store—"BARGAINS! BARGAINS!" (81–82)—ends up ironically serving as an advertisement for himself: the Tulsis are able to marry off their daughter to him without paying a dowry, and do not even pay him for painting the sign. The slogan he proudly dreams up for himself—"Give up sign-painting? And my independence? No, boy. My motto is: paddle your own canoe" (101)—is eventually used by the Tulsi family to mock him. When the house that he has been building for years in an attempt to be independent from the Tulsis falls apart in a storm, his brother-in-law Seth remarks snidely, "I suppose we have to bring the paddler home" (281).

The self-assertive, emancipatory tone of the phrase by which Mr Biswas links sign-painting with his own "independence" recalls the etymology of "slogan" noted by Cynthia Crossen in her discussion of the relation between the rhetoric of advertising and of political contest: "Like banana sellers, political candidates have long used slogans to market themselves. The word 'slogan' comes from the Gaelic, 'sluaghghairm', meaning 'war cry.'" But, despite Mr Biswas's bold and memorable attempt to forge a battle cry for his independence, the term "paddler" is henceforth used to refer to him only in the moments of his deepest humiliation. Thus, although Mr Biswas has mastered the flash and distinctiveness necessary to make an effective sign, he can no more control the entire universe of discourse in which he acquires significance than he can avoid the fact of his dependence upon a world hostile to his dreams. Without the signs of others, his own signs yield nothing; the debt that leads to his removal from The Chase and subsequent nervous breakdown is tellingly precipitated by Mr Biswas's failure to procure the signatures of his customers: "But they wasn't signed the last time either" (168).

Realism and the Detergent Purpose of Advertising

Mr Biswas, enchanted by the name, was disappointed to find.... (297)

By the time Mr Biswas arrives at the city of Port-of-Spain at the beginning of Part Two of the novel, he has come to realise the limitations of his autonomy: "If there was a place for him, it was one that had already been hollowed out by time, by everything he had lived through, however imperfect, makeshift and cheating" (303). Accepting the "imperfect, makeshift" and "hollow" nature of signs, he turns the editor's "No Hands Wanted" sign into an ironic joke upon himself, impressing the editor and landing a job at the Sentinel (310). After obtaining this new position of relative security in the world, other people come to depend on him, including his destitute relative Bhandat. The scene of Mr Biswas's visit to Bhandat is the climax of the use of advertising language in the novel. As Mr Biswas approaches the house where Bhandat is staying, the idealised language of "stylish advertisements" (429) that had previously portrayed landscape or scenery disappears, and is replaced by words describing a smelly, colourless reality: "broken", "rusty", "rancid", "many-accented smell", "wrinkled film of scum", "piercing, acrid smell", "black", "blank" (430).

Any trace of romanticised vision is taken over by "the gritty concrete" details of realism: dirty surroundings ("stale-smelling bed"), the touch of ageing and unkempt bodies ("unshaven chin scraping against his neck" and "dry lips on his cheek"), violence ("Bhandat had pulled sharply at his hair") and madness ("Bhandat hooted")—a state of affairs summed up in Mr Biswas's mind as "deafness, dumbness, insanity, the horror of the sexual act in that grimy room" (431–434). The overtly unaestheticised, unsentimental quality of this depiction serves to distance the novelistic portrayal of Bhandat's reality from what Naipaul describes in *The Middle Passage* as the popular standard for novels in Trinidad: "The Trinidadian expects his novels, like his advertisements, to have a detergent purpose" (69). The generic qualities of the novel and the advertisement are brought together once again, this time through the metaphor of a cleaning product that is intended to remove all traces of dirt, grime and use from the objects of daily life. Detergent seems to be precisely what the surroundings of Bhandat are in need of if they are to be transformed into the sanitised, aestheticised, orderly world that Mr Biswas had learnt to desire through advertisements. Indeed, when Mr Biswas first arrives at the home of Bhandat, Bhandat is trying to escape from his sordid situation by writing a winning advertisement slogan for Lux Toilet Soap:

> "Why do you use Lux Toilet Soap?"
>
> Mr. Biswas saw that Bhandat was staring at him earnestly.
>
> "Lux Toilet? I think we use Palmolive. A green thing –"
>
> Bhandat said in English, "I use Lux Toilet Soap because it is the soap used by lovely film stars."
>
> Mr. Biswas was disturbed.
>
> Bhandat ... handed Mr. Biswas a newspaper and Mr. Biswas read the details of the Lux slogan competition.
>
> "Help an old man, Mohun. Tell me why you use Lux Toilet Soap."

> Mr. Biswas said, "I use Lux Toilet Soap because it is antiseptic, refreshing, fragrant, and inexpensive."
>
> Bhandat frowned. The words had made no impression on him. And Mr. Biswas knew for sure then, what he had intuited and dismissed: Bhandat was deaf.
>
> "Write it down, Mohun," Bhandat cried. "Write it down before I forget it." (432)

Misunderstanding Bhandat's first question, Mr Biswas thinks that Bhandat is asking him a question about his actual habits, when, in fact, Bhandat is prompting him to provide an entry to a "slogan competition" (432). Yet, there is nothing in the words of the question themselves that would prevent Mr Biswas from hearing them this way; the world of the advertising competition and the world of actual product use intersect seamlessly in the form of consumer deliberation over a certain product. The slogan answers a question that a person in a supermarket might ask themselves or their friends. The only clues Mr Biswas has of his error are Bhandat's use of English, a foreign language, and his allusion to the glamorous world of "lovely film stars" in his current state of poverty. Indeed, the inherent surreality of their exchange seems to seep over into the ambiguity of the brand name itself, so that the "toilet" of "Lux Toilet Soap" connotes both a cosmetic act of grooming and a fixture for defecation and urination: excrement and luxury, filth and cleanliness, pollution and purification, smelliness and fragrance, all collide incongruously in this scene.[18]

---

18 In their summary of W. F. Haug's analysis of the "corruption or distortion of use values" through advertising in his book *Kritik der Warenästhetik*, Vestevgaard and Schroder state: "No one will want to buy a product unless it seems to be of use value to him, but since the seller's only interest in his commodity is selling it, he will be satisfied as long as the commodity appears to be of use value. The more attractive the product appears, the more people will want to buy it, and the shorter will be the lag between the time when the product leaves the factory and the time when the product is sold. This, according to Haug (ibid.) has led to an aestheticization of commodities (Warenästhetik.) This aestheticization may be inherent in the product itself in the form of design (cars for instance), smell (washing-up liquid), or colouring (beverages)–strictly irrelevant to the material use value of the product; it may appear in close connection with the product (the specially shaped bottles of beverages), or completely detached from the product, in the advertising" (9).

When Mr Biswas realises that Bhandat cannot even hear him talk, the slogan has to be "written down", thus, becoming the last advertisement Mr Biswas will ever write. Mr Biswas replaces Bhandat's suggested slogan with one that does not "promise the consumer that the acquisition and consumption of his product will give youth, love, recognition, and so on", but that hints more closely at some aspect of what we might think of as "the primary use value of [the] product", while nevertheless continuing to aestheticise the product in terms of its sensually appealing qualities.[19]

As Roland Barthes suggests in his essay on "Soap-powders and Detergents" in *Mythologies*, these very contradictions are exploited for the purpose of creating a highly suggestive and marketable image:

> As for foam, it is well known that it signifies luxury. To begin with, it appears to lack any usefulness ... it gratifies in the consumer a tendency to imagine matter as something airy, can even be the sign of a certain spirituality, inasmuch as the spirit has the reputation of being able to make something out of nothing.... What matters is the art of having disguised the abrasive function of the detergent under the delicious image of a substance at once deep and airy which can govern the molecular order of the material without damaging it. (37–38)

Like the elaborate fantasies of life that Bhandat spins for his audience without being able to hear himself, the slogan that Mr Biswas writes unveils a quest for something that might float delicately over the "material" of reality "without damaging it", or without, in this case, acknowledging the damage that has already been done to one's life and person.

Thus, when the detergent motif appears prominently in the interaction between Mr Biswas and Bhandat, it does so with an unexpected consequence that brings into sharp focus the interplay between advertising and novelistic text in the novel and reverses the dominant dynamic between them. Up until this point in the narrative, the novel seems to incorporate aspects of the formal and rhetorical aspects of advertising language into its text, blurring the distinction

---

19 Naipaul's choice of "Lux Toilet Soap" for this scene contains another allusion to the history of advertising, for as Beasley, Danesi and Perron note, the first products to be marketed with brand names were soaps: "Around 1880, soap manufacturers started naming their products so that they could be identified. The first modern-day brand names were thus invented. They included: Ivory, Pears, Sapolio, Colgate, Kirk's American Family, and Packer's" (29).

between the two genres; however, at this juncture, the novel turns abruptly away from the imitation of advertising in order to challenge it with the values of a different kind of mimesis.

Writing the slogan for Lux Toilet Soap affects Mr Biswas in a strange way, for, as soon as he returns home, he engages in a cleaning ritual, almost as if the advertisement had succeeded in triggering a desire for cleanliness. However, what he cleans out of his life is precisely the traces of his attempt to aestheticise his actual experience, to cover up and disguise its dirt and imperfection: "As soon as he got to the house he ... took out his unfinished *Escape* stories, the dreams of the barren heroine. He took the stories to the lavatory in the yard and stayed there for some time, creating a din of his own, pulling the chain again and again" (435). Literally enacting the textual turn from the elegant "toilet" of movie actresses in the slogan to the mundane "toilet" of everyday waste disposal in his home, Mr Biswas reduces his stories to an angry, one-word expletive that contrasts starkly with the artificial fantasy of his verbose and ridiculously elegant slogan: "antiseptic, fragrant, refreshing, and inexpensive" (434).

It is as if all his dreams of "*Escape*" collide with a messy and inescapable reality that he can no longer gloss over; he recognises, in his attempts to avoid a confrontation with reality, his denial of a part of his life that has literally been nothing but a waste. The "slogan competition" evokes Mr Biswas's desire to be a show-off, a wit, a wordsmith, reminding us that he has always badly wanted something he can be proud to show, something by which he can prove his talents and intelligence. After his "disturbing" encounter with the "small, unreliable" (431) fantasies of Bhandat's mind, however, Mr Biswas sees that he can no longer believe in "a familiar story of jobs acquired and lost, great enterprises which had failed, wonderful opportunities Bhandat had not taken because of his own honesty or the dishonesty of his associates, all of whom were now famous and rich" (432).

The only true memory that emerges from Bhandat's confused consciousness, besides his remembrance of having beaten Mr Biswas, is a memory of the rum they used to bottle together. In those days, Mr Biswas

> revenged himself by spitting in the rum when he bottled it, which he did early every morning. The rum was the same, but the prices and the labels were different: "Indian Maiden," "The White Cock," "Parakeet." Each brand had its adherents, and to Mr. Biswas this was a subsidiary revenge which gave a small but continuous pleasure. (59)

Mr Biswas, thus, bypasses the false labels and puts something of his own spiteful essence into otherwise indistinguishable spirits: spirits that are dispirited, like Mr Biswas in Part One of the novel, by being made generic. However, "spitting" into the bottles can be viewed not only as a childish form of "revenge" or self-assertion but also as a figure for the reproductive act—an act that ultimately distinguishes Mr Biswas, allowing him to realise one of his dreams. Like the detergent soap that Barthes describes, both foamy spit and semen suggest in their "abundant, easy, almost infinite proliferation ... [that] there is in the substance from which it issues a vigorous germ, a healthy and powerful essence, a great wealth of active elements in a small original volume" (37).

The metaphor of spitting into a bottle reminds us that Mr Biswas is not sterile, and that his creative capacity results in two children who win their independence through scholarships to study abroad. His son, in particular, learns to write prose with the actual literary qualities that Mr Biswas only hoped to achieve, and, realising this, Mr Biswas eventually abandons the "barren ... dreams" of his "*Escape*" stories and puts all of his energy into the education of his son (431); "his visions of the future became only visions of Anand's future" (474). The College Exhibition becomes the means by which Mr Biswas will eventually show what he is most proud of producing in his life: Anand.

Anand is not portrayed in the novel as an unqualified success, however, nor is his relation to his father romanticised. Unlike Mr Biswas, who does not deny Bhandat's fantasy, Anand does not indulge the comforting pretense of being "the only one ... of my worthless sons ever [to] come" and visit (432). Whereas, in the "Ideal School of Journalism", one might cover up or sugarcoat unpleasant facts in order to create something more commercially appealing, the Epilogue describes in plain, unsentimental language how Anand does not reply to his father's letters or visit him before his death (329). His letters home are described as alternately "impersonal, brief, empty, constrained" (562) and "strange, maudlin, useless" (563), as if the independence and privacy that Anand now enjoys have made him unable to share himself with others in the way that Mr Biswas—garrulous, comic, zealous, flamboyant—had always done. In its refusal to hide the ways that Anand fails his father, the ending of *A House for Mr Biswas* succeeds in showing that Mr Biswas does achieve at least one of his dreams when he says to Anand, "I don't want you to be like me" (359).

Considered in light of Naipaul's claim in *The Middle Passage* that "the Trinidadian expects his novels, like his advertisements, to have a detergent purpose", the novel's refusal to whitewash the fears and indignities that disturb Mr Biswas's last days is especially striking. In the short space of the five-page Epilogue, the temporary resolution and success that Mr Biswas seems to have achieved in owning his own house recede into the past. Anand does not come, and Mr Biswas is fired from his job at the Sentinel; he never receives the headline that he had hoped would report his death and the mourners who come to his funeral scratch and dirty the floors of his beloved house.

The mundane march of little tragedies continues its way across Mr Biswas's story, undeterred even by his death. Such an Epilogue may strike us as unnecessarily harsh and dismal, unless we understand that the novel as a whole works to establish its identity by starkly differentiating itself from the "detergent purpose" of advertising. Whereas advertising strives to present a sanitised, beautified, disinfected vision of the world, Naipaul's novel unflinchingly conveys the imperfections and contingencies of Mr Biswas's life in all of its suffering, disappointment and frenzied flights of folly. The fragments and scraps of advertising that litter *A House for Mr Biswas*, therefore, do not merely serve as trivial indicators of a larger cultural and historical context, but rather bear the weight of the aesthetic and moral issues that define the world of this novel.

Works Cited

"Advertisement." *The Oxford English Dictionary*. 2nd ed. CD-ROM. Oxford UP, 1992.

Alexander, Robert J. *A History of Organized Labor in the English-Speaking West Indies*. Praeger, 2004.

Barthes, Roland. *Mythologies*, translated by Jonathan Cape, Hill and Wang, 1972.

Baudrillard, Jean. *The System of Objects*, translated by James Benedict, Verso, 1996.

Beasley, Ron, Marcel Danesi, and Paul Perron. *Signs for Sale: An Outline of Semiotic Analysis for Advertisers and Marketers*. Legas, 2001.

Bhattacharya, Baidik. "Naipaul's New World: Postcolonial Modernity and the Enigma of Belated Space." *Novel: A Forum on Fiction*, vol. 39, issue 2, 2006, pp. 245–67.

Caudle, Fairfid M. "National Boundaries in Magazine Advertising: Perspectives on Verbal and Nonverbal Communication." *Global and Multinational Advertising*, edited by Basil G. Englis, Erlbaum, 1994, pp. 117–140.

Constantine, Mildred, and Egbert Jacobson. *Sign Language*. Reinhold, 1961.

Crossen, Cynthia. "Clever Lines / Make Us Crave / Return to Days / Selling Burma-Shave." *Wall Street Journal*, 20 August 2003, Eastern ed., Bl.

Crystal, David. *The Cambridge Encyclopedia of the English Language*. Cambridge UP, 1995.

Escalas, Jennifer Edson. "Advertising Narratives: What Are They and How Do They Work?" *Representing Consumers: Voices, Views, and Visions*, edited by Barbara Stern, Routledge, 1998, pp. 267–289.

Escalas, Jennifer Edson, and Barbara B. Stern. "Narrative Structure: Plot and Emotional Responses." *Psycholinguistic Phenomena in Marketing Communications*, edited by Tina M. Lowrey, Erlbaum, 2007, pp. 157–175.

Fathi, A. R. *The Language of Advertising and T. V Commercials*. Bahri, 1991.

Gandhi, Leela. "Made in England: V. S. Naipaul and English Fiction(s)." *England through Colonial Eyes in Twentieth-Century Fiction*, edited by Ann Blake, Leela Gandhi, Sue Thomas, Palgrave, 2001, pp. 128–142.

Gieszinger, Sabine. *The History of Advertising Language: The Advertisements in "The Times" from 1788 to 1996*. Lang, 2001.

Heyck, T. W. *Transformation of Intellectual Life in Victorian England*. Croom Helm, 1982.

King, Bruce. *V. S. Naipaul*. St. Martin's Press, 1993.

Leech, Geoffrey N. *English in Advertising*. Longmans, 1966.

Leonard, Garry. *Advertising and Commodity Culture in Joyce*. UP of Florida, 1998.

Li, David C. S. "Multilingualism and Commerce." *Handbook of Multilingualism and Multilingual Communication*, edited by Peter Auer and Li Wei, Mouton de Gruyter, 2007, pp. 423–443.

Marchand, Roland. *Advertising the American Dream: Making Way for Modernity*. U of California P, 1985.

Marcus, Sharon. "The Profession of the Author: Abstraction, Advertising, and Jane Eyre." *PMLA*, vol. 110, issue 2, 1995, pp. 206–219.

McKeon, Michael. *The Origins of the English Novel 1600–1740*. Johns Hopkins UP, 1987.

Mustafa, Fawzia. *V. S. Naipaul*. Cambridge UP, 1995.

Naipaul, V. S. "Foreword to *A House for Mr Biswas*." *Literary Occasions: Essays*, Knopf, 2003.

———. *Guerrillas*. Knopf, 1975.

———. *A House for Mr Biswas*. Vintage, 2001.

———. Interview Extract of Seminar 1974. *Banyan*. 1974, 28 March 2008.

———. *The Middle Passage*. Andre Deutsch, 1962.

———. *The Mimic Men*. Andre Deutsch, 1967.

Pandya, Indubala H. *English Language in Advertising: A Linguistic Study of Indian Press Advertising*. Ajanta, 1977.

Said, Edward. "Intellectuals in the Post-Colonial World." *Salamagundi*, vol. 70/71, 1986, pp. 44–64.

Seecharan, Clem. *Sweetening Bitter Sugar: Jock Campbell The Booker Reformer in British Guiana 1934–1966*. Ian Randle, 2005.

Steinlight, Emily. "'Anti -Bleak House': Advertising and the Victorian Novel." *Narrative*, vol. 14, issue 2, 2006, pp. 132–162.

Strachan, Ian G. *Paradise and Plantation: Tourism and Culture in the Anglophone Caribbean*. U of Virginia P, 2002.

Thornton, Sara. *Advertising, Subjectivity and the Nineteenth-Century Novel: Dickens, Balzac and the Language of the Walls*. Palgrave Macmillan, 2009.

Vestergaard, Torben, and Kim Schroder. *The Language of Advertising*. Blackwell, 1985.

Wadsworth, Sarah. *In the Company of Books: Literature and Its "Classes" in Nineteenth- Century America*. U of Massachusetts P, 2006.

Warner, William B. "Novels on the Market." *The Cambridge History of English Literature, 1660–1870*, edited by John Richetti, Cambridge UP, 2005, pp. 86–106.

Watt, Ian. *The Rise of the Novel: Studies in Defoe, Richardson, and Fielding*. U of California P, 1957.

Wicke, Jennifer. *Advertising Fictions: Literature, Advertisement, and Social Reading*. Columbia UP, 1988.

Williamson, Judith. "But I Know What I Like: The Function of 'Art' in Advertising." *The Communication Theory Reader*, edited by Paul Cobley, Routledge, 1996, pp. 396–402.

Chapter 10

CHARACTER AND REBELLION IN *A HOUSE FOR MR BISWAS* BY V. S. NAIPAUL

Gordon Rohlehr

> Ten weeks before he died, Mr. Mohun Biswas, a journalist of Sikkim Street, St. James, Port-of-Spain, was sacked. He had been ill for some time. In less than a year he had spent more than nine weeks at the Colonial Hospital and convalesced at home for even longer. When the doctor advised him to take a complete rest the Trinidad Sentinel had no choice. It gave Mr. Biswas three months' notice and continued, up to the time of his death, to supply him every morning with a free copy of the paper.
>
> —*A House for Mr Biswas* 1

It is worth asking: what is the social and universal significance of the rebellion of a mediocre, ridiculous man? Biswas certainly is this: an anti-hero moving through dimension after dimension of nearly epic absurdity. He is forever trying to arrange his world and ending up more deeply immersed in the absurd situation. Though there are signs at his birth, these are part of the grotesque pattern of events which will be his life. Like Oedipus, he is fated to kill his father. Unlike Oedipus, he fulfils this "prophecy" in the most ridiculous of ways. His father drowns in an attempt to retrieve from a pond the body of his son, who is hiding under the bed at home. Later on, Biswas is to be the Scarlet Pimpernel for a local newspaper stunt and is to read Samuel Smile's tracts on the dignity of labour and the virtues of being a self-made man. It is the nearest he comes to achieving epic status.

It is predicted that he will be a liar, a lecher and a spendthrift. Time proves him incapable of lechery, poverty preserves him from extravagance and he is incapable of falsehood since he constantly faces the harrowing facts of his condition. He is allowed no respite from the sense of his littleness. Riding like a Beckett character on his bicycle, moving countless times with his cumbersome furniture, savouring the bitter irony of his position as an investigator of "deserving destitutes", he is *l'homme absurd*. But Biswas is also *l'homme revolte*, since he is persistent in his desire to understand existence and make sense of his milieu. It is important to note that Naipaul has illustrated the rebellion of a weak, mediocre man, since, in writing elsewhere about West Indian society, he undervalues the quality of rebellion in a world which he rejects as mediocre.

The death of his father has left this absurd Oedipus homeless and emotionally bewildered. The early affection which he feels for his mother dwindles when embarrassment and decorum prevent her from showing him any affection in the presence of strangers. But Biswas needs to be mothered and uses his aunt Tara as a mother-substitute until he allows himself to be browbeaten into marriage. It is difficult to imagine one less capable of physical or emotional love. He looks at his "comic make-believe clothes", regards his body with disgust and swings his loose calf like a hammock or probes a stomach too distended to be fat. He confesses that he "don't look like anything at all" (143).

This sense of inferiority becomes particularly obsessive whenever Biswas is alone, and it leads to a grotesque exhibitionism which really indicates his need for love.

> There were whole weeks when he devoted himself to some absurdity. He grew his nails to an extreme length and held them up to startle customers. He picked and squeezed at his face until his cheeks and forehead were inflamed and the rims of his lips were like welts. When his skin became pitted with little holes, he studied these with interest and found the perfection of their shape pleasing. And once he dabbed ointments of various colours on his face and went and stood in the shop doorway greeting people he knew. (165)

Mark Spilka has written about the comic grotesque. The principle of humanity in comic villains becomes overt in Dostoevsky's fiction. The compulsion buffoon, Fydor Karamozov, insults and lacerates an entire monastery, and converts a pious businessman to his anti-faith. From the author's point of view, his buffoonery is defensive, a perverse display of his own inadequacy performed with comic zest. Like Quilp in *The Old Curiosity Shop*, Karamazov is a master of sadistic play; his clever insults, his acute perception of human weakness, are part of a general campaign to advertise his need for love. His conduct is roughly that of a child rejected by his parents, who deliberately accentuates his faults to gain attention. The result paradoxically is a brilliant demonstration of potential worth.

These comments are also true of Naipaul's Biswas. He needs a mother as well as a wife. Shama attracts him when she is mothering him, but he can't admit this. He is a difficult person to mother.

> As he was lying in bed one morning she came and placed her palm then the back of her hand on his forehead. The action offended him, flattered him, and made him uneasy....
>
> She undid his shirt and put her hand, large and dark and foreign, on his pale, soft chest.
>
> .... He wanted to scream.
>
> .... He was violently angry; never before had he been so disgusted by her. Yet he wished her to remain there. Half-hoping she would take him seriously, half-hoping only to amuse and bewilder her, he said in his quick, high-pitched voice, "something in my mind all right". (247)

He is in a state where he can neither give nor receive the love he needs.

Rebellion in Biswas is defined by his state as a cultural, psychological and social orphan. So often his revolt contains a childlike rage and grief at violated innocence; and a childlike need to prove that his suffering is always the fault of someone else. Indeed, he assumes that because he is oppressed he is, therefore, innocent. This assumption enables him to justify some of the less pleasant aspects of his revolt; like kicking the pregnant Shama in the belly, because he sees each new child as another Tulsi trap. "He develops a nausea at the idea of birth … almost immediately he began to hate her. Her pregnancy was grotesque; he hated the way she sat down; … he hated it when she puffed and fanned and sweated in her pregnant way" (246). This nausea never quite abandons him. When he dismissed Shama, he tells her to "[t]ake your girl children and go" (249). Later, as a writer of short stories, he has a recurrent theme:

> The hero, trapped into marriage, burdened with a family, his youth gone, meets a young girl. She is slim, almost thin, and dresses in white. She is fresh, tender, unkissed; and she is unable to bear children. Beyond the meeting the stories never went. (311)

He wants, then, a cessation of the entire process of birth, and hopes for a sexless, sterile world in which he can be alone. "He tried to think of landscape without people: sand and sand and sand, without the 'oses Lal had spoken about; vast white plateaux, with himself safely alone, a speck in the centre" (240).

He longs for inertia, a relapse into darkness, a bed which he will never have to leave, the enswaddling warmth of the bed in the Blue Room of Hanuman House. During the storm, Govind carries Biswas in his arms like a baby, while Anand walks in the rain. Beneath this self-laceration and play-acting, this assumption of the grotesque mask lies a fear of the future, of objects, of people; of time, place and mankind:

> And always the thought, the fear about the future. The future wasn't the next day or the next week or even the next year; times within his comprehension and therefore without dread. The future he feared could not be thought of in terms of time. It was a blankness a void like those—in dreams, into which, past tomorrow and next week and next year, he was falling. (171)

Biswas is living to an extreme degree the anxieties of the uprooted man. His elaborate poses, daydreams, assertion of self and evasion of responsibility are a result of the cultural social and psychological nowhereness produced by his position as an untalented second-generation Hindu in poverty-stricken colonial Trinidad. He is appropriately an orphan.

The comparison with Dickens' grotesques which was suggested earlier is not at all far-fetched. Biswas becomes an avid reader—of Dickens.

> Without difficulty he transferred characters and settings to people and places he knew. In the grotesques of Dickens everything he feared and suffered from was ridiculed and diminished, so that his own anger, his own contempt became unnecessary, and he was given strength to bear with the most difficult part of his day. (337–338)

One wonders whether the catharsis which Biswas seeks both in a real and a vicarious grotesqueness isn't a feature of Creole society in Trinidad. He seems to share with them a capacity to convert anxiety into absurdity and to make a grasp of the absurd dimension a part of his total psychology of struggle.

As an Indian in the Trinidad of the 1930s, Biswas is insecure and perhaps needs the support of the family or the clan. At no time in the book is he, or any of the Tulsis, able to come to any meaningful compromise with the Creole world, though he absorbs some of its spirit in his love for picong, mamaguy, repartee and caricature. When he marries into the Tulsi family, he is offered protection, the sort of job which he could scarcely get anywhere else, given his limited talents and lack of drive. Yet, he rebels and makes the Tulsis the target of his revolt.

To understand Biswas's rebellion, one must understand the social structure of Hanuman House. On the surface, the Tulsis have effected an admirable reconstruction of the clan in a strange and sometimes hostile environment. It has its leaders, its scheme of prescribed duties and responsibilities, its own law and order, its religious ritual and it tries to provide the individual with the sort of job for which his talents equip him. This is at least how it appears on the surface, and, in a sense, Biswas's rebellion is inexplicable when one considers his prospects in colonial Trinidad. Because he has no alternative to life in Hanuman House, his rebellion suffers from a lack of direction, and he has to return to the protective warmth of Tulsidom time and time again.

But, on closer examination, Hanuman House reveals itself not as a coherent reconstruction of the clan, but as a slave society, erected by Mrs Tulsi and Seth who need workers to help rebuild their tottering empire. They, therefore, exploit the homelessness and poverty of their fellow Hindus and reconstruct a mockery of the clan which functions only because they have so completely grasped the psychology of a slave system. Like the West Indies, Hanuman House is constructed of a vast number of disparate families, gratuitously brought together by the economic need of a "high-caste" minority. Men are necessary here only as husbands for the Tulsi daughters and labourers on the Tulsi estates. To accept Hanuman House is to acquiesce in one's slavery.

The Tulsi daughters have no choice since they have known no other world. It is only later in the book that education becomes a means of emancipation from Hanuman House since it places the Indians on par with the Creoles as competitors in the wider society of Trinidad. But the Tulsi daughters of two generations ago are inalienably bound to the rhythms and rituals of life in Hanuman House—the daily puja, the seasonal wedding, the occasional funeral. It gives them relief from the tedium and submissiveness of their daily lives. They have little real say in the running of Hanuman House but vie for the crumbs of authority which Mrs Tulsi allows to filter down to them from time to time. Competition for favours from Mai is keen, and Mai alone knows how to dispense these favours so as to prevent undue dissension.

She also knows that she must remain at the centre of her daughters' consciousness; they must see her as their sole reason for existence. There is something archetypal in the organisation of Hanuman House. Mrs Tulsi is a powerful mother figure and rules through an understanding of the psychology of slavery. She is constantly demanding to be loved and worshipped and is very good at staging strategic illnesses in order to inspire feelings of guilt in those who have failed in their worship. She has instituted an elaborate system of rules which make devotion easy on the would-be believer. Biswas, an inveterate enemy of ritual, assents. His deep scepticism preserves him from the necessity of paying the emotional blackmail which Mrs Tulsi constantly demands. A bad slave, he cannot be brought to feel grateful for his conditions or sorry for the trouble he causes.

> "You happy, eh, now that you make Mai faint?...
> Which foot you rub?"
> "You know, nobody hearing you talk would believe that you come to this house with no more things than you could hang up on a one inch nail...."
> It was a familiar attack. He ignored it. (115)

It is the first and last accusation of Hanuman House, the one in which it seeks to justify its methods. Biswas on the night of his final revolt bitterly shouts,

> "I curse the day I step into your house...."
> "You curse the day," Mrs. Tulsi said, "Coming to us with no more clothes than you could hang up on a nail."
> This wounded Mr. Biswas. He could not reply at once.
> "I am giving you notice," he repeated at last. (502)

One notices that Mrs Tulsi and her daughters only mention the fact that Biswas came to them. They never speak of their efforts to get him to join the system; of the original pressures which they applied to get him to marry Shama. It is important for the smooth running of the system that the impression be maintained that everyone joins Hanuman House of his own free will.

What Mrs Tulsi has grasped is the fundamental idea that a slave system must be able to prove and contain all the apparent evidence of its own legitimacy. As Albert Memmi observes in *The Colonizer and the Colonized*,

> In order for the colonizer to be the complete master, it is not enough for him to be so in actual fact, but he must believe in its legitimacy. In order for that legitimacy to be complete, it is not enough for the colonized to be a slave, he must also accept this role. (14)

Hence, Mrs Tulsi, good coloniser that she is, justifies her exploitation with the explanation that she is really doing her subjects good. Her argument is the one which ex-colonial peoples most bitterly resent, and also the one which gives them pause. Biswas "could not reply at once" partly because he suspects that part of what Mrs Tulsi says is true, and he cannot afford to admit that any good at all can proceed from so iniquitous a system. "Virtues are forced upon us by our impudent crimes", as T. S. Eliot's Gerontion puts it. It is this irony of the colonial process which paralyses Conrad's Marlow in *Heart of Darkness* and humiliates Mr Biswas. He knows at last that he has to forget all arguments of right and wrong, and leave the system once and for all: that too much energy has already been lost in debate and in working out the paradox of the master–slave relationship.

Mrs Tulsi is only one part of the power structure of Hanuman House. She can't rule alone. She needs Seth, who is as powerful a father figure as she is a matriarch. Mrs Tulsi divides power among the sisters and rules by checks and balances. By allowing her daughters the illusion of freedom and democratic rights, she practically controls their husbands. But she needs Seth, her counterpart, to complete and fulfil the psychological requirements of slave ownership. Not only a subtle manipulation of checks and balances but sanction, discipline, power obviously and ruthlessly wielded are necessary. Seth is almost an allegorical representation of Power. It is amazing, on reflection, how little we are told of Seth. Time and again we hear of his big military boots, see him in his khaki uniform, note his big hands and square fingers and hear his voice. He is almost above the struggle. He controls it. But he can rule without Mrs Tulsi no more than she can rule without him: for it is together that they fulfil the psychology of rulership.

Seth is aided in this job of preserving order by the husbands who accept their condition. The foremost of these is Govind who becomes a policeman for his master.

> He was tall and well-built and handsome though in a conventional, unremarkable way. Mr. Biswas thought it unseemly that someone so well-made should have been a coconut seller and should now do manual work in the fields. And Mr. Biswas was pained to see Govind in the presence of Seth. His handsome face became weak in every way. His eyes became small and bright and restless. He stammered and swallowed and gave nervous little laughs. (95)

Mr Biswas thought of Govind as a fellow sufferer, but one who had surrendered to the Tulsis and been degraded. Seth uses Govind to win Biswas into accepting an estate job. "'You should give up that sign-painting.... They looking for good drivers on the estate....' 'Give up sign-painting? And my independence?'" (96). Independence is the ideal which Biswas seeks, and which he equates with identity. The irony is that he will soon be behaving exactly like Govind before Seth, and that he will eventually accept an estate job.

But there is a difference between the weaknesses of the two men. Biswas continues to defy the system although circumstances force him to conform. Govind, on the other hand, beats up Biswas in order to achieve status in the eyes of the Tulsi world. It isn't that Biswas does not deserve punishment, but it is the mean way in which this punishment is administered; the way in which the weakest character aligns himself with the forces of law and order and helps teach others to conform. The children in Hanuman House are taught to ridicule the non-conformist in much the same way as creolised negro slaves were used to mock new arrivals from Africa into submission. It is worth noting, though, that Biswas wins the battle with Govind for, towards the end of the book, Govind too is a rebel of sorts. He refuses to welcome Owad when the latter returns from England; he disturbs the house by his loud unmusical singing and he comforts Biswas after the final encounter with Mrs Tulsi.

Besides Mrs Tulsi and Seth, there are the Tulsi sons, Owad and Shekar. In them, the hierarchy manifests its continuity, its indestructibility. Hierarchy is established, settled and perpetual, and the brothers-in-law accept that rebellion is physically, morally and psychologically impossible. Religious ritual, presided over by the young sons, or by Hari, the symbolically constipated negative and dying pandit, helps to seal the system together. As in slave society, the priest tightens the bonds between slave and master by inculcating a sense of moral obligation in the slave. The slave learns that his condition is divinely ordained and that rebellion is morally wrong.

Every feature of Tulsi society works towards a general end of conformity. Any sign of individualism is punished in the children by severe beating. Much is made of this ritual beating in the book, and it is illuminating to see how in this respect too Hanuman House conforms to classic slave society. Ralph Ellison shows how Southern Negroes suppress impulses of individuality in order to adjust their children to the Southern milieu. The people thus produced are termed by Ellison as "pre-individualistic", and they, in turn, perfect their elaborate defence mechanism.

Its function is dual: to protect the Negro from whirling away from the undifferentiated mass of his people into the unknown, symbolised in its most abstract form by insanity and most concretely by lynching; and to protect him from these unknown forces within himself which might urge him to reach out for that social and human equality which the white South says he cannot have. Rather than throw himself against the charged wires of his prison, he annihilates the impulses within him.

Ralph Ellison in *The Shadow and the Act* shows how:

> Even parental love is given a qualitative balance akin to "sadism." And the extent of beatings and psychological maimings meted out by Southern Negro parents rivals these described by nineteenth-century Russian writers as characteristic of peasant life under the Czars.

> The horrible thing is that the cruelty is also an expression of concern, love. (100–106)

The society of Hanuman House differs from this world in degree, but certainly not in kind. It also is pre-individualistic, and that is why Biswas's greatest crime is to have tried to be an individual. When he tries to make a sharp and complete break with Tulsidom, Biswas does go mad. Trinidad laws do not permit the Tulsis to lynch, but they do know how to commit symbolic murder. When Biswas, ignoring the pressures which the Tulsis bring to bear on the aspiring individual, gives his daughter a doll's house, he upsets the entire equilibrium of Hanuman House, and their rejoinder is to tear the doll's house apart.

> None of its parts was whole. Its delicate joints were exposed and useless. Below the torn skin of paint … the hacked and splintered wood was white and raw.… The edge of a wall scraped against his shoulder, tearing his shirt and tearing the skin below.… (197)

It is Biswas who is being torn apart, and this encounter with the full malice of the pre-individualistic world leaves him tired beyond irony, and beyond speech. "And suddenly his rage had gone. His shouts rang in his head, leaving him startled, ashamed and tired. He could think of nothing to say" (198).

This inner weariness too is a dimension of rebellion. This sudden apprehension of a silence that mocks the rhetoric of protest, and of a malice at the heart of things which paralyses both speech and pre-meditated action. The next stage is a retreat from complexity, a simplification of the issues and a blind commitment to action. Biswas lacks the strength to take this final step, and gains it only at the end of the book, when after another paralysed silence he decides to leave Hanuman House for good.

Chandra Jayawardena in his *Conflict and Solidarity on a Guianese Plantation* shows how the plantation system by requiring a large unskilled and uneducated labour force leads to egalitarianism of the underprivileged. The result of this is continual social conflict, which is most pronounced whenever anyone through industry, craft or thrift lifts himself a little above the rest of the community. Then complex feuds arise with almost ritual quarrelling in which the slighted party is really appealing to the solidarity of the group to join him in censure of the social climber. Biswas's experience of Hanuman House then is a more extreme version of what is still happening in those large segments of West Indian society where the patterns imposed by a plantation system still retain their strength and form.

It is, therefore, possible to see his rebellion, grotesque and strange as it is, as a paradigm of the perennial West Indian struggle for a more truly democratic society.

The nature of Biswas's rebellion is determined by his character, which, as we have noted, is saturated with the wit and irony of Trinidad speech. The Tulsis refer to Biswas as "creole"—which is the worst insult they know. "I hear they have made some creole converts. Brothers for you, Mohun!" (107). Throughout the book, Biswas rebels through the use of good, bad and sick humour, sarcasm, mamaguy. But the Tulsis come to regard his rebellion as a joke and accept him as a licensed buffoon, thereby, neutralising the effect of his wit. Like the traditional Negro comedian, Biswas is allowed to make those jokes which affirm his self-contempt and strengthen and justify the stereotype which his masters have created of him.

Yet, in the early stages of revolt, before the Tulsis learn that the best way to contain the rebel is to convert rebellion into a joke, Biswas's wit wins him temporary emancipation from Hanuman House. The Tulsis send him to the Chase to run a Tulsi shop, though there are several similar shops in that little village. It is a dubious sort of independence, given in conditions which guarantee failure. Biswas discovers that the task of changing from irony to construction, from the rhetoric of rebellion to the silent prosaic act of independence, is beyond him. In fact, he doesn't even know what to make of his freedom.

> How lonely the shop was! And how frightening! He had never thought it would be like this when he found himself in an establishment of his own. It was late afternoon; Hanuman House would be warm and noisy with activity. Here he was afraid to disturb the silence, afraid to open the door of the shop, to step into the light. (130)

Independence is a decaying rusty shop, with fly-blown groceries in a backward antediluvian village, where many other such shops are competing for the same customers. Moreover, the shop belongs to the colonisers, who have perfected the tradition of absenteeism and have learnt how to be invisible while they continue exploitation. So Biswas achieves only age in his six years of independence and has to return to Hanuman House for comfort and sanity, and for a definition of identity and status. He still judges himself for the most part by their standards and is grateful now for their good opinion.

His is the rebellion of the small, the weak, the acculturated. But his quest is nonetheless worthwhile. At the start, he tries to convert the rank and file of the Tulsis to his cause, since he instinctively realises that he isn't really at odds with them. He tries to convince people like Govind that his fight is really theirs, and his revolt the one they should be making themselves, until individual struggle broadens into revolution; for Biswas is possessed with the idea that every man should enjoy what Dostoevsky's Lebyadk in *The Possessed* considers the minimal right—the right to a cover over one's head. But the pre-individualistic Tulsis cannot recognise the value for which Biswas fights.

It is only when the Tulsi hierarchy begins to crumble that they rebel. Shekar, the elder son, marries. Owad, the younger, is in England. Seth quarrels with Mrs Tulsi; Hari, the pandit, dies. Autocracy has collapsed and so rebellion becomes possible. What follows is a general anarchic scrambling for wealth and power, the revolution of a rabble who have gained individuality without direction. The purity of motive and truth to instinct and necessity which marked Biswas's struggle against an apparently indestructible system make his rebellion an affirmation of universal values; this transforms it from being a sordid personal struggle to one undertaken on behalf of the group. Biswas doesn't know this, engaged as he is in the fight for a house; the Tulsis don't know it, engaged as they are in teaching their children to conform and mock at the rebel. It is not surprising, then, that, with the return of Owad, the sisters willingly return to the old system, the old ritual, the old death-in-life. The crowning irony is that when Biswas does gain his house, it is irretrievably mortgaged to his uncle Ajodha. To escape bondage to his wife's family, he is forced to enslave himself to his own. The absurd situation is worked out to the end, which suggests no resolution of the problems posed by the book, but a further vista into futility and rebellion.

No one can deny the danger of regarding Biswas as a figure representative of the Caribbean predicament. He is so strongly individual, and his limitations so grave. Moreover, if he resembles some of the grotesques of Dickens, he has been created by a writer who has a more contemporary sense of the themes of void, loneliness, meaninglessness and absurdity, so prevalent in modern European literature. Biswas's nowhereness may be something much more universal. Yet, as we have seen, he is representative enough of our local predicament: a man without a past, an orphan wavering between equally dubious cultural alternatives; winning a sort of independence and returning in humiliation to the people he is still forced to fight; turning anxiety into absurdity by using humour as a weapon and an escape; trying to create an identity from the void, and, sometimes, unknown to himself, exercising and expressing identity in the very act of searching for it.

Works Cited

Conrad, Joseph. *Heart of Darkness*. Signet Classics, 2008.

Dostoevsky, Fyodor. *The Possessed.* Barnes and Nobles Classics, 2004.

Eliot, T. S. *The Waste Land*, edited by Michael North, Norton Critical Editions, 2000.

Ellison, Ralph. *The Shadow and the Act*. Vintage, 1995.

Jayawardena, Chandra. *Conflict and Solidarity on a Guianese Plantation*. The Humanities Press, 1963.

Memmi, Albert. *The Colonizer and the Colonized.* 1974. Beacon Press, 1991.

Spilka, Mark. "The Necessary Stylist: A New Critical Revision." *Modern Fiction Studies*, vol. 6, no. 4, 1960, pp. 283–298.

Chapter 11

THE IMPLICATIONS OF TRANSTEXTUALITY IN V. S. NAIPAUL'S *THE MIDDLE PASSAGE: THE CARIBBEAN REVISITED*[1]

Zuzana Klímová Kršková

Sir Vidiadhar Surajprasad Naipaul—a Trinidad-born, British essayist, novelist and a Nobel Prize winner for literature—is often criticised, as Patrick French says, for "turning his back on his native land" or for siding with the imperial system according to postcolonial scholars (King 2008). After the publication of *The Middle Passage*, Naipaul attracted severe criticism for his allegedly offending re(-)presentation of societies described in the book.[2] The major controversy arose over Naipaul's choice of transtextual references—epigraphs and in-text quotations by Anthony Trollope, James Anthony Froude and Charles Kingsley who are usually categorised as representatives of high imperialism. Because of the sensitivity of the topic of the relationship between coloniser and colonised in a postcolonial context, Naipaul's decision to include passages by the "Victorian trio" aroused a lot of discussion about his cultural and social affiliations (Feder 89). Derek Walcott even accused him of perceiving the West Indies through "Victorian spectacles" (Walcott 18).

In this chapter, I would like to consider the complexity of the implications arising from transtextual references in *The Middle Passage* and argue against the simplistic views which denounce the text as pro-colonial. In order to open up the possibility of this wider interpretation

1 "The Implications of Transtextuality" in V. S. Naipaul's *The Middle Passage: The Caribbean Revisited* was originally published in Acta Universitatis Wratislaviensis, No. 3501, *Anglica Wratislaviensia* 51, pp. 19–23.

2 "re(-)present" is written in this way to show the double meaning of the term combining both Spivak's concepts of representation as *Vertretung* and *Darstellung*.

of the work, it is necessary to include other peritextual[3] and intertextual elements within the text in the analysis of *The Middle Passage*. For example, the frequent allusions to, or direct quotes from, authors such as James Joyce, Publius Cornelius Tacitus and Thomas Mann are usually ignored by Naipaul's critics. The quotes by Tacitus and Thomas Mann represent valuable sources that place the issue of colonialism into a worldwide context and show the British colonial influence in the West Indies as only a part of a greater scheme of power struggles whose victors and victims often interchange their roles.

In so doing, the chapter is intended to show the multifarious implications of Naipaul's book by considering his involved and highly personal approach to the creative process of writing from the point of view of a writer raised within a colonial society, whose primary loyalty is neither to the empire nor to the newly independent state, but above all to the individual conscience of the independent writer. Although such an approach to literature may be problematic in the political context of the postcolonial era, it can be perceived as a way towards true creative freedom, and as a means of breaking out of the vicious circle of either imitative (mimicking) or nationally oriented literatures typical of developing postcolonial cultures.

The Middle Passage was published in 1962—the same year that Trinidad and Tobago gained independence. Moreover, the idea of writing the book did not originate in Naipaul's mind. It was C. L. R. James who had suggested to Dr Eric Williams—the Premier of Trinidad and Tobago—that Naipaul was a suitable candidate for the writing of a non-fiction book about the Caribbean. James was sure that

> both the West Indies and its brilliant novelist would benefit from [Naipaul's] return to the region. The islands would benefit from Naipaul's critical insight into their history, identity and efforts at building new nations, while Naipaul himself would be rescued from alienation through a re-acquaintance with his origins. (James qtd. in Rohlehr)[4]

---

3 Genette calls epigraphs an example of "peritext"—textual elements such as titles, chapter titles, prefaces and notes. Together with "epitext" (interviews, private letters and other authorial and editorial discussion outside of the text) peritext forms the "paratext"—elements at the threshold of the text "which help to direct and control the reception of a text by its readers" (Allen 103).

4 Despite James's hopes, Naipaul was not "rescued", and it is emblematic of the perception of Naipaul's work that James should become one of Naipaul's critics after his expectations were not fulfilled. He says about Naipaul that he "is saying what the whites want to say, but dare not. They have put him up to it" (French 245).

Naipaul himself expressed doubts about the project. He openly admits in the foreword to *The Middle Passage* that he hesitated at first about whether to accept the offer. He had never written such a work before and felt constraints not present when writing fiction. His comments show a deep sense of unease as well as his awareness of possible expectations that might be aroused by a book whose writing was supported (including financial support) by the Government of Trinidad and Tobago and whose publication coincided with the achievement of political independence by Trinidad and Tobago. Under the turbulent political and cultural circumstances of the time, Naipaul assumed heavy personal responsibility concerning the effect the book might produce in the postcolonial societies of the Caribbean.

Accepting the challenge and the responsibility to write a non-fiction book about the newly emerging societies, the writer might have felt obligations towards the country in which he was born and which was now struggling to become fully independent not only politically, but also culturally. Naipaul seems to have decided not to follow the typical framework of national or anti-colonial works. To justify his approach to the material, he makes it explicit in the foreword that, although he got the idea from Williams, *The Middle Passage* "is in no way … an 'official' book. It sells nothing" (6). With the publication of *The Middle Passage,* however, it was clear that there had been a great discrepancy between the expectations of the postcolonial community about which he wrote and the author's own perceptions. The greatest challenge to these expectations appeared in the form of intertextual and peritextual references in the form of in-text quotations and epigraphs[5] from the well-known texts by the Victorian trio. These quotes outraged many postcolonial scholars, including Said, and many local ones, including Walcott.

Arguably, the possible reasons for including Froude's, Trollope's and Kingsley's texts in the non-fictional account dealing with the newly independent postcolonial country can be sought in Naipaul's own cultural and social background that gave rise to his very own peculiar understanding and experience of the postcolonial world in which the colonisers' accounts of the Caribbean society and history play an undeniable role. Trinidad's multiculturalism, which he experienced growing up, as well as his immigrant European experience clearly had a significant impact on the development of his worldview as well as

5 Epigraph is understood here specifically as "a quotation set at the beginning of a literary work or one of its divisions to suggest its theme" (*Merriam Webster*).

his approach to writing. In the circumstances of the 1960s, the role of the author within postcolonial societies had become complicated and it would have been difficult to stay detached from the political struggle. Naipaul seems to have chosen to be neither objective nor politically involved. Instead, his writing reflects his attempts to stay true to himself as an author who feels that the greatest need in West Indian society is individual acceptance of responsibility for his/her own life as inevitably connected to his/her colonial past.

Lloyd King is obviously of a similar view since he describes him as a writer who "felt that ethnic writing was a trap [offering] the temptations of facility and ephemeral solace.... His role would be to [scandalise] the English liberal establishment and the new black/African nationalisms." Naipaul, he claims, was determined to follow "a Conradian code: to be an accurate and unflinching observer with an absolute loyalty to his feelings and sensations". Naipaul himself continues to reveal an open distrust of ethnic writing. This is evident up to his much later works such as *The Enigma of Arrival* (1987). In his books, Naipaul strives to create "a synthesis of the worlds and cultures that had made [him]". He admits that separating those worlds would be easier, "but [he] felt it false to the nature of [his] experience" (Ray 113).

These views stand in contrast to Walcott's opinion of Naipaul wearing "Victorian spectacles" and denying the country of his birth (18). Although Naipaul is not very optimistic about the state in which he finds most postcolonial societies in the Caribbean, he does not simply prefer the colonial system. In fact, throughout his work, it is apparent that what he fears is that refusal to come to terms with the colonial past and its influence on the contemporary world can only hinder the already-arduous creation of independent postcolonial identities. In fact, many other Caribbean postcolonial writers and thinkers, such as Samuel Selvon, Wilson Harris and even their predecessor Frantz Fanon, see purely nationalistic works as directly reflecting the colonial order, if only in its reverse form. By ignoring the continuing presence of colonial influence in the institutions and strategies of development in the newly independent countries, nations merely recreate the oppressive power structures that nationalism was meant to destroy.

The presence of texts that come from the European literary canon in *The Middle Passage* certainly ensconces it not only in the context of Caribbean social circumstances but also in the literary history in which Naipaul is writing. The combination characterises the interwoven origins of present-day Caribbean societies. Complete exclusion of the imperial accounts would have had a similar effect on the final work as taking them for absolute authority. Any of the polarisations would have been unjust to the complicated West Indian experience in which

Naipaul shares. He is, therefore, inevitably emotionally involved, but he tries nonetheless to remain an exceptionally open and attentive observer interested in various points of view. He, therefore, rejects the position of the falsely objective historiographer of the European tradition as well as the blinded unilateral nationalist view.

It is, hence, most useful to conceive of Naipaul as a pedantic hardworking writer unsure of his own abilities, position or authority as an author, especially if one were to read *The Middle Passage* alongside his later memoir *Finding the Centre* and other creative works of non-fiction. In books like these, Naipaul drew not only on his personal experience but also undertook thorough research into existing accounts of the West Indies in order to add authority to his own work. The sources of authority were available only in the types of works that postcolonial scholars have condemned, in the works of Trollope, Froude and Kingsley, among others, who had visited the West Indies and whose texts had been considered for a long time to be the primary sources of evidence about the political and cultural situation in the region. Indeed, their travel books still represent some of the most reliable sources of information about the colonial period in the West Indies. In spite of the cultural biases and stereotypical views present in them, they provide significant evidence of the whole colonial system.

By including them in his book, Naipaul casts a new light on the understanding of these texts as testimonies of their age and, as Mohit Kumar Ray observes, manages to interlace "first-hand observation and commentary with references to the earlier authorities", thus, avoiding what would otherwise inevitably result in "naïve empiricism" (181). Reading of these "earlier authorities" within the postcolonial cultural context allows Naipaul deeper insight into the issues postcolonial societies are facing in the new phase of nationalist existence.

To contradict the simplistic "pro-imperial" interpretation of passages quoted within *The Middle Passage*, and to indicate the complexity of their transtextual relations, I will try to place the examples of texts chosen by Naipaul within their wider literary and social context. This approach will be used to show the possibility of reading the "colonial texts" as highly relevant and helpful works supporting the struggle for cultural independence to which Naipaul contributed despite what many consider his pessimistic vision and what Bowe calls "an almost brutally frank analysis".

The first epigraph in *The Middle Passage* that illustrates this situation well is taken from James Anthony Froude's *The English in the West Indies* (1888). It describes the West Indians as people who "were valued only for the wealth which they yielded, and society there has never assumed any particularly noble aspect ... there are no people there in the true sense of the word, with a character and purpose of their own" (*The Middle Passage* 7). Given that it introduces the whole book, the position of this epigraph suggests its importance within the rest of the text immediately.

But precisely because this passage can so obviously be interpreted as a criticism of the West Indians, we must consider simultaneously that it is highly unlikely that a person of Naipaul's background would be likely to deal with this material in a light-hearted and simplistic manner. Certainly, throughout *The Middle Passage* and in other books he has written we have evidence that Naipaul is severely critical of the colonial education system and European versions of the history of the region. Naipaul would also have been aware of the possible reactions of the audience to such a statement and yet he deliberately foregrounded it, thus, confounding the expectation of the reader. More importantly, we should observe that it is also the context that gives full meaning to the quotation itself. Considered independently, the passage sounds highly pro-colonial but placed back within the original text of *The English in the West Indies*, the overall understanding of the work itself easily changes.

Froude's account describes the situation as follows:

> It is strange to think how chequered a history these islands have had, how far they are even yet from any condition which promises performance. Not one of them has arrived at any stable independence. Spaniards, English and French, Dutch and Danes scrambled for them, occupied them more or less with their own people, but it was not to found new nations, but to get gold or get something which could be changed for gold … and heroic deeds were done there, but it was by adventurers who were in search of plunder for themselves. France and England fought among the Antilles, and their names are connected with many gallant actions; but they fought for the sovereignty of the seas, not for the rights and liberties of the French or English inhabitants of the islands. Instead of occupying them with free inhabitants, the European nations filled them with slave gangs. They were valued only for the wealth which they yielded. (306)

This passage does not criticise the colonised people, but is aimed rather at the colonial system that valued the people "only for the wealth they yielded". Although Froude shares many stereotypes about the colonised nations like the rest of his generation, his work is not without interest to the voices oppositional to the imperial order. Claudia Brandenstein reacts in a similar way to Charles Kingsley's *At Last: A Christmas in the West Indies* (1871). She says that it "is not the type of bedtime story that

Britain wants to tell itself, since in this text Britain is not fully figured as triumphant victor; its author is much too ambivalent towards the stock representations of colonialism popular at the time" (15). The ambivalent perception of these texts is a reaction to their symbolic value for they refer to the colonial enterprise with shame and ignorance on one side, and feelings of victimisation, hatred and disillusionment on the other. The topic is universally ambiguous and the imperial texts arouse consciousness and mixed emotions on both sides of the coloniser-colonised continuum. Naipaul seems to be aware of the potential of these texts to force readers to question stereotypes.

Like Froude's epigraph, the one by Anthony Trollope is also only intelligible within a wider context (this time mostly the context of the chapter it precedes). In 1860, Trollope describes then British Guiana as "the Elysium of the Tropics—the West Indian happy valley of Rasselas—the one true and actual Utopia of the Caribbean Seas—the Transatlantic Eden" (*The Middle Passage* 92). This "imperial introduction" is followed by Naipaul's description of the visit he paid to British Guiana. He sees some of the beautiful parts of the interior with their plateaus and waterfalls—"the lost world of Conan Doyle" (*The Middle Passage* 155)—but also the conflicts of "the society of six races", which contradicts the "paradisiacal proclamations" by juxtaposing them with the "subsequent documentation of the poverty, racial divisions, dependency, and political frustration prevalent in each society" (Strachan 157). Naipaul is clearly conscious of the remnants of three hundred years of extremely brutal slavery and the felt absence of the aboriginal Amerindians.

Naipaul's experience is, thus, a contrasting (re)interpretation of what Trollope described, and recognises it as one that is filled with understanding for an idealistic vision of a short-term visitor unaffected by the experience of longer residence in the colony. No matter how outdated this vision may seem, it represents one of the prominent images of the Caribbean held by the outside world up to today. Throughout *The Middle Passage*, this myth of the terrestrial paradise appears repeatedly as Naipaul travels throughout the Caribbean and sees the damage this myth imposes on the duality of the image that is now supported by the West Indians themselves in order to lure the tourists.

Charles Kingsley was also just a short-term visitor who saw in the Caribbean a terrestrial paradise. His letters, written during his 1870s journey to the West Indies and later published as *At Last: A Christmas in the West Indies*, share many of Trollope's positive views about the region. In spite of his overall positive impression, Kingsley saw quite clearly the negative sides of the colonial society and the effects of colonial rule. Like Froude in *The English in the West Indies*, Kingsley admits the dubious nature of the influence the British have had on the development of West Indian society. The intertextual reference chosen by Naipaul deals with the issue of "continual pilfering" (Kingsley) of material for the construction of houses by the black population:[6]

> On inquiry I found that the materials were, in most cases, stolen; that when a Negro wanted to build a house, instead of buying the materials, he pilfered a board here, a stick there, a nail somewhere else ... regardless of the serious injury which he caused to working buildings; and when he had gathered a sufficient pile, hidden safely away behind his neighbour's house, the new hut rose as if by magic. (*The Middle Passage* 78)

Were it not for the paragraph that follows, like Froude (and consecutively Naipaul), Kingsley would be easily read as the true pro-imperialist writer, the unconditional defender of colonial stereotypes. Kingsley, however, looks into the causes of such common practices. He offers a confession of a gentleman: "the very gentleman who complained" that this habit was simply an heirloom from the bad days of slavery, when the pilfering of the slaves from other estates was connived at by their own masters, on the ground that if A's Negroes robbed B, B's Negroes robbed C and so all round the alphabet; one more evil instance of the demoralising effect of a state of things which, wrong in itself, was sure to be the parent of a hundred other wrongs (*The Middle Passage* 78).

Kingsley foregrounds the moral decline of society as one of the most profound effects of colonialism. I have chosen one more paragraph from Kingsley's work to illustrate how complex his attitude towards colonised society and its relationship to the coloniser was. Despite the disillusioning experiences that I have just mentioned, in the following paragraph, he openly expresses his opinion of the black West Indians and their capability to actively participate in the creation and maintenance of culture.

> The West Indian peasant can, if he will, carry "la petite Culture" to a perfection and a wealth which it has not yet attained even in China,

---

6 The in-text quotation by Kingsley appears in the chapter on Trinidad, which is introduced by two epigraphs—by Thomas Mann and Tacitus. Both epigraphs, which are discussed later in the text, share the topic of the impact of cultural colonisation on everyday lives and rootlessness of the colonised, which is also present in Kingsley's text.

> Japan, and Hindostan, and make every rood of ground not merely maintain its man, but its civilised man. This, however, will require a skill and a thoughtfulness which the Negro does not as yet possess. If he ever had them, he lost them under slavery, from the brutalising effects of a rough and unscientific 'grande culture;' and it will need several generations of training ere he recovers them. (Kingsley 1871)

Although the majority of these assumptions about the skills and wit of the black population are in accord with the stereotypical ideas of the Victorian era, he also admits that no matter what the skills of "the West Indian peasant" were (or were not), the insensitive imposition of the "grande culture" would have inevitably led to their moral and cultural disintegration. Naipaul connects this subversive effect of the imposed social order to the loss of dignity and any sense of loyalty people might feel to their native country (*The Middle Passage* 78).

By acknowledging the complicity of the imperial power on the moral as well as cultural deterioration of the West Indian community, Kingsley gives Naipaul an important tool in the struggle for an independent postcolonial expression, because his writing (as well as those of Trollope and Froude) reflects the doubts coming from the heart of colonial power itself. Lillian Feder in *Naipaul's Truth: The Making of a Writer* asks whether it is not possible to interpret the quotations by the Victorian authors as Naipaul's way to "[introduce] a book on the rapaciousness and arrogance of the colonizers with the evidence of their own words" (89). I believe that Naipaul goes even further because the texts he chose not only represent the colonial past of the West Indies and the effects it has had on its development, but they also illustrate the considerable doubts about the system on the part of the colonial writers themselves.

Presenting the canonical figures of Trollope, Froude and Kingsley in an unexpected position opens new possibilities of reading and understanding their works within the new contexts of a postcolonial world. The transtextuality of their works in relation to Naipaul's is enriched by myriad new implications. Texts that were earlier associated only with the authority of the coloniser and the success of the civilising mission begin to allude more clearly to the seedier sides of history showing the less positive effects of colonisation during the period when it was actually in effect. Acceptance of responsibility by the colonising power (or its representatives) for the detrimental effects it had on the colonised societies can be crucial for the evolution of an independent postcolonial society. If only because of this, the postcolonial needs to come to terms with its past. Naipaul is in effect saying that in order to achieve cultural independence, postcolonial societies must accept

Western tradition as one of the aspects of its own tradition which enhances its richness rather than constricts or subjugates it.

The connotations that arise from reading these Victorian works in the context of *The Middle Passage* and against the historical and social background of the 1960s are further multiplied by parallels Naipaul draws between the colonisation of the West Indies by the British and that undertaken by other nations from earlier periods of history—particularly the Roman conquest of Britannia. He is suggesting in other words that to understand the question of an unconsciously accepted cultural colonialism as only a West Indian reality would be a mistake. Evidence of a similar kind of colonialism can be found in the former British Empire and Naipaul is not afraid to reveal it.

In the first part of my analysis of Naipaul's text, I said that the criticism of *The Middle Passage* is built mostly around the "Victorian trio" formed by Trollope, Kingsley and Froude. However, although they form an extremely important thought-provoking nucleus of the book, attention should not be concentrated solely on them, because the impact of the rich transtextuality of *The Middle Passage* would be significantly weakened by this simplification. Among the peritextual references throughout *The Middle Passage*, we can also find epigraphs by James Joyce, Thomas Mann and Publius Cornelius Tacitus.

Tacitus (56–120 AD) is one of the greatest historians and prose stylists of the Roman Empire. His epigraph comes from a biographical note about his father-in-law and the governor of Britannia—Agricola. Tacitus describes Agricola's campaign to Britannia with admirable insight. Naipaul's work, thus, moves the modern coloniser into the inverse position of the colonised, a fact often forgotten by postcolonial critics. To introduce the nexus of the passage chosen by Naipaul, I start below with parts from *Agricola* describing the people of Britannia and their position within the Roman Empire:

> Who were the original inhabitants of Britain, whether they were indigenous or foreign, is as usual among barbarians, little known.... The Britons, however, exhibit more spirit, as being a people whom a long peace has not yet enervated. Indeed we have understood that even the Gauls were once renowned in war; but, after a while, sloth following on ease crept over them, and they lost their courage along with their freedom. This too has happened to the long-conquered tribes of Britain; the rest are still what the Gauls once were.... The Britons themselves bear cheerfully the conscription, the taxes, and the other burdens imposed on them by the Empire, if there be no oppression. Of this they are impatient; they are reduced to subjection, not as yet to slavery. (Tacitus 11–13)

These descriptions conspicuously resemble the colonial imagery of the West Indies ranging from the accounts by Sir Walter Raleigh in his *Discovery of Guiana* to the Victorian trio discussed above. The population is seen as barbarian and primitive. The passage which was chosen by Naipaul focuses openly on "cultural colonialism", which has similarly severely impacted societies as direct political supremacy.

> In place of distaste for the Latin language came a passion to command it. In the same way, our national dress came into favour and the toga was everywhere to be seen. And so the Britons were gradually led on to the amenities that make vice agreeable – arcades, baths and sumptuous banquets. They spoke of such novelties as "civilization", when really they were only a feature of enslavement. (*The Middle Passage* 42)

Within the framework of the whole book this quotation is crucial. It reveals the multiplicity of views considered by Naipaul. His perception is not only regional but international. Naipaul's references to Tacitus evoke, in certain respects, *Heart of Darkness* where Joseph Conrad compares European expansion in Africa to the Roman colonisation of Europe. Moreover, one of Conrad's passages on the Roman colonisation is almost identical in its tone to the first quote by Froude, which describes the ruthlessness of the conquerors. Conrad describes the Romans as conquerors who

> grabbed what they could get for the sake of what was to be got. It was just robbery and violence, aggravated murder on a great scale.... The conquest of the earth, which mostly means the taking it away from those who have a different complexion or slightly flatter noses than ourselves, is not a pretty thing when you look into it too much. What redeems it is the idea only. (7)

Agricola shows the British in the same position as Trollope, Kingsley and Froude show the West Indians. Such a transtextual link allows Naipaul to connect the events of the 1960s (and recent past) to world history. *Agricola*, which presents British history from the then coloniser's point of view (showing the well-known coloniser as the subject), demonstrates the instability of authority which claims credibility for itself only. Such a juxtaposition, comprehensible for all parts involved, can bring societies closer to mutual understanding.

Naipaul goes even further with the second quote that accompanies Tacitus's *Agricola* as the introduction to the chapter about Trinidad. It is taken from Thomas Mann's *The Tables of the Law* from the Joseph series. Through the Biblical story of Joseph, Naipaul presents one of the oldest stories of subjection—that of the Israelites in Egypt—which represents a classical myth of Christian faith, and through that one of the roots of Western cultural tradition. The example helps Naipaul to deconstruct the image of a dominating Western colonial order. Both Tacitus's and Mann's examples help to widen the scope of transtextual implications present in *The Middle Passage*. They contradict the narrow interpretation of the work as openly pro-colonial. It is highly unlikely that Naipaul would have used these passages, if he wanted, as Rob Nixon says, to "promote racist and colonial prejudices" (*Naipaul's Truth* 89).

Thomas Mann is closer to Naipaul's view also because he was himself a writer in exile who felt the threat of the rise of fascism during the Weimar Republic—an ideology that proved to be one of the severest suppressive forces of the twentieth century. Moreover, to some degree, Mann also might have shared the racial awareness of many postcolonials through the origins of his mother who was born in Rio de Janeiro as the daughter of a German plantation owner and a Portuguese-Creole Brazilian. By stretching the topic out of the borders of the West Indies, Naipaul adds power to his work in his struggle to free it from the bondage of nationality and ethnicity. He shares King's idea that the basis for an independent society can be built neither on African or Indian or any other ethnic roots, nor on the mimicry of the coloniser's traditions.

The last epigraph that will be discussed in this chapter comments on the tormenting uncertainty of the writer about the language of the coloniser he adopts and the limitations it imposes on the work as well as the author. The epigraph that introduces the chapter on Surinam is taken from James Joyce's *A Portrait of the Artist as a Young Man*—a work by the well-known Irish author, exile and rebel against the traditional notions of nationalism and religion. In some respects, Stephen Dedalus—the main character of Joyce's novel—reflects Naipaul's own position within the colonial system and the "alienation from the traditional voices of authority in his life" ("James Joyce"). The historical struggle of Ireland against English domination portrays itself in the personal struggles of the hero. As Foley says, *A Portrait of the Artist as a Young Man* is not, however, "a story of revolutionary politics but of the quiet but dogged rebellion of a young man in search of his artistic voice". In both Joyce's and Naipaul's work the importance of the individual artistic voice is stressed over the escapism which can be temporarily found in nationalism, but which is nonetheless doomed to failure when adopted as the voice in which the writer speaks. Stephen's struggle begins early. For example, when he locates his place in the scheme of things in the following way: "I am Stephen Dedalus. I am walking beside my father whose name is Simon Dedalus. We are in Cork, in Ireland. Cork is a city. Our room is in the Victoria Hotel. Victoria and Stephen and Simon. Simon and Stephen and Victoria. Names" (16). The excerpt from Joyce's novel also deals with the problem of language imposition—a problem often found in the postcolonial context because the language brought by the coloniser "is his before it is mine" and such language cannot be spoken or written "without unrest of spirit" (*The Middle Passage* 179). When analysing Joyce's text in terms of anxiety for Ireland and its language, Declan Kiberd points out that although Joyce did not try to use Irish as a medium for his writing, he was deeply concerned with the transtextual echoes of writing in the language of the oppressor, which preserve the experiences of cultural dominance (*Inventing Ireland* 330–332).

West Indian authors also have to face the question of language imposition by the dominant discourse. Their position is, however, different in several respects. The most significant one is the geographical and cultural displacement of the language and literary tradition into a context in which it can be inauthentic. In his famous essay "Jasmine", Naipaul reveals the now classic symptoms of postcolonial writing. In *The Empire Writes Back*, this is expressed in the following terms, "[T] he experience of place and the language available to describe it forms a classic and all-pervasive feature of post-colonial texts" (*The Empire Writes Back* 9). Ireland, despite its long history of oppression by the English, still possesses strong links to its authentic language, and considerable homogeneity of its society (as far as the idea of self-identification with an ethnic group is concerned). The same is not true of the West Indies.

Ashcroft talks about a "permanently bifurcated situation" (*Key Concepts* 74), which, I believe, accurately describes the Irish position with "the continued opposition of the two discourses, ... their obsession with nationalism, [and] their unresolved passion for 'identity'" (*The Empire Writes Back* 74). The situation in the West Indies differs, with respect to language, especially in the absence of the one "original" language that has been forcefully substituted by the colonial code. Therefore, in contrast to Joyce's claim that the language "is [the coloniser's] before it is mine" (Joyce qtd. in *The Middle Passage* 179), Naipaul carefully states in his essay "Jasmine" that "the English language was [his]; the tradition was not" (26).

The cultural multifariousness of West Indian society played an important role in the development of specific forms of appropriation of language and literary tradition. As Ashcroft notes, by such appropriation, "the dominant language and its discursive forms [become capable of expressing] widely differing cultural experiences, and [interpolating] these experiences into the dominant modes of representation to reach the widest possible audience" (*Key Concepts* 19). I understand Naipaul's use of transtextual references as an example of such appropriation of dominant discourses by which he resists cultural colonialism.

Naipaul is the author who is able to come to terms with the problematic past—including the bitterness and disenchantment it brought. Gordon Rohlehr believes that Naipaul opposes, through his choice of literary inspiration and style, the stereotype of the postcolonial author. He refuses to be placed within a particular political and cultural situation, because such an approach would reduce the complexity of his attitude ("Confessional Element"). Although it is his own postcolonial background that provides Naipaul with the topics he deals with, and that gives him what Joseph Epstein calls a "racially secured licence" to criticise the Western as well as West Indian society, it is especially his individual approach to the literary material and his strong sense of personal responsibility to writing that allow him to transgress the limitations of cultural colonialism.[7] With the help of intertextual and peritextual references within *The Middle Passage,* Naipaul widens the scope of interpretation of the topics he discusses. The juxtaposition of similar events that appear throughout the history of humankind can help to reduce the feeling of anxiety experienced by the colonised. Through this creative approach to literature and the material he deals with it is possible to overcome the feeling of fear and shame of the past so typical of the West Indies (*The Middle Passage* 201).

Conclusion

Naipaul is surely a controversial author within the multicultural society of the contemporary literary world. In his works, he often criticises developing postcolonial societies, including his native Trinidad, as well as the colonial system. *The Middle Passage* belongs among his most criticised works for its alleged pro-colonial views. One of the most problematic and provoking characteristics of *The Middle Passage* is Naipaul's employment of transtextuality with his special focus on works of the Victorian icons—Froude, Trollope and Kingsley. Another aspect that contributes significantly to the interpretative ambivalence of this work is the fact that the original idea for writing a non-fiction book about the Caribbean came from the Trinidadian Premier

7 Epstein openly says that Naipaul "[only] can say things that ... in the mouths of others would straightaway be declared racism" (Gandhi 2005).

Dr Williams. Although Naipaul accepted the offer to produce such a text about a region striving for independence, it does not represent the type of postcolonial texts expected in the 1960s which were dominated by anti-colonial attitudes.

Naipaul had to face severe criticism from postcolonial scholars like Edward Said and Derek Walcott for some of his equivocal points of view. He was reproached for his attitudes towards the former British Empire and his alleged denial of his own community. But to explore Naipaul's ambivalent standpoint, it is necessary to consider the role and obligations (if any) of the writer within a wider multicultural community and to note that Naipaul refuses to retreat into the seeming stability of nationalism. Instead, he sticks to his personal views no matter how pessimistic or controversial they are. His highly emotional and daring account of the world is first and foremost a personal perception ignoring social expectations of either side of the postcolonial world. Looking more thoroughly and at a wider textual and historical context on his transtextual references in *The Middle Passage*, we can see this work as a valuable contribution to postcolonial literature which goes beyond the restricted point of view of either the formerly colonised or the colonising.

Works Cited

Allen, Graham. *Intertextuality*. Routledge, 2000.

Ashcroft, Bill, G. Griffiths, and H. Tiffin. *The Empire Writes Back*. Routledge, 2002.

———. *Key Concepts in Post-colonial Studies*. 1998. Routledge, 2001.

Bowe, Derek C. "The Caribbean through European Eyes: V. S. Naipaul's *The Middle Passage*." 2010. http://www.oakwood.edu. Accessed on 14 September 2012.

Brandenstein, Claudia. "Imperial Positions in Charles Kingsley's *At Last: A Christmas in the West Indies*". *Span*: *Journal of the South Pacific Association for Commonwealth Literature and Language Studies*, vol. 46, 1998, pp. 4–18.

Conrad, Joseph. *Heart of Darkness*. 1902. Hesperus Classics, 2002.

Feder, Lillian. *Naipaul's Truth: The Making of a Writer*. Rowman and Littlefield, 2001.

Foley, Barbara. "James Joyce *A Portrait of the Artist as a Young Man*: Stephen Dedalus - Rebel Without a Cause?." 2005. http://www.literature-study-online.com. Accessed on 15 September 2012.

French, Patrick. *The World Is What It Is: The Authorised Biography of V. S. Naipaul.* Alfred A. Knopf, 2008.

Froude, James A. *The English in the West Indies, or the Bow of Ulysses*. 1888. Green. http://www.archive.org. Accessed on 16 September 2012.

Gandhi, Leela. "A Complicated Occidentalism: Colonial Desire and Disappointment in V. S. Naipaul". *International Interdisciplinary Conference Occidentalism*. 2005. http://www.bulgc18.com. Accessed on 16 September 2012.

Kiberd, Declan. *Inventing Ireland: The Literature of the Modern Nation*. Vintage Books, 1996.

King, Lloyd. "Review: *The World Is What It Is: The Authorised Biography of V. S. Naipaul* By Patrick French." *Trinidad and Tobago Review*, 2008. <http://www.tntreview.com>. Accessed on 16 September 2012.

Kingsley, Charles. *At Last: A Christmas in the West Indies*. 1871. Project Guttenberg eBook, 2004. http://www.gutenberg.org. Accessed on 17 January 2011.

Mann, Thomas. "Thomas Mann - Autobiography." 1929. *Nobel Lectures, Literature 1901–1967*, edited by Horst Frenz, Elsevier Publishing Company, 1969. http://nobelprize.org. Accessed on 23 November 2010.

Naipaul, V. S. *Finding the Centre: Two Narratives*. Penguin, 1984.

———. "Jasmine." *The Overcrowded Barracoon*. Vintage Books, 1984.

———. *The Middle Passage: The Caribbean Revisited*. 1962. Penguin Books, 1975.

Ray, Mohit K. *V. S. Naipaul: Critical Essays*. Atlantic, 2007.

Rohlehr, Gordon. "The Confessional Element in Naipaul's Fiction." *Anthurium: A Caribbean Studies Journal*, vol. 5, issue 2, 2007. http://anthurium.miami.edu. Accessed on 16 September 2012.

"Stephen Dedalus." 2010. *Encyclopædia Britannica* Online. http://www.britannica.com. Accessed on 16 September 2012.

Strachan, Iain. G. *Paradise and Plantation: Tourism and Culture in the Anglophone Caribbean*. U of Virginia P, 2002.

Tacitus, P.Cornelius. 98. *Agricola*, translated by Alfred John Church, and William Jackson Brodribb, Macmillan, 1877.

Walcott, Derek. "History and Picong…in *The Middle Passage*." *Critical Perspectives on Derek Walcott*, edited by Robert Hamner, Three Continent Press, 1993, pp. 18–19.

Chapter 12

DID V. S. NAIPAUL HATE TRINIDAD?[1]

Kenneth Ramchand

Prelude: A Story with a Moral—Did James Joyce Hate Ireland?

James Joyce left Ireland in 1904 when he was twenty-two years old. He returned briefly on three occasions but he never set foot in Ireland after 1912. The Church and state hated him. On his death in 1941, his wife's offer to repatriate his body was refused, and the government instructed its ambassador not to attend the funeral.

Joyce hated and poured scorn on what he saw as the outlandish and confusing politics and the backwards cultural agenda of his country. He hated Catholicism for destroying individuality and creating decadence. Dublin was "the centre of paralysis" (*Selected Letters of James Joyce* 48).

Joyce also feared Dublin. He wanted to escape from it. If he stayed, he would end up like the failed writer Gabriel Conroy in the story "The Dead" in *Dubliners* (1914). He feared Ireland as a place that consumed its artists and other creative people. "You know what Ireland is?" he allowed the character, Stephen Dedalus, to declare in *A Portrait of the Artist As a Young Man*. "Ireland is the old sow that eats her farrow [newborn litter]" (185).

Dublin was, nevertheless, the physical setting of all his work, and it was the begetter of everything he wrote, including *Ulysses* (1922) and *Finnegan's Wake* (1939). He never disengaged from what he condemned. There is no more realistic and imaginative rendering of the Dublin of Joyce's formative years, its streets, its voices, its music and its spirit. Joyce left Dublin, but Dublin never left him. In the final reckoning, he loved Ireland and wanted it to find itself. This is where he stood: "Welcome, O life! I go to encounter for the millionth time the reality

1 The author dedicates this chapter to one of Trinidad and Tobago's foremost creative non-fiction writers, Tony Deyal, "whose sense of the topsy-turvy world worries me and makes me smile".

of experience, and to forge in the smithy of my soul the uncreated conscience of my race" (*Portrait* 253).

Joyce hated and feared Dublin, but he wrote about it all the time. He wanted to encounter the reality of experience and he wanted to forge the uncreated conscience of his race. Only a kind of love would have made him want to do that and to declare: "When I die, Dublin will be written in my heart" (Barry, *James Joyce: Occasional, Critical and Political Writing*).

Hate is complex in its manifestations and origins. Iago's malignity in Shakespeare's *Othello* is a wrathful and diabolic hate that wants to destroy only for the sake of destruction. Can we ever know where hate like that comes from? Thankfully, it is not that kind of hate that we are thinking about here. If the word "hate" is to be used regarding V. S. Naipaul's attitudes towards Trinidad, it would have to be classed as the kind of hate described by St Thomas Aquinas: "Nothing is hated, save through being contrary to a suitable thing which is loved. And hence it is that every hatred is caused by love" (128).

In this exploration of Naipaul's "cleansing-of-the-temple" attitudes towards Trinidad, the case of James Joyce stands as a useful precedent.

'Nothing Was Created in the West Indies'

Naipaul's justly deplored omission of the name of Trinidad from his list of acknowledgements on being awarded the Nobel Prize for literature in 2001 served as a reminder of an imagined wound that still festers. One sentence in *The Middle Passage* (1962) has become notorious for inflicting that wound. It is cited by all who want to indict Naipaul for being anti-West Indian and for hating Trinidad. The sentence is reproduced even for those who know it by heart:

"History is built around achievement and creation; and nothing was created in the West Indies."

The sentence comes at the end of a nationalistic discussion of the attitudes and behaviours of the Europeans who bossed slave society (*The Middle Passage* 27–29). With the help of telling quotations from British witnesses, Naipaul tags plantation whites as low-life, cruel and violent to those below them; as creatures with coarse appetites and vulgar sensualities; people with no learning, no interest in the arts and sciences; beings with no life of the mind, no idea of civilisation; creatures with no instinct to make a home of the place to which they had come.

The sentence does not imply denial or denigration of the folk culture of the enslaved and indentured peoples; or of the history of survival and resistance; or of the astounding outbursts of creativity and self-expression in song, story, calypso, dance, music, religion, festivals and carnival in the closing decades of nineteenth-century Trinidad. Naipaul's sentence is nothing to do with that. Nor is it a comment on twentieth-century Trinidad. The sentence is nothing more than part of a complaint about the whites in a slave society. It is restated forty-five years later:

> Europe had left behind nothing that could be called a civilisation, no great architecture, no idea of local beauty, no memory of style and splendour, nothing a man would wish to call his own. (*A Writer's People* 24)

If "Nothing was created" is read in context, it can be seen as a sentence in what was an implicit plea for us to discover and write our own history and build our own ships.

Elsa Goveia's brilliant *Slave Society in the British Leeward Islands at the End of the Eighteenth Century* (1965) defined the island societies as slave societies whose history could not be written and whose inner dynamics could not be understood if the shaping presence of slaves and free blacks was treated as peripheral. This dispassionate, scholarly and groundbreaking book inspired West Indian historians to turn research attention to the voiceless, nameless slave and to describe and analyse the hidden/suppressed cultures of the islands. Naipaul was clearly moving in this direction in *The Middle Passage* which appeared three years before Goveia's seminal contribution. By the time we come to the Epilogue to *The Loss of El Dorado* (1969), he calls—as does Wilson Harris in *History Fable and Myth in the Caribbean and the Guianas* (1970)—for an imaginative and researched history that would reconstruct the lives of the faceless, storyless, voiceless natives:

> Port-of-Spain was a place where things had happened and nothing showed. Only people remained. History was a fairytale about Columbus and a fairytale about the strange customs of the aboriginal Caribs and Arawaks; it was impossible now to set them in the landscape. History was the Trinidad five-cent stamp; Raleigh discovering the Pitch lake. History was also a fairytale not so much about slavery as about its abolition, the good defeating the bad. It was the only way the tale could be told. Any other version would have ended in ambiguity and alarm. The slave as slave was never real. Like the extinct aboriginal, he had to be reconstructed from his daily routine. So he remains, existing, like Vallot's jail (of which no plan survives), only in the imagination. In the records, the slave is faceless, silent, with an identification rather than a name. He has no story. (*The Loss of Eldorado* 375)

Will there ever be a non-partisan and rational discussion in the West Indies of "Nothing was created"?

SOUNDING THE MIDDLE PASSAGE

The whole account of Trinidad in Chapter Two of *The Middle Passage* has been held by some in the West Indies to provide detailed evidence of hatred of Trinidad and of the author's negative views of people of African origin. There are earlier tremors and symptoms, in Naipaul's fiction and in interviews, but this eruption came in 1962 with the publication of *The Middle Passage*. Trinidad was struck hard. The book reaches back to Naipaul's childhood, and its aftershocks are to be felt well into his later years. The first reason why *The Middle Passage* hits so hard, and makes people feel aggrieved, is because it chooses what to hit. It leaves alone many qualities of Trinidad and Trinidadians which make it a lovable country. Rereadings of *The Middle Passage*, even in tranquility, do not change the fact that Naipaul, in the book, is critical of the condition of Trinidad. But it is striking now to see in it how many positive things Naipaul says *en passant* about Trinidad and Trinidadians: the palpable energy in the air, the lust for life, the warmth and kindness of strangers, the natural anarchism and free self-expression of the Trinidadian. These are positive aspects that make the criticisms sound not like a rant but as something felt with sorrow and a sense of possibilities wasted.

It cannot be denied that the chapter on Trinidad leaves out positive aspects that Naipaul did not see, and does not emphasise some that he did see. What the seeing eye and darting mind took in, however, the pen sets before us with skill and style. It is distressing that the failings the book discerned are still with us, and the evils it uncovers are present fifty years later in a terrifyingly more virulent and extreme form. Today, Trinidadians are literally on the run; those who are abroad come back for a holiday with their return passage booked, or indulge in mainly food-based rituals to concoct a manageable Trinidad in the safe places where they reside. Those who stay know what Naipaul knew from early: there is nowhere to go. "Oh England is a pleasant place for them that's rich and high," says the old buccaneer. "Nah leaving," sings the calypsonian. Naipaul constructed his own private and largely unrecognised way of accepting home with its sorrows.

The early part of this discussion highlights four of the issues about Trinidad that are raised in *The Middle Passage*, all of them more or less accepted as true by Trinidadians, some being diverted by the humour, and some of them responding angrily—seeing it as ridicule. The issues are:

- the criticism of Trinidadians' "modernity"
- the description of Trinidad as a picaroon society
- the lack of nationalism

- the absence of African–Indian unity
- and, finally, a surprising one which I have titled "Naipaul's solutions"

Naipaul's descriptions of the things he hates are sharp and vivid. The things he hates prevent the society from being a society, and they do all manner of violence to the individual. There can be no doubt from his presentation, however, that he is interested in reform, so much so that he offers a number of practical suggestions about how this might come about. Certain notes are sounded that insinuate, at this stage, a concern that is a matter of life and death. The things that Naipaul hates endanger every individual, none more so than a boy in colonial Trinidad determined to make his way into the literary world, the larger world out there. To Naipaul, it amounts to threatening the writer with extinction.

Trinidadians' Modernity

Trinidad's self-satisfaction with its "modernity" is analysed as an escape from reality. It is "a constant alertness, a willingness to change, a readiness to accept anything which films, magazines, and comic strips appear to indicate as American" (*The Middle Passage* 46). To be modern is "to ignore local products" and to have a preference for foreign: "bad English potatoes" instead of yams and plantains. This modernity "turns out to be the extreme susceptibility of people who are unsure of themselves and, having no taste or style of their own, are eager for instruction". They drink deeply—intoxicated by commercial radio jingles, the advertising agencies and the other harbingers of American materialism. Naipaul, the satirist, calls it a life of fantasy and asserts that the fantasy is "cheating" and "masochistic". In this work, Naipaul wants to save the society and, notably, the calypso, which he recognises as a valuable tool in the search for self-knowledge: "It is only in the calypso that the Trinidadian touches reality." Even as he says so, however, he laments that the integrity and the social function of the native form are being undermined by self-caricaturing attempts to live up to "the ideals of the tourist brochure".

Naipaul's Solutions

It is surprising the number of times that Naipaul offers solutions to our plight. With respect to our so-called modernity, he laments our failure to look at ourselves critically, or to look inwards or to rediscover the past:

> Though we knew that something was wrong with our society, we made no attempt to assess it. Trinidad was too unimportant and we could never be convinced of the value of reading the history of a place which was, as everyone said, only a dot on the map of the world. Our interest was all in the world outside.... Our own past was buried and no one cared to dig it up. (*The Middle Passage* 41–42)

Later in the chapter, after describing the society as a picaroon society, there is a remarkable burst of youthful sermonising.

To bring political organisation to the picaroon society, with its taste for corruption and violence and its lack of respect for the person, has its dangers. Such a society cannot immediately become responsible, but it can be re-educated only through responsibility. Change must come from the top. Capital punishment and corporal punishment and incitements to brutality must be abolished. The civil service must be rejuvenated.

He then sketches out a code of conduct for civil servants, people serving the public in business places, in drugstores and even the police: "The policeman will see that he is more than a licensed bully" and all along the line no one will feel the need "to display his authority by aggression" (*The Middle Passage* 74–75). Finally, having conscripted the calypso into the educational process, he turns to the responsibility of the writer. They tend to flatter the prejudices of their group but they must check up on themselves. They can do better: "Living in a borrowed culture, the West Indian, more than most, needs writers to tell him who he is and where he stands" (*The Middle Passage* 68). How can anyone have reviewed this book under the title, "A pageant of apathy"?

Not Anancy but the Picaroon

Shunning the Anancy trope of West Indian writers in which the witty survival skills of trickster Anancy are given more emphasis than the cruelty and violence he suffers, the author of *Miguel Street* looks at the trickery, violence, brutality and sentimentality around him and defines the society as one in which slavery, the mixed population, the absence of national pride and the closed colonial system have recreated "the attitudes of the Spanish picaroon world".

A frightening place:

> This was an ugly world, a jungle, where the picaroon hero starved unless he stole, was beaten almost to death when found out, and had therefore to get in his blows first whenever possible; where the

> weak were humiliated; where [Kafka-esquely], the powerful never appeared and were beyond reach … where no one was allowed any dignity and everyone had to impose himself; an uncreative society where war was the only profession. (*The Middle Passage* 7)

This is one of the sources of the nightmare of being stranded in Trinidad that haunted Naipaul throughout his career. Yet, he can value the tolerance produced by the picaroon society ("How could one wish it otherwise?"); this tolerance is not the tolerance between castes and creeds which he insists does not exist on the island, but "something more profound: tolerance for every human activity, and affection for every demonstration of wit and style" (*The Middle Passage* 76–77).

The Lack of Nationalism

To the Naipaul of *The Middle Passage,* every clique saw itself as the elite, every individual was a guerrilla fighting his own war. Nobody had any loyalty to anything larger than himself—neither family, nor ethnic group, nor region, nor country. Each guerrilla was fighting for his place in the community, yet there was no community:

> We were of various races, religions, sets and cliques; and we had somehow found ourselves on the same small island. Nothing bound us together except this common residence. There was no nationalist feeling.… There was no profound anti-imperialist feeling; indeed, it was only our Britishness, our belonging to the British Empire which gave us any identity. (*The Middle Passage* 43)

When adult suffrage came in 1946, entrepreneurial individuals entered the lists because they saw "prodigious commercial possibilities". Naipaul did not add that they were succeeded by the biggest entrepreneurial entity of all, the modern political party. Naipaul sounds in these pages as if he could join a nationalist group fighting to turn a set of peoples into a people.

African–Indian Unity

There is no ambivalence in any of Naipaul's attitudes in his comments on the topics in the previous sections. Where there was disagreement about any of his pronouncements on any of the topics, it was rational and not *ad hominem*. But the author's comments on Africans, Indians and political unity have roused strong emotions as is usually the case when race and colour are part of the subject. The rumour took wing among Indians that Naipaul hated them. And, of course, he hated Africans too. These are subsets of hating Trinidad.

When Naipaul comes to discuss the two major ethnic groups on the island, the private anxieties and personal tensions sometimes sensed just below the choppy surface of *The Middle Passage* cannot be missed. Of the Indians of Trinidad, he generalises thus:

> A peasant-minded, money-minded community, spiritually static because cut off from its roots, its religion reduced to rites without philosophy, set in a materialistic colonial society; a combination of historical accidents and national temperament has turned the Trinidad Indian into the complete colonial, even more philistine than the white. (*The Middle Passage* 82)

This harsh dismissal of the Indians of Trinidad has some justice in it as a description of how things were. Not surprisingly, it led to cries by Indians that Naipaul hated them and, therefore, also hated himself. The severity of the tone suggests that Naipaul is attempting to distance himself from connections that in the colonial society of his boyhood were shaming, and full of threats to the self he wanted to become. The family organisation of the Indian was "an enclosing self-sufficient world absorbed with its quarrels and jealousies, as difficult for the outsider to penetrate as for one of its members to escape. It protected and imprisoned, a static world awaiting decay" (*The Middle Passage* 82). To the boy who wanted to become a writer, the Indian connection was entombment from birth.

Naipaul's analysis of the descendants of enslaved African peoples was done before the Black Power revolutions and before "black is beautiful" had set in. Naipaul complains of the self-contempt induced by slavery and colonial education; he cannot understand the obsession with whiteness; he is hostile to the mimicry that had spread to the Indians; he cannot understand why Africans continue to feel guilty about their blackness and their Africanity and he is appalled by the Africans' ignorance of Africa, which for them was not a continent of darkness but an arena of shame:

> Twenty million Africans made the middle passage, and scarcely an African name remains in the New World. Until the other day, African tribesmen on the screen excited derisive West Indian laughter … the darkie comic (whose values were the values of the Christian-Hellenic tradition) was more admired. In pursuit of the Christian-Hellenic tradition, which some might see as a paraphrase for whiteness, the past has to be denied, the self—despised. (*The Middle Passage* 67)

Marcus Garvey knew what Naipaul was talking about. It was he who uttered the words that Bob Marley turned into a redemption song: "We are going to emancipate ourselves from mental slavery because whilst others might free the body, none but ourselves can free the mind." Naipaul's analysis of the situation of descendants of Africans in Trinidad is an encouragement to work at freedom from mental slavery. There is no sign of hating Africans in all of that. But turbulence arrives.

The awakening that Naipaul encouraged in *The Middle Passage* was happening on island after island as he travelled to research the book, and he began to be afraid of what he was seeing. He saw these stirrings as disordered, lacking in rationality and likely to get out of control. There was paraphernalia of rebirth—slogans and symbols, loudspeakers and rallies, the beating of drums. Did he panic? There were roughly equal numbers of Africans and Indians in Trinidad. Would a West Indies-wide confederation of Africans with political control over an Indian minority come into being? I don't know if these were Naipaul's thoughts but the chapter on Trinidad ends ominously:

> I came to see that such eruptions were widespread, and represented feelings coming to the surface in Negro communities throughout the Caribbean: confused feelings, without direction; the Negro's rejection of the guilt he has borne so long; the last delayed Spartacan revolt, more radical than Toussaint L'Ouverture's; the closing of accounts this side of the middle passage. (*The Middle Passage* 85)

Some could see not the ethnic panic but saw instead a contemptuous tone. The fear never left Naipaul and it got stronger—stopping just short of open hysteria.

It does not impress Naipaul very much that certain attitudes shared between Africans and Indians speak of some accord between the races. Trinidadians from the two ethnic groups shared tastes in relation to food and to consumer items in the stores. Sadly, both groups are on the weary road to whiteness and competing for white approval. "But Trinidad, in fact, teeters on the brink of racial war. Politics must be blamed; but there must have been an original antipathy for the politicians to work on" (*The Middle Passage* 80). It is not known if anybody picked up on "an original antipathy" about which, incidentally, Naipaul says no more in *The Middle Passage.* The problem of recognising differences and working for social and political unity at the same time had come to him as a troubling subject.

An African–Indian political party that came to power in British Guiana in the early 1950s quickly split along racial lines, and then there were killings. With knowledge of the racial atrocities of Guyana's politics fresh in his mind, Naipaul wrote *The Mimic Men* (1967), a penetrating account of the failure of African–Indian politics in a country called Isabella (Trinidad in thin disguise). This novel explores all the awkward questions that have to be asked and answered at every level in the society if attempts at African–Indian political unity are not to end in the calamity of racial war. The novel is a courageous examination of the obstacles to political unity between the two races. Naipaul cares enough for Trinidad to want political unity. In this novel, too, Naipaul allows Ralph Singh to voice the worst fears of an Indian living in Trinidad:

> I belonged to a small community which in this part of the world was doomed. We were an intermediate race, the genes passive, capable of disappearing in two generations into any of the three races of men, with perhaps only a shape of eye or flexibility of slender wrist to speak of our intrusion. (*The Mimic Men* 57)

This is probably an anxiety that Naipaul shares with his fictional character.

The fear that drives the severe analysis of Trinidad society in *The Middle Passage* and elsewhere is not one fear but a tangled cluster of fears—including fear of racial annihilation, fear of the extinction of the writer and the existential fear of death. Naipaul's accounts of three visits to Trinidad from London allow us to see the continuity of a critical attitude ("hate") towards the behaviours of the people of the island and a consequential resorting to the landscape from which he fled in 1950. To put it dramatically, he pulls out of the actual landscape an alternative landscape, a country of the mind which at once sustains him and binds him to the original on which it is based.

An Old Fear, Old Personal Pain

The first of the journeys back took place in 1956: he had finished his studies and he had two novels awaiting publication. The account appears in *The Enigma of Arrival* (1987).

> The steamship made landfall in Barbados: Seeing the flat hot worn-out looking land, the narrow streets, the insubstantial houses and little children everywhere was like seeing very clearly an aspect of myself, and a past I thought I had outlived. The smallness of that past, the shame of that smallness.... (148–151)

After a morning tour, he was glad to return to the safety (his word) of the steamship which, leaving Barbados next morning, set him down on his own island where "everything, had shrunk to Barbados size", and he found himself looking "less at a landscape than at old personal pain". In the first sentence of *The Middle Passage*, a similar recoil is registered, in the account of the second return journey in 1960:

> As soon as the Francisco Bobadilla had touched the quay, the ship's side against rubber bumpers, I began to feel my old fear of Trinidad. I did not want to stay. I had left the security of the ship and had no assurance that I would ever leave the island again. (33)

(Interestingly, he is like the traveller in the Chirico painting of which Naipaul was to make thematic use many years later.)

Trinidad was menacing: "The world I thought I had left behind was waiting for me. It had shrunk, and I felt I had shrunk with it" (*The Enigma of Arrival* 163). We are told here that "the old fear" or the old personal pain "waiting for me", had apparently begun to be felt in childhood. He was twelve years old when he set down in writing his vow to leave the island within five years. Naipaul's fear of Trinidad is first of all fear of the power to hurt that lay in the social and political ills the writer targets in the book. The old personal pain refers to something else. A clue might lie in *A House for Mr Biswas*, a novel he tussled with during the four years after the 1956 visit to Trinidad.

The First Return: Glory Dead

For most of the year before the original departure in 1950, young Naipaul lived in nervous fear that somehow he would lose the scholarship that was to take him to England and Oxford which, he states, was "not a wish so much to go to Oxford as a wish to get out of Trinidad and see the great world and make myself a writer" (*The Middle Passage* 115). The abstract studies to which he had been subjected all his life and the conditioning of the Mother Country about what was literature and what kind of person a writer was had been converted into "an idea of a literary life in another country" leading to more and more withdrawal from Trinidad and the ties that bind: "My real life, my literary life was to be elsewhere" (*The Enigma of Arrival* 126). In 1950, "the excitement of departure" and the long journey to famous places, everything was tinged with the promise and the fantasies of the writing career and the metropolitan life. England was the first country of his mind.

Importantly, life in the extended family was a source of pain. When, to his embarrassment, members of the family converged on Piarco airport in 1950 to see him off, they could not have known what was going on in his head. Perhaps even he did not know where the phrase "my real life, my literary life" would take him. It had not taken long for the colonially self-created myth of a glorious literary life in England to die. England was now simply a place where he could make a modest living while trying to write. In 1956 Trinidad, his father was dead, the family was in straitened circumstances and he had no money. He returned to the uncertainty of England in winter on a banana boat from Jamaica with "an ache in my heart at my own insecurity" (*The Enigma of Arrival* 164).

The Ache of the Past

The four years after his return to England led to his release from the twice reawakened personal pain that was the Trinidad of his early life: "In those four years, out of the panic of that winter return to England, I had pulled much work out of myself, had written a book which I felt to be important" (*The Enigma of Arrival* 151).

It was more the ghosts of the visit to Trinidad in 1956 than the stress of the return to wintry England that harrowed him. The book he pulled out of himself was *A House for Mr Biswas.* In the long course of the writing of this book, he tusselled with his life in the Lion House, Chaguanas, and the transfer of much of it to the Capildeo houses in the city of Port-of-Spain, and he travelled over the beleaguered life of his father Seepersad Naipaul—the battles, the enthusiasms, the depression, the nervous breakdown and the anxious, life-long dream of being a writer. Near the end of the novel, disturbing memories and the long gestation of someone's early years are alluded to, until we come to this settlement: "So later, and very slowly, in securer times of different stresses, when the memories had lost the power to hurt with pain or joy, they would fall into place and give back the past" (581).

Freedom

My thesis is that the writing of *A House for Mr Biswas* freed Naipaul to develop a new relationship with the natural landscape of his birth. The fear of Trinidad remained. He says in *The Enigma of Arrival* that the human landscape had been "the landscape of anxiety, even panic, and sacrifice". As a child, he had never felt free. His education had been a race "in which the fear of failure was like the fear of extinction". Although *A House for Mr Biswas* was still to be published, he was confident in 1960 that with that book he had made himself a writer and could live as a writer. Hence, the visit to Trinidad (September 1960 to May 1961) was tinged with celebration. The island had fed his panic and his ambition and it nurtured his fantasies, but in 1960 he was confident enough to visit the scenes of early trauma, moving from place to place "to touch it with my mood of celebration, to remove from it the terror I had felt in these places for various reasons at different times" (*The Enigma of Arrival* 152).

But at this moment of seeming fulfillment, Naipaul begins to sketch out a new disposition. Though he had come "to the end of a particular kind of fear", he says, his relationship with the island was at an end; his interest in it could be "satisfied, even sated" in a day. He makes a distinction between the little island and its people who could no longer hold him; and, on the other hand, there was the British island of Muslims, Hindus and Africans that had given him, though he did not know it at the time, the great themes of displacement and the migration of peoples in the second half of the twentieth century. This side of the island eventually awakened in him a curiosity about the worlds of all the people who had come to it, worlds he recognised more and more like the worlds that had made him. The island put the whole world at the tip of his pen, sent him on journeys to all his connections and made him more metropolitan than he had ever dreamt possible in that deluded time when London was his home (*The Enigma of Arrival* 153).

The second element in the new disposition is the description of a two-fold landscape. He didn't need to say it, but he said that the Trinidad landscape the writer had created while living in England was not as accurate or full as he had pretended it to be. But the act of creation made him cherish the original. By the time we come to *The Loss of El Dorado* (1969), fabrication wins. Naipaul makes you feel that the Trinidad he created or discovered is more real than the degraded version in which he lived.

Country of the Mind

In his account of the writing of *The Loss of El Dorado* (*The Enigma of Arrival* 155–160), Naipaul describes a scholarly process that unearths suppressed facts in the island's history and prehistory and, at the same time, outlines a sustaining country of the mind. Through the documents, he makes himself feel the antiquity of his island, its global character and the continuity of its hidden and fractured life: the undiscovered country joined to Venezuela and South America by the Orinoco whose floods mingled with the Atlantic; the primordial landscape of the First Peoples; the connections through Columbus with medieval Europe and the Spanish Empire; the fantasies and the frenzy of European adventurers, the coming of Africa and the East. And the sagas of men with grand ambitions and huge flaws, chasing a dream and coming to grief. The narrating character thinks that this book is the book he was destined to write: "Ever since I had begun to identify my subjects I had hoped to arrive, in a book, at a synthesis of the worlds and cultures that had made me.... I felt in this history I had made such a synthesis" (*The Enigma of Arrival* 157).

It is possible that it was what he learnt and imagined about Trinidad in the writing of *The Loss of El Dorado* that led Naipaul to understand the hidden depths of his growing dissatisfaction with living in England. It is significant that it was while finishing the "history" of Trinidad that he decided to put "an end to my time in England" (*The Enigma of Arrival* 157). It was Trinidad that finally broke the hold that England had over him. The attempt to live in Canada was quickly aborted. The attempt to leave England failed. The man who wrote *The Loss of El Dorado* might have thought of trying to live in Trinidad, but the requirements of the writer came first. To avoid extinction, the writer in him had to go back to England. The man was convinced at last that his departure from his island in 1950, with all it implied of homelessness and drift and longing, was final.

Later, he would escape to Wiltshire and learn a love for the landscape and geography of rural county. That is a fiction to be examined elsewhere. For now, our subject is *The Loss of El Dorado* and how it reflects his attitudes to Trinidad, and, for that, we must turn to the visit to the island in 1968–1969. It lies between what was going to be the final departure from England and other journeys and accepting the freedom to move unencumbered from perch to perch, to be a roamer, to live the hotel life, to be free to say goodbye (*The Enigma of Arrival* 158).

The visit is in the nature of a farewell to the islands and it extends from Trinidad to St Kitts, Anguilla, Guatemala City and Belize City. He went first to his own island. "I wanted to see the island where I had been living in a new way in my imagination for the last two years, the island I had restored, as it were, to the globe and for which I felt a deep romance" (*The Enigma of Arrival* 158).

On this visit, the willful translation of the Trinidad landscape into a landscape existing in his head is completed. He saw "an island full of racial tensions and close to revolution", with an angry wish "to destroy a world judged corrupt and too full of pain", a wish "to turn one's back on it rather than to improve it". Hate for "the people and the anger that was like madness" is kept in check as he strives to see the landscape he had created in his imagination. He is determined to see the landscape he had created and to look for its aboriginal, pre-Columbus identity.

> The landscape of the past existed only in fragments. To see one such fragment, I looked at the drying-up mangrove swamp—green thick leaves, black roots, black mud [and] … From the top of Laventille Hill, among the shacks, I could imagine myself at the beginning of things if I looked selectively down the Gulf of Paria—grey, leaden, never blue—and the islets in the gulf. (*The Enigma of Arrival* 160)

Although he finds that this past existed only in fragments, he will not surrender the romance of the island that his research had divined.

On this visit, the narrating character sets above what is visible to common sight, the landscape he had brought into being in his writings:

> I had given myself a past, and a romance of the past. One of the loose ends in my mind had vanished; a little chasm filled. And though something like Haitian anarchy seemed to threaten my little island, and though physically I no longer belonged to the place, yet the romance by which I had attached it to the rest of the world continued to be possessed by me as much as the imaginative worlds of my other fictional books. (*The Enigma of Arrival* 164)

The hard-headed Naipaul's use of the word "romance" does not manage to trivialise an attitude to the island that James Joyce had to his country when he said: "When I die Dublin will be written in my heart."

James Joyce wrote only about his Ireland. Naipaul wrote about Trinidad and out of Trinidad even when the setting of a work was not Trinidad. Trinidad was the truth that kept interrupting the effort to belong elsewhere that Naipaul made in *The Enigma of Arrival.* He feared and, therefore, hated the social, cultural and political pressures in island society and family life that threatened the writer with extinction. Like all would-be reformers, he met resistance and the hate of those who did not understand his underlying purpose. He turned inwards for justification and could claim with Joyce: "Welcome, O life! I go to encounter for the millionth time the reality of experience, and to forge in the smithy of my soul the uncreated conscience of my race."

It might be difficult to ever convince those who hate him as being anti-Trinidad that he wrote out of a love for the island of his birth, wrote to help it achieve the self-knowledge that would set it free. Thomas Aquinas knew that Naipaul needed someone who understood: "Nothing is hated, save through being contrary to a suitable thing which is loved. And hence it is that every hatred is caused by love." The country of the mind is the model of the "suitable thing" that Naipaul loved.

Works Cited

Aquinas, Thomas. *Summa Theologica: First Part of the Second Part.* Devoted Publishing, 2018.

Ellmann, Richard. *Selected Letters of James Joyce.* The Viking Press, 1975.

Goveia, Elsa. *Slave Society in the British Leeward Islands at the End of the Eighteenth Century.* Yale UP, 1965.

Harris, Wilson. "History Fable and Myth in the Caribbean and the Guianas." 1970. *Caribbean Quarterly*, vol. 54, no. 1/2, The 60th Anniversary Edition: *Literature and Ideas*, March–June, 2008, pp. 5–38.

James Joyce: Occasional, Critical and Political Writing, edited by Kevin Barry, Oxford UP, 2000.

Joyce, James. *A Portrait of the Artist as a Young Man.* 1916. Granada, 1977.

———. *Dubliners.* 1914. Prestwick House, 2006.

———. *Finnegan's Wake.* 1939. Oxford World's Classics, 2012.

———. *Ulysses.* 1922. Vintage, 1986.

Naipaul, V. S. *The Enigma of Arrival* Picador, 1988.

———. *The Loss of El Dorado.* 1969. Vintage, 2003.

———. *The Middle Passage: The Caribbean Revisited.* Vintage, 2002.

______. *The Mimic Men* Andre Deutsch, 1967.

———. *Reading and Writing.* New York Review of Books, 2000.

_______. *A Way in the World.* Knopf, 1994.

———. *A Writer's People* Vintage, 2009.

Chapter 13

V. S. NAIPAUL AND THE 1946 TRINIDAD GENERAL ELECTION[1]

Aaron Eastley

> Precisely because history as the verbal representation by man of his own past is by its very nature so full of hazard, so replete indeed with the verisimilitude of sharply differentiated choices … it never ceases to excite. The historical discourse is the world's oldest thriller. (Guha 55)

On 1 July 1946, the first election featuring universal adult suffrage was held in Trinidad. As reported in the island's leading newspaper of the day, the *Trinidad Guardian*, the "privilege of a lowered franchise" expanded the electorate nearly tenfold, from approximately 30,000 to 259,000 eligible voters ("A Momentous Election" 4). This was a precipitous change, especially in a colony where voting even on a limited scale had only been instituted a couple of decades before, in 1925, in an era when lingering doubts about the qualifications of non-whites and women had motivated the institution of property, literacy and age requirements that disenfranchised all but about 6 per cent of the population (Caton 628; Malik, *East Indians* 69–70, 73, 75). According to Matthias Catón in "Trinidad and Tobago", only literate, English-speaking men over twenty-one and women over thirty were allowed to vote in the 1925 election and the elections of the 1930s and early 1940s. Furthermore, since Legislative Council posts were unpaid, only people with independent incomes could afford to serve in them. For most Trinidadians, government was a thing high up and far away, an in-house affair of the local elites (628).

---

1 "V. S. Naipaul and the 1946 General Election" was originally published in *Twentieth-Century Literature*, vol. 55, issue 1, pp. 135. Copyright 2009, Hofstra University. All rights reserved. Republished by permission of the copyright holder, and the present publisher, Duke University Press.

In 1946, these restrictions were lifted all at once. This election becomes a historical touchstone in the early fiction and journalism of Trinidad-born author V. S. Naipaul. Beginning in his first novel, *The Mystic Masseur*, Naipaul focuses considerable attention on it, a focus that returns in a key section of his first work of journalistic or travel writing, *The Middle Passage*.[2] As readers of *The Mystic Masseur* may recall, it is the 1946 election in which Naipaul's enterprising protagonist, Ganesh Ramsumair, transforms himself from a Hindu faith healer into a politician, initiating a personal metamorphosis that culminates in his becoming G. Ramsay Muir, M. B. E., a West Indian envoy operating in England and a shameless British mimic man (*The Mystic Masseur* 220).

"Nineteen forty-six" is heralded in the final paragraph of the novel's opening chapter as "the turning point of Ganesh's career" (18), and the election and its aftermath constitute the major focus of the book's final three chapters. Even more notably, in a brief but pivotal (and now famous) section of *The Middle Passage*, Naipaul invokes the 1946 election to showcase his vision of the "picaroon" individualism of late colonial-era Trinidadians—the vision of his compatriots as opportunistic survivors in a social environment "where it is felt that all eminence is arrived at by crookedness" (72). The journalistic analysis of *The Middle Passage* suggests the authenticity of a Ganesh-type character, while in the fictitious Ganesh, the Trinidadian picaroon finds a most personable and credible incarnation. This is an important recognition, for the notion that Naipaul's journalistic works represent a decisive break from previous fictional work is something of a commonplace in Naipaul studies—one contributed to even by such a careful critic as Rob Nixon, who contrasts the "fierceness of *The Middle Passage*" with the "bounteous comedy of the early fiction" (12).

The relationship between these texts is not just a literary curiosity, nor are the events of 1946 in Trinidad merely the minutiae of West Indian history. For, precisely because Naipaul introduces coherent interpretive paradigms from the authoritative subject position of a

2 This book is currently in print under two revised titles: *The Middle Passage: A Caribbean Journey* by Picador (2001) and *The Middle Passage: The Caribbean Revisited* by Vintage (2002). However, unless otherwise noted, references to *The Middle Passage* in this article refer to the original 1962 hardback edition published by Deutsch, the layout of which was replicated in the 1984 Vintage edition found in most US libraries. This distinction is occasionally more than academic, as later editions include some minor textual alterations. Whether these are intended revisions or simply printing errors is unclear.

societal insider, and because most of his readers are not in a position to bring any significant degree of parallel local knowledge to bear on his representations of places like the West Indies, his perspectives have attained a level of influence seldom achieved by modern literary discourse. What began at the inception of his career with representations of Trinidad has multiplied in a sweeping array of articles and book-length studies where Naipaul articulates the defining characteristics—as he sees them—of literally dozens of other societies, mostly in the so-called Third World. Factor into this equation that Naipaul's predominantly hostile assertions are delivered in crisp, unsparing terms, and it is little wonder that he has emerged as a polarising figure.

Those who are inclined to interpret Naipaul's acerbity as a sign of integrity hail him as a rare and courageous truthsayer, apparently accepting his assurances that in his journalism "nothing [is] falsified" ("Dark Visions" 71) and that in his work as a whole an admittedly "brutal sort of analysis" is deployed out of "concern" rather than "contempt" ("V. S. Naipaul: A *Transition* Interview" 59; "A Conversation with V. S. Naipaul" 20).[3] Others, however, accuse Naipaul of inveterate treachery of being a sort of Uncle Tom interpreter whose every word must be questioned. No less a figure than Edward Said, for instance, opines that "the most attractive and immoral move [...] has been Naipaul's, who has allowed himself quite consciously to be turned into a witness for the Western prosecution" ("Intellectuals" 53).[4]

Still, others qualify their appraisals of Naipaul with reflections on the complexity of his personal origins, the cogency of many of his

---

3 Numerous examples could be cited. To capture the general tenor, consider Adrian Rowe-Evans beginning his 1971 interview by telling Naipaul that "the most overwhelming impression I get from your books is of a pursuit of honesty above all things" ("V. S. Naipaul: A *Transition* Interview" 56). A further example would be the Swedish Academy's Nobel blurb in 2001, hailing Naipaul's "perceptive narrative and incorruptible scrutiny" ("Nobel").

4 Though Jeffrey Meyers' now well-known description of Naipaul as the "scourge of the Third World" is mitigated by its occurring in a passage questioning whether Naipaul has "mellowed" in a book like *India: A Million Mutinies Now* (1991), there is little ambiguity in a host of statements from other critics. In addition to Said, the most notable of these is Abdul JanMohamed, in whose view Naipaul's writing, beyond merely criticising the Third World (something that might be done sympathetically and productively), "reeks of contempt and reveals only the operation of colonialist mentality" (87).

general perspectives, and the inconsistency of his tone. For instance, Feroza Jussawalla, recent collector of many of Naipaul's most important interviews in *Conversations with V. S. Naipaul*, defends him, claiming that he "is not the man made out by his critics—a standoffish critic of the third world seeing all postcolonial countries as 'areas of darkness'" (xv). In her estimation Naipaul is instead:

> a man struggling with his own identity as well as his loyalty to his Indian family—at once a fierce, independent man struggling to break free of family, community, and identity and a little boy in need of solace, a desire to talk out and write out his psychological problems of family Indian and British, of nation and of the lack of belonging—a pull between home versus hybridity.[5] (xv)

Matching the vehemence and prodigious output of the author himself, the debate surrounding Naipaul has been intense and multifaceted, and its prolonged fervour highlights the need for additional studies that carefully ground their analysis in historical particularities. This is where an event like the 1946 Trinidad general election becomes of extraordinary interest: as an indicator, however partial or narrowly focused, of how Naipaul's representations—both fictional and journalistic—compare with lived experience insofar as it can be reconstructed from formal histories and, more especially, from historically contemporaneous sources, such as newspaper articles, interviews, diaries and government documents.

Vidiadhar Surajprasad Naipaul was fourteen years old and living in the Trinidadian capital of Port-of-Spain during the election year of 1946.

5 Somewhere between Jussawalla's and Said's is the view of Derek Walcott, whose 1992 Nobel Prize came almost a decade before Naipaul's in 2001. Walcott is typically lumped in with Naipaul's accusers, having coined the taunting moniker "V. S. Nightfall" in his 1981 poem "The Spoiler's Return". However, that poem, in singling out Naipaul for his cynicism, also defends him as an artist and empathises with his critique of the Caribbean, especially its general lack of appreciation for art ("This Country" 74, "Art of Poetry" 111): "I see these islands and I feel to bawl, / 'area of darkness' with V. S. Nightfall." Striking, perhaps, the most persuasive balance in recent scholarship, Bruce King offers a powerful defense of Naipaul's literary politics in "Naipaul's Critics and Postcolonialism," a chapter appended to the second edition of his adroit study *V. S. Naipaul*—a defense all the more compelling for King's admission in his introduction that Naipaul "has a history of ill-considered remarks which cannot be explained by politics and impatience" (3).

At this socially aware but impressionable age, he witnessed the election and its aftermath in person and also through the press as his father, Seepersad Naipaul, had worked on and off as a reporter for the *Trinidad Guardian* since before V. S. was born (White 27–29). His vantage point was in many ways ideal, but his views were obviously individual. And the same could be said of virtually all the extant primary texts touching on the election. The *Trinidad Guardian*, for instance, emerges as by far the most copious source of information; but, as a news organ founded in 1917 specifically to cater to the island's British elite, this paper is itself a highly situated source (Samaroo, "Vanguard" 3). As Ranajit Guha convincingly demonstrates in "The Prose of Counter-Insurgency", even ostensibly uncalculating primary documents or historical narratives "are not the record of observations uncontaminated by bias, judgement and opinion" (59) but are, in fact, "packed with comment" (65). Still, as Catherine Gallagher and Stephen Greenblatt put it, "there is something—the 'real'—outside of the historical narrative" (50), and we may productively seize "at least upon those traces" of the real that seem "close to actual experience" (30).

The challenge, then, becomes constructing a strategically authoritative version of events like the 1946 election from a limited pool of more or less highly situated primary documents. In attempting to do so, one discovers that the terrain is shifty but not impassable. Fundamentally, there is need not only for theoretical subtlety but also for disciplinary synthesis, for, in historicist research in the field of Naipaul studies, it quickly becomes apparent that although the disciplines of West Indian history and West Indian literary analysis are both well developed, these disciplines have often operated in relative ignorance of each other. The aim of this study, then, is to merge textual analysis and its attendant vital political concerns with close historical scrutiny.

What comes to light through this analysis is a pattern of insightful but ultimately unreliable narration by Naipaul. As both représenter (in writing) and representative (in person) of Trinidad, Naipaul opportunistically plays the picaro himself: acting in the now-familiar but ever-problematic role of the "native informant", he allows his fear of subaltern backwardness to turn much of his characterisation into noxious caricature (Spivak, *Critique* 6, 9). Writing in a matter-of-fact tone that evinces reliability, Naipaul metes out both insightful (but strictly false) generalisations in the guise of historical facts and strictly accurate (but simplistic and misleading) representations of lived experience. His journalism, thus, takes on the qualities of fiction; and his fiction, often reading like news or historical commentary, is marred by both the exaggeration and limitations of an anxious orientalism. Across the gamut of his early work, the slippage is uneven but persistent. Again and again, the legitimacy of Trinidad vis-à-vis England and America is diminished—often subtly, occasionally grandly and grotesquely—and the only apparent survivor is the représenter himself, who observes all things from an urbane, cosmopolitan, Oxford-educated distance.

The case against Naipaul may be said to begin where his explicit analysis of the 1946 election ends, in *The Middle Passage*. This curiously eclectic regional study, a text spangled not only with personal reminiscences and quotations from other travellers but also with calypso lyrics and frequent excerpts from the *Trinidad Guardian*, presents itself as a record of Naipaul's travels through the English-speaking West Indies and British Guiana in the early 1960s. It is sectioned out by country, and in the portion devoted to Trinidad, the political analysis is especially pointed. Running under the telltale heading "Trinidad—The Picaroon" in the 2002 edition (69), Naipaul's sketch of the political climate of the day maintains that in order to understand "the squalor of politics that came to Trinidad in 1946", one must know that the ordinary Trinidadian in 1946 "owed no loyalty to the island and scarcely any to his group" (72).

Elaborating this startling assertion with a memorable metaphor, Naipaul compares his countrymen to "the sixteenth-century picaroon of Spanish literature, [who] survives and triumphs by his wits in a place where it is felt that all eminence is arrived at by crookedness" (*The Middle Passage* 78). If there was unity in 1946, Naipaul would have his readers see, it was not rooted in sentimental solidarity or group loyalty but in a ruthlessly mercurial self-interest leading to the fleeting formation of ad hoc political alliances. Blatant pragmatism, it is suggested, was a legacy of colonial society, where "every man had to be for himself" and specifically had to "grasp whatever dignity and power he was allowed" (*The Middle Passage* 69).

So conditioned were Trinidadians by this state of affairs, so the argument goes, that when "after no popular agitation" the franchise was granted in 1946, "the privilege took the population by surprise", and, in the uncertainty of the moment, "old attitudes" prevailed (*The Middle Passage* 69). This sketch is delivered in rapid-fire sentence segments that bespeak a wish not to belabour details but rather to convey as quickly as possible the essential contours of events less important in themselves than as indicators of a supposedly atomised Trinidadian society. Naipaul's tone is that of an emotionally detached insider, an expert observer whose personal experience renders the society transparent, so that in this case the popular recourse to rank opportunism is "not unexpected" (*The Middle Passage* 72).

Given this self-assured tone, it is curious to note that, taken at face value, certain particulars of Naipaul's characterisation are obviously false. Perhaps the best example is Naipaul's claim that in the 1946 election, "[t]here were no parties, only individuals" (*The Middle Passage* 77). In fact, almost all of the major candidates in the election claimed some party affiliation, and the party concept was seen by many to be absolutely vital. At stake in the election were nine seats on the Trinidadian Legislative Council, the primary governing body of the colony. However, since the constitution stipulated that nine other seats would be filled after the election by appointees of the governor, himself a colonially appointed officer wielding a decisive tie-breaking vote on the council, the British Colonial Office in London and its local emissaries in the Trinidadian capital of Port-of-Spain maintained effectual control of the government (Malik, *East Indians* 74–76; "How the Constitution of Trinidad Developed" 3; "A Momentous Election" 4).

Indeed, in view of these systematic strictures carefully maintained by the constitution, the granting of universal adult suffrage in 1946 was not merely the culmination of political unrest that went back a decade or more. Historical evidence suggests that Trinidadians of various walks of life had been actively petitioning for greater local representation since at least the turn of the century (Malik 69–72). This stirring eventually led Under-Secretary of State for the Colonies E. F. L. Wood to visit the West Indies as a one-man commission in 1921, "to examine the whole issue of representative government in the light of changed conditions in this part of the empire" (70). Around the same time, in 1922 a legislative reform committee led by Trinidadian labour leader A. A. Cipriani argued that "the people of the colony were well advanced in the fields of education and political consciousness" and were "mature enough to be given a direct share in the representative bodies" (71). It was in the wake of these diplomatic exchanges that the first, limited extension of the franchise was granted in 1925. With an eye to the future, constitutional changes in 1950 and 1956 allowed for more real representation, and full internal self-government was finally achieved in 1961 (Brereton 253). Rather, it was a harbinger of the genuinely dramatic changes that brought political independence a decade or more later.

In 1946, this underlying reality of ongoing colonial control was not lost on either the people of Trinidad or on the local press, yet it seems not to have discouraged potential candidates, nearly fifty of whom came forward to vie for the nine open posts ("This Is Your Election" 1). Leading the way, in an effort to make the most of the political situation, was an alliance of nine hopefuls who called themselves the United Front. Amalgamated from pre-existing labour organisations representing both black and East Indian working-class Trinidadians (Brereton 194–195), the United Front contended that owing to the balance of power created by the constitution, only a team of elected representatives pledged to work together could have any real influence ("Women Tell South Back Kelshall" 5). The Front's agenda was outlined by their leader, leftist lawyer Jack Kelshall, who called for "responsible government, socialisation of the major industries, and mass education" ("Mr. J. B. Kelshall" 14). Kelshall was closely assisted in the pursuit of this agenda by United Front comrade Albert Gomes, former editor of the socialist-leaning literary magazine The Beacon and a labour union leader who already sat on the Legislative Council (Brereton 175; "Present Members" 1).

Their ultimate goal, voiced in numerous campaign statements, was unrestricted self-government of the island. Kelshall emphasised this point from the beginning. In his first recorded campaign speech on 9 April 1946, he spoke of the "dictatorial government" of Trinidad and clearly stated that the United Front "was created to rid the Colony of that form of government" ("Only Way" 2). Gomes was also a staunch advocate of self-government, asserting that a major aim of the United Front was to "precipitate constitutional crisis" with the goal of ending "rubber-stamp rule" ("Isolated Efforts" 3). In the short term, however, Kelshall appropriated the "popular-front strategy that was in vogue among left-wing groups in Europe" in the hope that a powerful party coalition would possess sufficient political clout to force more meaningful constitutional reform (Ryan, *Race and Nationalism* 73). Although the concept ultimately failed to yield an electoral sweep, Kelshall's United Front and a competing nine-member coalition rather grandly named the British Empire Workers and Citizen's Home Rule Party did each capture three of the nine open seats, and two other seats were won by candidates of the Socialist Party of Trinidad and Tobago (Brereton 194–195).

Strictly speaking, there was only one successful independent; parties played a major role. Indeed, the party politics of the election even find their way into Naipaul's novel *The Mystic Masseur*, whose publication predates *The Middle Passage* by half a decade. In the novel, Ganesh's Oxford-educated rival, Indarsingh, is presented as an affiliate of the "Party for Progress and Unity, the PPU", a political entity that sounds very much like the United Front (*The Mystic Masseur* 200). In light of these historical and literary facts, the notion that Naipaul simply misrepresented the situation out of ignorance is untenable. So when he quips that "there were no parties, only individuals" in *The Middle Passage*, it would seem that he is either blatantly prevaricating (perhaps counting on his readers not to know any better) or, more likely, writing metaphorically—suggesting that in effect there were only individuals. Such a likelihood is borne out by some of the particularities of the 1946 election, as the nomination system turned would-be nationalists like Kelshall and Gomes against their own countrymen—most notably a pair of charismatic opposition candidates who threatened the United Front's intended electoral monopoly. As I will show, these opposition candidates played an important role in the unfolding sequence of events surrounding the election and may also have inspired some of Naipaul's most notable characters and ideas.

Ostensibly the most dangerous opposition figure was the founder of the British Empire Workers and Citizen's Home Rule Party, famed oil-union agitator Tubal Uriah Buzz Butler. Butler had inspired a series of large-scale strikes in the mid-1930s (Brereton 172–173), and he claimed to have been chosen by God to lead the people ("Butler Claims" 2). Staunchly insisting on his full self-given title of "Chief Servant of the British Empire Workers and Citizen's Home Rule Party", Butler is now remembered by one prominent West Indian historian as merely a "sweaty demagogue", but his popular appeal in the 1940s and the 1950s was nevertheless tremendous, particularly among black working-class Trinidadians (Ryan, *Race and Nationalism* 45). That appeal was amplified in 1946 by his campaign promises to provide "free secondary education to all children, free books, free lunches, free milk and free uniforms—Butler uniforms—for all children attending school, bigger pay for workers, bigger old age pensions and the 'dole'" ("Speaker Urges" 2). As an individual personality, Butler was indeed a formidable political force, lending credence to Naipaul's notion that in the election individuals were more important than parties. Beyond Butler, moreover, the election was defined by a character much nearer to Naipaul's own East Indian roots, a dashing thirty-something-engineer-turned-politician named Ranjit Kumar.

Kumar's previous political activity had been limited to a short stint on the Port-of-Spain City Council, but, in early April 1946, he announced that he would likely stand for election to the Legislative Council in North Port-of-Spain, Victoria or the Eastern Counties ("Asked to Stand" 2). Unlike Butler, who made a serious tactical error in seeking to represent North Port-of-Spain, a district far removed geographically and socially from his power base in the oilfields of central and southwestern Trinidad, and the stronghold of his political archenemy, the already "Hon'ble" Gomes ("Butler Will" 2), Kumar wisely chose to run in the predominantly East Indian agricultural district of Victoria, where, despite his apparent lack of organisational backing as an independent, he captured more votes than any other single candidate, easily outpacing his United Front rival for the

Victoria seat ("Kumar Gains" 1). This was precisely the result that the politically savvy Gomes had feared. Travelling the country in support of his United Front colleagues in the months preceding the election, he had relentlessly championed the doctrine of electoral unity, asserting that "unless a team gets into the Legislature, then the election is lost and the very force of adult suffrage is vitiated". He specifically warned voters that if they could not unite in support of all nine United Front candidates, they could expect "the Colony for another five years to beat its chest in impotent rage because individual glamour boys seduced their way to the Legislature" ("Keep Out" 3).

The handsome young Kumar was almost certainly the target of this barb, and his sensational victory makes him a fitting poster boy for the Naipaulian hypothesis that in the election there were only individuals and that picaroon ingenuity prevailed, more especially because his appeal seems to have been grounded not only in youthful good looks but in the conscious pursuit of an arguably opportunistic ethnic solidarity. Along these lines, it is fascinating to uncover in a 1982 interview the recollection of Pundit Ragbir of El Dorado, Trinidad, that on the 1946 campaign trail, Kumar posed with a bow and arrow in symbolic reenactment of the familiar Hindu drama of Ram and Seeta (La Guerre 190). Such a dramatic gesture would have been unmistakable: he was signalling his predominantly Hindu and largely illiterate would-be constituents that he could be relied on to promote their interests. The United Front's sensible political logic was ultimately no match for this—despite the fact that a mere week before the election, the Front seemed to be enjoying considerable popularity even in Victoria.[6]

As it turned out, certain of the "old attitudes" Naipaul alludes to did seem to prevail. For as historian Selwyn Ryan maintains, speaking of the two decades preceding the election—from 1925, when the vote was introduced on a limited basis, to 1945—"the rural Indian in particular was not yet able, or in fact willing, to identify with abstract

---

6 To wit, on Tuesday, 25 June, the *Trinidad Guardian* reported that the previous Sunday, the leadership of the United Front (Gomes, Kelshall and others) had toured Victoria, delivering their platform to "about 1,000 enthusiastic electors" in one community, and then to another "large waiting audience" at a prominent road junction ("United Front Tours Victoria" 2). This second session was reported to have been an unplanned gathering made up of people so "anxious to hear the Front's programme" that they "demanded a meeting and listened attentively throughout". On the same day, the Front's leaders also addressed a "packed hall" in San Fernando, the prominent city in the southern part of the island (2).

institutions like 'council' or 'party'" but "it was still very much a case of *apanjhat*—Indian for Indian" (*Pathways to Power* 5–6). Early evidence of the persistence of such feelings is scattered but portentous. To cite just one example, the *apanjhat* mantra was echoed in 1946 by the East Indians of a small village called Debe, where, in the midst of widespread regional enthusiasm for the United Front, a mostly Indian audience "declared they were 'voting Indian', and broke up the [Front's] meeting" ("United Front").

Running parallel to the *Guardian* column, touting the United Front's Victoria tour just one week before the election, was a small announcement of seven "lectures" to be delivered during the final week by Pundit Basdeo Misir at Hindu temples throughout the island. The pundit's topic was "How to Vote" ("Indians to Be Told" 2). The *Guardian* may not have seen this as something worthy of emphasis, either because it really was deemed insignificant or because editorial bias made its emphasis undesirable, but Indians were actively encouraged to "vote Indian", and they were in any event probably predisposed to do so. If Ryan's appraisal is to be credited, the Indian voter of the day still "thought mainly in terms of persons who could understand his language and his problems, and who would safeguard and promote his ethnic interests" (*Pathways to Power* 6). This certainly seemed to have been the case on election day, as the incumbent Gomes convincingly defeated Butler in North Port-of-Spain, while Kelshall, in contrast, was even more convincingly defeated by East Indian challenger Timothy Roodal in St Patrick. East Indians also won seats in Caroni and St George ("Election Results at a Glance" 3). In Victoria, the predominantly East Indian voters of the district shied away from the plans of lawyer, experienced legislator and demagogue alike, apparently seduced by the "glamour boy" with the bow and arrow.

The complaint in *The Mystic Masseur* of Ganesh's PPU rival Indarsingh, who may be seen as a stand-in for Gomes just as Ganesh may be seen as a stand-in for Kumar, becomes prescient: "Funny people in Trinidad, old boy. No respect for ideas, only personalities" (*The Mystic Masseur* 212). In further defense of Naipaul's claim that there were "only individuals", not only did the hope of a unified electoral bloc fail to materialise in 1946, but the parties that contested the election subsequently broke up, raising the possibility that they weren't quite real parties to begin with.

In fact, much of what Naipaul says of the PPU in *The Mystic Masseur* could be said of the United Front as well. The PPU is carefully described as "an organization hastily slung together two months before the elections", and shortly thereafter it dies (200). When the credulous Indarsingh looks to the PPU after the election to make good on its promise to cover his deposit (an official entry fee required of all candidates), he finds that the party has "just disappeared" (204). Similarly, the United Front coalition was also assembled only months before the election, and in effect ceased to exist almost immediately thereafter. Even its three elected members did not consistently vote as a body in Council matters as they had pledged to do (Brereton 196; Ryan, *Race and Nationalism* 78–81).

If the essential characteristic of a political party is that it endures over time while individual candidates come and go, the parties that existed nominally in Trinidad in 1946 hardly qualify. For although four of the five parties that contested the 1946 election also went on to sponsor candidates in 1950, and although Butler's party remained a force until 1966, none were ever really more than the political fronts of other organisations, such as labour unions or religious fraternities, or the political fiefdoms of key individuals (Catón 637). And this was understood locally. Just a few months before the 1950 general election, for instance, Kumar cited the absence of a functional party system in a speech before the Legislative Council which caused no confusion whatsoever ("More Provision" 5). Thus, Naipaul's synopsis, in retrospect, may be seen to astutely highlight the importance in the 1946 election of individuals who could appeal to particular ethnic blocks—an insight in harmony with responsible histories, which convey that the election was indeed a "confusing" affair, "reflecting the undeveloped state of party politics in Trinidad, the importance of personality and leadership struggles and the divisions in the society" (Brereton 195).

There is a big difference, however, between saying that party politics in Trinidad were "undeveloped" and saying that "there were no parties". For, while Trinidadians and others acquainted with the country might appreciate the metaphoric insight of such a synopsis, outside readers almost certainly will not, and their view of the political legitimacy of late colonial-era Trinidadian society will be coloured accordingly. Put plainly, the historian's representation of "undeveloped" party politics implies a complex situation needing further exploration in order to be understood. Naipaul, in contrast, presents a simplified reality—one that just happens to mesh with orientalist assumptions of Third World "backwardness" and to darken the outline of his ever-developing "picaroon" panorama (Said, *Orientalism* 205). The rhetorical dynamic at work here is all the more reprehensible because it is not "ignorance, shared and unstated" that is at play, as in most misleading representations of subaltern experience originating with Western first-world writers (Chakrabarty 28). Naipaul is not ignorant, either historically or rhetorically.

On the one hand, his familiarity with Trinidad in the 1940s is intimate. On the other hand, having lived for over a decade in England before writing *The Middle Passage*, he can hardly have failed to recognise how his words would likely be misread by a British or American public. Yet, he seems willing to allow and even to facilitate such misreading, especially when it lends credence to the pet metaphors of his fundamentally interpretive prose. It is not ignorance but orientalism that structures the rhetorical relationship between Naipaul and many of his readers. In addition to the ironic portrayal of a putative lack of sophistication in Trinidad's political structure and social organisation in 1946, *The Middle Passage* makes claims that are rather more personal, reflecting poorly in a much more direct way on the people of Trinidad.

Naipaul asserts, for example, that universal suffrage was declared in Trinidad "after no popular agitation" (*The Middle Passage* 72). This is strictly true. No suffragist riots, rallies or protests as such occurred in Trinidad in the years immediately preceding 1946. On the contrary, Trinidad as a country can only be called a loyal supporter of Britain in World War II. However, it is fatuous for Naipaul to imply that Trinidadians were generally satisfied with their living conditions and had little real interest in political self-determination—a state of affairs that would account for their "surprise", as he characterises it, when the vote was granted (*The Middle Passage* 72). In fact, the vote came as a culmination of decades of popular struggle in various forms. Most directly, the granting of the franchise in 1946 had its origins in the strikes led by Butler in 1937. In these strikes, workers from both the oil and sugar industries of Trinidad acted in solidarity, having been brought to the limits of desperation by abysmal living conditions made finally intolerable by increasingly inadequate wages in the face of rising inflation—privations suffered even as the major corporations declared double-digit dividends for their shareholders.[7]

Uniting in protests that began peacefully but ended in violence, Trinidadian labour agitators succeeded where other colonials had failed in gaining the attention of the British Parliament. As the official record of the debates that ensued in the House of Commons in 1938 reveals, the unrest in Trinidad became a point of discussion partly because Trinidad's oil industry made the country more important to the empire

7 Several oil and sugar companies operated in Trinidad in the 1930s, but the dominant oil producer was Apex Oil, which declared a dividend of forty-five per cent to its shareholders in 1937, and the leading sugar producer was Trinidad Leaseholds Limited, which paid out a thirty per cent dividend to its shareholders in the same year (Ryan, *Race and Nationalism* 61–62).

than most colonies, partly because of the charismatic quality of Butler's defiance, and partly because in Trinidad there was a dramatic "loss of life" (*Parliamentary Debates* 334–338, 766–858). The protests led to a dozen civilian and two police deaths, most notably the brutal murder of black policeman Charlie King by Butler's supporters on 19 June 1937 (Forster et al. 107).

On that day King, a much-hated man by all accounts, showed up in plain clothes at a Butler rally in the oilfield shantytown of Fyzabad, apparently intending to arrest Butler. Slightly differing accounts have been published concerning the killing that followed, but all agree on the cardinal facts that King was first stoned and then burned alive after Butler confronted him with a declaration that went something like: Hello Charlie King! I hear you come to arrest me, with your gold teeth shining like a circus clown. Go and tell those colonial bastards that I, Butler, will turn the British Empire upside down if they don't give the workers their just due[8] (Johnson 6).

Reports of this vivid spectacle seem to have elevated English public and official interest in the strikes, prompting the formation of the Commission on the Trinidad and Tobago Disturbances, whose findings were formally published as the Forster Report. When this report was released in January 1938, it sparked a fierce debate in the British House of Commons, with numerous Labour MPs using Trinidad as a case in point to decry the moral bankruptcy of their country's colonial policies. Labour MP W. Lunn initiates the discussion by suggesting: "It is a rare thing for any event that takes place in any British Colony to get any sort of publicity in this country", but "the disturbances in Trinidad, the loss of life that resulted from them, the appointment of the Commission and their report, are an exception to the general rule" (*Parliamentary Debates* 778). Lunn points out the difficulty of getting so much as a copy of the report, or even of the minutes of the House debates from the week before, when the issue of Trinidad was first raised. Yet "this sort of thing has been going on in many parts of the West Indies for a long time", he insists, "for weeks and months" (778).

MP Riley expands on this perspective, calling attention to "the circumstances out of which these disturbances took place and the fact

8 In a 2005 interview, eyewitness Elbert Redvers Blades, born 1902, recounts Butler's statement this way:

Ah Charlie King, ah hear you come to arrest me, your gold teeth shining in the sunlight like a circus clown. Go and tell those bastards of yours if they do not give the workers their just due, I Uriah Butler will turn the British Empire upside down (Fraser, "Eruption of the Working Class").

that successive Governments have known of these conditions for the last 40 years" (807). The overriding sentiment among Labour MPs, voiced in succession by Lunn, Riley and especially MP Benn is that the British government has failed its colonial subjects in the West Indies, neither protecting their interests in the House of Commons by insisting on good administration through the Colonial Office nor allowing them local political representation (844–845). With this in mind, Riley asks point-blank: "What are [sic] the Government going to do to give an increased measure of responsible democracy throughout the West Indian islands? What are they going to do to make the franchise easier for these people?" (807). Of Butler, MP Maxton concludes that he "performed a service not merely to this House of Commons [...] but he performed a great service to coloured workers in every part of the British Empire [...]. Three cheers for Butler!" (82, 1–22). This enthusiasm, along with the inclination to address the underlying economic and social issues in the West Indies through an extension of the franchise, was shared by Labour MPs as a body. "I, like every other Member on this side", MP Gallacher sums up in closing the debate, "am for the people of Trinidad", and "everyone has the right to the franchise" (855).

These MPs called particular attention to the truly "extraordinary" fact that the commissioners "could not find out anything about the profits of this or that industry, or whether the natives wanted to have the vote", leading to the direct assertion by MP Benn that "the right and the approved method of defending the interests of these people is to give them the chance to defend their own interests by giving them the vote" (841–845). The clear impetus for these comments, Naipaul's retrospective dismissal notwithstanding, was the popular agitation of ordinary Trinidadians led by an extraordinary elocutionist in the person of Tubal Uriah Buzz Butler. Calling Butler "an inspired negro genius", MP Bevan asserts near the end of the debates that "had it not been for the speeches and agitation of Uriah Butler [...] we should be ignorant in regard to the miseries of these people" (849). And from the outset, MP Maxton had maintained that "This particular Debate would not have taken place if there had not been an agitator called Uriah Butler" (816).

It is ironic that Naipaul would specifically elect to use the word "agitation" in his denial when Butler was so often identified as an agitator of the first order. The very governor of Trinidad at the time of the strikes, Sir Murchison Fletcher, recognised and admired Butler's unique ability to rouse the populace, avowing that "Butler is an agitator [...] a person who stirs things up. I have tried to stir things up; and Butler has done it so much more effectively than I have been able to do"

(Ryan, *Race and Nationalism* 57). It was precisely this debate, driven home by the findings of a second commission under the oversight of Lord Moyne in 1939—in this case, specifically charged with looking into the issue of the franchise in the West Indies as a whole—that led to the appointment of a Franchise Committee in Trinidad in 1941 and a recommendation in 1944 that the vote be given to all adults (Ryan, *Race and Nationalism* 65; Samaroo, "Politics" 90). In due course, a 1945 Order in Council made the proposed changes to the Trinidadian constitution official, and as soon as the war was well over the first election with universal suffrage was announced for 1 July 1946 (Brereton 193–194).

Simply put, the timetable was a bit drawn out, but the vote in 1946 came not as a gift dropped inexplicably from clear colonial skies but as a direct result of a political domino effect set off by the popular agitation of 1937. It might be argued, to be sure, that this agitation was not specifically for the vote, and that it was Labour MPs in London, rather than the people of Trinidad, who seem to have most expressly petitioned for the change. The Forster Report, in fact, is dismissive of the claim made by some Trinidadians that "inadequate representation" was a significant underlying cause of the 1937 "disturbances", instead citing "the working and living conditions of the labouring people" (Forster et al. 79). But this assertion, virtually unassailable at one level (who can doubt that their daily working and living conditions were of paramount importance to the Trinidadian strikers?), betrays a logical fallacy of colonialist mentality similar to that detected by Ranajit Guha in the official British renderings of peasant uprisings in India. As Guha argues in "The Prose of Counter-Insurgency," the various discourses of recorded British imperial history in India tend to agree in their erroneous presumption that peasant insurrections are "purely spontaneous and unpremeditated affairs" (45). Revolts in places like India are seen to "break out like thunderstorms, heave like earthquakes, spread like epidemics"—all metaphoric interpretations that connote "a very low state of civilization" (46).

By comparison, the Forster Report is progressive in its recognition of material motivations. But in suggesting that the underlying economic causes were functionally separate in the minds of the strikers from the larger issue of inadequate representation, the report still implies a form of action more emotional than strategic: action merely as reaction "sparked" by the rhetoric of a fiery Butler. Yet, as in Guha's reading of India, there was far too much at stake, and far too well-ingrained a pattern or experience of subaltern subjugation, for the "rural masses" to take decisive (and especially violent) action in anything less than a "motivated and conscious undertaking" (Guha, "Prose of Counter-Insurgency" 45–46).

Trinidadians had a great deal to lose in the killing of Charlie King, for example, but they were motivated to action by his attempt to arrest and thereby silence Butler, a man who had courageously spoken out in the cause of their material interests against employers intent on preserving their advantage under a system in which they were under no legal obligation to allow their workers to organise and negotiate for better conditions. Trinidadian workers were not so naive as to fail to discern that their suffering was a direct product of their voiceless status, and that having locally elected leaders could be useful either in dictating improved conditions directly or in pressuring officials in industry and government to allow the formation of unions that could effectively lobby for such changes. Furthermore, if there was ambiguity about whether ordinary Trinidadians specifically wanted the vote, it seems most likely to have arisen not because the people were ignorant of possible advantages but because the minority populations of the island were uncertain about what local democracy would look like. East Indians in particular feared that universal suffrage could result in an Afro Trinidadian power grab under which Indian interests might suffer even more than they already did under the British colonial regime (Ryan, *Race and Nationalism* 69).

Along these lines, it might be noted that the immediate impetus for Trinidadian East Indians to "Vote Indian" in 1946 would have been well known to a figure like Albert Gomes, who served as a key member of the European and Afro Trinidadian-dominated Franchise Committee that initially recommended that adult suffrage be extended only to those citizens who could understand spoken English (Ryan, *Pathways to Power* 7–8). This move was accurately viewed by East Indians as a blatant attempt to disenfranchise Hindi-speaking people, who made up a large segment of the Indo Trinidadian population. So intent were the non-Indians on pushing through this policy that it ultimately took an Order in Council from London, overriding both the governor and the committee, to eliminate the language requirement and pave the way for regional Indian victories in 1946 (Samaroo, "Politics" 90).

This Order in Council itself came as a result of Indian activism, adding a final touch of irony to Naipaul's proclamation in *The Middle Passage* that the vote was granted after "no popular agitation". Perhaps, the surest conclusion that can be reached from this data is that the sociopolitical situation in Trinidad in the 1930s and the 1940s was extremely complex. It is this complexity, as much as the particular denial of the existence of political parties or the neglect of events that might be seen as popular agitation, that Naipaul's representation of the situation elides. In reading his neat synopsis, one is led to conclude that Trinidad was simply politically immature in the sense that most of the colony's people were ambivalent about non-local issues and did not believe that participation in a democratic process would yield material advantages in their daily lives.

Again, in creating this impression, Naipaul glosses over the complexities of a history he knew only too well—an offense that even the conservative Colonial Secretary serving in the late 1930s, the Rt. Hon. William George Arthur Ormsby-Gore, did not commit, insisting in defense of his handling of the 1937 uprising that "the position [in Trinidad] is intensely complicated, and the climate is the hottest in the West Indies" (*Parliamentary Debates* 824). Ormsby-Gore was clearly not talking about the weather but about a society that was intensely frustrated by conditions that reflected a lack of political power. This tension and complexity are utterly lost in the themed rhetoric of *The Middle Passage*. And as suggested in the early stages of this essay, in this regard, the book is very much the stepchild of Naipaul's first, overtly fictional foray into the 1946 election, *The Mystic Masseur*.

While *The Middle Passage* tends to be summarily dismissive of the complexities of Trinidadian lived experience, drawing all analysis of the 1946 election back to the metaphor of the picaroon, *The Mystic Masseur* seems intent on turning any and everything Trinidadian into a farce, with feckless picaroon shysters generating most of the laughs. The political parties that would later be dismissed out of hand in *The Middle Passage* are the butt of a grand joke in *The Mystic Masseur*. Beyond simply dismissing the PPU as a transitory organisation, the novel belittles the genesis of party politics in Trinidad through a damning account of the formation and evolution of an East Indian political organisation called the Hindu Association.

The Hindu Association is born out of the rivalry between Ganesh and a fellow East Indian competitor, Narayan, in the spiritual healing business. Narayan raises the political stakes of their rivalry by founding a local periodical called "The Hindu". The tone of disdain toward this paper in the novel is unmistakable. It is "a ragged thing, [...] printed atrociously on the cheapest paper", which besides its central section—an editorial opinion column innocently titled "A Little Bird Tells Us", in which Narayan regularly blasts Ganesh—is filled primarily with "repeated urgings to 'Read The Hindu'" and quotations from scripture (151–152). Through this dubious medium, Narayan reaches out to like-minded Indians (that is, enemies of Ganesh) and forms a "party": the Hindu Association (*The Mystic Masseur* 166).

The illegitimacy of the Hindu Association as a party is as clearly communicated as that of the newspaper. When Ganesh first hears of it, he derisively tells his friend Beharry: "You and me know what sort of thing Indian associations is in this place. Narayan and those people just like little girls playing doll house" (166). Ganesh's opinion signifies little on its own, but his verdict is quickly backed up by the main narrative. "Ganesh's judgment was sound", readers are informed, for, besides electing Narayan president at its first general meeting, the Hindu Association also elects "four Assistant-Presidents, two Vice-Presidents, four Assistant Vice-Presidents; many Treasurers; one Secretary-in-Chief, six Secretaries, twelve Assistant-Secretaries" (166). Every interested individual is recognised with an official position, cementing the party's identity as a childish make-believe alliance of dignity-starved picaroons, temporarily united by their jealousy of Ganesh.

Yet, just as Naipaul's disdain for the parties of 1946 proves factually strained, this ridiculous portrayal of the Hindu Association looks tendentious in light of the fact that many actual Indian associations had a long and distinguished history of influence in Trinidad. A short list of these would include the traditionally orthodox Sanatan Dharma Association, the Arya Samaj, the Kabir Panth, and the Seunerinis or Siva-Narayanis (a name Naipaul appropriated—a phenomenon of which there is more to come) (Niehoff and Niehoff 112–113). Each of these groups had its own religious tenets, but politically the Sanatan Dharma was dominant, especially after it united with another major Hindu organisation to form the explicitly political Sanatan Dharma Maha Sabha (Singh 54). Such religiously oriented traditionalist groups were but part of an organisational scene that also featured progressive secular organisations like the Young East Indian Party, the Trinidad Labour Party, and various trade union groups (Samaroo, "Politics" 83).

A number of these organisations dated back to the late nineteenth and early twentieth century; many more had their origins in the East Indian cultural renaissance that began in Trinidad around 1930 (Campbell 119). While Naipaul's novel does not mislead in giving the impression that these bodies reflected and exacerbated schisms in the larger East Indian community, it certainly diminishes their scope and the seriousness of the divisions they reflected and caused (Ryan, *Race and Nationalism* 72). Narayan's party throughout the novel becomes more and more a joke, significant only when the *Trinidad Sentinel* (Naipaul's stand-in for the *Trinidad Guardian*) ignorantly supposes it represents East Indians as a group and begins to report on the party's activities (*The Mystic Masseur* 166). This notoriety irks Ganesh, and, in retaliation, he conspires with three friends to found The Dharma (helpfully glossed for non-Hindi readers as "the faith"), an organisation that informed readers cannot fail to connect with the real-life Sanatan

Dharma Association. Ganesh is elected business manager, his friends Swami and Partap editor-in-chief and editor respectively, and Swami's nephew subeditor—as in Narayan's party, everybody involved is granted a title (*The Mystic Masseur* 179–180).

Likewise, Ganesh and company use their own rag to launch a rival party, the Hindu League (186–189), which ultimately takes over the Hindu Association through a bit of political skullduggery and muscle (*The Mystic Masseur* 193–197). This action is reminiscent in its results of the real merger that formed the Sanatan Dharma Maha Sabha, yet the formation of Naipaul's fictional super-party occurs under the most questionable of circumstances. Once the dust settles, Ganesh is elected president of the new organisation, and in the wake of Narayan's forced retirement, he enters the 1946 election running against Indarsingh, a former Narayan supporter and Oxford graduate who has switched his allegiance to the PPU.

This picture of party politics, ludicrous at best, clearly underlies the claim soon to follow in *The Middle Passage* that there were "no parties, only individuals" in the 1946 election. It also paves the way for more hilarious machinations of the picaroon when the political neophyte Ganesh handily defeats Indarsingh, who makes the mistake of campaigning as if he were running for office in England or America. In the race between these two "enterprising individuals", to borrow a phrase used to describe the 1946 candidates in *The Middle Passage*, each proceeds to distinguish himself as laughably inept in his own way (72).

Ganesh's ineptness comes of never even trying to approach the election as a serious political process. He fights "the cleanest election campaign in Trinidad history" because he has, in fact, "no platform" (*The Mystic Masseur* 199). His experiences in the faith-healing business have taught him that getting ahead in Trinidad is best done by playing to the prejudices of the people. So instead of political rallies, he simply holds a series of "prayer-meetings" in which he "quite casually" announces his candidacy in Hindi. This programme, a caricature of the lecture series offered by Pundit Ragbir in real life, is inept by Euro-American standards but locally effective.

In contrast, Indarsingh's politically progressive platform is delivered in "long, carefully thought-out" lectures that he later publishes as "Colonialism: Four Essays—about the Economics of Colonialism, Colonialism in Perspective, The Anatomy of Oppression, The Approach to Freedom" (*The Mystic Masseur* 200–201). But his reward for such intelligence and energetic idealism is that he utterly fails to connect with the people, who instead gravitate towards the familiarity of Ganesh's picaroon buffoonery. This is Kelshall and Gomes versus Kumar and Butler all over again but reduced to farce. Indarsingh becomes known as the "Walking Dictionary", and Ganesh's wife wonders aloud why those pestered by his big words "don't throw something big at his head" (*The Mystic Masseur* 201). Even his published lectures cannot compare in the minds of the people with Ganesh's book on Profitable Evacuation—a text cleared for printing only because authorities, too lazy to read it, assume from the title that it relates to the war. It does not. But the book trumps Indarsingh's highbrow anticolonial lectures because it is attractively "printed on thick paper, with a cover of brightest yellow decorated with a lotus" (*The Mystic Masseur* 165).

The people of Trinidad in this novel are not impressed with real intellectual depth or politically progressive ideas but rather with appearances, with personalities and with a paltry but cunningly pragmatic approach to life similar to their own. *The Middle Passage* looms on the horizon: Naipaul's only figure for the modern Trinidadian is, quite simply, the picaroon. The trouble, again, is that this metaphor drastically simplifies the actual situation in 1946. It wasn't that simple, and those elected by the people of Trinidad to the Legislative Council in 1946 bear little resemblance to Naipaul's harlequin band of failed mimic men.

In his fictional narrative, by holding up equivalents of the newly elected members of the Legislative Council (MLCs) to ridicule, Naipaul moves from satirising systems—criticising Trinidad's party structure and social organisations—to satirising individuals. This is, perhaps, most vividly seen in the farcical representation of a state dinner that takes place at Government House after the election. Naipaul here has a heyday with the well-worn trope of the lower classes trying to leapfrog into the circle of the elite. Ganesh's "first experience as an M.L.C.", the state dinner is "a mortifying one" for the characters and the country they ostensibly represent (*The Mystic Masseur* 206). Throughout the scene, the inferiority of the new members "speaks" for itself through their heavily inflected local dialect. Words are left out that British and American readers associate with grammatical completeness, and several mans and you knows are thrown in, making the speakers appear simpleminded or almost illiterate.

Most prominently mocked at first is the clothing of the new councillors, described as "a treat for the photographers" (*The Mystic Masseur* 207). Ganesh (again, perhaps, the character most similar to Kumar) opts to show up in a dhoti; a member from Port-of-Spain (Gomes's area) chooses a khaki suit and sun helmet (a British imperial touch); another wears jodhpurs (an Indian look again, but in this case a colonial one); another "still adhering for the moment to his pre-election principles" comes in a working man's shorts and open shirt; "the blackest M.L.C.", a man named Primrose, comes in a "three-piece suit trimmed out with yellow gloves and a monocle". "Everybody else, among the men, looked like penguins, sometimes even down to the black faces" (*The Mystic Masseur* 208–209). Clearly, racist in tenor, these descriptions betray a general embarrassment for such socially inept people.

Similarly articulated is the limited knowledge of British table manners in this group. Several of them, including Ganesh, attempt to cover their ignorance by rudely refusing various items, claiming religious scruples or palate preferences. Others furtively look to the waiters for hints. Unable to catch their attention, however, one complains: "Is why black people can't get on. You see how these waiters behaving? And they black like hell too, you know" (*The Mystic Masseur* 208). As befitting a gathering of picaroons, at this dinner it appears to be mostly a case of every man for himself, a point emphasised when the "blackest" MLC falls victim to "unoriginal disaster" when his monocle falls into his soup. This man's lack of social grace in particular is highlighted as he immediately calls this blunder to the attention of the Governor's lady who, possessing contrasting dignity, has politely looked away. Ironically, when the other MLCs, momentarily forgetting their own troubles, "looked on with sympathy", he turns on them and says "What all you staring at? All you ain't see nigger before?" (*The Mystic Masseur* 209).

The dinner is a grand humiliation, revealing the new MLCs as failed mimic men. The only possible exception is an "elderly Christian Indian" who brings as his partner a four-year-old daughter and plies her with morsels of the food the others are too baffled to approach. Even his confidence is marred, however, by the spectacle he creates in bringing a child to a state dinner, and still more by his disclaimer that he could not bring his wife because he has never married (*The Mystic Masseur* 207–208). All this is clearly done for comic satirical effect; but the satire is one-sided: only the new politicians and their partners are mocked. In stark contrast, the Governor's lady "moved with assurance and determination among the members and their wives. The more disconcerting the man or woman, the more she was interested, the more she was charming" (*The Mystic Masseur* 207). It is as if Naipaul is saying to his British and American readership, "Despite any outward trappings of office, I know that if you could mix with and really come to know our politicians you would find them hilariously, and at times disgustingly, unrefined" (*The Mystic Masseur* 209).

However, although *The Mystic Masseur* maligns the speech, dress and social graces of the winning candidates of the 1946 election, in reality they were well educated (by any standard), highly articulate (always in English, and for the Indian candidates in Hindi and sometimes other

South Asian languages as well), familiar with a wide variety of social graces (including British table manners) and sincere in their pursuit of serious political goals. In short, they were the equals in the political realm of V. S. Naipaul in the literary. This is especially true of Ganesh's doppelganger, Ranjit Kumar, and Indarsingh's possible double, Albert Gomes. Evidence of the general articulateness of the candidates abounds in the election guide printed as a supplement to the *Sunday Guardian* on 26 May 1946, which included a wide selection of invited statements submitted by leading candidates.

These statements universally address serious political issues in good prose. Postelection press coverage of debates in the Legislative Council also provides ample evidence that the elected members were quite fluent in standard British English. This is not to suggest, of course, that other dialects of English or other languages are in any way inferior, but simply to raise questions about Naipaul's portraying his MLCs speaking in a local dialect that he could rightly assume many of his readers would see as a marker of ignorance. The intellectual credentials of the successful candidates were also nothing to scoff at. Gomes, along with such notable figures as Alfred Mendes, R. A. C. de Boissiere and C. L. R. James, was a leading figure in the Trinidadian cultural renaissance of the early 1930s, a movement built around the magazine *The Beacon*, which Gomes founded and edited, in addition to editing in 1937 an anthology of Trinidadian creative work (Brereton 175–176).

Kumar, the son of a wealthy Punjabi banker, took his BSc degree as an engineer at the age of eighteen from the Imperial College of Science in South Kensington in 1930 (Kumar, *Thoughts and Memories* 2). While Naipaul mocks his MLCs' dress and dining etiquette, the frontpage election results coverage in the *Trinidad Guardian* on 2 July 1946 includes photos of all nine winners, all dressed impeccably: eight in Western suits and ties, one (Mr Abidh) in a high-collared traditional Indian formal. Gomes, in particular, was a natty dresser: in what may be termed his trademark picture (reproduced literally dozens of times in the *Guardian* over the years) he sports a fancy tie, a conservative suit and a distinguished looking pipe. As for Naipaul's mockery of the MLCs' dining etiquette, no mention of any official state dinner at the governor's residence appears in the *Trinidad Guardian*, but the Sanatan Dharma Association did celebrate the victories of Kumar and the other East Indian winners with a formal banquet held in their honour near the end of July ("Sanatan Dharma" 3).

This was a serious political gathering, and it featured no trouble of note with table manners or utensils. On that score, Kumar, in particular, in contrast to Ganesh would have had no trouble whatsoever, no matter what was served. Following his formal education in England, he had returned to India as an officer in training for the Indian Imperial Police, and as such was instructed in law, drill manoeuvres, riding, polo, hockey and, above all, dining etiquette. “Most important was dinner in the mess at night”, he recalls in his autobiography: “strict English etiquette had to be observed as if we were dining at Buckingham Palace. The most important things as a British officer in India were the social graces” (*Thoughts and Memories* 8). Eventually, as mess secretary, Kumar himself was in charge of meals and “became expert at foods and wines”, giving several banquets that were attended by, among other local dignitaries, the Governor of Punjab (*Thoughts and Memories* 8).

To label these tastes and attainments as mimicry is to stretch the bounds of that concept into hyperbole. Naipaul might have fairly and perhaps productively satirised the political leaders’ social distance from the majority of their constituents, but instead he represented them as crude versions of the most uneducated of those constituents. Again, this is not to suggest that sophistication is definable only by a Euro–American standard. But in making his jokes, Naipaul consistently portrays the leading non-European figures of Trinidadian society in ways that prompt non-Trinidadian readers to see these figures and their society as inferior. This is all the more clear when one considers that there were, in fact, many examples of bad behaviour among rank-and-file Trinidadians in the political melee leading up to the 1946 general elections—behaviour that Naipaul might easily have appropriated for farcical representation in *The Mystic Masseur*. Most notable were several instances of heckling at political rallies.

On 4 May 1946 (approximately two months before the election), for instance, the *Trinidad Guardian* reported that Butler was unable to hold a meeting owing to interference from Kelshall supporters (“Butler Gets” 3), who on another occasion “made a straw and rice bag effigy of [Butler ally] Timothy Roodal and thrashed it” (“Mr. Roodal Whipped” 2). Butler was again heckled and booed for a half hour straight as he tried to speak on 12 June (“Butler Booed” 2), and candidate Vernon Wharton faced “incessant heckling” on 19 June (“Hecklers Busy”). The problem quickly became so widespread that the Guardian ran a special column on it on 22 June (“Hecklers Breaking up Election Meetings”), citing numerous examples of what appeared to be “organized groups in every constituency” using heckling “as a means of breaking up meetings”. The candidates themselves, as one might imagine, were incensed—one even called the heckling “the sort of conduct that leads to Hitlerism”. Unruliness apparently reached its apex about a week before the election, as reports came in on 23 June of hecklers throwing rotten eggs ("Hecklers Throw").

Such accounts may help to explain why a writer like Naipaul would disparage "the squalor of politics that came to Trinidad in 1946" (*The Middle Passage* 72). Certainly, there were many who questioned the policy of universal suffrage from the beginning. Trinidad estate owner Sir Norman Lamont, for instance, speaking in Glasgow in early February 1946, opined: "it is strange indeed that, in an age and generation which pay so much lip-service to education, the franchise alone should be free for all, however ignorant or misguided" ("Sir Norman" 14). "This is the offspring", he concluded, "of that bastard conception of democracy which assumes a peculiar inspiration in the opinions of the uneducated" ("Sir Norman" 14).

Though more strident than most, Sir Norman voices a sentiment that seems to have been prevalent among Trinidadian and foreign elites. Consider, for instance, a series of statements made in the months leading up to the election by foreign visitors and local dignitaries alike, all of whom seemed concerned that perhaps the common people were being endowed with a greater privilege and responsibility than they deserved. One of the most notable of these observers was A. J. Pelletier, a Canadian who had organised the first general election in the West Indies (in Jamaica in 1945) and was subsequently imported to arrange the Trinidadian event. Pelletier is headlined in the *Trinidad Guardian* urging voters to "justify the new trust" that had been placed in them ("Mr. Pelletier Says" 8).

Similarly, Dr S. M. Laurence, in an editorial piece published about a month before the election, speaks of the "high responsibility" of the vote, and suggests that "Trinidad is within a few paces of a political crossroads" ("Trinidad Has Arrived" 6). "The privilege of the vote is a sort of coronation of the dignity of the human person", another foreign visitor observed, and "Real men, I know, will weigh well before voting" ("Visitor Says" 2). Such statements were essentially hopeful but betray trepidation that the "privilege" of the franchise was perhaps a pearl being cast before swine.

Sir Norman's arguments recall the extreme prejudice revealed in the majority recommendation of the Franchise Committee that only those Trinidadians with demonstrable English language literacy should be allowed to vote. Such prejudices continued to surface as the election approached, reflected for instance in a system of symbols devised to aid illiterates in voting. Figure 13.1 shows a sample ballot employing this system. Figure 13.2 is a cartoon that mocks it.

Fig. 13.1. "Symbols Aid Illiterates to Vote." Trinidad Guardian, 21 April 1946, p 2.

Fig. 13.2. Cartoon by P. Lelong. Trinidad Guardian, 24 April 1946, p 4.

Although the system focused on the illiterate voter, an assumption of general ineptness is implied. It seems unlikely that Naipaul, well-educated himself even at age of fourteen and eager to eventually prove his worth in a cosmopolitan literary arena (*Middle Passage* 41; "Prologue" 43–44; Naipaul, *Reading and Writing* 3), would have been untouched by such powerful structures of feeling, pervasive in his island community. Certainly they pervade *The Middle Passage*, where the returning Naipaul memorably concludes that "the history of the islands can never be satisfactorily told" because "history is built around achievement and creation; and nothing was created in the West Indies" (29). These sentiments had mellowed somewhat by the mid-1990s, when Naipaul published *A Way in the World*, but he still maintains there that "the problem" with writing in the 1950s and the 1960s about "a place like Trinidad was that black people were simply not a subject" (96).

He apparently saw quite clearly that when it came to local West Indian life, in that early postcolonial era, "no one was interested in the subtleties" (*The Middle Passage* 96). Yet, his initial response to this rhetorical no-win situation in *The Middle Passage* is to convey to his British and American audiences that he can be trusted because he is a traitor—because he has local knowledge but shuns local loyalties. As Rob Nixon has convincingly shown, Naipaul's self-fashioned ethos is exceptional. Through the medium of his journalism, in particular, Naipaul has forged an image of himself as an "expert" observer, one "possessing a penetrating, analytic understanding of Third World societies" (4). This is indeed a "reputation of a different order" from that enjoyed even by most other postcolonial writers, whose representations are often perceived to be biased in favour of their native lands, while the contrarian Naipaul emerges "as a figure [...] untrammeled by ideologies and beholden to nobody" (10).

Just before introducing his vision of the Trinidadian picaroon, he speaks of a "yearning" among West Indians "to be thought different and worthy" (64). This "is not a new thing", Naipaul explains, and progress can be made "only when writers cease to think about letting down their sides" (64–65). He specifically suggests that "many a writer" from the West Indies "has displayed a concern, visible perhaps only to the West Indian, to show how removed his group is from blackness, how close to whiteness" (*The Middle Passage* 65). Others have done this, it is suggested, by whitewashing their group for outside readers.

This, Naipaul implies, he will not do. Yet, in the very act of boasting that he is above such things, Naipaul does for himself alone what he accuses others of doing more generally. He shows just how far removed he is from the "blackness" of his group. This is accomplished all the more effectively in *The Mystic Masseur*, by Naipaul's making light of the candidates rather than the electorate, inasmuch as the candidates were more particularly his equals—and thus his rivals.

To conclude, then, the fictional representations in *The Mystic Masseur*, much like the sweeping visions of *The Middle Passage*, convey a spurious simplicity and attendant impression of backwardness, suspiciously targeting Naipaul's erstwhile associates. Yet, here again, now that we are supplied with a wider array of textual examples and historical analysis, we must circle back to the core issues raised by Naipaul's surprising assertion of the "picaroon" nature of Trinidadian society. Has Naipaul through his early fiction and journalistic work provided a skeleton key that unlocks for the uninitiated the underlying absurdity of mid-twentieth-century Trinidadian life? Does his satirical fiction, offensive as it might be to contemporary sensibilities, actually illuminate shadowy truths? And could it at least be argued that his journalism, with all its exaggeration and elision, is more insightful than misleading? Might Trinidadian politics on the whole, for instance, possibly be viewed as being much less serious in their inception than surviving historical records seem to suggest? Given that all sources are situated, could Naipaul's representations be regarded as just as authoritative or valid as those records? Ultimately, does Naipaul's situation as a societal insider trump the logic of multiple examples of apparently colonialist ideological renderings?

The danger here is that an insider's perspective will tempt us to suppose that by virtue of a privileged source the past has become knowable and grounded. Even naturally critical readers are predisposed to give extra credence to lived experience and the journalistic medium, and in doing so may, as Gayatri Spivak cautions, "allow the complicity of the investigating subject [...] to disguise itself as transparency" ("Can the Subaltern Speak?" 90). This is problematic because, as Raymond Williams puts it, the "always moving substance of the past" inevitably swirls in powerful undercurrents beneath the visibly placid waters of the "fixed, explicit, [and] known" (128). Although "perhaps the dead can be reduced to fixed forms" by living interpreters for their own purposes, "their surviving records are against it", and "the living will not be reduced", Williams wryly observes, "at least in the first person; living third persons may be different" (129).

Williams' caution is apt; the postcolonial author, like any author, represents or "speaks for" a constituency much as a politician does—a concept signified by Marx's term *vertreten* (Spivak, "Can the Subaltern Speak?" 70). At the same time, the author is a literal représenter through the medium of art (*darstellen*). This "double session of representations", as Spivak labels it, hinges on the distinction "between a proxy and a portrait". That distinction invokes the dual problematic discourses of authorial detachment and authorial omniscience: discourses arising in works, whether creative or critical, that imply either that a functional gap exists between texts and their subjects or that authors can "imagine"—and, therefore, represent—"the kind of Power and Desire that would inhabit the unnamed subject of the Other" (70–71, 75).

The internationalisation of English literature in the wake of mid-twentieth-century colonial independence struggles in South Asia, Africa, the Caribbean and elsewhere has created a literary environment in which readers often know comparatively little about the lived experiences behind fictional and journalistic representations. In this environment, where literary texts themselves often serve as the first and perhaps only introduction to other places, cultures and experiences, the power of the représenter is clearly accentuated. This raises the question: what responsibilities devolve upon the postcolonial writer?

Spivak's cautionary insights noted above are typically administered as correctives for first-world academics intent either on absolving their responsibility for the interventions made by their texts or on recklessly (and often selfishly) seeking to lend their voices to the silenced. Yet they apply as well, Spivak posits, to "native informants", locally knowledgeable "elites" whose insider status tempts readers to forget "that the colonized subaltern subject is irretrievably heterogeneous" (79). In reality, to "confront" the subaltern "is not to represent (*vertreten*) them but to learn to represent (*darstellen*) ourselves" (84).

Thus, postcolonial artists ought never to be viewed as natural representatives of places or people in subjugated or formerly subjugated regions of the world, nor should their works be received as transparent images of subaltern lived experience. Receiving them that way perpetuates a fundamental tenet of orientalism, which Said perceives as a worldview "more particularly valuable as a sign of European–Atlantic power over the Orient than it is as a veridic discourse about the Orient (which is what, in its academic or scholarly form, it claims to be)" (*Orientalism* 6). Academic or journalistic objectivity is an orientalist illusion. In reality, the works of postcolonial artists, again like those of any others, most directly represent the artists themselves.

This is true, I would argue, in a special way with regard to Naipaul, who has gone further than any other postcolonial author in seeking to escape the shadow of his own complicity with orientalism. The posed objectivity of a text like *The Middle Passage*, where he insists that one must be "icily detached" in order to tell the story of one's own country (29), seems too convenient a personal distancing for a writer whose first novel depicts a protagonist evolving as need demands, ultimately casting off his Trinidadian identity in favour of a British cosmopolitan facade. Trinidadians living and dead are reduced by Naipaul's thematic journalism in both *The Middle Passage* and *The Mystic Masseur*, and these texts are much more telling about their author than his island.

Nixon's suggestion that the "fierceness of *The Middle Passage*" contrasts markedly with the "bounteous comedy of the early fiction" thus seems misleading (12). For while there are distinct tonal differences, to be sure, in their key "functions and indices" (Guha, "Prose of Counter-Insurgency" 54), the texts are twins: Naipaul's representation of the 1946 election in *The Middle Passage* is essentially a continuation of his original portrayal in *The Mystic Masseur*. In the novel, the genesis of party politics in 1946 is belittled, the very notion of serious agitation in Trinidad is belied and the lived complexities and larger nationalistic and imperial significance of island politics are severely elided. This becomes crucial in light of the impression of reliability conveyed first by the quasi-historical novel and later (to a much greater degree) by the journalistic travel book: the one-two punch of *The Mystic Masseur* and *The Middle Passage* implies that the grand jokes of the fictional narrative closely reflect actual experience. And in a readerly environment where historical credulity mingles easily with ideological prejudice and deference to perceived expertise, this makes all the difference.

In winning the Nobel Prize for Literature in 2001, Naipaul was hailed by the Swedish Academy for "having united perceptive narrative and incorruptible scrutiny in works that compel us to see the presence of suppressed histories" ("Nobel"). In view of my analysis, this statement is about half right. His early narratives are indeed perceptive, but his scrutiny is hardly incorruptible, and in revealing suppressed histories he seems to have suppressed a lot of history. Read as metaphor, Naipaul's first journalism and first fiction are insightful. Read as metonymy, they are misleading. Read as verisimilitude, they are utterly reprehensible.

Works cited

"Asked to Stand." *Trinidad Guardian*, 1 Apr. 1946, p 2.

Brereton, Bridget. *A History of Modern Trinidad 1783-1962*. Heinemann, 1981.

"Butler Booed Through Speech." *Trinidad Guardian*, 12 June 1946, p 2.

"Butler Claims He and Roodal are God-Chosen Leaders." *Trinidad Guardian*, 2 June 1946, p 2.

"Butler Gets Noisy Greeting." *Trinidad Guardian*, 4 May 1946, p 3.

"Butler Will Fight Gomes for North Port-of-Spain Seat." *Trinidad Guardian*, 4 Apr. 1946, p 2.

Campbell, Carl C. "The East Indian Revolt against Missionary Education 1928-1939." La Guerre, John, editor. *Calcutta to Caroni: The East Indians of Trinidad*. The University of the West Indies, 1985. pp 117–131.

Catón, Matthias. "Trinidad and Tobago." *Elections of the Americas: A Data Handbook*, edited by Dieter Nohlen, vol. 1, Oxford University Press, 2005, pp. 627–646.

Chakrabarty, Dipesh. *Provincializing Europe: Postcolonial Thought and Historical Difference*. Princeton University Press, 2000.

"Election Results at a Glance." *Trinidad Guardian*, 3 July 1946, p 3.

Forster, John, et al. *Trinidad and Tobago Disturbances 1937: Report of Commission*. HMSO, 1938.

Fraser, Tony. "Eruption of the Working Class." *Trinidad Guardian*, 2005. Accessed on 17 October 2020. <http://www.guardian.co.tt/archives/2005-06-16/Tonyfraser.html>

Gallagher, Catherine, and Stephen Greenblatt. *Practicing New Historicism*. University of Chicago Press, 2000.

Guha, Ranajit. "On Some Aspects of the Historiography of Colonial India." *Selected Subaltern Studies* edited by Guha, Ranajit and Gayatri Spivak . Oxford UP, 1988 pp. 33–44.

———. "The Prose of Counter-Insurgency." *Selected Subaltern Studies* edited by Guha, Ranajit and Gayatri Spivak . Oxford University Press, 1988 pp. 45–84.

Guha, Ranajit, and Gayatri Chakravorty Spivak, editors. *Selected Subaltern Studies*. Oxford University Press, 1988.

"Hecklers Breaking Up Election Meetings: Candidate Gangsterism." *Trinidad Guardian*, 22 June 1946.

"Hecklers Busy in the East." *Trinidad Guardian*, 19 June 1946

"Hecklers Throw Rotten Eggs." *Trinidad Guardian*, 23 June 1946

"How the Constitution of Trinidad Developed." Trinidad, *Sunday Guardian Election Guide*, 1946 p 3.

"Indians to Be Told." *Trinidad Guardian*, 25 June 1946, p 2.

"Isolated Efforts." *Trinidad Guardian*, 26 June 1946, p 3.

JanMohamed, Abdul R. "The Economy of Manichean Racial Difference in Colonialist Literature." *Critical Inquiry*, vol. 12, no. 1, 1985, pp. 59–87.

Johnson, Kim. "Mob Pounced on Charlie King." *Trinidad Guardian*, Sunday 28 November 1999, p 6.

Jussawalla, Feroza. Introduction. *Conversations with VS. Naipaul*. University Press of Mississippi, 1997, pp. ix–xvii.

"Keep Out 'Individual Glamour Boys.'" *Trinidad Guardian*, 26 June 1946, p 3.

King, Bruce. *V. S. Naipaul*. 2nd ed., Palgrave, 2003.

"Kumar Gains Easy Win." *Trinidad Guardian*, 2 July 1946, p 1.

Kumar, Ranjit. *Thoughts and Memories of Ranjit Kumar*. Inprint Caribbean Publishers, 1981.

La Guerre, John, editor. *Calcutta to Caroni: The East Indians of Trinidad*. The University of the West Indies, 1985.

Malik, Yogendra K. *East Indians in Trinidad: A Study in Minority*, Oxford University Press, 1971.

Meyers, Jeffrey. "Dark Vision": Rev. of *India: A Million Mutinies Now* by V. S. Naipaul. *Virginia Quarterly Review* Winter 1992. Accessed on 5 Mar 2018. <https://www.vqronline.org/dark-vision >.

"A Momentous Election." *Trinidad Guardian*, 30 June 1946, p 4.

"More Provision." *Trinidad Guardian*, 29 Apr. 1950, p 5.

"Mr. J. B. Kelshall Thinks Electorate Should Be Allowed to Recall Representatives." *Trinidad Guardian, Election Guide Supplement*, 26 May 1946, p 14.

"Mr. Pelletier Says Citizens Must Try to Justify New Trust." *Trinidad Guardian*, 11 Apr. 1946, p 8.

"Mr. Roodal Whipped in Effigy." *Trinidad Guardian*, 24 Apr. 1946, p 2.

Naipaul, V. S. "A Conversation with V. S. Naipaul." Interview with Bharati Mukherjee and Robert Boyers. *Salmagundi*, vol. 54, 1981, pp. 4–22.

———. "Dark Visions of V. S. Naipaul" Interview with Charles Michener. *Conversations with V. S. Naipaul*, edited by Feroza Jussawalla. University Press of Mississippi, 1997, pp. 63–74.

———. "Prologue to an Autobiography" *Finding the Centre: Two Narratives.* Andre Deutsch, 1984.

———. Introduction. *East Indians in the West Indies: Colonialism and the Struggle for Identity*, edited by Bridget Brereton and Winston Dookeran. Kraus, 1982. pp. 1–9.

———. *The Middle Passage: The Caribbean Revisited.* Vintage, 2002.

———. *The Middle Passage: Impressions of Five Societies, British, French, and Dutch - in the West Indies and South America*. Deutsch, 1984, pp. 15–86.

———. *The Mystic Masseur* Andre Deutsch, 1957.

———. *Reading and Writing*. New York Review of Books, 2000.

———. "V. S. Naipaul: A *Transition* Interview. Interview with Adrian Rowe-Evans. *Transition*, vol. 40, 1971, pp. 56–62.

———. *A Way in the World.* Knopf, 1994.

Niehoff, Arthur, and Juanita Niehoff. *East Indians in the West Indies.* Public Museum Publications in Anthropology 6, 1960.

Nixon, Rob. *London Calling: V. S. Naipaul, Postcolonial Mandarin*. Oxford University Press, 1992.

"Nobel Prize in Literature 2001: V. S. Naipaul." *Nobelprize.org*. 11 Oct. 2001. The Swedish Academy 20 July 2005. http://nobelprize.org/literature/laureates/2001/press.html.

"Only Way." *Trinidad Guardian*, 9 Apr. 1946, p 2.

Parliamentary Debates: Fifth Series - Volume 332. House of Commons Official Report: Fifth Session 1937-38. HMSO, 1938.

"Present Members of Legislature". *Trinidad Guardian, Sunday Guardian Election Guide*, 26 May 1946, p 1.

Ryan, Selwyn. *Pathways to Power: Indians and the Politics of National Unity in Trinidad and Tobago*. Caribbean Paper and Printed Products, 1996.

———. *Race and Nationalism in Trinidad and Tobago: A Study of Decolonisation in a Multiracial Society*. University of Toronto Press, 1972.

Said, Edward. "Intellectuals in the Post-Colonial World." *Salmagundi*, Vol 70–71. 1986, pp. 44–64.

———. *Orientalism*. Vintage, 1979.

Samaroo, Brinsley. "Politics and Afro-Indian Relations." *Calcutta to Caroni: The East Indians of Trinidad*. Edited by La Guerre, John, The University of the West Indies, 1985. pp. 77–93.

———. "'The Vanguard of Indian Nationalism in Trinidad': *The East Indian Weekly*, 1928–1932." Presented to the Ninth Conference of Caribbean Historians, Cave Hill, Barbados, 4–7 Apr. 1977. Typescript University of the West Indies Library, St. Augustine, Trinidad.

"Sanatan Dharma Association Fetes Four Legislators." *Trinidad Guardian*, 30 July 1946, p 3.

Singh, Kelvin. "Indians and the Larger Society." *Calcutta to Caroni: The East Indians of Trinidad*. Edited by La Guerre, John, *Calcutta to Caroni: The East Indians of Trinidad*. The University of the West Indies, 1985. pp. 33–61.

"Sir Norman Lamont Sees Bastard Idea of Democracy." *Trinidad Guardian*, 3 Feb. 1946, p 14.

"Speaker Urges Vote as Butler Directs." *Trinidad Guardian*, 5 May 1946, p. 2.

Spivak, Gayatri Chakravorty. "Can the Subaltern Speak?" *Colonial Discourse and Post-Colonial Theory: A Reader*, edited by Patrick Williams and Laura Chrisman. Columbia University Press, 1994, pp. 66–111.

———. *A Critique of Postcolonial Reason: A History of the Vanishing Present*. Harvard University Press, 1999.

"This Is Your Election." *Trinidad Guardian*, 26 May 1946, p 1.

"Trinidad Has Arrived at Political Crossroads." *Trinidad Guardian*, 26 May 1946, p 6.

"United Front Tours Victoria." *Trinidad Guardian*, 25 June 1946, p 2.

"Visitor Says There Must Be No Selling of the Vote." *Trinidad Guardian*, 30 June 1946, p 2.

Walcott, Derek. "The Art of Poetry 37: Derek Walcott." Interview with Edward Hirsch. *Paris Review*, vol. 101, 1986, pp. 196–230. *Conversations with Derek Walcott*, edited by William Baer. University Press of Mississippi, 1996, pp. 95–121.

———. "The Spoiler's Return." *Collected Poems 1948-1984*. Farrar, 1986, p 433.

———. "This Country is a very Small Place." Interview with Anthony Milne. *Sunday Express* (Trinidad), 14 Mar. 1982, pp. 18–19. *Conversations Derek Walcott*, edited by William Baer, University Press of Mississippi, pp. 70–78.

White, Landeg. *V. S. Naipaul: A Critical Introduction*. Macmillan, 1975.

Williams, Raymond. *Marxism and Literature*. Oxford University Press, 1977.

"Women Tell South Back Kelshall." *Trinidad Guardian*, 19 May 1946, p 5.

Chapter 14

COLONIAL FANTASY SHATTERED, COSMOPOLITAN DREAM BROKEN: V. S. NAIPAUL'S *MR STONE AND THE KNIGHTS COMPANION*[1]

Weiwei Xu

Introduction

The metropolis is conventionally viewed as the site where cosmopolitanism is created and located, and its economic and cultural dominance becomes central to the cosmopolitan imagination. Mike Featherstone, for instance, points out that "cosmopolitan dispositions are closely associated with cities", more importantly with Euro–American metropolises such as London, Paris and New York, since they have long been "the sites for markets and the mixing of people, commodities, ideas and cultures" and "the homes of a wide range of intellectual and artistic social and cultural movements and institutions" (1–2).

Gary Bridge posits: "It is in the burgeoning transnational neighbourhoods of the global cities that the best prospects of cosmopolitanism are to be found: cosmopolitanism as a form of reason lived daily in the city of difference" (158). Leonie Sandercock argues for "a cosmopolitan urbanism as a normative project that is a necessary response to the empirical reality of multicultural cities" (39). Mica Nava further suggests that cosmopolitanism is "an ordinary everyday aspect of metropolitan UK culture" (134). The typical cultural form of the metropolis is cosmopolitanism understood as an exposure to a mix of many kinds of cultural and social frames of reference,

1 First published in the *International Journal of Applied Linguistics & English Literature*, vol. 5, no. 1, January 2016 ISSN 2200-3592 (Print), ISSN 2200-3452 (Online) Australian International Academic Centre, Australia. The research was financed by Chongqing Social Science Planning Fund Program. No. 2014QNWX30 and the Fundamental Research Funds for the Central Universities. No. SWU1509173, SWU1409348.

thanks to which the individual has the simultaneous experience of both proximity and distance.

However, metropolitan-centrism in cosmopolitan theory—the elitist, normative conception that metropolitan culture is a prerequisite for cosmopolitan imagination—has been challenged and refuted. On the one hand, cosmopolitanism identified with the metropolis can quite easily become synonymous with a kind of urban sophistication, and cosmopolitan possibilities are classed, gendered or racialised. Tim Butler describes how white, middle-class gentrifiers in north London appropriate a discourse of belonging that accentuates and celebrates diversity, whilst their lives in practice are characterised by social exclusivity.

The cosmopolitan is thus presented as white and middle class, standing out in a multi-ethnic metropolis because of their whiteness. Butler concludes that despite their "long rhetorical flushes in favour of multiculturalism and diversity" (2469), white and middle-class residents of north London regard ethnic minorities as "a kind of social wallpaper" (2484). They do not engage with the dialectical or transformative process that a cosmopolitan ethos entails; instead, their "metropolitan habitus—of feelings, attitudes and beliefs" transforms the metropolis into "the natural habitat for a section of the new (urban-seeking) middle classes" (2484).

On the other hand, the cosmopolitan experience of individuals in the metropolis (especially immigrants) cannot be equated with the cosmopolitan nature of the city. Daniel Hiebert draws on his study of transnational communities in Vancouver to illustrate that transnational connections and exchanges in themselves do not necessarily foster cosmopolitanism amongst labour migrants or elite professionals. Hiebert even contends: "In fact, in certain cases transnational lifestyles may actually inhibit cosmopolitanism" (210).

Ranji Devadason reaches a similar conclusion in her analysis of the extent to which London engenders cosmopolitan values amongst its established minorities and ethnic majority. Devadason reminds us: "Cosmopolitanism is not something which can be inferred from diversity in itself; it requires transformation in 'structures of meaning' both for the individual and the political community" (2960). *Mr Stone and the Knights Companion*, Naipaul's only novel set entirely in London, dealing with exclusively English characters, is the ideal text to examine how the postcolonial writer imagines and constructs the metropolis. I would argue that Naipaul's earlier colonial fantasy that cosmopolitanism only exists in the metropolis and is accessible to the privileged individuals is severely shattered.

Colonial Fantasy Shattered: The Dull London Life

When he was still at work on *A House for Mr Biswas*, Naipaul narrated how he experienced London in his essay "London". He emphasises his sense of being continually excluded from London, because "everything goes on behind closed doors" there (*Overcrowded Barracoon* 14). His engagement with London seems spoiled by his inability to penetrate beneath its surfaces and to discover the substance of London life. Naipaul admits that his knowledge of London and of England remains profoundly unsatisfactory:

> I feel I know so little about England. I have met many people but I know them only in official attitudes—the drink, the interview, the meal. I have a few friends. But this gives me only a superficial knowledge of the country, and in order to write fiction it is necessary to know so much: we are not all brothers under the skin. (*Overcrowded Barracoon* 14)

Describing several nights out at the restaurant, nightclub and theatre, which end with him lonely, looking for a bus, haunted by a sense of disappointment and waste, he complains about the depressing "privacy of the big city" and the lack of "communal pleasures" (*Overcrowded Barracoon* 15). He confesses:

> But after eight years here I find I have, without effort, achieved the Buddhist ideal of non-attachment. I am never disturbed by national or international issues. I do not sign petitions. I do not vote. I do not march. And I never cease to feel that this lack of interest is all wrong. I want to be involved, to be touched even by some of the prevailing anger. (*Overcrowded Barracoon* 16)

Naipaul concludes the essay by recording the "barrenness" of his life in London and the impact it might have on his imaginative faculties: "Unless I am able to refresh myself by travel—to Trinidad, to India—I fear that living here will eventually lead to my own sterility; and I may have to look for another job" (*Overcrowded Barracoon* 16).

Mr Stone and the Knights Companion shows that Naipaul tries to register his self-consciously peripheral engagement with the metropolis and sense of being defrauded by and displaced from its substance. At first glance, Naipaul's earlier characters in steaming, chaotic Trinidad would be literally unimaginable in Mr Stone's cool, ordered world of middle-class London respectability. For the boy narrator of *Miguel Street*, for Ganesh and Mr Biswas, London and England epitomise civility and order, the fountainhead of all inspirations. Mr Stone possesses all that is desirable to them—a house of his own in suburban London, a steady and respectable job and a pension after his retirement.

While the image of the house in *A House for Mr Biswas* is frequently used to convey the disorder, haphazardness and transience of Trinidad, Mr Stone's house is a much more substantial affair, a regulated space that happily records a long history of occupancy. Mr Stone takes pleasure

> in the slow decay of his own house, the time-created shabbiness of its interiors, the hard polish of old grime on the lower areas of the hall wallpaper, feeling it right that objects like houses should age with their owners and carry marks of their habitation. (*Mr Stone* 22)

His well-ordered life, upon which he reflects with some frequency, is a source of satisfaction:

> Mr. Stone liked to think in numbers. He liked to think, "I have been with Excal for thirty years." He liked to think, "I have been living in this house for twenty-four years." He liked to think of the steady rise of his salary, since he had gone into industry, to its present £1,000 a year; and he liked to think that by earning this sum he was in the top five per cent of the country's wage-earners (he had read this fact somewhere, possibly in the Evening Standard). He liked to think he had known Tomlinson for forty-four years. (*Mr Stone* 18)

Mr Stone enjoys his rootedness in the milieu of middle-class London suburbia. The financial and social security into which he was born is supported by and contributes to a highly stable society with a set of dependable norms and rights, a coherent culture, and an accessible history. His surname "Stone" perfectly suggests the "solidity, continuity and flow" not only of his own ready-made identities and positions but also of the grandeur of London and England (*Mr Stone* 20).

Nevertheless, Naipaul presents Mr Stone's life as insular and dull, "possibly the price of order in a well-regulated society", to acknowledge and unravel his assumption of the "perfection" of the metropolis (Mustafa *V. S. Naipaul* 91). At the opening of the novel, Mr Stone is introduced as an old bachelor with few attachments. He only briefly visits his widowed sister Olive who provided him with female attention after their mother died when he was seventeen while fixing his "distaste" for Olive's daughter Gwen (*Mr Stone* 28). He has a friend with whom he "annually renewed" (10) friendship, a housekeeper with whom he barely communicates, and a few colleagues with whom he has "only an office relationship" (47). He even refuses to "bid anyone on it [the street where Mr Stone lives] good-day for fear that such greeting might be imposed on him in perpetuity, leading to heaven knows what intimacy" (*Mr Stone* 36).

Mr Stone purely cultivates and is strict with his never-rushed habitual actions, which border on dreary routines. He always shaves the right side of his face first and puts on his right shoe first. He reads the first page and no more of the *Telegraph* at breakfast and buys two evening newspapers from a particular vendor at Victoria to read at leisure after dinner, not on the train. He does not even savour the news, for he instantly forgets most of what he reads. He treats it "as part of a newspaper, something which day by day produced itself for his benefit during this after-dinner period, an insulation against the world out of which it arose" (*Mr Stone* 20). In the office, he recognises the days of the week from the regular changing of his assistant's business outfits. At home, his housekeeper Miss Millington shops every Thursday morning and goes to the cinema every Thursday afternoon.

The only thing that intrudes upon his settled existence is his neighbour's cat, a creature of free will. Its daily "obscene scuttlings and dredgings and buryings" on his flowerbeds require frequent reparations (6). Armed with cat pepper, Mr Stone is at war with it. "Stone", in fact, symbolises the rigid, ossified order. Finding himself living a drab life in London, Naipaul makes Mr Stone's insular, ritualistic existence a story that "we have come to associate with the English provinces after the war, when English writing turned inward from larger issues and was fascinated by the manners, morals and lives of the drab rather than the sophisticated and cosmopolitan" (King *V. S. Naipaul* 62).

Post-War London Transformed by Immigrants

The shadow of the war still hangs implicitly over England in *Mr Stone and the Knights Companion*. Mr Stone realises that "he was surrounded by women—Margaret, Grace, Olive, Gwen, Miss Millington—and that these women all lived in a world of dead or absent men" (131). If the Knights Companion scheme that he creates for the welfare of the retired is "for the protection of the impotent male", the post-war Empire in terminal decline is just like that male (84). It is not only substantially ruined by the ravages of the war, but also ultimately transformed by its immigrant communities as a result of exultant decolonisation movements around the world. Towards the end of the first chapter of the novel, Mr Stone goes to visit Margaret Springer whom he is soon to marry:

> Mrs. Springer lived in Earl's Court. A disreputable, overcrowded area Mr Stone had always thought it, and he thought no better of it now.

> The entrance to the Underground station was filthy; in a street across the road a meeting of the British National Party was in progress, a man shouting himself hoarse from the back of a van. Behind neon lights and streaming glass windows the new-style coffee houses were packed; and the streets were full of young people in art-student dress and foreigners of every colour. (*Mr Stone* 32)

The visible ethnic pluralism and cultural admixture incubating in post-war London are indicators of cosmopolitanism as "a sociocultural condition" linked to large-scale migration, which facilitates a multiplication of cultural contacts and social exchanges bringing the English closer to other physically and psychologically distant cultures (*Conceiving Cosmopolitanism* 9). John McLeod interprets Naipaul's depiction of Earl's Court as "the shattered colonial fantasy of decorum and the disturbing muddle of contemporary, cosmopolitan London—where the certainties of English place are challenged by the spontaneous and contingent transformations of subaltern renegotiations of space" (71).

In other words, elements that used to be marginal or peripheral with respect to those dominant ones now express the formation of a cosmopolitan culture in the metropolis. Naipaul may not celebrate the positive dimension of cosmopolitanism that politically and socially challenges ethnocentric or national narratives, but it would be over-simplistic to interpret it as his nostalgic longing for a homogeneous, pure English culture. He points up here that the opening-up of the political-social space of the metropolis cannot necessarily cultivate an open, cosmopolitan vision among the metropolitan locals who, in fear of the death of their local and national identities, shun others. As Craig Calhoun has argued, "While cities can be places of creative disorder, jumbling together ethnicities, classes, and political projects, most people claim only familiar parts of the diversity on offer" (104). Mr Stone obviously carries a general dislike of the coloured immigrants infiltrating Earl's Court, "a symbol of a nascent multiracial society beginning to impinge on the homogeneous, older England Mr Stone represents" ("Naipaul's English Fable" 499–500).

The new, heterogeneous urban populace contributes to the making of London's physicality that does not necessarily square with, even betrays, the promise of English order, which guarantees continuity between England's past and present, its colonial possessions overseas and metropolitan heart. To Mr Stone, cosmopolitanism assumes a threatening dissolution of his identity. Mr Stone is only reassured to find out that the private hotel off the Earl's Court Road where Margaret lives appears to be a bastion against incursions—"a small typewritten 'Europeans Only' card below the bell proclaimed it a refuge of respectability and calm" (32). The ignorance of the surrounding demographic change and smooth retreat into white supremacy (an almost fascist proclamation of national and racial exclusiveness) articulate the irony of the author, himself a coloured immigrant depressed by the impenetrability of the metropolis.

Cosmopolitan Dream Broken: Travel, Cosmopolitan Curiosity and English Insularity

In *Mr Stone and the Knights Companion*, Naipaul adopts an overall cool voice with detached irony to criticise the conservatism and cultural remoteness of Englishness and the insularity of the English. Englishness becomes self-possessed, even ignorant, since the English, who have difficulty in getting over "the barrier of self-consciousness" in their activities and responses, withdraw into themselves rather than look outwards (15). This is most evident in their contacts with other cultures through travel. A common feature of cosmopolitanism is the lionisation of travel as the key to self-enhancement and the cultivation of a sophisticated, worldly outlook. In the words of Barry Curtis and Claire Pajaczkowska, travel implies "a journey of metamorphosis and transformation, in which the self is changed by the experience of alterity encountered in a dialectic of difference" (206). Calhoun points out that "cosmopolitanism has considerable rhetorical advantage", because "it seems hard not to want to be a 'citizen of the world'" when exposed to other geographies and cultures through travel (89).

Nonetheless, Naipaul suggests that travel does not necessarily lead to a greater level of cosmopolitanism, which is supposed to be marked by an open stance towards difference and an inclusive consciousness. Ulf Hannerz points out that "we often use the term 'cosmopolitan' rather loosely, to describe just about anybody who moves about in the world" (238). Rosabeth Moss Kanter also warns us that "it is not travel that defines cosmopolitans—some widely traveled people remain hopelessly parochial—it [cosmopolitanism] is mind-set" (23).

In contrast to Naipaul's earlier Trinidadian characters who have no chance to travel at home or abroad, the English characters in *Mr Stone and the Knights Companion* enjoy the privilege conferred by the dominant power of their country to travel anywhere of their free will, even in a luxurious style. But unfortunately, they do not move mentally or psychologically. We are told that

> Mr Stone preferred to spend his holidays in England. He had thought after the war that he would go abroad. In 1948 he went to Ireland; but the

> most enjoyable part of that holiday was the journey from Southampton to Cobh in a luxurious, rationing-free American liner. (60)

When Mr Stone describes this journey to Gwen, Olive comments that it is "too self-conscious and namby-pamby" (148). Travelling in Paris, Mr Stone does not display an appreciation for the French cultural milieu into which he is inserted, and all that is left in his head are unpleasant memories:

> A fortnight in Paris two years later had been, after the first moment of pleasure at being in the celebrated city, a tedious torment. He had dutifully gone sightseeing and had been considerably fatigued; he often wondered afterwards why he followed the guidebook so slavishly and went to places as dreary as the Pantheon and the Invalides. He had sat in the cafes, but hated the coffee, and to sit idling in an unfamiliar place was not pleasant, and the cups of coffee were so small. He had tried aperitifs but had decided they were a waste of time and money. He was very lonely; his pocket was playfully picked by an Algerian, who warned him to be more careful in future; everything was hideously expensive; the incessant cries from men and women of le service, monsieur, le service! had given him a new view of the French, who he had thought a frivolous, fun-loving people made a little sad by the war. And for the last two days he was afflicted by a type of dysentery which made it impossible for him to take anything more solid than mineral water. (*Mr Stone* 60–61)

Similarly, Grace Tomlinson's trip to Paris, "not surprisingly", gives her "little pleasure" (130). In a metropolis like Paris where cosmopolitanism is ideally marked by people's appreciation for cultural diversities and exchanges, the close-mindedness of Mr Stone and Grace is accentuated. Naipaul implicitly makes the point in the novel that the metropolis does not necessarily foster cosmopolitanism, that people's open, cosmopolitan outlook should be the key to therapy for parochialism. Failing to shed the bias of their own home culture, Naipaul's English characters in *Mr Stone and the Knights Companion* are really what Hannerz calls "anti-cosmopolitans ... people who are locals at heart", who see and judge anything in other parts of the world as a kind of evil contamination through their local, parochial lens (241).

Lacking the deeper curiosity about the world outside the self, they become the counter-image of Naipaul, who alludes to an enjoyment of "the experience of travel and human discovery for its own sake" as it "broadened my world view; it showed me a changing world, and took me out of my own colonial shell" (*Finding the Centre* 11–12).

Naipaul implies that insularity strangles the English's capacity to look at the world with the possibility of cultural diversity. Their unwillingness to pay a necessary cost to get involved with other European cultures shows their hidden assumption about the ranking of cultures, in which only English culture stands at the top of the pyramid. It is unimaginable how they would rank other marginal, subaltern cultures. Whereas, the Trinidadian insularity in Naipaul's first four novels is about inferiority and self-abasement under the intimidation of colonialism, the English insularity presented in *Mr Stone and the Knights Companion* is about self-consciousness and arrogance.

The Hegemonic, Fraudulent Metropolitan Culture

At the same time, Naipaul is aware of the prevalent, dangerous homogenising power of the English insular parochialism intolerant of difference. In *Mr Stone and the Knights Companion*, a Jamaican family moves into Mr Stone's neighbourhood. Their intrusion into the territory of middle-class London suburbia (like the presence of foreigners in Earl's Court) indicates that the metropolis begins to look like a mosaic. Yet, it is not very cosmopolitan. The Jamaican family tries to demonstrate their "ferocious respectability" by receiving "no negro callers", accepting "no negro lodgers for the room they let", keeping a budgerigar and having their house repainted by English decorators until "its gleaming black-pointed red brick was like a reproach to the rest of the street" (140). Here, Naipaul presents the hegemonic nature of the metropolitan culture. As long as England's cultural universalisation supports its insularity, coloured immigrants can only be acceptable if they spontaneously respect the particular sense of Englishness, acting, dressing, eating and talking as native-born Britons. They are expected to mimic their allotted roles, to become the mirror of a homogeneous England and to enter and uphold the English order. Their particular histories (cultural, ethnic, racial and religious) have to be negated. Assimilation is their only way to avoid exclusion.

While the immigrants want to assimilate into English society by imitation, the middle- and lower-class English succumb to the mimicry of upper-class respectability in *Mr Stone and the Knights Companion*. The English characters for the most part are shallow mimics, lacking a genuine self to be falsified by posturing. Their role-playing comments on the insincerity and fraudulence built into the fabric of the metropolis. At the beginning of the novel, Margaret Springer is introduced by her unsuitably stagy dressing at the Tomlinsons' annual Christmas dinner party—"Mrs Springer was over fifty, striking in her garnets, a dark red dress of watered silk, cut low, the skirt draped, and a well-preserved gold embroidered Kashmir shawl" (*Mr Stone* 12). She establishes herself as a wit in an obvious display of theatricality—"her manner went contrary to her dress; it was not a masculinity she attempted, so much as an arch and studied unfemininity. Her deep voice recalled that of a celebrated actress, as did her delivery" (12). Her statement that "the only flower I care about … is the cauliflower" greatly impresses Mr Stone (13). So Mr Stone does have some reason to expect that Margaret will provide him some intellectual and social stimulation.

Upon marrying Mr Stone, however, Margaret discards her party manner and attaches "the greatest importance to her functions as a woman and a wife" until she appears to possess no true character of her own (46). She encourages Mr Stone to keep up and reinforce the empty routines of his former life: he becomes the Master to Miss Millington and is cajoled into taking up gardening as a hobby. She also encourages him to undertake socially acceptable formalities, such as hosting a dinner party "which to a large extent recreated one of the Tomlinsons' dinner parties" (47). The dull, meaningless dinner party at which wine is sipped like a liqueur, women play music and sing, and men clown and jest is a pathetic imitation of the lifestyle of the upper class.

Gwen entertains the guests by reciting a scene from *The Importance of Being Earnest* "in imitation of the celebrated actress, for the female", and the court scene from *The Merchant of Venice*, speaking rhetoric "as though it were everyday speech" (51–52). Later, after Mr Stone's social eminence grows with his Knights Companion scheme, Margaret adjusts once again "as easily as she had always taken on new roles" (87). She becomes the self-effacing wife "who encouraged and inspired her husband in his work" (87). To keep up with her new status as a socialite, she collects a formal wardrobe, talks about making changes in the house or moving to the country after Mr Stone's retirement, and envisages dinner parties spreading out on the lawn in summer. Margaret's mimicry of the elite illustrates one of Naipaul's central themes—human beings always imitate their social superiors. The English are no exception as well. This echoes Naipaul's comment that

> England is the least-educated country in Europe … it's so many people here, living at a very high material level, who have allowed their minds to go slack. The English bourgeoisie are mimicking their former roles. They express their soul by the colour of their walls. They put dreadful pictures on their walls and stagger them. (Michener "Dark Vision" 64)

Superficial Cosmopolitan Consumption

The upper-class respectability represented by the Tomlinsons and mimicked by Margaret and Gwen is actually superficial and fraudulent because it assumes that access and openness to difference are only signalled by the consumption of cultural diversity and the attendant sense of sophistication. In the novel, Naipaul criticises this kind of elitist model of cosmopolitanism. The most successful cultural element in the spread of cosmopolitan ideals is what Calhoun calls "consumerist cosmopolitanism", enacted through the consumption of exotic cultures (105).

Elaborating on the cosmopolitan construct, Douglas B. Holt highlights cosmopolitanism as a style of consumption that creates and maintains status distinctions between high-cultural-capital and low-cultural-capital consumers. The high-cultural-capital consumers are said to possess a cosmopolitan habitus—a nexus of internalised and naturalised predispositions or proclivities towards cosmopolitan consumption practices that reflect a history of class-based socialisation. Holt's informants from "the upper tier of the middle-class—the highly educated, urbane New Class", for example, "express Cosmopolitan tastes even when they are not participating in the activities that they deem essential for that lifestyle" (338–339). They gravitate towards exotic food and music and are highly dissatisfied with the parochial cultural offerings of their own community. On the contrary, those informants possessing lower levels of cultural capital are not favourably inclined towards cultural fare deemed exotic; instead, they remain content in their local cultural milieu, and their consumption patterns are governed by strong preferences for the familiar and traditional.

Ghassan Hage portrays cosmopolites as the elite pursuing refined consumption. Just as important as his/her urban(e) nature, the cosmopolite is a class figure and a white person, capable of consuming and appreciating "high quality" commodities and cultures, including "ethnic cultures" (201). But Calhoun cautions us: "Food, tourism, music, literature, and clothes are all easy faces of cosmopolitanism. They are indeed broadening, literally after a fashion, but they are not hard tests for the relationship between local solidarity and international civil society" (105). Hannerz gives a similar warning:

> Cosmopolitanism has two faces. In its aesthetic and intellectual dimensions, it can become a kind of consumer cosmopolitanism, a cosmopolitanism with a happy face, enjoying new cuisines, new musics, new literatures. Political cosmopolitanism is often a cosmopolitanism with a worried face, trying to come to grips with

> very large problems. We may suspect that it is entirely possible for people to be pleased with their experiences and their personal levels of connoisseurship in regard to cultural diversity without having any strong sense of civic and humanitarian responsibility transcending national borders. (71)

Both Calhoun and Hannerz recognise that consumerist cosmopolitanism evades cultural openness to and ethical, political responsibility for others. Pnina Werbner summarises the elitist nature of cosmopolitanism as a consumer orientation as follows:

> A cosmopolitan is, historically, an elect member of his or her society, familiar with the languages and high cultural products of European and American literature, art and music, able to converse about world history, philosophy, classical music, ballet, theatre and human rights. Culturally, such a cosmopolitan is an aesthetic consumer, living an elegant lifestyle, a connoisseur of good wine, haute cuisine and haute couture; a fashionable person with immaculate table manners, a sophisticated conversationalist and bon vivant, au fait with the latest novels and world current affairs. In other words, the "true" cosmopolitan—unlike many anthropologists—is a man or woman of the world, but of a very specific world—that of Western, and especially European, elites. He or she is usually also a collector of world art. (50)

Cosmopolitanism becomes a conglomeration of self-interested individuals whose primary aim is the personal satisfaction of an insatiable consumption of consumer goods. In *Mr Stone and the Knights Companion*, cosmopolitanism is revealed as the superficial aestheticisation and stylisation of metropolitan life through the depiction of the Tomlinsons' Christmas dinner parties. As Tony Tomlinson is "a figure of some importance in his local council" who never jokes about "his territorial decoration" such as his initial followed by the letters T. D., the couple's Christmas dinner parties increase "in severity and grandeur with the years" to match their superior status as the social elite (*Mr Stone* 10–11).

The dinner party at the beginning of the novel shows that the Tomlinsons narrowly and superficially view their access to and consumption of exotic cultures in their everyday life as an indicator of their status-defining cosmopolitan orientation and aesthetics. The tarnished relics of an Austrian holiday that they turn into their "traditional decorations" appear to demonstrate the sophistication of their cultural interest (15). But the dinner party arrangements (candles, carved wood, manger scenes and pine trees), the floral decorations and

Grace Tomlinson's corsage that gains admiration from the guests turn out to be the result of a brief course at the Constance Spry school in St John's Wood.

When the conversation among the guests comes around to the subject of films lately seen, the narrating voice informs the reader in a slightly ironic tone that Tony raises the discussion "to a more suitable intellectual level", which is "acknowledged as his prerogative and duty" (13). Tony then announces that he watches Rififi "on the recommendation of a person of importance" (13). This cosmopolitan aesthetics seems to differentiate him from the middle- and lower-class (for instance, Miss Millington who goes to the cinema to the cheap show for pensioners), but it is revealed as only posturing. He tries hard to attract his audience by "losing nothing of his suffering appearance, looking at none of them, fixing his eyes on some point in space as though drawing thoughts and words out of that point", whereas, all the comment that he can produce is the repetition of "extraordinary" and "no dialogue" (13–14). This scene discloses Tony's lack of the intellectual ability that a real cosmopolite possesses. The Tomlinsons imbricate conspicuous signifiers of their identity as cosmopolitans through the display of luxury. Their expenditure on resources and cursory consumption of cultures do not commit to a genuine cosmopolitan attitude or outlook. It is a fraudulent deployment of cosmopolitanism.

Xenophobia underneath Cosmopolitan Openness

While the Tomlinsons' seemingly cosmopolitan aesthetics and consumption are self-deceptive, the young PRO Whymper in the novel, "a man without a family, someone who belonged only to the city", is a trickster, adopting superficial cosmopolitan attitudes and tastes to conceal his xenophobia towards immigrants and to achieve social superiority (109). The urban deceit that Whymper embodies is identified by his house, furniture and food. His undistinguished terrace house with no garden is in Kilburn, but its location on the side of the High Road gives him a respectable Hampstead telephone number. He lives on the ground floor, renting out both the basement and other floors. His front room, decorated with two "perfunctorily modern" armchairs, a bullfighting poster, a jumbled bookcase of paperbacks, old newspapers and copies of *Esquire*, *Time* and *The Spectator* and "a neat shelf of green Penguins", projects the image of urban sophistication (110).

Inviting the Stones to dinner, Whymper displays his cosmopolitan consumption practice by serving them "cold sliced beef below a thick layer of finely chipped lettuce, cabbage, carrots, capsicums and garlic, all raw" with olive oil, Polish black bread that he thinks "ten times as good as our cotton wool", Greek retsina, biscuits with brie and camembert, and Turkish coffee (110–111). Ironically, he sniffs at the food in his plate "with mock disgust" and asks desperately for tomato ketchup, complaining: "Those dirty foreigners, eating all this garlic and grease" (111). Later, Whymper's posturing cosmopolitan taste is further exposed by his illiberal attitude to race. He is driven into fury by "the sight of black men on the London streets" and spends the whole of one lunchtime walk "loudly counting" those whom he sees (114).

Nevertheless, when Mr Stone quarrels with and insults a typist of Polish origin in the office in public, Whymper the xenophobe gives an exaggeratedly righteous performance defending the typist and criticising Mr Stone. Mr Stone cannot even believe Whymper is "the man who during those lunchtime walks had spoken with so much feeling about 'foreigners cluttering up the place'" (128). Whymper's hypocritical adoption of an open, cosmopolitan attitude covers up his quintessential rejection of foreigners and wins him the advantage needed in the job market. At the end of the novel, Whymper takes all the credit for Mr Stone's original creation of the Knights Companion scheme to get a top executive position of publicity director in another company. Karl Miller comments, however, that Naipaul "takes pleasure in the deals and treasons of Mr Stone's circle, and makes of it a sort of sooty, strangulated, boring Miguel Street, with its own fragmented, none-too-organic community life" (123).

Conclusion

In *Mr Stone and the Knights Companion*, Naipaul for the first time confronts and questions his long-held colonial fantasy about the reassuring metropolitan purpose and desirable cosmopolitanism seen from afar. His depiction of the dull middle-class London life challenges metropolitan-centrism in cosmopolitanism. In his observation, the multiplication of cultural contacts and exchanges facilitated in the metropolis does not necessarily mean that the metropolitan locals exposed to it are predisposed towards cosmopolitan openness. The English, for example, in fear of the death of their local and national identities, shun immigrants, even in the face of the inevitable break-up of their homogeneous social world. Lacking the deeper curiosity about other cultures, they view the world through a local, parochial lens, even in their privileged travel that cosmopolitanism assumes to cultivate a sophisticated, worldly outlook.

Using a detached, ironic tone, he criticises the English insularity as self-conscious and ignorant and implies that people's open, cosmopolitan vision should be the key to cosmopolitanism. He discusses the allure and danger of cosmopolitanism: consumption of various cultural products and luxurious stylisation of metropolitan life are superficially understood as signals of access and openness to differences. From the perspective of an immigrant, Naipaul points out that under such a consumer orientation may actually lurk xenophobia towards others. Respectability becomes a mere facade. Naipaul's sense of disillusionment can be best illustrated by the dream that he has not long after his return to London from his second journey to India recounted at the end of *An Area of Darkness*:

> An oblong of stiff new cloth lay before me, and I had the knowledge that if only out of this I could cut a smaller oblong of specific measurements, a specific section of this cloth, then the cloth would begin to unravel of itself, and the unravelling would spread from the cloth to the table to the house to all matter, until the whole trick was undone. Those were the words that were with me as I flattened the cloth and studied it for the clues which I knew existed, which I desired above everything else to find, but which I knew I never would. (289–290)

An analogous sense of London and England as a trick pervades *Mr Stone and the Knights Companion*, and many of Naipaul's subsequent novels (for example, *The Mimic Men*, *A Bend in the River* and *The Enigma of Arrival*) are suspended between such a colonial dream of perfection and the knowledge of its fraudulence.

Works Cited

Bridge, Gary. *Reason in the City of Difference: Pragmatism, Communicative Action and Contemporary Urbanism*. Routledge, 2005.

Butler, Tim. "Living in the Bubble: Gentrification and its 'Others' in North London." *Urban Studies*, vol. 40, issue 12, 2003, pp. 2469–2486.

Calhoun, Craig. "The Class Consciousness of Frequent Travellers: Towards A Critique of Actually Existing Cosmopolitanism." *Conceiving Cosmopolitanism: Theory, Context, and Practice*, edited by Steven Vertovec and Robin Cohen, Oxford UP, 2002, pp. 86–109.

Curtis, Barry, and Pajaczkowska, Claire. "Getting there: Travel, time and narrative." *Travellers' Tales: Narratives of Home and Displacement*, edited by G. Robertson, M. Mash, L. Tickner, J. Bird, B. Curtis, and T. Putnam, Routledge, 1994, pp. 199–215.

Devadason, Rajen. "Cosmopolitanism, Geographical Imaginaries and Belonging in North London." *Urban Studies*, vol. 47, issue 14, 2010, pp. 2945–2963.

Featherstone, Mike. "Cosmopolis: An Introduction.". *Theory, Culture & Society*, vol. 19, issue 1–2, 2002, pp. 1–16.

Hage, Ghassan. *White Nation: Fantasies of White Supremacy in a Multicultural Society*. Pluto Press, 1998.

Hannerz, Ulf. "Cosmopolitans and Locals in World Culture." *Theory, Culture & Society* 7, 1990, pp. 237–251.

———. "Cosmopolitanism." *A Companion to the Anthropology of Politics*, edited by David Nugent, and Joan Vincent, Blackwell Publishing, 2007, pp. 69–85.

Hiebert, Daniel. "Cosmopolitanism at the Local Level: The Development of Transnational Neighbourhoods." *Conceiving Cosmopolitanism*, edited by Vertovec and Cohen, pp. 209–223.

Holt, Douglas B. "Poststructuralist Lifestyle Analysis: Conceptualizing the Social Patterning of Consumption in Postmodernity." *Journal of Consumer Research*, vol. 23, issue 4, 1997, pp. 326–350.

King, Bruce. *V. S. Naipaul*. Palgrave Macmillan, 2003.

McLeod, John. *Postcolonial London: Rewriting the Metropolis*. Routledge, 2004.

Michener, Charles. "The Dark Vision of V. S. Naipaul." *Conversations with V. S. Naipaul*, edited by Feroza Jussawalla, UP of Mississippi, 1997.

Miller, Karl. "V. S. Naipaul and the New Order." *Critical Perspectives on V. S. Naipaul*, edited by Robert D. Hamner, Three Continents P, 1977, pp. 111–125.

Moss Kanter, Rosabeth. *World Class: Thriving Locally in the Global Economy*. Simon & Schuster, 1995.

Mustafa, Fawzia. *V. S. Naipaul*. Cambridge UP, 1995.

Naipaul, V. S. *Mr Stone and the Knights Companion*. Andre Deutsch, 1963.

———. *The Overcrowded Barracoon and Other Articles*. Andre Deutsch, 1972.

———. *Finding the Centre*. Penguin, 1985.

———. *An Area of Darkness*. Picador, 2002.

Nava, Mica. *Visceral Cosmopolitanism: Gender, Culture and the Normalisation of Difference*. Berg, 2007.

Sandercock, L. "Cosmopolitan Urbanism: A Love Song to Our Mongrel Cities." *Cosmopolitan Urbanism*, edited by J. Binnie, J. Holloway, S. Millington, and C. Young, Routledge, 2006, pp. 37–52.

Thieme, John "Naipaul's English Fable: *Mr Stone and the Knights Companion*." *Modern Fiction Studies*, vol. 30, 1984, pp. 497–503.

Vertovec, Steven, and Robin Cohen. "Introduction: Conceiving Cosmopolitanism." *Conceiving Cosmopolitanism*, edited by S. Vertovec, and R. Cohen, pp. 1–22.

Werbner, Pnina. "The Cosmopolitan Encounter: Social Anthropology and the Kindness of Strangers." *Anthropology and the New Cosmopolitanism: Rooted, Feminist and Vernacular Perspectives*, edited by Pnina Werbner, Berg, 2008, pp. 47–68.

Chapter 15

NAIPAUL'S ENGLISH FABLE: *MR STONE AND THE KNIGHTS COMPANION*[1]

John Thieme

V. S. Naipaul's fourth novel, *Mr Stone and the Knights Companion*, may appear to be something of an oddity in his work in that it is his only novel that does not demonstrate an immediate and obvious concern with Third World society. The Trinidadian milieux of his earlier novels are forsaken for an account of the effect imminent retirement has on an elderly London bachelor; the broader postcolonial themes of his later work have yet to appear. As a result, *Mr Stone* has received less attention than most of Naipaul's other works. It has been viewed as his attempt to escape from being regarded as a regional writer (Thorpe 18; Naipaul, *The Overcrowded Barracoon and Other Articles* 9–16; Naipaul, "The Regional Barrier")[2] and as a "minor" (Walsh 45) or "transitional" (L. White 127) work between the twin masterpieces of *A House for Mr Biswas* (1961) and *The Mimic Men* (1967). Moreover, comments Naipaul has made on the composition of *Mr Stone* have tended to suggest that there was something rather perfunctory about it. Although he speaks of *A House for Mr Biswas*, his previous novel, as having totally absorbed him for three years ("It was like a career—I've been feeling unemployed ever since") (Bates 13), *Mr Stone* appears to have been written in a completely different spirit: "I had to write another book, to prove to myself that I could write, that it wasn't all over, that one had

---

1 This chapter originally appeared in *Modern Fiction Studies*, vol. 30, issue 3, 1984, pp. 497–503. and is reprinted here with permission from the copyright holder.

2 Michael Thorpe, *V. S. Naipaul* (Longman/British Council, 1976), p 18. Naipaul discusses the problem of the regional writer in London in *The Overcrowded Barracoon and Other Articles* (André Deutsch, 1972, pp. 9–16). This article was originally published as "The Regional Barrier" in *The Times Literary Supplement*, 15 August 1958.

a talent. It wasn't written out of anything else but that and the subject did present itself to me" (Plomley).

Nevertheless, although *Mr Stone* may have been less a labour of love than *Mr Biswas*, and, although it is only of novella length, it exhibits the same sureness of touch as the previous novel while exploring similar themes from a slightly different angle of vision. These themes include the struggle of the "little man" protagonist to overcome his sense of displacement, a struggle worked out particularly through his attitude to accommodation, both literal and metaphorical, and through his relationship with the landscape in which he lives. Like *Mr Biswas* and *The Mimic Men*, *Mr Stone* explores these themes through the use of recurrent house and tree images. Such parallels have not passed unnoticed (Garebian 32–33; Morris 38–51),[3] but as yet critics have not commented on the Condition of England aspects of the novel.

Despite its spare, naturalistic mode, *Mr Stone* is, like Naipaul's previous novels, a fable about cultural identity (Thieme 13–15),[4] and *Mr Stone* is as much a displaced person in his native English environment as any of Naipaul's earlier colonial protagonists were in theirs. If it is true that the novel represents an attempt to overcome the supposed stigma of being regarded as a regional writer, then it does so not through the cultivation of a vague universalism but through the employment of precise circumstantial details shaped with a consistency that lends itself to allegorical interpretation. Naipaul has said that he believes the novel genre to be "a form of social inquiry" (Naipaul, *India: A Wounded Civilization* 18) and, in *Mr Stone,* the specific inquiry is into the nature of English society in the third quarter of the twentieth century, the years of the winds of change. This is not to say that the novel does not also have more general resonances, only to suggest that as in all Naipaul's other fiction, it is the accretion of concrete detail, localising the work in time and place and the concern with a cultural identity that provides the foundation.

---

3 See, for example, Keith Garebian, "V. S. Naipaul's Negative Sense of Place." *Journal of Commonwealth Literature*, vol. 10, issue 1, 1975, pp. 32–33; and Robert K. Morris, *Paradoxes of Order: Some Perspectives on the Fiction of V. S. Naipaul.* University of Missouri Press, 1975, pp. 38–51.

4 See my article "V. S. Naipaul's Third World: A Not So Free State." *Journal of Commonwealth Literature*, vol. 10, issue 1, 1975, pp. 13–15, for a discussion of *A House for Mr Biswas* as an allegory of this kind.

The novel is set mainly in south London,[5] and Mr Stone is first presented as an almost fanatically conservative suburban little man (Brooke, "Two Comedies" 934; Brooke, "Sunk in Suburbia 385; Allen 21)[6] who resents the violation of his garden by his neighbours' cat and who regards these neighbours as interlopers because they have only lived in the street for five years. His watchwords are "solidity, continuity and flow" (Naipaul, *Mr Stone and the Knights Companion* 17); he amuses himself by writing out curricula vitae (even though he is sixty-two and hardly likely to change his job as a librarian in a large commercial firm), and every evening he engages in an after-dinner ritual of reading the newspaper as "an insulation against the world out of which it arose" (16). It is almost as if Mr Stone begins where Mr Biswas left off, with the eponymous hero enjoying the calm, orderly possession of his own house, which Naipaul's earlier "Mr" craved so desperately (Shenfield 95–100; Fido 30–37; Naipaul, "The Book Programme").[7] Mr Stone's attitude to his house typifies his view of the human predicament.

He detests the "home-making" instincts of two of his neighbours, feeling that they deny the atrophy that lies at the heart of the human

5 The exact location of Mr Stone's house is never mentioned, but his journey home in the final chapter—by a No. 109 bus he boards in Brixton—suggests that he must live in the Streatham Hill area where Naipaul himself lived (in Wyatt Park Road, London SW 2) around 1960 and where he wrote *A House for Mr Biswas*. Mr Stone's assistant, Miss Menzies, lives in Streatham.

6 When *Mr Stone* first appeared, reviewers were quick to identify the protagonist as, like Mr Biswas, a version of the "little man" stereotype. He was particularly compared with Pooter of the Grossmiths' *Diary of a Nobody*. See Jocelyn Brooke, "Two Comedies." *The Listener*, 30 May 1963, p 934; "Sunk in Suburbia." *The Times Literary Supplement*, 31 May 1963, p 385; and Walter Allen, "London Again." *The New York Review of Books*, 19 March 1964, p 21.

7 The use of the "Mr" prefix would seem in the case of *A House for Mr Biswas* to be an allusion to Wells's *History of Mr Polly*. Parallels between the two works are discussed in a number of articles, most notably in Margaret Shenfield, "Mr. Biswas and Mr. Polly." *English*, vol. 23, Autumn 1974, pp. 95–100; and in Martin Fido, "Mr. Biswas and Mr. Polly." *Ariel*, vol. 5, issue iv, 1974, pp. 30–37. "Compare Naipaul's comments in a 1979 television film profile: "During that winter of '57 there was a tree at the back of the flat in Muswell Hill.... I saw the tree get bare and then in the spring I saw it putting out shoots. That was a great rebuke. It was also for me after more than seven years my first experience of the seasons" ("The Book Programme," BBC 2, 24 March 1979).

condition (Naipaul, *Mr Stone and the Knights Companion* 18). These neighbours, whom he mentally nicknames "The Male" and "The Monster", seem within the Condition of England scheme to be new suburban archetypes, whereas, Mr Stone, who takes pleasure in "the slow decay of his own house", may be seen as representing the decline of an older England (Naipaul, *Mr Stone and the Knights Companion* 18). Although Mr Stone is initially portrayed as satisfied with his lifestyle, the limitations of his sequestered existence are quickly made manifest as thoughts of his imminent retirement lead him, for the first time in his life it would appear, to contemplate the changing of the seasons in the form of the metamorphoses of a tree he can see from his back window (Naipaul, "The Book Programme").[8]

This image of seasonal renewal leads him to ponder whether there is any possibility of his enjoying a late spring. Although this passage suggests a concern with the fundamental existential problem of growing old, it is complemented by specific English detail. Towards the end of the first chapter, Mr Stone goes to visit the woman he is soon to marry, Margaret Springer. Margaret lives in Earl's Court, an area he has always thought "disreputable" and "overcrowded" and that now seems to serve as a symbol of a nascent multiracial society beginning to impinge on the homogeneous, older England Mr Stone represents (Naipaul, *Mr Stone and the Knights Companion* 26). This older England is here seen as being infiltrated by coloured immigrants, the new youth culture and continental European influences:

> The entrance to the Underground station was filthy; in a street across the road a meeting of the British National Party was in progress, a man shouting himself hoarse from the back of a van. Behind neon lights and streaming glass windows the new-style coffee houses were packed; and the streets were full of young people in art-student dress and foreigners of every colour. (Naipaul, *Mr Stone and the Knights Companion* 26)

In contrast, the house in which Margaret lives appears as a bastion against these incursions, "The address Mrs. Springer gave turned out to be a private hotel in one of the crescents off the Earl's Court Road.

8 Compare Naipaul's comments in a 1979 television film profile: "During that winter of '57 there was a tree at the back of the flat in Muswell Hill.... I saw the tree get bare and then in the spring I saw it putting out shoots. That was a great rebuke. It was also for me after more than seven years my first experience of the seasons" ("The Book Programme," BBC 2, 24 March 1979).

A small typewritten 'Europeans Only' card below the bell proclaimed it a refuge of respectability and calm. It also turned out to be a refuge of age" (Naipaul, *Mr Stone and the Knights Companion* 26). This house's dual function as a "refuge of respectability and calm" and as "a refuge of age" is significant and parallels the fusion of conservative English values and age in the character of Mr Stone.

So, although the novel may initially appear to be concerned with the problem of ageing in a fairly general way, it also has clear social reverberations, with Mr Stone (like George Lamming's Old Dowager in *Water with Berries* [1971], a much more obviously allegorical novel) representing an aging England—the monolithic social world suggested by his name. Subsequently, there are no less than three more, apparently gratuitous, references to black immigrants, references which, though they initially appear to be purely incidental, taken together can only suggest the changing nature of British society (Naipaul, *Mr Stone and the Knights Companion* 90, 111, 125). And there are also several references to the inroads continental culture is making into English life, with Europe being characterised largely in terms of unsavoury eating habits and read as a symbol of illusory romance (Naipaul, *Mr Stone and the Knights Companion* 87–88, 47).[9]

So Mr Stone finds he no longer feels secure in his slowly decaying, homogeneous social world. He looks for some form of renewal, and the first chapter ends with "the coming of Spring" in two senses: he marries the ironically named Margaret Springer, and the tree at the back of his house sprouts white buds (Naipaul, *Mr Stone and the Knights Companion* 20). His marriage is a false spring and, instead of bringing renewal, initiates him into a world of social role-playing, which divorces him from the expression of his innermost feelings. Consequently, the tree increasingly comes to serve as a reproach, reminding him that the seasonal rebirth of the natural cycle has no parallel in his human cycle. In a mood of growing despair and disillusion, he goes with Margaret on a belated honeymoon to Cornwall, where the central epiphany of the novel occurs. From this epiphany the Knights Companion scheme, with its allusions to the Arthurian legend (the definitive English myth), is ultimately born. Significantly, however, the Stones do not go to the Arthurian sites of Tintagel and Castle Dore but to Penzance and the harsh, rugged peninsula of Penwith, a "stone-bound land, which remained to speak of discord between man and earth" (Naipaul, *Mr Stone and the Knights Companion* 48).

---

9 See particularly the accounts of Whymper's home and the dinner he serves to the Stones, pp. 87–88, and of Mr Stone's Paris holiday, p 47.

So, again human life is portrayed as being out of step with nature, and the Celtic reality Mr Stone encounters is a world away from the Celtic romance of the matter of Britain. This is particularly evident when he and Margaret visit the Iron Age village of Chysauster on a cold and windy day (O'Neill Hencken 237-284).[10] In this setting, which provides an archetypal image of man's need to house himself, with all that this seems to imply in Naipaul's work from *Mr Biswas* onwards, Mr Stone reflects on the distance between these dwellings and those of his suburban neighbours: "How thick the walls, how clumsy, how little space they enclosed, as though built for people sheltering from more than the elements! Mr Stone thought of the Monster and her watering can, the nest-building of the Male: this was not their setting" (Naipaul, *Mr Stone and the Knights Companion* 49). With the statement, "As though built for people sheltering from more than the elements!" Naipaul reminds us that the inhabitants of Chysauster were farmers and probably also tin smelters, who had no need for defence from enemies but built their walls up to fifteen feet thick, supposedly to protect themselves from the elements in their exposed hilltop situation (Childe 230).[11]

Naipaul, however, hints that the thickness of the walls also indicates a desire for a more fundamental kind of defence, perhaps born out of inner fears that their homogeneous community was threatened. Before leaving the site, the Stones experience a bizarre "hallucinatory moment" as they follow a strange, silent man—who appears to be showing them the way—into a cloud of smoke that robs them of all sense of reality and contact with the earth (Naipaul, *Mr Stone and the Knights Companion* 50). This is the quintessence of the Cornish trip. Earlier, Cornwall had seemed like a landscape of death to Mr Stone, and now he feels this moment is "like an experience of nothingness, an experience of death" (Naipaul, *Mr Stone and the Knights Companion* 50). And, while they are still in Cornwall another, more mundane, incident further disturbs Mr Stone's equanimity. A visit to a tea shop, where he sees a recently

---

10 Chysauster, reputedly the oldest village in England, survives because the houses were built of local stone, not the wood characteristic of the period. It was inhabited from circa 100 BCE to the third century CE. It was excavated between July and September 1931. See H. O'Neill Hencken, "An Excavation by H. M. Office of Works at Chysauster, Cornwall, 1931." *Archaeologia*, vol. 83, 1933, pp. 237–284.

11 They were also probably afforded protection by the hill-fort at Castle-an-Dinas half a mile away. See V. Gordon Childe. *Prehistoric Communities of the British Isles*. Chambers, 1940, p 230. See also Hencken.

retired man, in the care of two female "keepers", serves not only to heighten his fear of ageing but also to accentuate his feeling that the roles women impose on their menfolk, forcing them to play the parts of tame, domestic animals, exacerbate the problems faced by elderly men (Naipaul, *Mr Stone and the Knights Companion* 52). So the Cornish trip brings Mr Stone's uneasiness about retirement, death and playing the role of a man, which Margaret has assigned to him, into sharp focus. He realises that social role-playing offers no respite from the process of ageing and intuitively senses that meaningful self-renewal can only be achieved through independently undertaken creative activity.

He finds this when he conceives his project, which subsequently becomes known as the Knights Companion, to help former employees of his firm, Excal. Under the scheme, active pensioners are to visit inactive ones. Mr Stone is not, in fact, responsible for the name of the project. This is the brainchild of Whymper, the young public relations officer assigned to the scheme, and Whymper also draws on well-known Arthurian details when he adds such touches as a Round Table dinner at which the Knight Companion of the Year will be presented with an Excalibur sword. None of the Arthurian or other medieval motifs associated with the scheme emanates from Mr Stone. True to his name, he provides the basic idea, whereas the embellishments—the sword drawn from the stone—are the products of Whymper, a man who sees himself as "a processer of raw material" (Naipaul, *Mr Stone and the Knights Companion* 63). Nevertheless, the original impulse of the scheme comes from Mr Stone's disturbing experiences in Celtic Cornwall and hence have their roots in an older Britain.[12]

Moreover, he does eventually come to feel that the name of Knights Companion is appropriate, once the project becomes a genuine "crusade" (Naipaul, *Mr Stone and the Knights Companion* 79). His initial conception has been chivalric, even though, as he wryly observes, it inverts the gender roles of the courtly code because, in this instance, men are coming to the rescue of men, not of damsels in distress, and in some cases saving them from the ministrations of their womenfolk (Naipaul, *Mr Stone and the Knights Companion* 76). So the chivalric name is fitting, even if the novel draws attention to the ironies inherent in the employment of such terminology. Such ironies largely arise because Mr Stone's project is appropriated by Whymper, a latter-day Merlin who represents the threat the public relations world poses both

12 Compare Patrick White's use of Cornwall to represent a different kind of cultural identity from the rest of England in *A Fringe of Leaves* (Jonathan Cape, 1976).

to individual creativity and integrity and to the conservative English order Mr Stone epitomises. Thus, although the Knights Companion scheme is a success and temporarily provides Mr Stone with a sense of renewal, it is adulterated virtually from the start. The use of the Arthurian allusions is an index of this: in essence, they related the project to one of the noblest of English ideals; in practice, they are no more than superficial "packaging" that makes it a success in a consumer society but that trivialises the chivalric frame of reference (Naipaul, *Mr Stone and the Knights Companion* 97). In this context, it is interesting to note that Sir Harry, the modern-day knight who heads Excal, is a man best known for writing letters to *The Times* on such subjects as the number of pins in new shirts and the quality of London Transport bus tickets.

So the Arthurian motifs with which Mr Stone finds his scheme invested come to represent a betrayal of his original humanitarian impulse and, one might argue, of the mythic imagination. Like the role-playing into which his marriage has initiated him, the mythic allusions of the tale within this tale are treated ironically and serve as an index of the urban man's alienation from elemental folk experience. Towards the end, Mr Stone arrives at the conclusion that "nothing that was pure ought to be exposed" and the public relations world's appropriation of the Knights Companion scheme may be viewed as an allegory of the fate the artist suffers at the hands of the communications media in a consumer society (Naipaul, *Mr Stone and the Knights Companion* 118).[13] More generally, it suggests, as Anthony Boxill has observed, the difficulty of "trying to be creative ... in a society which is too highly ordered, in which natural responses have been replaced by stereotyped ones" (Naipaul, *Mr Stone and the Knights Companion* 28).

The final chapter sees Mr Stone making his way home from central London on the day of a transport strike. This breakdown in communications further underscores the isolation of the suburban little man, and, as Mr Stone walks along the Embankment and across the Thames, he seems like one of the anonymous city-dwellers in "The Burial of the Dead" section of *The Waste Land*, consigned, like the Dantean trimmers to whom Eliot alludes, to exist in a midway state between life and death (*The Waste Land*, I, 60–76). Gradually, during his journey home, he comes to feel that destruction, not creativity, is the only meaningful form of human activity.

13 Allen, "London Again", calls *Mr Stone* "a parable about art" (p 21).

The creative impulse that gave rise to the Knights Companion scheme is now a thing of the past, but the novel ends with Mr Stone recognising that his present mood is also transitory and that "in time calm would come to him again" (Naipaul, *Mr Stone and the Knights Companion* 126). Although this low-key ending may seem inconclusive, it is much in keeping with the tenor of the whole work, which argues the impossibility of perennial renewal within the human cycle. Mr Stone is no "once and future king", but rather an old dog who has had his day late in life and is now beginning to come to terms with this (Ashe 17–18).[14] On the level of national identity, the novel suggests the inevitability of the break-up of homogeneous social worlds and the displacement of the contemporary English little man, with Naipaul evincing more than a little nostalgia for the older England his hero represents.

Mr Stone and the Knights Companion may be read as an allegory about the little man's alienation in the modern world, the impossibility of perennial renewal in the human cycle, the fate of art in a consumer society or the death of the mythic imagination. But, in each case, it has distinctively English ramifications that make it as much an investigation of contemporary cultural identity as any of Naipaul's works more obviously treating this subject.

Works Cited

Allen, Walter. "London Again." *The New York Review of Books*, 19 March 1964, p 21.

Ashe, Geoffrey. *The Quest for Arthur's Britain*. Praeger. 1968.

Bates, David. "Portrait Gallery." *Sunday Times Magazine*, 26 May 1963, p 13.

Boxhill, Anthony. "The Concept of Spring in V. S. Naipaul's *Mr Stone and the Knights Companion*." *Ariel*, vol. 5, issue 4, 1974, pp. 21–29.

Brooke, Jocelyn. "Two Comedies." *The Listener*, 30 May 1963, p 934.

———. "Sunk in Suburbia." *The Times Literary Supplement*, 31 May 1963, p 385.

Childe, V. Gordon. *Prehistoric Communities of the British Isles*. Chambers, 1940.

14 This phrase, popularised as the title of the T. H. White's 1958 tetralogy on the matter of Britain, is an exact translation from the Latin epitaph *Hic iacet Arthurus, rex quondam rexque futurus*, which, according to Malory, was widely believed to be inscribed on Arthur's tomb. Arthur's symbolic function as a force for national renewal is evident in the folk tradition that he would come again. See Geoffrey Ashe. *The Quest for Arthur's Britain*. Praeger, 1968, pp. 17–18.

Eliot, Thomas Stearns. *The Waste Land*. Edited by Michael North, Norton, 2000.

Fido, Martin. "Mr. Biswas and Mr. Polly." *Ariel*, vol. 5, issue 4, 1974, pp. 30–37.

Garebian, Keith. "V. S. Naipaul's Negative Sense of Place." *Journal of Commonwealth Literature*, vol. 10, issue 1, 1975, pp. 32-33.

Morris, Robert K. *Paradoxes of Order: Some Perspectives on the Fiction of V. S. Naipaul*. U of Missouri P, 1975.

Naipaul, V. S. *India: A Wounded Civilization*. André Deutsch, 1977.

———. Interview. "The Book Programme." BBC 2, 24 March 1979.

———. *Mr Stone and the Knights Companion*. Penguin, 1973.

———. *The Overcrowded Barracoon and Other Articles*. André Deutsch, 1972.

———. "The Regional Barrier." *The Times Literary Supplement*, 15 August 1958.

O'Neill Hencken, Hugh. "An Excavation by H. M. Office of Works at Chysauster, Cornwall, 1931." *Archaeologia*, vol. 83, 1933, pp. 237–284.

Plomley, Roy. "Desert Island Discs." BBC Radio 4, 5 July 1980.

Shenfield, Margaret. "Mr. Biswas and Mr. Polly." *English*, vol. 23, Autumn 1974, pp. 95–100.

Thieme, John. "V. S. Naipaul's Third World: A Not So Free State." *Journal of Commonwealth Literature*, vol. 10, issue 1, 1975, pp. 10–22.

Thorpe, Michael. *V. S. Naipaul*. Longman/British Council, 1976.

Walsh, William. *V. S. Naipaul*. Oliver and Boyd, 1973.

White, Landeg. *V S. Naipaul: A Critical Introduction*. Macmillan, 1975.

White, Patrick. *A Fringe of Leaves*. Jonathan Cape, 1976.

Chapter 16

FAILURES IN DECOLONISATION AND THE RETURN TO THE PAST: READING V. S. NAIPAUL[1]

Mahesh Hapugoda

The aim of this study is to interpret and contextualise selected works by V. S. Naipaul which depict the social transformation process called decolonisation. According to the *Oxford Dictionary*, decolonisation is "the withdrawal from its colonies of a colonial power, the acquisition of political or economic independence by such colonies". The *Oxford Companion to Politics of the World* defines decolonisation, on the other hand, as "a change in sovereignty in which a state recognizes the independence of a segment of the people formerly under its rule" (193). In more radical terms, the concept of decolonisation is taken to mean "the ending of colonialism and the liberation of the colonized" by the dismantling of colonial government and social systems which exercise social control and exploitation of indigenous communities (Hill 20).

These ideas inform how decolonisation is conceived in this study. But the concern is that when previously colonised societies engage in the transformation from traditional to modern, failed projects of decolonisation drive citizens to return to the ideological comfort of the traditional instead of generating the modern, secularised individuals which they seek to nurture. This study observes, as evidenced in the works of Naipaul, that the humiliation, dislocation, anxiety and jealousies regarding the luxuries associated with modern secularism have made previously colonised subjects respond violently to modernity in their existing lifeworlds. This trend destroys the democratic public sphere of colonised nations and creates untenable forms of nationalism by "negating social life itself, the erosion of its foundation" (Hardt and Negri 113).

Most importantly, when traditional societies with pre-modern values coexist and fight against "westernized" modernity and secularism "by

1 A version of this essay was first published in *Sabaragamuwa University Journal*, vol. 14, no. 1, May 2015, pp. 59–85.

means of pre-political traditional religious form of protest" (Žižek, *End Times* 281), I argue, against Dipesh Chakrabarty, that the archaic traditional ideologies and practices themselves become anti-progressive in terms of universal emancipatory politics. Therein, Naipaul's representation of societies "torn between modernism and the return to tradition" shows that there is a greater movement towards remaining "faithful to the universal/secular project of modernity" (Žižek, *End Times* 280). Chakrabarty's ideas of "organic unity" within such societies which fail to take into account any periodic historical change and deny the "incompleteness" of pre-modern political practices could thus be contested in the light of empirical evidence cited by Naipaul.

Contemporary decolonisation processes have sometimes failed to generate the advanced cognitive space in which individual's potential for living "in a state of constant vigilance, apprehension, and criticism to reject everything that was not true, not justified by free reason" is fostered (Marcuse 43). People's potential to make rational judgements about their lifeworld is undervalued. The capacity for higher judgements arrived at independently based on individual conceptual and discursive capacities is not exercised in a majority of postcolonial contexts where they are often most urgently needed—for example, in those with serious ethnopolitical divisions coupled with geographical sensitiveness.

Though Western societies also experience and have experienced such anti-enlightenment tendencies within their historical development, especially in the twentieth century, and are now subject to confrontation with the rise of religious reason,[2] the nature and the intensity of the crises generated by religious ideologies derived from tradition seem more serious, politicised and threatening in previously colonised nations. Therefore, in the West, it is often believed that when such crises occur, the death of reason and the rise of authoritarianism will last for a brief period and then the system will return to normal. Contrarily, some of the postcolonial nations in which this occurs may not see the end of ultranationalistic fundamentalism for a long time. In these contexts, it is evident that reasoning is superseded by inherent biases in traditional ideologies derived from myths, ancient chronicles and even colonial historical interpretations. Anything that does not fit into the framework of thinking and practice that these ideologies generate or affects the sentiments of the traditionalist is negated, looked down upon

2 For more on this, see Rawls, "Idea of Public Reason Revisited"; Audi, "Religious Argument"; Habermas *Theory of Communicative Action* and "Religion".

and sometimes leads to punishments of barbaric nature in extreme circumstances.

The anti-enlightenment tendencies in the once colonised world thus thwart the logic that drove the revolutions and resistance to colonialism in favour of traditionalism. Often backed by tremendous politico-militant power and ideological support, these supposedly "organic" societies appear determined to destroy all that they deem western, secular and modern and, at these ideological frontiers, it would seem to be our scholarly responsibility today to intervene if only with the understanding proffered by Jürgen Habermas:

> [T]hat neoconservatism is confused in its understanding of the relation between culture and society. It attributes to cultural modernism all those pathological or dysfunctional syndromes, such as hedonism, narcissism, lack of social identity, withdrawal from status and achievement competition, that are in reality the product of a successful capitalist modernization of the economy and society. (d'Entreves 3)

At this juncture, it is possible to turn to Naipaul for literary evidence to identify the vulnerable identity issues of colonial subjects. Naipaul is acknowledged as an author who initially wanted to move away from a limited colonised world to metropolitan spaces that manifest "the idea of our modernity and development" (*A Bend in the River* 269). This desire resulted in a wide geographical drifting fueled by a sense of not-belonging. In the process, he became a writer who effectively used an insider-outsider point of view to understand and express "the larger truth through not being partisan" (Park 243). Of those who have truly explored the anarchical and nihilistic aspects of "transitional and makeshift" postcolonial societies where serious identity issues create deeper sociopolitical calamities, Naipaul unarguably emerged as a pioneer (*The Mimic Men* 6).

Given this scenario, this discussion puts together two significant literary and ideological developments of the twentieth century. To analyse Naipaul in the context of decolonisation, this reading will primarily draw literary evidence of events in the transitional postcolonial world from Naipaul's works.[3] The evidence will then be interpreted in

3 In this study, transitional societies are taken to be ones which are undergoing serious sociocultural dilemmas and challenges during the process of transforming from traditional (early modern, feudal or semi-feudal) to modern and postmodern societies. To draw on what Samuel P. Huntington observes in relation to post-Communist Central European contexts after the Cold War, once the iron grip of the colonial masters that

light of contemporary politico-philosophical interpretations, firstly about decolonisation and postcolonialism and secondly about the rise of totalitarianism. This will be drawn from the works of a range of intellectuals including Frantz Fanon, Samir Amin, Douglas Kellner, Aijaz Ahmad, Michael Hardt and Antonio Negri, as well as Tariq Amin Khan. Studies of the rise of totalitarianism from which the arguments are drawn include ones by Hannah Arendt, Herbert Marcuse, Matthew Sharpe, Geoff Boucher and Slavoj Žižek.

Thus, in this study, a rereading of Naipaul's literary journeys is proposed to understand failed projects of decolonisation, from the return to tradition to the rise of totalitarianism developed from within the dialectic coordinates of modernity itself. Based on the fictional evidence in Naipaul's work and the different responses to it from contemporary literary critics, this study attempts to theorise the anxiety, dislocation and the jealousies towards modern secularism that drive deprived and alienated colonised subjects to seek the ideological comfort of history and tradition, and most dangerously, respond as a consequence with barbaric violence against supposedly Western modernity.

To reiterate, therefore, this study investigates how subjects in postcolonial transitional societies have shown post-independence symptoms of subjugation by returning to tradition and indulging in a kind of deceptive mental comfort for a sense of security. It explores how these societies violently try to re-establish the archaic values of a fantasised past and force it on others. The study also touches on the education systems operated under colonialism and ever afterwards which did not prepare individuals who emerged from traditional, sometimes feudal, societies to develop the cognitive capacities to "re-negotiate the meaning in time" (Bauman, *Liquid Modern Challenges* 2). This deficiency similarly applies to failures in political institutions. This study shows how these failures in the decolonisation process result

---

kept all the conflicting interest groups together either collapsed or was released due to the pressure from indigenous politics in the mid-twentieth century, a violence crisis emerged within many independent nations based largely on ethnic, religious and linguistic lines (22). Most of these societies have undergone centuries of colonialism and now entertain independence but still struggle to discover or recover their own form and shape to face the future. Most identifiable issues in these nations are fundamentally centralised among ethno-nationalistic, cultural and religious adaptabilities and problems of assimilation; therefore, the nature of their crisis is usually more ideological than material.

in symptomatic totalitarian development within transitional social contexts. It briefly identifies how short-sighted political strategies exploited in decolonising societies aimed at regaining the past contribute to the ideological strengthening of fundamentalist totalitarianism. The study, thus, contributes to the theorisation of contemporary dictatorial political developments in the postcolonial world.

Liberal capitalism has been the main force in changing traditional forms of life during and after imperialism and introducing modernisation of the lifeworlds of traditional communities. Capitalism, because of its place as a "stage in the development of human civilisation" and in "the development of the forces of production", and its association with an "equitable distribution of income", also stands as the sole agent of a legitimate economic order today (Amin, *Implosion* 107).

Secular education under imperialism brought about significant changes to traditional ways of thinking but with serious limitations both in relation to its objectives and outcomes. Since missionary education, for example, did not have a grand plan and was often fragmented and contradictory, colonial education was often "limited to a basic elementary level—extending no further than the transmission of minimal literacy and numeracy skill" (Paisley and Reid, *Critical Perspectives* 9). It served at best the needs of the colonial master who wanted a kind of literate social layer whose members could be employed for their subordinate minor administrative works. This kind of education was not part of the "enlightenment project" in which free individuals are supposed to use their critical thoughts and analytical skills for their own advancement but was intended rather for maintenance of the existing status quo on a larger systemic scale.

After the imperialist stage of capitalism, as we know, the expansion of liberalised economic forces created the grounds for globalisation. However, globalisation only further united the market forces, creating profound social inequalities.[4] The marginalised and unprivileged segments of society generated by globalised capital started reacting to its forces that widened divisions and inequalities. The violent reaction to modernity promoted under these conditions of globalisation emerges from the deprivation and disappointment of the underprivileged. The systemic failure of capitalism thus undoubtedly plays a significant role in the failures of decolonisation processes.

---

4 See, for example, the statements in this regard in Bauman, *Liquid Modernity*; Stiglitz, *Globalization and Its Discontents*; Amin, *Capitalism in the Age of Globalization; The Implosion of Contemporary Capitalism* and Dierckxsens, *The Limits of Capitalism.*

The failure of the neo-liberal model of globalisation is also attributed to the phenomenon called neo-feudalism[5] that springs up mostly in the Third World. Despite the limitless authority of capital and globalised culture propagated through market forces, feudal systems still remaining in the transitional societies rejuvenate to foster anti-democratic and neo-fascist movements. Historically, the origin of economic anti-democratic trends, as Wim Dierckxsens observes, sprung up from the market crisis in a liberal order. He points out,

> Liberalism hit bottom during the crisis of the 1930s with the stock market crash and the ruin of many companies. Since it was no longer useful to the bourgeoisie it was substituted by nationalist protectionism. Corporate, authoritarian and anti-democratic state power was born, based on the same atomizing individualism that characterized economic liberalism. (120)

Thus, capitalism expanded across the globe after World War II and widespread application of the logic of capitalism threatened "the national systems of production created by the previous historical period" (Amin, *Capitalism* 16). Under the new system, global production and markets grew across borders and forced peripheral nations to restructure their political systems to match the new inflow of capital. The novel "networked society" and the universalisation of consumerism "supplanted the local cultures and traditions", which meant that the cultures that existed within certain geographical boundaries had to make way for the new global culture (Kellner 285). More than with the direct methods used under imperialism, local communities experienced quick and radical changes which completely uprooted the traditional world order and its values. Unlike under colonial imperialism, the intensity to introduce material secular values desired by global consumerism was profound, empathic and unavoidable. The interpretations of living proposed to individuals by tradition were no longer applicable in the complex brand-new situations and "the historical narratives appeared outdated and illegitimate" (Hennayake 80).

Global capitalism not only challenged traditionalism but almost all the principal values cultivated by modernity itself. As Hardt and Negri observe, this new empire constitutes "a new planetary order" and "we

5 This concept theorises that the rebirth of policies of governance, economic activities and public and cultural life of individuals are restricted because of the remnants of feudal societies. For further insights, see Andreas Rahamatian's *Copyright and Creativity: The Making of Property Rights in Creative Work*, p 263.

are confronted no longer with the local mediations of the universal but with the concrete universal itself" (19). They also point out, "it deploys a powerful police function against the barbarians and the rebellious slaves who threaten its order" (20), and the marginalised segments from which those rebels and slaves originated during the previous system, both under the colonial and decolonial processes, are further alienated by the new. Those who did not or are reluctant to acquire the necessary skills to survive under the new inflow of liquidated capital became outcastes who rely on the fantasy of ahistorical narratives to ideologically defend their existence and radical actions against the new enemy.

Two historical phenomena—the dissolution of local culture in the face of the new universalism and the insecurity of consumer secularism unexpectedly merged as the pre-modern and the post-modern both collectively—stand together to fight the spirit of modernity. The loss of legitimacy in traditionalism is paralleled by the collapse of metanarratives (loss of master signifiers) in the postmodern era.

The Return to the Past and the Rise of Totalitarianism

The return to the past is more than a simple nostalgic revisit to an idealised past for psychological comfort; ideologically, it is a political process in which subjects in transitional contexts often try to violently materialise the past in the present. The end result of this ideological attempt demands total submission and tolerance of individuals during the process to regain the supposedly lost superiority of the past. In other words, an anti-democratic movement emerges with the intention of taking total control of every aspect of the social life of the individual, be it economic on a macro basis or sociocultural at a micro level.

Hannah Arendt observes that the threats and demands of a totalitarian regime are mostly indirect and veiled. However, the barbaric and banal form of fundamentalist totalitarianism today functions in a very obvious manner. It insists more on cultural submission than political obedience; the latter being more commonly addressed via an ultra-military mode. But it nonetheless manipulates what Arendt calls the idea of "eternal laws of nature and life" with an urgency about missing the train of history unless one partakes right now in the collective utopia of its given ideologies (*The Origins of Totalitarianism* 345–346). The threat of an irreparable and mysterious deterioration of a historical heritage, bloodline or totemic religious legacy is held out as the prospect for the non-conforming.

In its attempts to completely take control of the cultural life of an individual, totalitarian regimes can sadistically employ violence to maintain complete individual obedience, demoralise democratic institutions and make their authority seem beyond questioning. Rational thinking may thus cease to exist when one truly desists from suspecting or querying the very foundation of totalitarian ideologies and their functions in society. Hence, the faculty of thinking based on reason, judgements based on rational understanding and critical evaluation, the search for truth and evidence; in short, the whole exercise of scholarly opinion is directly or indirectly either prohibited or discouraged.

Totalitarianism is, thus, in its broadest sense, a phenomenon in which the "banality of evil has accentuated the whole relationship among the faculty of thinking, the capacity to distinguish between right and wrong, the faculty of judgement, and their moral implications" (Assy 1). Totalitarianism, in the context of this essay, therefore, refers to the unconditional obedience to a regime which holds total authority over the society and seeks to control all aspects of public and private life. Such a body of authority "fills the gap opened up by the modernist dissolution of all traditional organic social links". But unlike postmodernist thinkers, this concept of totalitarianism does not see it as the "necessary outcome of the modernist Enlightenment" (Sharpe and Boucher 88–89).

A major difference can, in fact, be drawn between the two. In the totalitarian systems in which this study is interested, the unquestioning subjugation of individuals to the infinite authority of the state and its use of terror against freedom and democracy take place in a society that silently tolerates or neglects to see the obvious reality of the various suppressions. As Žižek reminds us in *For They Know Not What They Do: Enjoyment as a Political Factor*, individuals cynically and ritualistically maintain an inner distance in relation to the manipulation of the entire social process and even rationalise such manipulation. In short, the system functions through the suppression of the public use of reason by hystericising the crowd "to hold them in obedience with a mixture of threat and promise" (244). However, such totalising potential is derived and shared through a single Ego Ideal, for example, in the name of the master symbol of king and father.

Trends which emerge in postcolonial nations are often termed "anti-modernist movements, resurgences of primordial identities and values" and "can be conceived as a kind of historical backflow, a de-modernization" (Hardt and Negri 146). Presently, however, religious revivalism and its fundamentalist movements in challenging modern secularism and rationalism can even be found in Western civilisations "washing away or at least levelling the thresholds hitherto assumed to pertain between 'tradition' and 'modern' societies" (Habermas, "Religion" 2).

Hence, Habermas attributes the rise of fundamentalism to the "long-term impact of violent colonisation and failures in decolonisation" (1). On this phenomenon, he further notes, "Under unfavourable circumstances, capitalist modernization penetrating these societies from the outside then triggers social uncertainty and cultural upheavals" (1).

The state of returning to the remnants of the past and to the comfort of tradition is also reviewed in Yannis Stavrakakis' *Lacan and the Political.* Stavrakakis sees it as a phenomenon resulting from the "dislocation of traditional forms of organizing and making sense of society, a dislocation inflicted by the increased hegemony of secularism, liberalism, socialism and industrialization" (103). The impact that the mega social projects of modern civilisation, such as global forms of liberal capitalism and socialism, in the first half of the twentieth century, had on traditional and postcolonial nations was immensely powerful and, subsequently, created serious rivalries, marginalisation and polarisations in these societies.[6] At the same time, as Marshall McLuhan observes, the luxuries of modern secularism in the west generated anxieties and jealousies in those who could not materialise them. Therefore, both marginalisation and jealousies in transitional traditional societies generated deep divisions between modern secularist and traditional world views while generating violent reactions towards secular nations.

As Matthew Sharpe and Geoff Boucher remind us, postcolonial subjects in these situations are often interpellated by some kind of "perfect final stage of mankind ideology", such as Aryan triumph or the power of the proletariat (94). The nostalgia for historical heritage and bloodlines fit into the category. Indeed, this is the way fascists gained support from established aristocratic and business classes to successfully function as "reactionary-modernist" regimes and were able to manipulate the most developed modern media, industrial and military technology to reach their targets. As Sharpe and Boucher put it, "However, fascism is predicated on a reactionary criticism of the decadence or 'nihilism' of liberal society, and the way that the intrinsic dynamics of capitalist economies break up traditional, organic, racially and culturally unified communities" (95).

Sharpe and Boucher's statement about fascism is equally applicable as a bedrock for understanding one of the greatest paradoxes that

---

6 See, for example, Fanon, *The Wretched of the Earth*; Wallerstein, "Dependence"; Amin, "Global Polarization"; Huntington, *The Clash of Civilizations*; Kellner, "Theorizing Globalization"; Ahmad, "Imperialism of Our Time".

postcolonial nations have to live with even today, that is, broken up traditional societies arising as reactionary fundamentalist to the secular tendencies of liberal capitalism from within the coordinates of liberal capitalism itself. This trend has historically challenged, sometimes through its sheer physical energy, and often threatened to destroy the only and the most sustainable change agent of modernity—education. As Samir Amin helps us to recognise in *The Implosion of Contemporary Capitalism* and other works, during and after long periods of imperialistic capitalism and now that globally expanding mercantile capital is at its advanced stage, modern education introduced by the imperialists, albeit with grievous limitations, still remains the most important change agent for developing nations (and most postcolonial states are included in this category).

As Patrick Ziltener and Daniel Künzler correctly observe, missionary education, modern healthcare, the judicial system, democracy, technology, transportation, commercial agriculture, new social structures, including new economic models and market places, etc. created a new social world for traditional communities. Hence, if the concept of "decolonisation" is to mean something more than the biophysical and is supposed to reconstruct the relationship between meaning and the constitution of forms of life, the danger of the subordination of the individual to futile conditions of meaning should be carefully avoided. But the empirical evidence today bears witness that those who were finally freed of colonial masters have surrendered to irrational violence and totalitarianism, primarily, as Amin notes in *The Arab Revolutions*, by ideologically returning to tradition and Naipaul's work is of great significance in exploring these types of sociopolitical scenarios.

Naipaul's Representations of Failed Projects of Decolonisation

The critical literature about Naipaul's works basically falls into two main categories. First, there is the literary criticism which articulates common postcolonial themes, such as alienation, exploitation and identity crises of once colonised subjects, while others critically concentrate on how the previously colonised are entangled by Western forms of modernity and secularism in his works.[7] Interestingly, many current postgraduate

7 Further on this, see A. Singh, *Literary Secularism*; B. Singh, "Naipaul's India"; Park, "An exploration of the outsider's role"; Harode, Postcolonial Chaos in *Mimic Men*; Cader "Homelessness and Exiled Identity".

students are working in this area. The other category, somewhat smaller in number, is critical about Naipaul's Westernised world view towards postcolonial, sociopolitical and cultural developments.[8] These two categories both talk about the impact of colonialism on indigenous cultures and the implications of decolonisation. Neither, however, seems to pay significant attention to how the ideological return to tradition bring about violent repercussions in the present. This is strange because if we look at fundamentalist tendencies in the postcolonial world today, we see that various situations have become much more serious and dangerous than what Naipaul prophesied during his days a few decades back. A rereading of his works is therefore deemed much needed in the present context, recapped in Figure 16.1.

Figure 16.1 attempts to illustrate how the anxious and often schizophrenic postcolonial subject ideologically returns to the past for psychological comfort. This emergence constitutes a violent return of tradition because it is evoked eagerly to compensate for lost glory. This return, as we experience it today, is often excessively violent and there seems to be no end to its revenge on modern rationality. It is in this conjuncture that this study contextualises Naipaul as a writer who bears witness to the misadventures of modern postcolonial man.

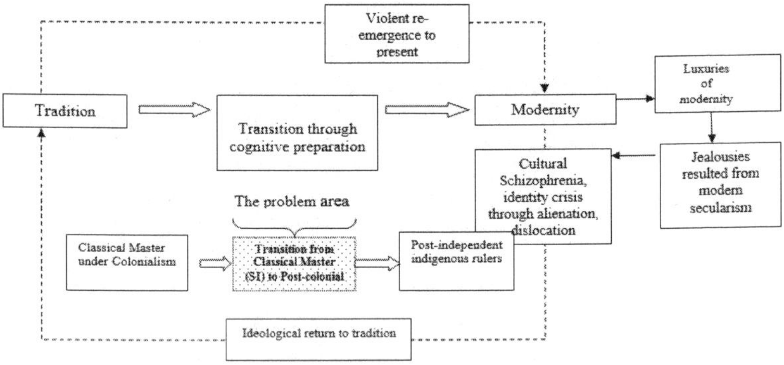

Fig. 16.1: A Pathway of Return to Tradition. (Hapugoda)

Within what is usually referred to as postcolonial literature today, failures in processes of decolonisation are illustrated by many writers including Chinua Achebe, Salman Rushdie, Wole Soyinka,

8 See, for example, Said, *Culture and Imperialism* and "The intellectual in the post-colonial world"; Bhabha, "Signs taken for wonders"; Eid, "Naipaul's Bend in the River"; Johnstone, "Politics and V. S. Naipaul"; and Cudjoe, *V. S. Naipaul.*

Arundhati Roy, Bapsi Sidhwa, Shyam Selvadurai and many others. But it is Naipaul who digs deep, especially into Asian feudal hierarchies, in his many fictional and non-fictional works produced over a time span of fifty years. Despite criticism about his male-chauvinism made by, among others, Champa Rao Mohan and his supposed celebration of the triumph of colonialist moment that Homi K. Bhabha talks about, Naipaul has succeeded in depicting a postcolonial reality that we all easily recognise. He focusses on those which fail in building the righteous society of universal emancipation oriented towards the ideals of truth, freedom and justice through the reasonable application of the rules of law and order.

Regardless of his supposedly Western orientation, even Edward Said had to concede in *Culture and Imperialism* that he is "ruthlessly honest" in portraying colonial and decolonising projects (19). Some of his works, as Sudipta Chakraborty notes, obviously progress from an "exploration of alternative spaces of modernity and belonging" (26) and "the imposition of British colonialist-imperialist values upon colonial people" (58). Naipaul makes visible in his work "the impact of imperialism on the life and personality of the colonized individuals" (Harode 3). In his wide range of independent writings, he analyses and interprets his own past and experiences over five decades so that he could produce a compilation of a kind of spiritual and psychological autobiography. As a result, when we read his work, comparisons across texts are possible and social evolution can subsequently be traced. Similarly, we can examine irrational political domination in the light of "the substitution of theology for education and suppression of all individuality" that Lillian Feder notes as a focus in much of his work (135).

There are thus significant features that distinguish Naipaul's work from his contemporaries and make him perhaps the most appropriate choice of author in the context of this research. As mentioned previously, throughout his works, Naipaul maintains an insider-outsider point of view. He looks at the rational secular motives of the colonisation project while illustrating the catastrophic elements within it. He discloses the imperialistic motives of the colonists in a dialectical manner which reminds us of Walter Benjamin's assertion that "there is no document of civilization which is not at the same time a document of barbarism" (256). For example, in one of his most famous novels, *A Bend in the River*, Naipaul has his narrator explain,

> But the Europeans could do one thing and say something quite different; and they could act in this way because they had an idea of what they owed to their civilization. It was their great advantage

> over us. The Europeans wanted gold and slaves, like everybody else; but at the same time they wanted statues put up to themselves as people who had done good things for the slaves. Being an intelligent and energetic people, and at the peak of their powers, they could express both sides of their civilization; and they got both the slaves and statues. (19)

If modernisation means a break from the past and its metaphysical, mythical and traditional teachings, as Donald Rutherford asserts, then we can see that Naipaul agrees with him. However, Naipaul sees it as a kind of conversion and notes that "[t]o be converted you have to destroy your past, destroy your history. You have to stamp on it, you have to say 'my ancestral culture does not exist, it does not matter'" (M. A. Khan 172). This perspective in his works is extremely useful for a study that is attempting to interpret the social transition processes he examines in his writings. Because of his own sense of not belonging and self-distancing from all nations, he has become an important witness to the disintegration, ingenuity and inauthenticity of the world.

To understand this, it is important to understand the social setting in which he was born and raised. When he was born on the island of Trinidad, it was still a British colony comprised of a majority population descended from the enslaved Africans and "a large minority of Indians, descended from indentured laborers who were imported to replace the slaves when slavery was officially abolished in the British Empire", as well as numerous smaller minorities of Chinese and European groups (Dooley 2). His exposure to this range of persons in a very early stage of his life seems to have made a tremendous impact on his world view which is reflected in his works. However, he was a writer who was also "disenchanted by his past and his native background" (Deodat iv) and he recognised his inability to become part of the Trinidad society when he was just eleven. In the meantime, Naipaul's own scholarly potential was recognised in the early stages of his life and it helped him as he was trying to make an exit from the small world into which he happened to be born. As Gillian Dooley notes, "from an early stage he saw the possibility this provided of escaping from the limited society of Trinidad to the 'real' world abroad" (2). This situation is true for many a postcolonial subject and it illustrates a pertinent postcolonial psychological dilemma with which he struggled from very early in his own life.

At first, he used to think that colonial cultures are trapped by their own histories, practices, biases and traditions. In his works, Naipaul, thus, illustrates the cultural dilemmas of colonised nations in which people are caught between powerful historical narrations of traditions and modernisation. Though Naipaul talks about this complex and conflicting interrelationship between tradition and modernity, he did not particularly belong to either camp. He has been an "observer rather than participant, the witness who describes, not prescribes" (Johnstone 108). It is the chaotic nature of the experience of these colonial nations that makes Naipaul's realism a unique one. In this regard, according to Bruce King,

> Besides the complexity of characterization and the mixture of criticism with sympathetic understanding, there is often a profound substrata of literary and cultural associations giving Naipaul's realism, and social and psychological analysis, roots in history, archetypes, myths and symbols. (202)

The time and setting of his works are mostly in the post-independent periods of those societies he explores and this is the era of decolonisation examined in my study. In this case, I look specifically at the psychoanalytical significance of his thematic observations of colonisation, alienation, dislocation, hybridity and, most importantly, the failures of Western secular values in the colonised Third World. As many critics argue, indigenous communities experience a major psychological breakdown due to the dislocation and identity crisis incurred by the imposition of two totally dissimilar and incompatible worlds. Reeta Harode, in her article, "Postcolonial Chaos in V. S. Naipaul's *Mimic Men*", notes for example that:

> The natives who are devoid of their own cultures, customs and traditions, religions, and race consider themselves to be inferior to those of their masters and try to identify themselves with the empire. As they are far away from their original homeland, their own original traditions and religions have become meaningless to them and being completely different from the master in cultural, traditional, racial and religious backgrounds, they can never successfully associate themselves with the colonized other. They suffer from dislocation, placelessness, fragmentation, and loss of identity. As these psychological problems remain unsolved even after independence is achieved, independence itself becomes a word but not a real experience. Without the colonizer, the colonized see themselves as lost in their postcolonial society that fails to offer a sense of national unity and identity. (7)

The in-betweenness of not belonging either to a traditional way of life or secular modernity causes, in other words, a kind of psychological paralysis in previously colonised subjects. In spite of living a modern life which values individual freedom, secular values and democracy, the previously colonised live a life full of ambivalence (Noor 2013). In depicting this condition, Naipaul "goes beyond the bounds of regionalism and also avoids the trap of nationalism" (Park 181) to observe as an outsider. Over the course of his writing career, therefore, some of the themes that Naipaul writes about were to appear for the first time in postcolonial literature and his perspective of them changed even as his understanding of the situations changed but remained ever new. As Mohan points out,

> The themes of alienation, homelessness and mimicry still preoccupy Naipaul but the perspective has changed. They are now viewed as a universal condition of the modern world afflicting both colonized and colonizers alike. Besides the familiar themes that still haunt Naipaul's pen, there are themes that appear for the first time- the broader post-colonial themes of power and freedom and neocolonialism. (81)

The psychology of the colonised and how they respond to new postcolonial situations was one of the major concerns of the novel *The Mimic Men*. As Naipaul succinctly reminds us in this work, "The empires of our time were short-lived, but they have altered the world forever; their passing away is their least significant feature" (32). As a writer, Naipaul was actually trying to understand this confusing and profound social conundrum. He puts the dilemma in the words of his protagonist like this:

> It was during this time, as I have said, that I thought of writing. It was my hope to give expression to the restlessness, the deep disorder, which the great explorations, the overthrow in three continents of established social organizations, unnatural bringing together of people who could achieve fulfilment only within the security of their own societies and the landscape hymned by their ancestors, it was my hope to give partial expression to the restlessness which this great upheaval has brought about. (32)

Naipaul clearly perceives the process of colonisation and the political changes after independence as consequent waves of history which kept on changing the way people lived without their consent or their ability to understand what was happening to them. Those who do try to stop and understand prove to be ineffective and inefficient at ever doing so, like Ralph Kripalsingh in *The Mimic Men*. In the novel *A Bend in the River*, similarly, the protagonist declares, "We had lived our lives in our way, done what we had to do, worshipped God and obeyed his commandments. Now—to echo Indar's words—another tide of history was coming to wash us away" (22).

In the postcolonial world, the lifestyles, beliefs, practices, ideologies, political structures and modes of authority and power shifted from one master to another in quick succession, from traditional masters to colonial and then back to the traditional. These transformations took a minimum of two centuries. As far as contemporary structural changes are concerned, these two centuries must be considered the most influential period of the present social fabric of these postcolonial nations because these structural changes altered people's way of thinking. In Naipaul's view, the only way to move on from this position is to consciously build now "a universal civilisation based on the rights and responsibilities of the individual" (Mohan 69). To get to this new order, however, requires vanquishing older hierarchical authoritarian structures. For this reason, Naipaul often turned his attention to the effects of dictatorial rule.

The sustaining ideological fantasy produced by the discourse of the master is that the master is the bearer of a second body which is an embodiment of the sublime object of ideology, as Žižek asserts in *For They Know Not What They Do*. In other words, in him, the masters' subject believed that there is more than himself. As King, for example, he was believed to be made of some special stuff derived from some hereditary legacy which gives him a special right to rule. Such a ruler uses his sublime-ideological mandate to the full to achieve an even more sublime authority over his subjects (Sharpe and Boucher 92).

Sometimes, it may be royal blood that gives the necessary justification for such a ruler to be considered unique amongst the ordinary or to be elevated above the ordinary as seen, for example, in the claims made by the archetypal African dictator in the character Jean-Bedel Bokassa in Wole Soyinka's *Opera Wonyosi*, which illustrates perfectly that "traditional authority was based on what we could call the *mystique of the Institution*. Authority based its charismatic power on symbolic ritual, on the form of the Institution as such" (Žižek *For They Know Not What They Do*, 249; emphasis in original).

The liberal-bourgeois principle of rational authority is transformed to irrational and unconditional authority in the post-liberal totalitarian postcolonial context. In other words, bureaucratic knowledge in the previous system becomes "madness" which operates "by itself" without reference to anything real to symbolically justify its authority. As a result, such authority may not be willing to tolerate agencies which stand for justice, human rights or freedom of expression and all the other aspects of a universal civilisation of which Naipaul speaks or any other bodies which pass judgements about law and order.

Under such rulers, people easily find an externalised enemy or traitor who conspires to steal the essence of the nation, which it derives mostly from a nostalgic history. Gradual isolation, changes in language policy, restructuring of the colonial education system and structures of governance, often referred to as radicalisation, and the generation of policies in order to return to so-called tradition and a consequent intolerance for criticism are symptomatic political developments in such a context. Naipaul illustrates this through the journeys of the character Salim in *A Bend in the River*, who as a trader travels into the interior of the African setting and gradually experiences the stages of such developments. The subsequent attitudinal changes in the indigenous African characters, such as Metty and Ferdinand, in the wake of authoritarianism under a nationalistic banner are represented in the novel as unconscious obedience to the irrational call of this voice.

Naipaul, thus, shows that postcolonial societies imagine themselves as traditional ones when they are obviously caught in a whirlwind of fundamentalism, anti-secularism and blind obedience to one usurping master voice while they face grave changes in the tradition itself that they think they are upholding. He illustrates the point that there is no way out for them in this paradoxically positioned evolution of mutual antagonisms. Even those who are exposed to education in the hope of making a successful transition to modernity are unable to completely withstand the irrational elements introduced by the demand to return to a supposedly traditional social order. When those educated otherwise achieve positions of power in the new political system, even they succumb to its irrationality.

For example, Ferdinand in *A Bend in the River* becomes an administrator after his successful completion of school but this does not help him to promote a world view of a universal civilisation. The pathway to this failure is in fact one of the main stories the novel is interested in illustrating. In the beginning of the novel, we see that like any mother in the postcolonial world who wants a better life for her son, Zabeth too wants Ferdinand to go to lycée as she wishes "something better for her son" (41). This is how Ferdinand is introduced into the story of the protagonist Salim. Zabeth wants Ferdinand to go to school in the town and she arranges for him to board at Salim's place because she thinks that Salim is a foreigner and "English speaking as well, someone from whom Ferdinand could learn manners and the ways of the outside world" (41). Zabeth represents what traditional society has become over the course of imperial subjugation. The protagonist sees the difficulties of the lifeworld she inhabits and understands that she does not want this for her son. Salim says,

> It seemed to me natural that someone like Zabeth, living such a hard life, should want something better for her son. This better life lay outside the timeless ways of village and river. It lay in education and the acquiring of new skills; and for Zabeth, as for many Africans of her generation, education was something only foreigners could give. (41)

The potential of education for freedom from hardship is a role it plays in the transformation of society by inculcating higher cognitive levels of thought and action. The generations under imperial rule who could not acquire this education recognised this potential and negotiated in whatever ways they could with the foreigners from whom it could be taken. Zabeth, therefore, makes Salim a European agent, despite his African–Indian origins which are not as different from hers in relation to the Europeans as she thinks, because he can speak English and appears to her as a spokesperson of European values. He could, thereby, easily be established by the people at the borders of the river and the forest where his business is located as some sort of ego-ideal for the people who have been settled there eons before. He is perceived as one who can help them to fulfil the dream of going beyond tribal boundaries.

These boundaries have demanded a certain kind of subjectivity from Zabeth because she has had to find ways to fend for and protect herself and her son from others. Naipaul imagines some of these in fine detail, for example, in the narrator's description of her survival techniques during her days-long river journey:

> She came and went with her vanity case and no one molested her … there was something else about Zabeth. She had a special smell. It was strong and unpleasant, and at first I thought—because she came from a fishing village—that it was an old and deep smell of fish. Then I thought it had to do with her restricted village diet…. Metty said that Zabeth's smell was strong enough to keep mosquitoes away. I thought myself that it was this smell that kept men away from Zabeth … but the smell was meant to keep people at a distance. (10–11)

This is one good instance of the not-so-"organic" cultural practices which operated in supposedly traditional communities in which women had to use what we may call rather primordial methods to safeguard themselves. Zabeth must transform her very gender identity in order to survive. Whereas, other women might use perfumes to attract others, the kind of ointment that Zabeth uses intentionally repels. The picture that Naipaul gives us of the social structure in the communities he represents in *A Bend in the River* can be visualised by means of the following Figure 16.2.

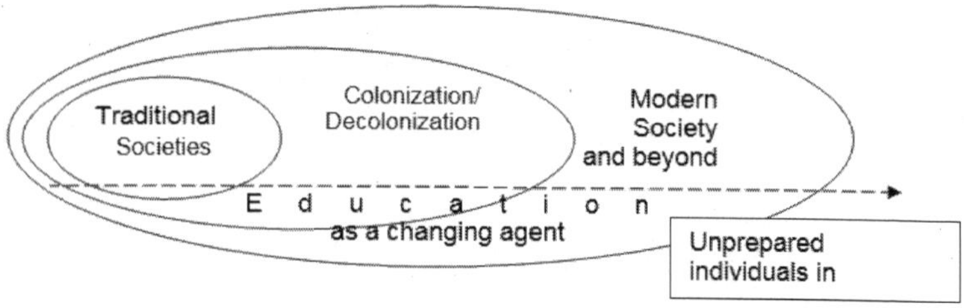

Fig. 16.2: Function of Education in Social Transformation (Hapugoda)

Fig. 16.2 illustrates education functioning as a changing agent in transitional contexts. One of the major responsibilities of those who guide the decolonisation process is the establishment and articulation of a strong system of secular education to ensure that individuals are able to cope with the complexities of modernity. This is a necessary process, as discussed previously, because when persons are cognitively unprepared to adapt to the new postcolonial situation, this may generate the need for comfort zones leading to supposedly traditional justification albeit within the coordinates of modernity. What is required is critical education which offers individuals freedom to question existing ideologies and practices.

Naipaul has represented the need for this not only in *A Bend in the River* but in many other novels. For example, in *A House for Mr Biswas*, the significance of education, termed "education frenzy" is highlighted as everyone recognises that the children must be able to "read" and "learn". "They still want their children to go to Port-of-Spain schools, and Mrs Tulsi fulfilling a duty that had been imposed in a different age.... The cries of "Read! Learn! increased" (463). Naipaul realises that often feudal values and social frameworks in transitional societies suppress the individual's authentic desire to interrogate the existing status quo, but that modernity's impetus for education operates against this oppression. The real tragedy of education in Naipaul's work, therefore, is that it becomes a lost opportunity when those who are ostensibly educated still succumb to the call of the totalitarian master and his irrational dehumanisation agenda.

As pointed out previously, the totalitarian master seeks the obedience of the crowd by hystericising them with a mixture of threat and promise. The nature of nationalisation and radicalisation that were introduced by many postcolonial rulers during that critical decolonisation point during the immediate post-independence period often occurred in the form of threat and promise. As Amin reminds us in *Capitalism in the Age of Globalization*, a wave of radical economic reformation influenced by left-wing political developments occurred during the 1960s and 1970s in the Third World.

The income that nationalisation produced was first channeled "to expand the new middle classes" (32). As we know, however, nationalisation always runs the risk of falling into the pit of "national consciousness" which results from "the intellectual laziness of the national middle class" (Fanon 149). Most dangerously, there is ample historical evidence that this can result in nationalistic motives being channeled into an articulation of solely ethnocentric aspirations of a certain majority by over-determining the ethnic otherness of other groups as competitive enmity.

Rather than humanistic universalism and respect for difference, postcolonial societies often establish singular identity standards. This is evident, for example, in the postcolonial plantation and land reforms in Sri Lanka. As Oddvar Hollup observes,

> Land reform and nationalization of plantation must be analysed in connection with the emergence of Sinhala-Buddhist fundamentalist ideology and political patronage. The ideology, based on mytho-historical interpretations of the past, helped to create greater homogeneity by constructing a 'singular identity' among Sinhalas while at the same time excluding others. (84)

The development of phenomenon of nationalism in Sri Lanka has been the subject of a substantial number of studies over last twenty years.[9]

A Bend in the River represents nationalisation mechanisms in ways that allow us to ponder situations like these in the real-world context of Sri Lanka. The novel illustrates the mechanisms as effecting an absolute radicalising of the existing status quo. As common to any totalising project of the ethno-nationalistic variety, it excluded the so-called foreigners. Needless to say, the excluded feel that they do not belong anymore. As the novel puts it, "Nationalization: it had been a word. It was shocking to face it in this concrete way" (300). The narrator comments that the so-called revolution which necessitates the kind of reformation he observes is deemed "rotten" by the natives themselves (301). These rotten aspects of systemic change made way for blind totalitarianism where supposed foreigners were treated as a threat and forced to flee. Their property, including their land, and business pursuits were taken over by the government and granted to those deemed indigenous or local and in many instances the state also demanded that the original owners continue to work for those who now owned their business enterprises. The President ordered: "you will continue as managers" (301).

9 See, for example, Roberts, *Sinhala-ness and Sinhala Nationalism*; DeVotta, *Sinhala Buddhist Nationalist Ideology*; and Wijeyeratne, *Nation, Constitutionalism and Buddhism in Sri Lanka*.

These symptoms of postcolonial radicalisation which excludes ethnic otherness were happening everywhere: “What was happening to me was happening to every other foreign businessman” (246). The simple totalitarian principle operative behind this radicalisation process is: “the President issued a statement, just to let everybody know that what Big Man gives the Big Man can take away. He gives and he takes back” (302). This means that everything belongs to the ruler. But the most cynical logic is that everything is taking place for the good of the majority or according to the use of egalitarian logic. As a result, the majority embraces the irrational logic and its violent application in their lifeworlds. As Naipaul shows, the reason Ferdinand and Metty and countless others do not decisively oppose the Big Man and his political manoeuvres and fundamentalism, his destruction of the previous harmony of the society, is because they too participate in the unconscious fantasy of return to a paradisiacal traditional past.

As illustrated extensively in *A Bend in the River*, the ethnocentric nationalisation that was being propagated across many parts of Africa confiscated all properties that belonged to people of non-African origin as well as traders like Salim who saw himself as African. The nationalisation project proceeded without rationally investigating such persons’ roles in ensuring Africa and Africans a place of dignity in international relations and global affairs. What this process finally meant was that under the new political dispensation, every aspect of the people’s lifeworlds was influenced by the new “unquestionable authority” of what is considered the “hidden truth of the discourse of the pre-modern masters” (Sharpe and Boucher 92). Naipaul allows us to understand the psychological disassociation from which people suffer in these circumstances by allowing us to view events from the perspective of the victims.

Salim says, for example, “It was strange. He wanted me to acknowledge him as his boss. At the same time, he wanted me to make allowances for him as an uneducated man and an African. He wanted both my respect and my tolerance, even my compassion” (308). Salim is psychologically tortured by the fact that he is supposed to be there physically and witness the downfall of his own business through the (mis)management of someone unfit for the task. He is also expected to be remorseful about his ownership of the business and be willing to help the one to whom the generations of his community’s hard work has simply been handed over for no other reason than that the Big Man has said so. Salim, therefore, discovers that one of the most dangerous aspects of totalitarianism is people’s need to pretend that they believe in the rotten system in power even though they don’t. One has to act as if one does not recognise the true evil in the political body.

Another feature of fundamentalist totalitarianism is the anti-educational motive which prohibits critical thinking and questioning. In *A Bend in the River* the characters fear that "They are going to kill everybody who can read and write, everybody who ever puts on a jacket and tie" (322). Drawing on the energy of anti-imperial resistance towards colonial education that underpinned the demands for independence, postcolonial educational systems foreclose on the very possibility of education that would develop the capacity for rational thought and analysis. Outside of the formal education system, this subsequently turns on the excluded ethnic other to destroy them not only because they do not belong to a certain dominant social group but also because they become the containers for rational thought which is inimical to the survival of Big Man politics. To combat this fact, the totalitarian ruler grants sadistic permission to his followers to violate all universal conventions about humanity and employ the banality of evil against the other despite the "worth of the other man" (136). This establishes the ground not for tribal warfare as commonly asserted but the mass slaughter of anyone who does not support the Big Man by those who do. The limit of people's evil is the limit of their knowledge. Salim is assured, "They haven't done anything to you in jail. That's only because it hasn't occurred to them" (319).

Conclusion

This study has shown that what is most problematic about our present is due to profound structural failures in decolonisation processes. The symptoms of returning to the past, as illustrated in Naipaul's works, drive unprepared subjects of postcolonial nations to subjugate themselves to the irrational call of totalitarian masters who speak in the voice of what is assumed to be tradition although it emerges within the coordinates of Liberal Capitalism. The education system which was seen by those who fought for freedom from colonial rule as a tool and avenue for their fight is handicapped in order for totalitarianism to succeed. Reading Naipaul's works helps us to see in detail how these processes work.

Works cited

Arendt, Hannah. *The Origins of Totalitarianism*. Harvest Books, 1951.

Ahmad, Aijaz. "Imperialism of Our Time." *Socialist Register*, vol. 4, 2004, pp. 43–62, https://socialistregister.com/index.php/srv/article/view/5810/2706. Accessed 6 May 2020.

Amin, Samir. *Capitalism in the Age of Globalization: The Management of Contemporary Society* Zed Books, 1998.

———. *The Implosion of Contemporary Capitalism*. Monthly Review Press, 2013.

———. *Samir Amin: Pioneer of the Rise of the South*. Springer, 2014.

———. "The Arab Revolutions: A Year After." *Interface: A Journal for and about Social Movements*, vol. 4, issue 1, 2012, pp. 33–42.

———. "The Future of Global Polarization." *The World Today*, vol. 23, no. 1/2, 1994, 5–13, https://www.jstor.org/stable/29766921. Accessed 6 May 2020.

Assy, Bethania. "Eichmann, the Banality of Evil, and Thinking in Arendt's Thought." Seminar Proceedings Spring 1997 in the Department of Philosophy, New School for Social Research, https://www.bu.edu/wcp/Papers/Cont/ContAssy.htm. Accessed 22 June 2014.

Audi, Robert. "The Place of Religious Argument in a Free and Democratic Society." *San Diego Law Review*, vol. 30, 1993, 677–701, https://digital.sandiego.edu/sdlr/vol30/iss4/4/. Accessed 6 May 2020.

Benjamin, Walter. "Theses on the Philosophy of History." *Illuminations: Essays and Reflections*. Vintage, 2011.

Bhabha, Homi K. (1985). "Signs taken for wonders: Questions of ambivalence and authority under a tree outside Delhi, May 1817," *Critical Inquiry*, vol 12, no. 1, 1985, pp. 144–165.

Bauman, Zygmunt. *Liquid Modernity*. Polity Press, 2000.

———. *Liquid Modern Challenges to Education*. Padova University Press, 2011.

Cader, Roshan. "V.S. Naipaul: Homelessness and Exiled Identity." M.A. Dissertation, University of Stellenbosch, 2008, https://scholar.sun.ac.za/handle/10019.1/2031. Accessed 6 May 2020.

Chakrabarty, Dipesh. *Provincializing Europe: Postcolonial Thought and Historical Difference*. Princeton University Press, 2000.

Chakraborty, Sudipta. "Space and Cultural Geography: A Study of V. S. Naipaul's Representation of India in His Travel Narratives." PhD Dissertation. University of Burdwan, West Bengal Calcutta, n.d., https://shodhganga.inflibnet.ac.in/bitstream/10603/21932/1/sudipta%20chakraborty,%20ph.d%20thesis.pdf. Accessed 6 May 2020.

Cudjoe, Selwyn R.*V.S. Naipaul: A Materialist Reading*. University of Massachusetts Press, 1988.

Deodat, Rovindradat. "V. S. Naipaul's Fiction, 1954–71: Fragmentation and Rootlessness. M.A. Dissertation." Simon Fraser University, 1979, http://summit.sfu.ca/system/files/iritems1/3297/b12245367.pdf. Accessed 6 May 2020.

d'Entreves, Maurizio Passerin. "Introduction." *Habermas and the Unfinished Project of Modernity*, edited by Maurizio Passerin d'Entreves and Seyla Benhabib. The MIT Press, 1997, pp. 1–36.

d'Entreves, Maurizio Passerin and Seyla Benhabib, editors. *Habermas and the Unfinished Project of Modernity: Critical Essays on the Philosophical Discourse of Modernity*. The MIT Press, 1997.

DeVotta, Neil. *Sinhala Buddhist Nationalist Ideology: Implication for Politics and Conflict Resolution in Sri Lanka*. East West Centre Washington, 2007.

Dierckxsens, Wim. *The Limits of Capitalism: An Approach to Globalization without Neoliberalism*. Translated by Jayne Huchcroft, Zed Books, 2001.

Donghyun, Kim. *Reason, Tradition, and Authority: A Comparative Study of Habermas and Gadamer*. University of Glasgow, 2011.

Dooley, Gillian. *V.S. Naipaul: Man and Writer*. USA. University of South Carolina Press, 2006.

Eid, Haidar. "Naipaul's Bend in the River and Neo-colonialism as a Comparative Context." *CLC Web: Comparative Literature and Culture*, vol. 3, issue 3, 2000, pp. 2–12.

Fanon, Frantz. *The Wretched of the Earth*. Translated by Constance Farrington, Grove Press, 1963.

Feder, Lillian. *Naipaul's Truth: Making of a Writer*. Rowman and Littlefield, 2001.

Gadamer, Hans George. *Truth and Method*. Continuum, 2006.

Habermas, Jurgen. *The Future of Human Nature*. Polity, 2007.

———. "Religion in the Public Sphere." *European Journal of Philosophy*, vol. 14, issue 1, 2006, pp. 1–25.

———. *Modernity: An Incomplete Project* http://designspeculum.com/POD/habermas.pdf Accessed on 6 May 2020.

Hardt, Michael, and Antonio Negri. *Empire*. Harvard University Press, 2000.

Harode, Reeta. "Postcolonial Chaos in V.S. Naipaul's *Mimic Men*." *IRWLE*, vol. 8, issue 1, 2012, pp. 1–8.

Hennayake, Nalani. *Culture, Politics and Development in Postcolonial Sri Lanka*. Lexington Books, 2006.

Hill, Gord. *Colonization and Decolonization: A Manuel for the Indigenous Liberation in 21st Century*. Warrior Publications, 2006.

Hollup, Oddvar. "The Impact of Land Reforms, Rural Images, and the Nationalist Ideology on Plantation Tamils." *Buddhist Fundamentalism and Minority Identities of Sri Lanka*, edited by Tessa Bartholomeusz and Chandra R. De Silva, State University of New York Press, 1998.

Huntington, Samuel P. *The Clash of Civilizations and Remaking of World Order*. Simon and Schuster, 1996.

Jaggi. Maya. "V.S. Naipaul: A Singular Writer." *The Guardian*, 8 Sept. 2001, http://www.theguardian.com/education/2001/sep/08/artsandhumanities.highereducation/. Accessed 10 Apr. 2014.

Johnstone, Richard. "Politics and V.S. Naipaul." *Journal of Commonwealth Literature*, vol. 14, issue 1, 1979, pp. 100–108.

Kellner, Douglas. "Theorizing Globalization." *Sociological Theory*, vol. 20, issue 3, 2002, pp. 285–305.

Krieger, Joel. *The Oxford Companion to Politics of the World*. Oxford University Press, 2001.

Khan, M. A. *Islamic Jihad: A Legacy of Forced Conversion, Imperialism and Slavery*. iUniverse, 2008.

Khan, Tariq Amin. *The Post-Colonial State in the Era of Capitalist Globalization*. Routledge, 2012.

King, Bruce. *V.S. Naipaul*. Palgrave Macmillan, 2003.

Marcuse, Herbert. *Technology, War and Fascism: Collected Papers of Herbert Marcuse*, edited by Douglas Kellner, Routledge, 1998.

McLuhan, Marshall. *Medium is the Message: An Inventory of Effects*. Ginkgo Press, 2001.

Miao, Ching. "Transformative Learning and Social Transformation: A Cross Cultural Perspective." Master's Dissertation, Toronto, National Library of Canada, 2000, https://tspace.library.utoronto.ca/bitstream/1807/13774/1/MQ50488.pdf. Accessed 6 May 2020.

Mohan, Champa Rao. *Post-colonial Situation in the Novels of V.S. Naipaul*. Atlantic Press, 2004.

Naipaul, V.S. *A Bend in the River*. Picador, 2002.

———. *A House for Mr Biswas*. Penguin. 1967.

———. *In a Free State*. Andre Deutsch, 1971.

———. *The Mimic Men*. Penguin. 2002.

Noor, Samira. "The futile struggle for self-determination in Naipaul's protagonists." B.A. Thesis Department of English and Humanities, Brac University, Bangladesh, 2013,

http://dspace.bracu.ac.bd/xmlui/handle/10361/2762?show=full. Accessed 6 May 2020.

Paisley, Fiona, and Kirsty Reid. *Critical Perspectives on Colonialism. Writing the Empire from Below*. Routledge, 2014.

Park, Jong Seong. "An exploration of the outsider's role in selected works by Joseph Conrad, Malcolm Lowry, and V. S. Naipaul." PhD Dissertation, Queen Mary and Westfield College, University of London, 1996, https://core.ac.uk/reader/30695680. Accessed 5 May 2020.

Rahamatian, Andreas. *Copyright and Creativity: The Making of Property Rights in Creative Work*. Edward Elgar Publishers, 2011.

Rawls, John. "Idea of Public Reason Revisited." *The University of Chicago Law Review*, vol. 64, issue 3, 1997, pp. 765–807.

Roberts, Michael. *Sinhala-ness and Sinhala Nationalism: A History of Ethnic Conflict in Sri Lanka*. Marga Institute, 2001.

Rutherford, Donald, editor. *The Cambridge Companion to Early Modern Philosophy*. Cambridge University Press, 2006.

Said, Edward. *Culture and Imperialism*. Vintage Books, 1993.

———. "The intellectual in the post-colonial world." *Salmagundi*, issue 70/71, 1986, pp. 44–64.

Sharpe, Matthew, and Geoff Boucher. *Zizek and Politics: A Critical Introduction*. Edinburgh University Press, 2010.

Singh, Amardeep. *Literary Secularism: Religion and Modernity in Twentieth Century Fiction*. Cambridge Scholars Publishing, 2006.

Singh, Bhupinder. "Naipaul's India: A Million Mutinies Now: A Political Perspective." *International Journal of Scientific and Research Publication*, vol. 3, issue 1, 2013, pp. 1–3.

Soyinka, Wole. *Opera Wonyosi*. Indiana University Press, 1986.

Stavrakakis, Yannis. *Lacan and the Political*. Blackwell, 1999.

Stiglitz, Joseph. E. *Globalization and Its Discontents*. Norton, 2002.

Wallerstein, Immanuel. "Dependence in an Independent World: The Limited Possibilities of Transformation within the Capitalist World Economy." *African Studies Review*, vol. 17, issue 1, 1974, pp. 1–26.

Wijeyeratne. Roshan de Silva. *Nation, Constitutionalism and Buddhism in Sri Lanka*. Routledge, 2014.

Žižek, Slavoj. *Did Someone Say Totalitarianism? Five Intervention in the (Mis) Use of a Notion*. Verso, 2011.

———. *Enjoy Your Symptom*. Routledge, 2008.

———. *For They Know Not What They Do: Enjoyment as a Political Factor*. Verso, 2002.

———. *Interrogating the Real*. Continuum, 2005.

———. *Living in the End Times*. Verso, 2014.

Ziltener, Patrick, and Daniel Kunzler. "Impact of Colonialism: A Research Survey." *Journal of World System Research*, vol. 19, no. 2, 2013, pp. 290–311, https://jwsr.pitt.edu/ojs/index.php/jwsr/article/view/507. Accessed 14 May 2020.

Chapter 17

V. S. NAIPAUL AND HISTORICAL DERANGEMENT[1]

Sanjay Krishnan[2]

In an essay on V. S. Naipaul that appeared in the *New Yorker*, critic James Wood recounts the hostile scrutiny to which he was subjected when they met:

> The public snob, the grand bastard, was much in evidence when I interviewed V. S. Naipaul in 1994, and this was exactly as expected. A pale woman, his secretary, showed me in to the sitting room of his London flat. Naipaul looked warily at me, offered a hand, and began an hour of scornful correction. I knew nothing, he said, about his birthplace, Trinidad; I possessed the usual liberal sentimentality. It was a plantation society. Did I know anything about his writing? (Wood, "Wounder and Wounded")

Wood does not tell his reader what Naipaul said during that "hour of scornful correction". This is regrettable, for what stands out is not the anecdote about the author's nasty personality—a tired reality effect of middlebrow journalism produced with Naipaul's cooperation—but the telling reference to "a plantation society". Sensitivity to this context, Naipaul seems to say, rather than mere sympathy for the plight of

1 "V. S. Naipaul and Historical Derangement" was originally published in *Modern Language Quarterly*, vol. 73, issue 3, September 2012, pp. 433–453. Copyright 2012. All rights reserved. Republished by permission of the copyright holder, and the present publisher, Duke University Press www.dukeupress.edu.

2 I am indebted to Marshall Brown, Joe Cleary, Jed Esty and Colleen Lye for their criticisms and suggestions. I am also grateful to Siraj Ahmed and Tim Watson for reading an early draft of this chapter. A section of it was expanded and given as a talk at the Thirtieth Annual West Indian Literature Conference, University of the West Indies, St Augustine, Trinidad. My thanks to Laurence Breiner, Raphael Dalleo, Alison Donnell, Vijay Maharaj and Gordon Rohlehr for their remarks.

downtrodden people, is critical to a grasp of his aims as a writer. These two comportments need not be mutually exclusive, of course, though some critics have argued that Naipaul acts as if they were. At any rate, what Naipaul conveys to the metropolitan critic, contemptuously stereotyped as a prisoner of his good intentions, is the critic's inability to assess the productive force of this past on Naipaul's work.

This image of Naipaul is never emphasised in postcolonial or progressive circles. Instead, there exists a consensus among critics, notably Edward W. Said and Pascale Casanova, as well as historians such as Sanjay Subrahmanyam and Michael Gilsenan, that Naipaul is a gifted writer whose distorted accounts of non-European societies are calculated to ingratiate him with his metropolitan patrons (with the exception of the *New Yorker* crowd, presumably). The unchallenged view among progressive-minded critics that the postcolonial writer must be on the side of the oppressed often prevents them from grasping the original ways in which Naipaul's untypical writings are attuned to the periphery's historicity. To sum up, the relationship between Naipaul's Eurocentrism and his past is more complicated than such readers would have us believe.[3]

Naipaul's premise is that subjects in the periphery are shaped by complex pasts that they are not well placed to comprehend. For historical reasons, peripheral societies lack the institutions and social practices required for an adequate grasp of modernity's profoundly disruptive effects. The globalising forms of colonialism and capitalism diverted the social trajectories of the peasant formations of the precapitalist world. Such groups found themselves enslaved, displaced, indentured or colonied—in short, violently inducted into modern institutions of production and exchange. These peoples adapted to their new historical circumstances—some even thrived, materially speaking—but they could not reclaim or assert control over their disrupted social trajectories. The institutions and norms of their societies were deranged by modernity.[4]

---

3 For important exceptions to the dominant critical view, see the subtle accounts of Edward Baugh, "'The History That Had Made Me': The Making and Self-Making of V. S. Naipaul", and Rhonda Cobham-Sander, "V. S. Naipaul, C. L. R. James and *A Way in the World*", in *Created in the West Indies: Caribbean Perspectives on V. S. Naipaul*, ed. Jennifer Rahim and Barbara Lalla (Ian Randle, 2011), pp. 3–11, 51–78.

4 The modern colonial state was an external power of a unique sort. It used "a social conceptualization that was fundamentally alien to [local] arrangement[s].... [The European order] had totally different moral, political, and, most significantly, cognitive values" (Kaviraj 15). An

Naipaul's work implies that the forms of derangement and subjective disorientation in such societies cannot be thrown off as an alien or oppressive ruling power might be. In the wake of colonial modernity, thinking and being underwent a fundamental transformation. Horizons of worldly involvement, conceptual frameworks, and norms and values were remade in uneven, contradictory ways that had a profoundly disorienting effect on the non-European world. According to Naipaul, these deranging effects are precisely what the artist should excavate. Writers born of this historical milieu must also note how their writing partakes of the order it describes. Those who explore their formation in this way may discover new ways of seeing the affiliations between subjected parts of the world. In this light, derangement also assumes a productive force: it makes available perspectives derived from shared but diverse expressions of peripheral historicity.

Few literary examples, literal and allegorical, can be found of derangement, for it frames the terms in which seeing takes place. An instance of misreading gets closer to the heart of the matter. Rob Nixon upbraids Naipaul for asserting in *The Loss of El Dorado* (1969) that the seventeenth-century disappearance of an Amerindian tribe called the Chaguanes is unimportant; "it is part of nobody's story": "What is disturbing is [Naipaul's] decision to abide by the standards of importance and unimportance that he finds in the colonial sources" (*The Loss of El Dorado: A History* xiv; Nixon 125). As it happens, Nixon is mistaken. Naipaul is being heavily ironic in this passage.

He makes it clear that he regards the Amerindians as precursors to his forebears, the East Indian indentured labourers (also "part of nobody's story") who were shipped to Trinidad in the nineteenth century to work the sugar plantations. The Chaguanes recur in Naipaul's work for a reason. Naipaul recalls how, while he was working in the archive of the British Library in the 1960s on the early history of Trinidad, he came upon a letter from 1625 with instructions from the Spanish king to a military commander that contained an ominous reference to the Chaguanes, from which, Naipaul suddenly realised, the name of his hometown of Chaguanas derived:

> This was more than a fact about [the Chaguanes]. It to some extent altered my own past. I could no longer think of the Ramlila [peasant staged performances of the archaic Ramayana on the clearings of

established view is that colonialism and semicolonial rule constituted "a triple assault on other societies: on indigenous institutions of governance, on longstanding patterns of generating and distributing economic assets, and on ideas and values that gave meaning to life" (David B. Abernethy 12).

> sugarcane fields near Chaguanas] I had seen as a child as occurring at the beginning of things. I had imaginatively to make room for people of another kind on the Ramlila ground. Fiction by itself would not have taken me to this larger comprehension. ("Reading and Writing" 35–36)

Behind this portentous juxtaposition lies a simpler confession, which offers a glimpse of the historicity from which Naipaul's peripheral style emerges:

> I suppose I was shocked by this discovery in 1967 about my birthplace [Chaguanas] because I had never had any idea about it. But that was the way most of us lived in the agricultural colony, blindly. There was no plot by the authorities to keep us in darkness. I think it was more simply that the knowledge wasn't there. ("Two Worlds [The Nobel Lecture]" 186)

Derangement can take a variety of forms in the periphery. One clue to its presence here is the writer's inability to decide which is more significant: the discovery that the Chaguanes are precursors or the realisation that there had been no way to access that knowledge, let alone assimilate it.

Knowledge about that past arrived artificially, circuitously, accidentally, many years later. It took a visit to the British Library for the putative colonial historian to learn a rudimentary fact about the origins of his hometown's name. The deranged artist then had to discover how to activate this feeling of unease so as to bring that disjunction into focus. Naipaul suppressed this awareness at the time, but he returned to it decades later, in part to ironise or undermine the authoritative persona he had assiduously cultivated in his early years as a novelist and traveller. In his later incarnation, Naipaul explores instead the links between himself and his subjects in light of pasts in which "the knowledge wasn't there". The extinction of the Amerindians overtaken by events beyond their comprehension, the ignorance and indifference of the hapless East Indian labourers several centuries later, the absence of institutions for the propagation and assimilation of such knowledge in the plantation colony that subsequently developed—these elements constitute a genealogical chain from which Naipaul must claim descent and through which he necessarily frames the terms of historical seeing and saying. Naipaul's point, formulated only in his later years, is that peripheral writing should find a way to formally register the impact of such constitutive derangement.

This marks a departure from the perspectives adopted in the important works of realist fiction, notably *A House for Mr Biswas* (1961) and *A Bend in the River* (1979) that consolidated Naipaul's reputation as one of the great chroniclers of global colonial and postcolonial conditions. It also deviates from the studiously authoritative tone of the disenchanted travel writing for which Naipaul gained fame and notoriety, not least *The Middle Passage* (1962) and *India: A Wounded Civilization* (1977). In the 1980s, Naipaul's persona appears to have fundamentally changed. He began experimenting more openly with forms that mingle history with autobiographical fiction, travelogue with essay, that implicated him in his stories of people inducted into a modernity that they were not always equipped to understand.[5] One might say that he began searching for a form adequate to his belated and disorienting "discovery" of the Chaguanes.

The Brazilian critic Roberto Schwarz insightfully discusses how historical circumstances impose constraints on the formal choices made by peripheral writers. But Schwarz also remarks that artists do not passively "register" these constraints. They mould the social processes, or the "preformed material", that define them: "In shaping it, in turn, the writer superimposes form upon form, and the depth, force and complexity of the artistic results will depend upon the success of this operation, of this relation to the preformed material in which the energies of history lie" (*Misplaced Ideas* 31). Naipaul's relationship to the "preformed material" that he takes as his object in his later writing gains complexity and significance from his refusal to shape it into fiction (a move more typical of other creative writers). He seeks instead to discover its effects on the writer and the man, something that "fiction by itself" would not have allowed him to do.

In the later Naipaul, this "preformed material" is the object of literary excavation, not the point of departure for artistic invention. While he displays few outward signs of sympathy for or identification with the wretched of the earth, his prose implicates him in the (de)formation it describes. Its evocation of a shared condition is usefully unsentimental. Of his return from England to Port-of-Spain in 1956, Naipaul recalls his anxiety at the rise of racial politics in Trinidad:

> I was full of nerves on this return, for all kinds of reasons—but I believe I was only amplifying something that was true. The history of the place was known: its reminders were all around us; scratch us and we all bled. The wonder was that it had taken so long for black people to arrive at this way of feeling. In our colonial set-up the champions

5 See, for example, *The Enigma of Arrival*. Knopf, 1987, p 146; *India: A Million Mutinies Now*. Vintage, 1990, p 31 and *Beyond Belief: Islamic Excursions among the Converted Peoples*. Random House, 1998, p 67.

> of black people had been white men or coloured men like Belbenoit. Black men, with their self-distrust, had looked to such people to be their leaders. Political life had come late to black people; confidence had come late; too many generations had had to bury or mock their emotions in barber-shop gossip. (*A Way in the World* 33–34)

The muted tone of this passage is in striking contrast to that of *The Middle Passage*, Naipaul's satirical account of his return to the West Indies, which appeared more than three decades earlier. The later Naipaul takes care to mark his interpellation as a member of the racial minority. We do not know if what he says is factually accurate. Everything depends instead on learning to read, rather than judge, his presuppositions and on exploring how he engages his fears and his prejudice.

Castigating Naipaul for his political views would not, in this instance, do justice to his attempt to imagine the messy, uneven constitution of race relations in the periphery. Standing in Woodford Square, Port-of-Spain, on the eve of political independence, listening to the speeches from which he felt deliberately excluded, Naipaul describes a novel disorientation overlaying the still- unresolved effects of the colonial period: "Every black or African person from my past altered. And I felt a double distance from what I had known" (*A Way in the World* 34). Up to this point, Naipaul plays the role of a prejudiced, if self-pitying, returnee who offers a jaundiced explanation of the historical tensions underlying the mass gathering. Suddenly, however, the tone of melancholy resignation or anxiety is transformed:

> At the meeting I had gone to in the square I had seen a white family walk out in an interval between the speeches. They were an old trading family. I had had some slight dealings with them. For a few weeks [before leaving for Oxford in 1950] I had been a tutor to one of their children. I felt I had been tricked by them into accepting very low payment for what I did.... Old shame and rage (an aspect of the very mood of the meeting in the square) came back to me. (34)

Layers of hidden emotions associated with indenture evidently catch Naipaul by surprise and connect his mood with the populist anger in the square, giving him a kind of sympathy with the black people. The words "trading family" and "tricked" graft something hitherto unmentioned onto the merely racial sentiment Naipaul perceives: colonial commerce and slavery. Thus, even though Naipaul calls it politics as "racial sacrament", this disdain does not alter the fact that his views are "an aspect of the very mood" of the people (31). This engagement adds a layer of complexity to the phrase "imagined community", with its utopian view of nationalism's initial form in the periphery (Anderson, *Imagined Communities: Reflections on the Origin and Spread of Nationalism*). Naipaul's mixed feeling accedes to the filigree of epistemic and affective dislocations on which the modern postcolony was created and run. In the increasingly polarised spaces of the periphery—where expressions of political empowerment are mobilised by identitarian claims centred on race, ethnicity and religion, especially where these claims serve more complicated political histories and economic interests—Naipaul accesses self-implicating structures of feeling that do not "falsify" (125).

Thus, Naipaul stretches realism into a form through which the periphery's critical and imaginative resources, the pre-comprehended form and constraints that define its historicity, become available to it. Older, defective ways of apprehending the world are evinced by his helpless shame and rage at the sight of the white family. Naipaul's combination of factual and fictional forms animates historical conditions that would otherwise seem mere expressions of mutual hostility or resentment. The elaborations opened up by his approach cannot be confined to the narrow terms of his prejudices and shortcomings.

His writing stages (in Antônio Cândido's phrase) the "internal causality" of literatures produced across a global context, albeit in a manner that is not legible to recent theorists of world literature whose frameworks of analysis derive from macroscopic models of core–periphery antagonisms (131). Naipaul's peremptory treatment of Wood, then, reflects his impatience with readers whose praise for his work belies an insufficient interest in the shaping force of peripheral historicity. It may be that such perceived biases are not unique to metropolitan literary critics and writers. The anthropologist Sidney W. Mintz once declared that he did not understand why, given the Caribbean's "special social history", scholars "of this portion of Latin America should have concluded that Caribbean peasantries closely resemble those of the European subcontinent" (140). Discussing the "reconstituted peasantry" (140) that developed in this region after the end of slavery in the mid-nineteenth century, Mintz expresses a view that resonates with Naipaul's dissatisfaction at being the object of misdirected praise and condemnation:

> We wish to discover how people drawn from many different ancestral pasts, and subjected in most cases to one or two centuries of intense repression, could establish their own ways of life, synthesized from their various pasts and from their learning experiences in their new homelands. We deal, in other words, with peoples whose social histories in situ are short; whose prior social relationships were colored by their subjection to naked force; and for whom the

> establishment of peasant life was in most instances a mode of escape or a mode of resistance [to the plantation], or both. (140)

Mintz's observation provokes questions that bear on the constitution of one part of the periphery. A more global aspect of that peripheral condition can be discerned in Stuart Hall's assertion that the "Eurocentrism" of certain expressions of Marxist theory did not engage fully with the conditions in which capitalism and colonial ideology unfolded in the colonies:

> The model at the center of most developed parts of Marxist theory ... suggested that capitalism evolved organically from within its own transformations. Whereas I came from a society where the profound integument of capitalist society, economy, and culture had been imposed by conquest and colonization. (1901)

We can draw on Mintz's and Hall's intuitions to make a connection with the peculiar character of peripheral writing. Novels written out of such situations represent a uniquely "reconstituted" form of the metropolitan novel, inasmuch as they respond to a historical situation—what Mintz calls a "special social history"—that differs qualitatively from that presupposed by the metropolitan novel.

Naipaul's conception of himself as a peripheral writer is very much informed by the history of nineteenth-century imperialism. Stamped by Britain's victories in the Seven Years' War (1756–1763) and the Napoleonic Wars (1795–1815), the British imperial order came into being through conquest, not settlement, and was defined by racial subjugation and economic exploitation. The Trinidad that Naipaul grew up in resembled many British colonies in Asia, Africa and the Americas: populated by polyglot, nonwhite groups that (in J. S. Furnivall's phrase) mingled only in the marketplace. "Society" in these contexts was created by fiat ("direct" and "indirect" rule), its character primarily determined by the demands of an international market (318–330). The forms of civic association and consensus that arose in these plantation colonies were fragile at best. Civility and tolerance based on mutual incomprehension between groups of peasant origin congealed over time and, under colonial tutelage, gave civil society its enduringly segmented and polarising character in the periphery.

This historical make-up can be usefully contrasted with the context that Schwarz offers of the independent settler colony of Brazil. Schwarz argues that the importation of the European novel form into nineteenth-century Brazil was complicated by the fact that the metropolitan realist novel (defined by its bourgeois ideology) could not be reconciled with the material conditions of slave-owning Brazil (*Misplaced Ideas* 19–33).

The reproduction of social relations between the propertied classes and writers was governed by favour and patronage. Through the ideology of favour, Brazilian writers unconsciously circumvented the apparently insuperable challenge that the institution of slavery posed to their claim to be modern. Favour allowed them to obscure society's obvious dependence on slave labour. Thus, Brazilian writing discovered a way to claim metropolitan values—the rule of law, individual rights, artistic autonomy, free labour and so on —even though socio-economic reality contradicted them. As Schwarz notes, "Slavery gives the lie to liberal ideas; but favour, more insidiously, uses them for its own purposes, originating a new ideological pattern" (22).

No critical account of comparable systematicity can be extracted from Naipaul's depictions of Caribbean society. Whereas, Schwarz demonstrates the creation of a bridging mechanism, an epistemic interface, in a manner that enabled the Brazilian novelist to import metropolitan ideologies in twisted form, Naipaul's task was complicated by the lack of a unitary historical framework to which to align himself. In this context, autobiographical details assume a new significance. Naipaul gravitates to historically disenfranchised and unorganised viewpoints that Schwarz deems "absent" (*Misplaced Ideas* 20). In a sense, Naipaul is interested in conceptual or figurative resources available to those from the margins of the periphery (Chaguanas is not São Paolo or Calcutta). For the writer who seeks out perspectives deriving from the enslaved, the indentured and the colonised, the likelihood of discovering an ideological or epistemic interface is limited.

In *A Way in the World,* Naipaul obliquely explores these concerns in a fictionalised account of his encounter with C. L. R. James, the radical historian and public intellectual whom Naipaul here names Lebrun.[6] Naipaul recounts first meeting Lebrun, a brilliant Trinidadian several decades his senior, at a dinner party in London during the 1960s when he, Naipaul, was trying to establish himself as a writer. Lebrun, already

6 See Kent Worcester, C. L. R. James: *A Political Biography*. State U of New York P, 1996, pp. 173–175; and Gordon Rohlehr. "Intersecting Q. R. C. Lives: James, Williams, Naipaul." *Transgression, Transition, Transformation: Essays in Caribbean Culture*, Lexicon Trinidad, 2007, pp. 199–233. Naipaul recalls first meeting Lebrun in London: "I thought him a prodigy. I was moved by the fact that such a man came from something like my own background. I began to understand his great reputation among middle- class black people. How, considering when he was born, had he become the man he was? How had he preserved his soul through all the discouragements of the colonial time?" (A Way in the World, 117).

the author of a famous historical account of an early modern revolution in the Caribbean and a personality in progressive circles, had just written an incisive review of Naipaul's early work:

> [Lebrun's] method was original. He ignored the comedy, over which I had taken so much trouble—such care in the mounting of many scenes, such judgement in the matter of language and tone. He looked through all of that to the material itself—the people, the background—and he considered that with complete seriousness. He said I was writing about people impoverished in every way, people on whom history had played a cruel trick. My characters thought they were free men, in charge of their own destinies; they weren't; the colonial setting mocked the delusions of the characters, their ambitions, their belief in perfectibility, their jealousies. The books, light as they were, were subversive, the article said, and remarkable for that reason... I knew immediately what he meant by the helplessness of my characters; I realized that I had always known it; I had grown up with that knowledge in my bones. (113–114)

Naipaul adds, "The revelation of Lebrun's article became a lasting part of my way of looking" (114). Having said that, Naipaul confesses to his inability to understand why James, in his classic *The Black Jacobins* (1938), would have made substantive claims that appear to contradict these valuable insights, especially as they pertain to a discussion of the world-historical significance of the Haitian slave revolt in the wake of its heroic overthrow of French rule. Most notably, Naipaul declares himself "puzzled" by Lebrun's unrealistic insistence on the "industrial nature of slavery in the Caribbean" (126) and by his belief that a modern revolution could have arisen from the working conditions on the slave plantation despite the near-complete absence of civil society's mediating institutions.[7]

Naipaul skeptically summarises Lebrun's claim that the slaves who led the revolt could be likened to a class of revolutionary peasants comparable to the modern proletariat in preparation and organisation (126; see also James, 85). A fateful simplification of the colony's predicament follows from the importation into the periphery of a template derived from a European story of historical progress:

---

7 See James's harsh assessment of "town life" in *The Black Jacobins: Toussaint L'Ouverture and the San Domingo Revolution*, 2nd ed., Vintage, 1961, p 31. For a thoughtful interpretation of the figure of peripheral modernity in *The Black Jacobins* that differs from mine see David Scott. *Conscripts of Modernity: The Tragedy of Colonial Enlightenment*. Duke University Press, 2004, pp. 112–119.

> [Lebrun's] purpose in writing the book in the 1930s had been to prove his old point about the revolutionary nature of the islands; to give himself and his ideas a great past, to link the revolutionary stir of the 1930s to the stir caused in the region by the French Revolution; to lift the islands from the end-of-empire smallness in which they had been becalmed since the abolition of slavery, and to attach them once again to the great historical processes of the continent. (132)

Naipaul does not only believe that James is wrong to claim that a political revolt undertaken in the absence of modern institutions and social practices could impel a transformation of mental habits and dispositions shaped by long servitude. He wishes to understand how a man of James's sagacity could make such an outlandish claim. To the extent that Naipaul's objection is justified, it parallels Schwarz's view that in the periphery "the test of reality and coherence did not seem to be decisive", because the ideologies involved "do not describe reality, not even falsely" (*Misplaced Ideas* 24–23), but rather always already rest on a distorted appropriation of an alien historical template. Whereas Brazilian favour concealed the fact of slavery, for the colonised intellectual elite of the Second British Empire, of which James was an outstanding example, the ideology of anticolonial nationalism effectively obscured the effects of derangement. In this light, Lebrun's importation of the template of enlightenment progress into the Haitian revolution and his attempt to cast the slaves as precursors of the "modern proletariat" assumed the potential to empower and to mislead.

Writing as an engaged intellectual in the 1930s, a time of global economic depression and political unrest, James could hardly have avoided making the assertions that Naipaul challenges. For his part, Naipaul affirms the achievements of anticolonial struggle when he celebrates the spirit captured in James's work. But Naipaul is also wary of the affirmative spirit and the effortlessness with which James's cosmopolitan style at once critiques and assimilates alien templates. However, identifying this distortion is one thing; discovering an adequate response to it is quite another. Here Schwarz gives insight into Naipaul's artistic project when he asserts that the peripheral writer has to "repeat this [ideological] dislocation at a formal level if he is to keep up with the objective complexity of his material".[8]

8 Roberto Schwarz, "The Importing of the Novel to Brazil and Its Contradictions in the Work of Alencar." *Misplaced Ideas,* translated by John Gledson and Peter Anti, in Gledson, p 41.

Naipaul does not attack James squarely. Instead, he slyly enters into an imagined account of Lebrun the supremely gifted historian–artist who represses the historicity of his formation, that is, the everyday forms through which the great ideas from the metropole must have disjunctively presented themselves to him in the periphery. Naipaul controversially suggests that a psychological need must have occasioned Lebrun's "stress" on the "universality, and even [the] precedence", of slavery (*A Way in the World* 126). According to Naipaul, this need was revealed to him at the dinner party in Maida Vale when they first met. Lebrun told a story about his mother's uncle, a coachman, who had been treated kindly by the white servants in the famous Tichborne house in England. The coachman was especially impressed that a friend of his, a black man who worked for the house, had married a white servant girl. "When [the coachman] was very old he was still talking about the black man in the big house in London who had married the white woman and nobody minded, and he was still talking about the white servants who always made him welcome and gave him tea and cake." Lebrun continues:

> My mother's uncle, the old coachman, and a very proud man, used to say, "It had no trouble in those days. Black people and white people was one." And that was what I grew up believing too, that in the old days things were better. When I was old enough to understand what the old coachman had taught me, I was ashamed. I tried to forget. From various things I deduce that the old man was born in . This was six years after the abolition of slavery. This means that his mother had been a slave, and all the older people around him. It also means something else. The slave trade was abolished in 1807. So when my mother's uncle was ten or twelve there would have been people of sixty-five or seventy in Barbados who had been brought over from Africa. And still the old man thought that things were better in the old days, and had got me to believe it.
>
> I was tormented by this memory, until I arrived at my own political resolution, and saw it for what it was. (118–119)

With this move, Lebrun's insights into the "helplessness" of Naipaul's characters come full circle. Lebrun himself, like Naipaul earlier, is made into a victim of the deranged historical conditions he describes. Lebrun's "torment" resembles Naipaul's feelings in Woodford Square.

Because affects are unmediated, they are also taken for a "truth" that needs to be finessed. Naipaul's and Lebrun's experiences are united by a shame that differs from the sort experienced by Schwarz's Brazilians vis-à-vis their metropolitan cousins (128). The impression one receives is not that Lebrun cannot think objectively or that the coachman story compromises the value of his resolution. Rather, Lebrun's response is, like Naipaul's search for a form proper to peripheral historicity, the outcome of a confrontation with a past marked by derangement. Despite their ideological differences (to Naipaul, the ascent of "racial leaders" [129] in the 1950s and 1960s makes Lebrun's revolutionary optimism irrelevant), it is when Naipaul "discovers" this fact about Lebrun that he feels closest to the man:[9]

> The confession had been impressive: every black man, he had said, had some tormenting secret like that. Yet the words, "political resolution," had appeared to conceal something. And now I felt—with shame, grief, sympathy, admiration, recognizing something of myself in his struggle—that, as much as the uneducated old coachman of ninety years before.... Lebrun had always needed to find some way of dealing with the past. With his fine mind, and his love of knowledge, his need might even have been greater. (126)

Rather than accept Naipaul's interpretation, I wish to reflect on the style of excavation and comparison that he undertakes as a writer marked by derangement. In Naipaul's view, the peripheral writer cannot make a direct intellectual claim to the discourse of historical transition, which emerges from the "organically" European account of capitalist development (Hall, 1901).[10]

For Naipaul, as for Lebrun, there is no alternative to the forms of representation that are imported from the imperial metropole. Because historical reflection and critical practice are necessarily underdeveloped in the plantation colony, Naipaul attends to unbidden, pre-rational, affective reactions that repeat the ideological distortion at the level of form. Applications of transition, think to the periphery occlude its peculiar historicity, in the way that the youthful Naipaul trained himself to become a writer using "false" European models that he could

---

9 See also Walton Look Lai, "C. L. R. James and Trinidadian Nationalism." *C. L. R. James's Caribbean*, edited by Paget Henry and Paul Buhle, Duke University Press, 1992, p 198.

10 The histories of decolonisation suggest that this lesson mostly went unheeded. "To the Asian modernists, modernity seemed attractive precisely because it posed no Hegelian riddle, it held no Rousseauesque terrors, nor did it require the massive Marxist intellectual enterprise of knowing history. Modernity was simplicity itself, a simple conflict between superstition and knowledge, error and science, in which, moreover, a benign history had arranged victory for science and truth in advance" (Kaviraj 122).

not, all the same, have done without. For us, today, a few guidelines for the reading of the peripheral novel suggest themselves if we adopt Naipaul's perspective. Literary forms in the periphery partake of the deficient order they describe. Critical and historical reflection must work through the enduring effects of this underdevelopment. Whereas, the West's induction into modernity is narrated through the category of transition, the periphery's induction should be grasped through the figure of derangement.

The peripheral novel's emergence—here I am referring to Naipaul's rather than Schwarz's conception of the periphery—in the context of colonialism points to an absence of social institutions that might enable characters to comprehend the effects of colonial capitalism.[11] The point to draw is not the usual social–evolutionist one. I am not suggesting that the European novel was a seamless outgrowth of capitalism, whereas, the peripheral novel was its hapless opposite. My desire here is only to note that metropolitan and peripheral novels are shaped by distinct (but related) forms of derangement; as modes of writing, they accordingly respond to distinct historical predicaments. Yet I do not believe that the different "meanings" of this transformation in different parts of the world can be explained away by hybrid or alternative modernities.[12]

Colonial domination deranged the pre-existing cognitive norms and trajectories of non-European societies. Epistemic fracturing was the defining condition of the resulting historical order. This fracturing cannot be fully assimilated to the coexistence of "nonsynchronous" elements in an emergent mode of production (Bloch 22–38). Such templates are drawn from the historical experience of Europe's peasantry, not from that of the colonised periphery. Thus, it is useful

11 This point can be made by means of an against-the-grain reading of Benedict Anderson's argument in "A Time of Darkness and a Time of Light," in *The Spectre of Comparisons: Nationalism, Southeast Asia, and the World*. Verso, 1998, pp. 77–80. What is noteworthy is the immense, if unexplained, gulf between Anderson's account of the disorientation or incomprehension implicit in the mid-nineteenth-century Javanese court poet Ronggawarsita's description of the colonial presence as "a time of darkness", on the one hand, and the transition-think implied by the ideals of nationalist freedom asserted in 1908 by the student members of Budi Utomo, on the other.

12 The alternative-modernities argument is unsatisfactory because it confuses cultural differences with epistemic engagement. See Dipesh Chakrabarty. "Adda: A History of Sociality." *Provincializing Europe: Postcolonial Thought and Historical Difference*. Princeton University Press, 2000, pp. 180–213.

to point out the difficulty of assimilating analyses such as the following in peripheral situations where their applicability, objectively speaking, might be thought greatest:

> Periods of transition are ... characterized by the coexistence of several modes of production, as well as by these forms of non-correspondence.... Thus it seems that the dislocation between the connexions and instances in transition periods merely reflects the coexistence of two (or more) modes of production in a single "simultaneity," and the dominance of one of them over the other. (*A Singular Modernity* 242)

Fredric Jameson, who quotes this passage from Louis Althusser and Étienne Balibar's *Reading "Capital"*, explains it as follows:

> We thus have two distinct systems coexisting (means of production, forces of production, categories of property, etcetera) in such a way that the dominance of the first over the second will gradually be overturned into a dominance of the second over the first. It is clear that this scheme is motivated by the intent to exclude continuity and "evolutionism": in it the elements of the old system do not gradually evolve and "turn into" the elements of the new. Rather, they coexist from the outset, and it is merely the preponderance of the one set or combination over the other that changes. (Jameson 242–243)

Coexistence suggests an interface between norms and practices of earlier and later modes of production.

For Jameson, the idea of transition as progress was itself a creative response to a particular historical predicament. But the European discourse of transition emerged in response to a very different predicament from that faced by a global peasantry broken into modernity by genocide, slavery and colonisation. Transition was a way to make sense of the deranging effects peculiar to the West's induction into modernity. In the periphery, we are confronted not by coexistence but by something akin to the flexible overlay of radically disjointed cognitive norms and social trajectories. The peripheral work is defined by the absence or failure of the epistemic interface we are treated to by Cartesian rationality.

The challenge posed by incommensurable modes of being-in-the-world was not made into an object of reflection in these contexts. The peripheral novel is, therefore, drawn from a social context that may have learnt to write its own history but is inarticulate as regards its historicity. This tradition is most painfully apparent in the official discourse of postcolonial states, in which modernity is thought to be synonymous with economic modernisation. It does not presume "the availability of a wider learning" in the sense taken for granted by general accounts of the historical transition to modernity in the West ("The Writer and India" 51). The differences between East and West should not be exaggerated, given the diversity of colonial experience and the forms of "coinvention" through which colonisation took place (Mbembe 262). Nonetheless, the peripheral novel encodes how new habits, dispositions and cognitive frameworks overlaid (rather than, to recall Jameson, "coexisted" with) precolonial evaluative and interpretive frameworks quite differently from events in the European context.

Just as a discourse of historical transition enables accounts of the rise of the metropolitan novel, the empirically diverse forms taken by historical derangement ought to form the basis of any history or theory of the peripheral novel. It is uncontroversial to observe that the beautifully serene and self-contained opening pages of Chinua Achebe's *Things Fall Apart* (1958) and *Arrow of God* (1964) are belied by a sense that characters like Okonkwo and Ezeulu cannot adequately grasp the rationality of the colonial order. It is not simply that such men are defeated by a technologically superior power but that the rules of the new game are unintelligible to them.

In Raja Rao's *Kanthapura* (1938) and Pramoedya Ananta Toer's *Child of All Nations* (1980), a peasant order is broken up as a consequence of its attempt to insert itself in forms of protonationalist resistance whose logics are entirely unfamiliar. The story can be told as the effect of a breakdown centred on the individual—Mustafa Sa'eed in Tayeb Salih's *Season of Migration to the North* (1966), Imam Ibrahim in Amitav Ghosh's *In an Antique Land* (1992)—or collectively experienced by subjected groups, as in Jean Rhys's *Wide Sargasso Sea* (1966), George Lamming's *In the Castle of My Skin* (1953), Maryse Condé's *Segu* (1987) or Assia Djebar's *Fantasia: An Algerian Cavalcade* (1985). The origins of the peripheral novel are embedded in this structure of historical disorientation. In some cases, the novel of the periphery reveals itself as marked by the epistemic fracturing it purports to describe.

These forms of writing dramatised the objective forms that derangement took as well as its subjectively disorienting expressions. But that is not why they came to be studied by anticolonial thinkers and postcolonial scholars alike. The political imperatives of anticolonialism necessitated an empowering rhetoric determined to make the colonial situation immediately legible to the colonised. Accordingly, all expressions of disorientation or failure broached by the peripheral novel were instrumentalised to serve political arguments against colonial capitalist domination and exploitation, on the one hand, and to uphold affirmations of cultural self-representation and autonomy, on the other.

Naipaul's writing enables us to revise this received account and to consider how novels from the periphery are products of and reflections on derangement.

This is a framework of interpretation for literary and cultural critics that parallels the one adumbrated by Jameson, a makeshift tradition to be critically embraced. In this light, Naipaul's infamous lack of sympathy with the postcolonial world may be recast as an excavation of the epistemic fracturing in which he is implicated. His work obliquely serves as a call for styles of reasoning and institutional forms required for the emergence of cultures that work through, rather than suppress, their deranged pasts. In the periphery, metropolitan conceptions of critical thinking and practice will be imagined through the figure of derangement. Habits of reading and analysis may then attend to the dialogue and sympathies that arise from the perceived deformations of self and other. It is, therefore, important to see how literary texts from the periphery enable us to imagine the effects of epistemic fracturing from a position of intimacy and complicity. A style of interpretation eventually attentive to the historical situation of the periphery is the object of such an enterprise.

Works Cited

Abernethy, David B. *The Dynamics of Global Dominance: European Overseas Empires*, pp. 1450–1980. Yale UP, 2000.

Althusser, Louis, and Balibar, Étienne. *Reading Capital*, translated by Ben Brewster, NLB, 1970.

Anderson, Benedict. "A Time of Darkness and a Time of Light." *The Spectre of Comparisons: Nationalism, Southeast Asia, and the World*. Verso, 1998, pp. 77–80.

———. *Imagined Communities: Reflections on the Origin and Spread of Nationalism*. Verso, 1990.

Baugh, Edward. "'The History That Had Made Me': The Making and Self-Making of V. S. Naipaul." *Created in the West Indies*, edited by Rahim, Jennifer, and Barbara Lalla, Ian Randle, 2011. pp. 3–11.

Ernst Bloch, "Nonsynchronism and the Obligation to Its Dialectics." *New German Critique*, translated by Mark Ritter, no. 11, 1977, pp. 22–38.

Cândido, Antônio. "Literature and Underdevelopment." *On Literature and Society*, edited and translated by Howard S. Becker, Princeton UP, 1995.

Chakrabarty, Dipesh. "Adda: A History of Sociality." *Provincializing Europe: Postcolonial Thought and Historical Difference*, Princeton UP, 2000, pp. 180–213.

Cobham-Sander, Rhonda. "V. S. Naipaul, C. L. R. James, and *A Way in the World*." *Created in the West Indies*, edited by Rahim, Jennifer, and Barbara Lalla, Ian Randle, 2011 pp. 51–78.

Furnivall, J. S. *Colonial Policy and Practice: A Comparative Study of Burma and Netherlands India*, Cambridge UP, 1948.

Hall, Stuart. "Cultural Studies and Its Theoretical Legacies." *The Norton Anthology of Theory and Criticism*, edited by Vincent Leitch et al., Norton, 2001.

James, C. L. R. *The Black Jacobins: Toussaint L'Ouverture and the San Domingo Revolution*, 2nd ed. Vintage, 1961.

Jameson, Fredric. *A Singular Modernity: Essays on the Ontology of the Present*. Verso, 2002.

Kaviraj, Sudipta "On State, Society, and Discourse in India." *The Imaginary Institution of India: Politics and Ideas*, Columbia UP, 2010.

Look Lai, Walton. "C. L. R. James and Trinidadian Nationalism." *C. L. R. James's Caribbean*, edited by Paget Henry, and Paul Buhle, Duke University Press, 1992.

Achille Mbembe, "African Modes of Self-Writing." *Public Culture*, translated by Steven Rendall, vol. 14, no. 1, 2002, pp. 239–273.

Mintz, Sidney W. *Caribbean Transformations*. Aldine, 1974.

Naipaul, V. S. *A Way in the World: A Novel*. Knopf, 1994.

———. *Beyond Belief: Islamic Excursions among the Converted Peoples*. Random House, 1998.

———. *India: A Million Mutinies Now*. Vintage, 1990.

———. "Reading and Writing." *Reading and Writing: A Personal Account*, New York Review of Books, 2000.

———. "Two Worlds (The Nobel Lecture)." *Literary Occasions: Essays*, Knopf, 2003.

———. *The Loss of El Dorado: A History*. Penguin, 1981.

———. *The Enigma of Arrival*. Knopf, 1987.

———. *The Middle Passage: Impressions of Five Societies—British, French, and Dutch—in the West Indies and South America*. Andre Deutsch, 1962.

______. "The Writer and India" *The New York Review* 04.03.1999. https://www.nybooks.com/articles/1999/03/04/the-writer-and-india/ Last accessed 14.01.2021

Nixon, Rob. *London Calling: V. S. Naipaul, Postcolonial Mandarin*. Oxford UP, 1992.

Rahim, Jennifer, and Barbara Lalla. eds. *Created in the West Indies: Caribbean Perspectives on V. S. Naipaul*, edited by Ian Randle, 2011.

Rohlehr, Gordon. "Intersecting Q. R. C. Lives: James, Williams, Naipaul." *Transgression, Transition, Transformation: Essays in Caribbean Culture*, Lexicon Trinidad, 2007, pp. 199–233.

Schwarz, Roberto. "Misplaced Ideas: Literature and Society in Late Nineteenth-Century Brazil." *Misplaced Ideas: Essays on Brazilian Culture*, edited by John Gledson, translated by Edmund Leites and Roberto Schwarz, Verso, 1992.

Scott, David. *Conscripts of Modernity: The Tragedy of Colonial Enlightenment*. Duke UP, 2004.

Wood, James. "Wounder and Wounded." *New Yorker*, December 1, 2008, www.newyorker.com/arts/critics/books/2008/12/01/081201crbo_books_wood. Accessed on 14 January 2021.

Worcester, Kent. *C. L. R. James: A Political Biography*. State U of New York P, 1996.

Chapter 18

AMONG THE UNBELIEVABLE: RAGE, FAITH AND REASON IN SELECTED WRITINGS BY V. S. NAIPAUL[1]

Robert J. Balfour

> ...my experience had banked up, and the idea now came to me of expanding on that experience and doing a large book, full of people, a ... panorama which (since I believe that the present, accurately seized, foretells the future) would contain or explain in a broad way most of what might happen in the country for the next twenty or thirty years. (*India: A Million Mutinies Now* 12)

I believe a rereading of the travel texts written by V. S. Naipaul and the literary critical reception of these are justified in relation to selected analyses of Islam as offered by sociologists and historians. At the turn of the new century, religious strife, together with Western interference, often seems to lead to escalation in violence. That escalation points to the need to re-examine perspectives adopted as authoritative in order to ascertain whether the critique of Naipaul is merited. The article is structured in terms of an introduction and four sections to explore this argument.

The second section examines the complexity of Naipaul's subject positioning with reference to four travel texts: *An Area of Darkness* (1964), *Among the Believers* (1981), *India: A Million Mutinies Now* (1990) and *Beyond Belief* (1998). The possibilities offered by Naipaul to the reader are framed and filtered at a number of levels, even though his ostensible focus appears to be Islam. In this section, I show that the delimitation of subject position and the selection of interviewees make for a highly selective reading of Islam. Section three entitled 'transitions to faith,' concerns itself with perspectives offered by the narrator and his interviewees on the effects of conversion to Islam, whilst the fourth section explores faith and its relationship to the state. Naipaul suggests

1 This essay was first published in 2014 in *Literator*, vol. 35, issue 1.

that intellectual tolerance of difference is associated with modernity and so the fourth section provides a discussion of faith in relation to intellectual work. In this section, I also suggest that the filtering process described in the first section makes for a series of insights revealing of the author's perspectives on faith and tolerance. The fifth section explores the associations between faith and daily life.

The methodology here is twofold: I first describe Naipaul's interrogation of the legacy of Orientalism and colonialism in relation to Islam with some reference to the literary critical reception of Naipaul already well documented. Secondly, by drawing on historical texts concerning Islam, I demonstrate that the discourse and ideas evident in political analyses do not differ substantively from the analyses offered by Naipaul in the travelogues. Naipaul, despite shifting between seeming neutrality and cutting criticism, is deeply compassionate about the dilemmas and choices offered to the convert, which he views at best as ambiguous, and at worst as a corrupted distortion of the past, of identity and of future possibilities.

In order to support this argument, I consider the work of certain literary and social commentators from the following perspectives on Naipaul's writing on Islam—Nixon, Said, Bhabha and Feder—in relation to these descriptions of Islamic states in transition in the context of decolonisation—Waines, Ahmed, Zakariyya and Mazrui. While the first four are literary critics, the latter four scholars are historians or political scientists, and, with the exception of Waines, are Muslim themselves. Re-reading Naipaul from the perspectives of such scholars enables me to consider afresh the literary reception of the Islamic travels.

Naipaul and Authorial Subjectivity

I began by suggesting that Naipaul's representation of Islam is revealing of his own subjectivities and, indeed, anxieties. Naipaul has been described as "[o]ne of the greatest living writers in the English language" (Donadio 1). Every book is prefaced with a statement concerning the major prizes accorded to his work, including, in 2001, the Nobel Prize. He has been described by William Boyd in the *Times Literary Supplement* and Norman Rush in *The New York Review of Books* as an influential opinion maker with regards to the postcolonial world; a prophet no less of Third World affairs (Donadio 1). It is well-known that his views of the postcolonial are not positive: Naipaul has on occasion described postcolonial states as half-made, and as being in the process of unmaking (see, for example, *A Bend in the River* 31).

Because of the acerbity of his comments (see Anjum), he has also been criticised for being neurotic, contemptuous and even racist. In short, he remains a controversial figure as well as a celebrated one, and, in the aftermath of 9/11, his writing on the relationship between Islam and its converted peoples is again receiving a great deal of attention in the field of postcolonial literary scholarship. Rereading Naipaul's Islamic travels from the perspective of his subject-positioning suggests that the literary critical perspectives offered may have neglected this dimension.

Naipaul reveals something of his role as narrator in relation to the subject of the text. In *Beyond Belief*, a collection of travel stories undertaken while visiting non-Arab Muslim countries in 1995, he argues that "[t]his book is about people. It is not a book of opinion" (1). According to Naipaul, "Islam … makes imperial demands", requiring converts to forget or reject the past; a problematic demand in the context of a present which arises from past diasporas and conflicts which similarly demand recognition in their consequences for people (*Beyond Belief* 1). He claims that in these books, he is in the background; he is "a discoverer of people; a finder-out of stories … the most important thing about travel, for the writer, was the people he found himself among … the writer retreats; and I become … a manager of narrative" (*Beyond Belief* 2). Of the kind of person he is, even if a character implicit in the travel narratives, very little is suggested.

In *Among the Believers*, he recounts a visit to the Diamond Market in Lahore (a prostitution area): "In the old days I would have grown dizzy with excitement here. Up to my mid-thirties I had been attracted to prostitutes.… My memories of those times were not really of pleasure, however; they were more of enervation" (*Among the Believers* 283). Candour such as this, which reveals degrees of distress and enervation that translate into anxiety, is rare in the travel books, and is illuminating for reasons elaborated upon later.

Who is this V. S. Naipaul? What is he? And what psychic baggage accompanies the Islamic journeys? These questions are useful for two reasons. First, the occlusion of his subject-position as author who dictates the script, evokes and edits is skilled and subtle. With the exception of the fiction, the travel narratives contain extended interviews with subjects. It is interesting to note that Naipaul seldom provides the reader with his questions, nor does he provide any of the promptings necessary to elicit the interviews described. The writer becomes the interlocutor whose questions are never articulated, but whose nature is evident in the narrative of the interviewee. Feder suggests aptly that Naipaul brings a strong set of beliefs to the interviews and risks becoming "less of an inquirer of himself as well as of his informants" (139), but I would argue that the selection of interviewees and the evident direction the narrative and interview material takes suggest a powerful control over the narrative despite the anxiety of his own position as stranger; a point to which I return in later sections.

A second observation concerns the "subjectivity" offered to the reader. With few exceptions, Naipaul offers a Western gaze in which the attachment to religious belief is paired with an aversion to modernity, and an oppression to intellectual endeavour or freedom to question belief. Much has already been suggested by Rob Nixon who noted that Naipaul trades on the common identification of author and reader with a Western persona. And yet, he is also a "colonial": the identity of race is one which allows him access to eminent Islamic figures for whom race, because of the association of whiteness with Western imperialism, is a barrier to communication. Naipaul, on another level, is also a subaltern (Spivak 271). The position of the subaltern is complicated and presents few and delimited possibilities. The first of these is the possibility of resistance, whereby the subaltern rejects the inferior identity imposed on him by the colonial world. The rejection can be total and, in its totality, can lead to new forms of oppression and self-denigration.

By alerting the reader to the inconsistencies and compromises interviewees accept, one becomes aware as literary critic that this focus has implications for the author of the text, by reflecting on choices and their implications concerning his credibility and identity. Alternatively, there is the possibility of the stereotype defined by Said (*The World, the Text, and the Critic* 58) or the mimic articulated by Bhabha (85). For Bhabha, while the mimic entails an almost wholesale adoption of the values, identity markers and performance of a colonised subjectivity, it may become an expression either of resistance (in which case the mimicry is subversive and destabilising of colonial assumptions and terms of engagement) or assimilation, which can never be total and which appears to lead to nervous anxieties.

These observations suggest that Naipaul presents himself either as insider or outsider depending on the context in relation to the objectives of the text. For example, in order to access his subjects, he must appear to be an insider to some extent. In post-revolutionary Iran, a white and Western journalist would be unlikely to gain access to religious authorities, let alone dissidents; thus, it is sufficient to assume that Naipaul trades on his appearance to gain insider access. There are evidently risks associated with this, and the reader becomes aware of the tenuousness of the interaction between interviewer and interviewee, and of frequent misunderstandings—another source of anxiety.

The reader, which Naipaul also is, remains outsider in these encounters, and in that context, the preoccupation with Islam becomes interesting from a number of perspectives. For example, through the presentation of ironic insights that make use of the contrivances of pillory, satire and joke knowledge, Naipaul presents to the reader an argument about Islam with three major premises (Coovadia 4). First, that the spread of Islam is the equivalent to the historical spread of (Western) colonialism. Second, that Islam demonises and obliterates the historical, legal and religious past of a people, and persuades and coerces them to accept in its place an Islamic and Arabic past. Third, as argued by Feder, the journeys through nations in which Islamic revolutions have occurred seem to reveal that where religion and the state fuse, there exist few possibilities of alternatives (137). Furthermore, conversion to Islam and the distortions and simplifications imposed by it enable people (the converts) to construct ideas about observance that participate in a fantasy life which seems to imprison the intellect. Religion then changes attitudes to behaviour, sex, commerce, law and observance. The issue to raise is whether the distortions as depicted are enabled by faith or arise from the author's subjectivity and tension.

Another aspect of Naipaul's positioning is revealed in the relationship of the author to authority. Consider, for example, that all the works produced by Naipaul are prefaced by the same list of literary prizes, honours bestowed (the knighthood and Nobel Prize) in the English-speaking literary establishment. It would not seem unfair to suggest that the foregrounding of this list serves two additional purposes in relation to the establishment and maintenance of the subjectivity, both offered to, and concealed from, the reader. Paul Theroux suggests that the reiteration of the list of prizes is an appeal to authority (the cultural, social and institutional forms of authority in the West) (366). On the other hand, Naipaul claims on the grounds of gender and race authority to speak for, and write about, the East (or the decolonised world in general). At the same time, the concealment of race, gender and cultural milieu (Naipaul's Brahmin heritage) serves a second and third purpose.

Race has already been mentioned, but gender requires further exploration. In his interviews, the removal of what Naipaul terms as his "opinion" combines with a deliberate selection of subjects to be interviewed (mostly male, almost always selected as a consequence of their exemplar status), and always through the mediation of someone young (a younger male, most often a student (for example, Aziz in *An Area of Darkness* 102, and Furqan in *Beyond Belief* 73). There is only one interview with a woman in the texts (*Beyond Belief*)—and the texts themselves present, for observation only, all the other women in purdah. The interview with the one woman occurs because she is emancipated (in fact a divorcee).

Therefore, the positioning of the reader occurs in relation to the positioning of the interviewed subject; both are managed through an equally complicated and nuanced sensibility. That said, there is an implicit use of race and gender. The interviews themselves are often translated by an intermediary (Mehrad performs the role as intermediary for Naipaul in Qum in *Beyond Belief* 215) used by Naipaul to not only identify subjects to be interviewed, but also to enable access to subjects whom he seeks to interview (for example, Ayatollah Khalkhalli in Qum (Iran) [*Beyond Belief*]). Thus, the subjectivity offered by Naipaul to his interlocutors is not the same as that offered to the reader; both subjectivities are tacit and the dissonance between them problematic.

Thirdly, access to the author-narrator is also concealed, and when Naipaul is questioned about what it is that he is, or what it is that he seeks, the responses are often muted, misdirected or deflected in order to enable access to the narrative Naipaul seeks in his travel writings. Thus, the deference to authority (that Western, enabled, male and educated authority) and "establishment" allows for access to the audience of his adopted context, while the appeal made to interviewees occurs on the basis of assumed affinities. As the author straddles inside/outside, so too does the period in which these writings have been located span the end of decolonisation and the emergence of globalisation.

Naipaul must have been aware at the time he wrote the Islamic travel books of earlier less prejudicial associations with the East; what Said refers to as "the idea of Orient" associated with the "romance, exotic beings, haunting memories and landscapes, [and] remarkable experiences" (*Orientalism* 2), since he refers to the antiquity and mystique of selected Iranian cities like Qum (*Beyond Belief* 221). Nevertheless, the complex straddling suggests, also that for Naipaul, these precolonial associations with the East have, as Said has noted, fast disappeared in the popular twentieth-century Western imagination (2).

No doubt this occurred because of the perceived threat posed by Islamic states, control of oil reserves and the resistance (sometimes in the form of terrorism, nuclear threat, the popular press) against the alleged exploitation of the Islamic states by West as noted by cultural and literary critics writing in the 1990s (GoGwilt 68). Said states that the Western notion of the Third World in the East (whether Middle, Near or Far) forms a more discursive terrain not only because the "triumph of nationalism" has occurred there only in half-measure, but because it has been overshadowed by responses to the impact of Islam, what Said refers to as the "attack ... on the third world for its religious fanaticism" (*Orientalism* 320).

In short, it can be argued that for Naipaul, conversion, and his particular interest in the transition from the old faiths to the new, is also a means for interpreting his own experience of the anxiety of transitions from colonisation, decolonisation and neo-colonisation: "[it] is still going on ... the extra drama [in the] background, like a cultural big bang, the steady grinding down of the old world" (*Beyond Belief* 3). I return to this idea in the concluding sections of the article. The next section explores further those transitions between outsider/insider to insider/outsider perspectives on Islam and its relationship with modernity in order to argue that the representation of modernity as offered by political or sociological scholars of Islam, such as Ahmed, echoes that offered by Naipaul. This suggests that the negative criticism by literary scholars of Naipaul's representation of Islam is, if not misplaced, based on a decontextualised and ahistorical reading of Islamic societies in transition.

Transitions to Faith

Since this article is concerned with faith, it is useful to begin very briefly with Naipaul's sense of his faith—its purpose and characteristics. "In Trinidad, with its many races, my Hinduism was really an attachment to my family, an attachment to my own difference" (*Among the Believers* 15). Critically then, faith, like culture and its markers, is a means of location and relationship to the land and its communities but, in this instance, faith is an almost absent stain, a barely discernible watermark and its showing is as much the evidence of a Trinidadian history, as it is the abandonment of this for the possibilities offered by Western metropolitan culture. However, there is another side to the representation of faith: faith which is living, and which motivates action. Naipaul presents such faith in a later travel book as something which appears to defy reason:

> It had been hard for me, emerging from the soft lake world of ... waterways and lotus, to believe what I had so suddenly come upon: bloodied bodies, blood soaked clothes, chains, whips tipped with knives and razor blades, the exalted, the deficient faces of the celebrants, and their almost arrogant demeanour.... I hadn't understood the religious-historical charge of the occasion, the underlying grief it sought to express. (*India: A Million Mutinies Now* 507)

Naipaul perceives India as a place of faiths in conflict:

> [T]he liberation of sprit that has come to India could not come as release alone. In India, with its layer below layer of distress and cruelty,

> it had come as disturbance. It had come as rage and revolt. India was now a country of a million little mutinies ... supported by twenty kinds of group excess, sectarian excess, religious excess, regional excess ... people were always ready in India to let religion carry the burden of their pain. (*India: A Million Mutinies Now* 517–518)

Already in 1990, the idea that faith, or the absence of faith, can motivate rage is evident in the literary and political scholarship of the time. And, not unsurprisingly, in the relationship between faith and the faithful (especially the converted peoples in the travel texts), there is also this transmission of rage; rage rather than passion which is how the political commentator Ahmed describes the resurgence of Muslim protest in the 1990s (95). For Naipaul, there is a similar perspective, though its range is extended to cover both the past and the present:

> A convert's world view alters. His holy places are in Arab lands; his sacred language is Arabic. His idea of history alters. He rejects his own; he becomes ... a part of Arab history. The disturbance for societies is immense, and even after a thousand years can remain unresolved; the turning away has to be done again and again. People develop fantasies about who and what they are; and in the Islam of converted countries there is an element of neurosis and nihilism. These countries can easily be set to boil. (*Beyond Belief* 1)

The attitude displayed by Naipaul to Muslims and their reactions to the West is not without compassion, but also verges on disdain as shown in this extract from *Among the Believers*. Faith was a:

> … turning away from the life of intellect and endeavour [Feri and the doctor] have come together in an Iranian death pact. In the emotions of their Shia religion, so particular to them, they will rediscover their self-esteem.... They will no longer have to be last.… Other people in spiritually barren lands [the West particularly] will continue to produce the equipment.… That expectation—of others continuing to create, of the alien, necessary civilisation going on—is implicit in the act of renunciation, and is its great flaw. (19)

The location of the West as present, but unknowable, and intellectually inaccessible is rendered for the reader in the binary associated with the labour and technology to produce innovation, and the relative lack of technological sophistication required to use it.

Some eighteen years after *Among the Believers*, Naipaul returns to the theme of conversion and its implications in *Beyond Belief* and problematises the relationship between the convert, faith, gender and race.

In a passage in which he describes an Indonesian convert's efforts to convert an American man (who himself is about to wed an Indonesian woman), the following quotation is illuminating, since faith is shown to have its limits when offset against other essentialising elements of identity, for example, race or gender. The convert Imaduddin says: "'It's amazing how you've changed. You don't look like an American. You already look like an Indonesian.' The Oklahoman, straightening a sock over a foot, and looking down, said in a voice that didn't carry far, 'Still white'" (*Beyond Belief* 49).

If faith is shown to have an intensely private and radicalising dimension in terms of behaviour and thought for the convert, it is equally meaningful for political movements of the period to be able to harness its passions (or rages), as described in the paragraphs to follow, in which the relationship between faith and the state in transition from a colonial dispensation to modern nation state is explored. This is important because literary scholars have focused on Naipaul's view of modern postcolonial states as half-baked and or inadequate, but failed to note that colonialism and Western intervention are the primary causes of endemic instability.

Faith and the State

Akbar Ahmed suggests that after years of despotic rule, corruption and nepotism, supported in many instances by Western imperial or multinational capitalist companies, modernity had come to be identified by Muslim thinkers as un-Islamic (33). "Muslims … asked if God had abandoned them. Other Muslims turned the question round: had they abandoned God? The answer pointed in the direction of Islam" and, therein, lay Islamic resurgence and a rejection of the West (33). Ahmed argues further that "[p]ostmodernism, with its emphasis on globalisation, equality and tolerance" presents a dilemma to Islam precisely because it demands the acknowledgement that Muslims live in an interconnected world in which diversity is both accepted and rejected (191). Such dilemmas lie on the surface in the interviews conducted by Naipaul (the Oklahoman referred to earlier, for example).

Revolution in Islamic states has come to be associated with economic, social and religious reform. Ali Mazrui notes that economically, there has been a need to break the monopoly held by Western (colonial) power and multinational corporations on the wealth of Islamic nation states. In *Beyond Belief*, Naipaul interviews an Iranian who lived through the 1979 Revolution. Mehrad "remembered that at the beginning of the revolution the cry was the communist one of 'Nun,

Kar, Azadi', 'Bread, Work, Freedom'. Within a year it had changed to 'Bread, Work, and an Islamic Republic'" (147). But, having described the quick transition from a concern with social issues to a concern with religious observance, Naipaul suggests that the role of faith as political movement or as ascendant over the secular state is damaging and corrupt: "We went to the blood fountain. It used to be famous… and it was intended to stimulate ideas of blood and sacrifice and redemption. The fountain didn't play now…. There had been too much blood" (*Beyond Belief* 152). Even Muslim historians of Islamic states, such as Zakariyya, acknowledge that far from being concerned with social issues plaguing such countries, the new religious "movements … focused on superficial issues … the beard, the veil … issues of sexuality and sexual purity…. [T]he mass appeal of the Islamist movements … is a clear expression of the totality of defeat [after 1967 by Israel]" (125). Of critical significance though, faith became a vehicle for defiance in the absence of other viable political alternatives not associated with the West.

In terms not dissimilar to Zakariyya's, Naipaul depicts the association between faith and the state in *Among the Believers* as follows: "[A]fter the centuries of despotism, they really believed [in Pakistan] ... that the state was something apart, something that looked after itself and was ever restored. And even while with their faith they were pulling it all down—hotel, city, state—they were waiting for it to start up again, to be as it was before" (37).

Such ideas have also been expressed by postcolonial and other commentators. For example, Michael Hardt and Antonio Negri suggest that while the nation appeared in the early twentieth century to be the necessary vehicle for political modernisation, it has become "the poisoned gift of national liberation" (132–134). Participation in a global order has created internal tensions for new nation states, as Mahmood Mamdani points out in his analysis of the despotic power of postcolonial African states, suggesting that previous forms of despotism made for difficult conditions in the transition to democracy (26).

Waines, an American and non-Muslim historian of Islamic theocratic societies, characterises Muslim society as one in which Islamic revolutions focused on a return to the faith, and an ever-deeper understanding of its centrality in daily life (215). In contrast, in the West, innovation is associated not with mastery of religious learning, but rather of technological and societal organisation, often accompanied by spiritual loss. The fundamentalists believe that renewal would be forthcoming from the Shari'ah. As I argued earlier in relation to the less prejudicial Western associations with the East, Waines also points out that until the 1870s, Muslim attitudes towards the West were generally positive and characterised by curiosity rather than hostility, and that borrowing technologically from the West was permissible within the religio-spiritual superiority of Islam (216).

Waines suggests that the withdrawal of imperial power from the Middle East in the nineteenth century and the rise of the Zionist movement sowed the seeds of discontent with the West. Furthermore, Western technological advantage came to be associated with a new crusading project, a belief not dispelled by missionary activities in the colonies (Waines 238). This contextualisation explains the desire to establish a religious purity in the aftermath of Western colonisation, a phenomenon problematised by Naipaul:

> Mr Jaffrey had had a dream of the *jame towidi*, the society of believers. This was a dream of re-creating things as they had been in the earliest days of Islam … and the spiritual and the secular were one. It was like a dream of an ancient city state, and in the modern world it was a dangerous fantasy.… [It was] in this awareness of his own piety, which was like pride, his constant rejection of the impure, that the tyranny of the religious state began.... (*Beyond Belief* 154–155)

In *Beyond Belief*, Naipaul notes that control in Iran had become ever more stringent and led to social absurdities: "The revolution had bred strange children," he writes with reference to a new generation of Iranians, sexually defiant and more strangely radical (245). Naipaul, while in Iran, learns that that the young Iranian Nazis torment the Jews of Tehran. In Pakistan, "[t]he state withered. But faith didn't.... [T]he state failed ... because men had failed the faith. A purer and purer faith began to be called for. Extraordinary claims began to be made for Pakistan: it was founded as the land of the pure; it was to be the first truly Islamic state...." (*Among the Believers* 87). Of Iran, Naipaul notes that Ayatollah Khalkhalli said, "The mullahs are going to rule now. We are going to have ten thousand years of the Islamic Republic" (*Beyond Belief* 214).

The society of believers is characterised by submission to obedience, extortion of property or wealth by petty criminals legitimised by the theocratic state because of their faith; policing of demeanour, dress, aspect: in effect reducing the dignity of the person to a function of the state, to be defined, and changed at will. As much is described in relation to Pakistan, which Naipaul suggests, "could be contemplated in the same way ... economically stagnant, despotically ruled … [its] people close to hysteria ... cherished as a pioneer of the Islamic revival. Politics is combined with religion in Islam" (*Beyond Belief* 82).

The state becomes self-devouring: "certain fantasies had taken hold … the Powers had decided to foist Khomeini on the Iranian people…. The establishing of an Islamic state … was an anti-Islamic plot by the Powers, to teach Muslims a lesson" (*Beyond Belief* 241).

For the author-narrator, the fusion of faith with the state offers few possibilities for even mild expressions of difference, let alone dissent:

> [S]uch a state could always be manipulated, easy to undermine, full of simple roguery. The mullahs would always hold the ring, would limit inquiry. All history of the ancient land would cease to matter … the history of Pakistan would become only an aspect of the history of Islam…. It is a dreadful mangling of history … too much has to be ignored or angled; there is too much fantasy. (*Beyond Belief* 329)

One has to question why it is that political or social alternatives seemed rare. Zakariyya speaks of secularism as having a special meaning in Islam: for Muslims active in society in the 1970s, secularism meant the pursuit of technology and progress rather than the separation of church and state as it had meant for centuries in the West. Thus, "Arab secularists advocated technological and scientific progress while resolving to eject European colonialism" (16). After independence, the oil and mineral wealth of the East became evident, and Zakariyya suggests that in this, the nationalists and leftists vied for power, but were eclipsed by what he terms the "Islamists" who were focused on the establishment of the theocratic state (for example, Iran and Sudan, who introduced the Shari'ah), with its regulation of the curriculum, suppression of women's rights, policing of dress, behaviour and sexuality, and its state nationalisation of institutions of finance, the economy and learning.

According to Naipaul, the "faith could not acknowledge secular associations or divisions" (*Among the Believers* 102). Thus, the vacuum created by decolonisation also created the conditions necessary for religious and political absolutism. What is evident in the anxieties expressed by his interviewees is Naipaul's own anxiety about the fate of postcolonial peoples caught up in or not conforming to the new regimes, the origins of which, whilst apparently internal to the "religion", find their sources beyond the nascent postcolonial state.

Though the scholarship describes social and political developments in ways which echo the interviewee's accounts, what remains noticeable in Naipaul's work is the absence of any deviation from a narrative of Islamic-pessimism—a matter for which he has been severely critiqued (Al-Quaderi and Habibullah 23). The section to follow explores this perspective further in relation to those instances where faith does offer some possibilities other than dissolution or corruption; I argue against the general literary critical reception of Naipaul, and suggest that the anxiety attendant on the postcolonial condition is experienced both by the author and the interviewee.

Faith and Intellectual Work

Is faith the antithesis of intellectual enquiry? The author-narrator visits two newspapers shortly after the Iranian Revolution; both are anxious places: "Remember that director. Remember that busy office.... Six months later when I went back to Tehran, that office was desolate" (*Among the Believers* 34). The destruction of the press in Iran is well-documented as is the heightening of censorship in every form (already a feature of the Shah's government) (Mazrui 24). Universities, schools, curricula and even student political activity all came to be regulated. In his travels, Naipaul sought to ascertain where centres of learning continued to thrive.

Qum, the city renowned for learning in post-revolutionary Iran, offers an opportunity to recall the scholarly affinities between the East and the West, acknowledging that eminent Muslim scholars and philosophers once influenced every aspect of learning in the West. For example:

> On the pavement outside the Turkish Embassy turbaned medicine men sat with their display of powders and roots ... I had seen other[s] in Tehran and had thought of them as Iranian equivalents of the homeopathic medicine men of India. But the names these Iranians were invoking as medical authorities—as Beshad told me, after listening to their sales talk to a peasant group—were Avicenna, Galen, and Hippocrat. Avicenna ... it had never occurred to me that he was a Persian.... [A] thousand years before ... Muslim civilisation was the central civilisation of the West. (*Among the Believers* 12)

Of the learning produced in the aftermath of decolonisation and the birth of the radical Islamic state, the narrator finds evidence in a contemporary publication: "One of the English-language magazines I bought was published from the holy city of Qum. It was *The Message of Peace*, and, as its title warned, it was full of rage" (34). Absolute faith and devotion became both a vehicle for political rage against Western exploitation, as well as for spiritual desire for a new beginning and new identity.

As regards learning and the marginalised groups (for example, women), Naipaul records when visiting oil-rich Indonesia, Paydar's mother as saying, "You will never gain anything from following these religious people. We have known them. These are the people who didn't let me learn reading and writing" (194). For women and other marginalised groups, the new Islamic state seems to offer little. The only people who appear to have benefitted in the Islamic Republic are the clerics and men in general, a matter confirmed by Ahmed.

Intellectual work, where it can be found, is shown to be narrow and redundant. For example, Naipaul refers to the "antique learning" of Avicenna and Farrabi, which remains key to the philosophy curriculum in Qum (*Among the Believers* 221). Later, on a visit to a theological school, he finds a historian who is writing a history of World Philosophy, convinced of the ubiquity of Zionism (*Among the Believers* 233). This description recalls Said's (*Orientalism* 270) observation concerning scholarship developed in a vacuum where it cannot "critically ... examine the assumptions and principles on which ... [intellectual] work depended" (275).

If intellectual work arising in the context of the new Islamic state is thwarted because of faith, then the likelihood of faith being a binding, progressive and unifying force for Muslims is diminished. What Naipaul describes is the ossification of a curriculum increasingly at odds not only with secular Islamic impulses, but also the non-Islamic world. For example, in *Beyond Belief* Naipaul says of Imaduddin's ability to reconcile Western technological advances with Islam: "Always out there, the United States, an unacknowledged part of the world picture of every kind of modern revolutionary: the country of law and rest, and which at the end of the day a man who proclaimed himself to be on the other side—in politics, culture, or religion—could make peace and on whose goodwill he could throw himself" (*Beyond Belief* 17). Whilst Naipaul is aware of the influence of political change on the lives of those whom he interviews, the perspectives offered are tragic rather than inflammatory, pathetic rather than preoccupied with rage.

Faith and Living

Faith and the role it plays in the travelogues is ambiguous but I believe that the literary critical reception of the travelogues has undermined that complexity. Naipaul provides four different perspectives as regards faith, living and modernity. He notes that even in the oil rich secular states of the East, faith and superstition appear to sit in uneasy proximity: "Kamran, in spite of his cynicism, about things generally, had begun to grumble that in the morning ... he hadn't put anything in an alms box.... That was why he had had trouble with the ignition … the prayers [he] offered were for a safe run back" (*Beyond Belief* 234). In Malaysia, Nasar, the former Muslim youth group leader turned successful businessman, says: "What they had been looking to religion to do for them in 1979, simple power, simple authority, had done for them later" (*Beyond Belief* 391).

In Kuala Lumpur, while noting the new wealth of the state, Naipaul notes also the fate of the immigrant Chinese, who "without protection" had been absorbed into Malay society, either as converts to Islam or Christianity: Philip was now "liberated from those kitchen gods" (*Beyond Belief* 395). For Nadezha, a Westernised woman married to a Malaysian with a rural family, "There were no cultural interests in the *kampong* (village). Life was shallow. There was only religion" (*Beyond Belief* 403). Both husband and wife abandon religion and get divorced.

And finally, there is Rashid, a Christian Malay, descended from an Indo–Chinese Taoist–Buddhist traditional healer, whose conversion to Islam had meant purpose and delivery: "Without Islam … his life would have been without point" (*Beyond Belief* 415). However, Rashid still appreciates the old customs; he was "pleased … that other members of the family would be carrying on [his mother's] worship of her Malay Datuk spirit in her kitchen, and doing the rituals on the family altar" (*Beyond Belief* 419). In all four perspectives, faith sits in uneasy proximity to the possibilities offered by wealth and technological advances, offering both protection and a measure of authenticity to its adherents.

The traces of old religions and observance appear difficult to erase completely even within the context of the wealth of the new state. Naipaul notes that "[i]n Jakarta, the new wealth could at times feel oppressive … new money, new luck made every weekend festive; and on Sunday mornings in the Borobudur Hotel, the rich folk, Chinese and others, from the Bethany Successful Families, one of the few American Evangelical faiths, … sang hymns, clapped hands … praying for that luck to last" (*Beyond Belief* 419).

And, as if almost by accident, there is in Rashid's account, a description of faith that appears to be sincere in its purpose, and which is rendered compassionately by Naipaul (Feder 136). Rashid tells the narrator that his mother's love of community and her Islamic faith were what enabled his father to live in dignity in their home throughout the twenty-three years of his illness. "Without her he would have been thrown into the madhouse and he wouldn't have lasted two years. As it was, he lived in his two worlds for twenty-three years" (*Beyond Belief* 437). Faith to live by, faith enabling compassion for the suffering of others and faith ensuring a humble and dignified approach to life and death are described almost tangentially. Why should this be so? Does Naipaul find in the turmoil of the Middle and Far East an expression of his own rage against the violence associated with imperialisms of different forms, what Feder describes as Naipaul's "truth": "Islam, almost from the start, had been an imperialism as well as a religion?" (Feder 11).

The oblique references to the possibilities offered by faith when not contorted by power, or reactionary politics, or defiance against an externalised and alien "West" are enabling and inspire a depth of feeling and compassion in the author and indeed in the interviewees. Caught-up in the aftermath of dramatic and violent change, Naipaul is clearly deeply affected by the context and the people whom he meets. Evidence of his perceptions can also be seen as equally responsive (and sometimes equally reactionary) to these circumstances. It is possible, as a result of this rereading of Naipaul, to argue that Islam becomes the vehicle for the narrator's rage against imperialism and that the religion cannot patently address the many layers of distress experienced by converts desperate to remain connected to ideas of authenticity, place, purpose and value. Religion then becomes an inadequate vehicle for forgetting the violence of colonialism and the destruction of holy places associated with conversion and religious conflict (Marangoly-George 197).

Reflections

I began by speculating on the strategies deployed by the narrator in terms of the selection of persons to be interviewed, the erasure of questions posed by the narrator, the ambiguity of the narrator as insider-outsider and postcolonial subject, and the ways in which these positions and strategies construct a perspective on faith in Islamic societies in transition. What emerges in the texts discussed is that far from being oblique, the subject-position taken by the author-narrator is at once intrusive and obscured, authoritative and fragmented. Though not the overt subject of the four travel texts, it is clear that the texts form a dialogue between Islam and the "West" as rendered by the author-narrator.

Far from consenting or even being party to perspectives articulated by the interviewees, the narrator's manipulation of perspective serves a twin purpose: first, the creation of an authorial as well as political dialectic in which the contrast between the author-narrator's and interviewee's perspective places a distance between reader, author-narrator and interviewee. Second, by allowing for a reading of Naipaul's travelogues to be contrasted with selected contemporary commentary (social, political and historical), I have shown that the discourse crafted by Naipaul is by no means associated with anti-Islamic, or pathological perspectives adopted by the West in relation to the East (a point argued by Said and other postcolonial scholars).

Naipaul is not simply a Western mimic of stereotype or prejudice. Ghazoul contends that Said finds himself between "two civilizational modes … [partaking] of American and Arab culture", and that this positioning, similar to that which applies to Naipaul, is not necessarily voluntary or complacent (158). Naipaul argues that the rage experienced in those Islamic societies he visited is at once the rage at loss of civilisation, and at the erasure of more authentic and local histories in favour of a seeming vacuity associated with universal religion in which what is local needs to be replaced. This is a convert's choice (and also unforeseen fate) when conversion occurs in the context of wider social and political development in which alternative forms of identity are not recoverable from the past, and not offered by the possibilities suggested in the present.

To some extent, it is ironic that Naipaul draws comparisons between colonialism and an Islam in which he sees faith as filled with distortions and simplifications. The question to be asked in the context of the travelogues is whether the conversion is enabling? The answer to this is "yes/no" and it is the tensions between the "yes/no" that Naipaul explores to demonstrate that the distortions of reality, identity, sexuality and gender offered power to some and alienation to others. What is significant in this rereading of Naipaul against his critics and in light of the sociopolitical commentary of scholars outside of postcolonial studies is the extent to which such a rereading reveals that the distortion of the narrative reflects as much the author-narrator's rage at the violence and loss, as well as his attempts to refuse to grant it importance.

Works cited

Ahmed, Akbar. S. *Postmodernism and Islam: Predicament and Promise*. (rev edition). Routledge, 2004.

Al-Quaderi, Golam Gaus, and Mohammed Habibullah. "Travels in Absurdity: Islam and V. S. Naipaul." *Journal of Postcolonial Cultures and Societies*, vol. 3, issue 1, 2012, pp. 22–37.

Anjum, Z. "A Convert's Complaint: Analyzing Naipaul's Views on Islam." 26 Feb. 2002, http://www.chowk.com/articles/5246. Accessed 23 July 2010.

Bhabha, Homi. *The Location of Culture*. Routledge, 1994.

Boyd, William. "V. S. Naipaul: A Misanthrope Abroad." *The Times Literary Supplement*, 6 Oct. 2010.

Coovadia, Imran. *Authority and Authorship in V.S. Naipaul.* Palgrave, 2009.

Donadio, R. 2005. "The Irascible Prophet: VS Naipaul at Home." *The New York Times.* 7 Aug. 2005.

Feder, Lillian. *Naipaul's Truth: The Making of a Writer*. Rowman and Littlefield, 2001.

Ghazoul, Ferial. J. "The Resonance of the Arab-Islamic Heritage in the Work of Edward Said." *Edward Said: A Critical Reader* edited by Michael Sprinker. pp. 157–172.

Gibbons, Fiachra. "VS Naipaul launches attack on Islam." *The Guardian*, 4 October 2001, http://www.guardian.co.uk/world/2001/ oct/04/afghanistan. terrorism9. Accessed 23 July 2010.

GoGwilt, Christopher. *The Invention of the West: Joseph Conrad and the Double Mapping of Europe and Empire.* Stanford University Press, 1995.

Hardt, Michael and Negri, Antonio. *Empire*. Harvard University Press, 2001.

Marangoly-George, Rosemary. *The Politics of Home: Postcolonial Relocations and Twentieth-century Fiction*. Cambridge University Press, 1996.

Mazrui, Ali A. *Islam: Between Globalisation and Counter-Terrorism.* James Currey Press, 2006.

Mamdani, Mahmood. *Citizen and Subject.* Princeton University Press, 1996.

Naipaul, V. S. *An Area of Darkness.* Penguin Books, 1964.

———. *A Bend in the River.* Penguin Books, 1979.

———. *Among the Believers*. Penguin Books, 1981.

———. *India: A Million Mutinies Now*. Minerva, 1990.

———. *Beyond Belief.* Little, Brown and Company, 1998.

Rush, Norman. "Naipaul's Mysterious Africa." *The New York Review of Books*, 11 November 2010.

Said, Edward. *The World, the Text, and the Critic.* Vintage Press, 1991.

———. *Orientalism.* Penguin Books, 1991.

———. *Culture and Imperialism.* Vintage, 1994.

Sprinker, Michael, editor. *Edward Said: A Critical Reader.* Blackwell Press, 1993.

Spivak, Gayatri C. "Can the Subaltern Speak?" *Marxism and the Interpretation of Culture*, edited by Cary Nelson and Lawrence Grossberg, University of Illinois Press, 1988, pp. 271–313.

Theroux, Paul. *Sir Vidia's Shadow: A Friendship across Five Continents.* Mariner Books, 1998.

Waines, David. *An Introduction to Islam.* Cambridge University Press, 2003.

Zakariyya, Fouad. *Myth and Reality in the Contemporary Islamist Movement.* Translated by Ibrahim M. Abu-Rabi, Pluto Press, 2005.

ABOUT THE EDITOR AND CONTRIBUTORS

Editor

J. Vijay Maharaj is a lecturer in the Department of Literary, Cultural and Communication Studies at the University of the West Indies, St Augustine. In the course of filling this role over more than two decades, she has developed deep expertise in one field—literacy—which includes the sub-categories of cultural and technological literacy but, more importantly, it encompasses the traditional literacies of reading, writing, speaking and listening. Her publications and presentations try to exemplify this.

Contributors

Gollamudi Radha Krishna Murty is currently working for IUP Publications, Hyderabad, India, as Managing Editor. Earlier, he worked at Andhra Pradesh Agricultural University for five years as entomology research assistant and later as an officer with the Bank of India for twenty-six years. He has published several papers in science, banking, management, insurance, literature and education journals, besides authoring seven books: *Soft Skills for Success*; *Currency Market Derivatives; Reflections on Free Market: Economy, Capital Markets; Banking, Forex Markets and Governance; HRM in Knowledge Economy; Banking and the Law; Leadership: The Shakespearean Way* and *Epic Leadership: Timeless Lessons from the Valmiki Ramayana.* He has co-edited the book *Select Issues in Macroeconomics: A Quantitative Approach* with two others.

Roxana Elena Donçu graduated from the University of Bucharest with a degree in English and Russian studies. She completed her PhD in cultural and literary studies from the same university, with a thesis entitled *Transformers and Mimic Men: An Analysis of Subjectivity in the Postcolonial Fiction of V. S. Naipaul and Salman Rushdie*. She is currently a lecturer in the Department of Modern Languages at the "Carol Davila" University of Medicine and Pharmacy in Bucharest. Her research interests cover areas like postcolonial and post-communist studies, world literature and medical humanities. She is a member of the international research group on literary modeling at the University of Münster, where she has recently been invited to teach at the graduate school on British, American and Postcolonial Studies.

Bhoendradatt Tewarie began lecturing at the University of the West Indies in 1977 in the Department of Language and Linguistics. In 1992, he became Executive Director of the Institute of Business at University of West Indies. He remained in this position until 2001 when he became Pro Vice-Chancellor and campus Principal of St Augustine. Outside of academia, Dr Tewarie has had a varied career. He was a secondary school teacher and cabinet minister. He has served on a number of government policy-making committees—chairing these committees on a few occasions. He has also served as a director in a number of private and public organisations.

Kenneth Ramchand is Professor Emeritus of West Indian Literature, the University of the West Indies and Professor Emeritus of English, Colgate University, New York. He has also been Senior Fulbright Scholar affiliated to Yale University and the University of Tulsa, Oklahoma, Visiting Professor at Indiana University and Fellow of the Guggenheim Foundation. He also served as President of the University of Trinidad and Tobago where, as Associate Provost, he established that university's Academy for Arts, Letters, Culture and Public Affairs. Born in 1939, Kenneth Ramchand was educated at Naparima College, San Fernando, and the University of Edinburgh, where he began his career as a lecturer in English in 1964. He authored the pioneering work *The West Indian Novel and its Background*, and numerous other publications. He was a literary-cultural columnist in *The Trinidad Guardian* and served for more than ten years as an independent senator in the Government of Trinidad and Tobago. In 1996, Ramchand was awarded a Trinidad and Tobago Chaconia Medal Gold for his work in literature, education and culture. In 2012, Ramchand was honoured with a NALIS Lifetime Literary Achievement Award.

Mariacristina Petillo is a lecturer at the University of Bari Aldo Moro where she teaches English Language and Translation. Her current research interests include audio-visual translation, the relationship between music and poetry and opera surtitling, topics on which she has written extensively (*La traduzione audiovisiva nel terzo millennio*, 2012; *Reflecting on Audiovisual Translation in the Third Millennium: Perspectives and Approaches to a Complex Art*, 2014). She has also dealt with literary translation and postcolonial translation, with particular reference to V. S. Naipaul and Andrea Levy ("Problemi traduttivi in Miguel Street di V. S. Naipaul", 2008; "Dai margini dell'Impero al cuore della Madrepatria: Small Island di Andrea Levy", 2009 and "'You see the sort of thing woman is': Riflessioni di gender sulla traduzione italiana di Miguel Street", 2010).

Paula Morgan is Professor at the University of the West Indies, St Augustine. Her inaugural professorial lecture was titled "Healing the Hurts of my People Slightly: Discourses of Societal Violence and Trauma", and is a summation of the work she has done over a long career in academia. Her recent publications include: *The Terror and the Time: Banal Violence and Trauma in Caribbean Discourse* (2014) and *Writing Rage: Unmasking Violence in Caribbean Discourse* (2008), with Valerie Youssef. Her edited collections include: *The Arc Memory in the Aftermath of Trauma* (2019); *Reassembling the Fragments: Voice and Identity in Caribbean Discourse* (2013), co-edited with Valerie Youssef; *The Culture of Violence: A Trinidad and Tobago Case Study*, co-edited with Valerie Youssef; *In a Fine Castle: Childhood in Caribbean Imagi/Nations* (2010), an online edited collection with a focus on the impact of violence on children, published in *Tout Moun: Caribbean Journal of Cultural Studies.*

Weiwei Xu is Associate Professor at the College of International Studies, Southwest University, China. She received her BA in English from Southwest China Normal University in 2005. She earned her MA in English from Newcastle University in 2006 and her PhD in English from Macquarie University in 2013. She has more than twelve years of teaching experience, and her research interests include cultural studies and postcolonial literature. Dr Xu has produced over ten peer-reviewed journal papers and undertaken four research projects and grants.

Yi-Ping Ong is the author of *The Art of Being: Poetics of the Novel and Existentialist Philosophy* (2018). Her research explores questions at the intersection of literature and philosophy, with a focus on self-knowledge, ethics, *bildung* and old age. She is Assistant Professor of Comparative Thought and Literature at Johns Hopkins University and co-editor of the Comparative Literature issue of *Modern Language Notes.*

Gordon Rohlehr is Professor Emeritus at the University of the West Indies, St Augustine. He was born in Guyana in 1942, graduated in 1964 from the University College of the West Indies, Jamaica, with a first-class Honours degree in English Literature, after which he wrote a doctoral dissertation titled *Alienation and Commitment in the Works of Joseph Conrad* at Birmingham University, England.

He has been Visiting Professor at Harvard, Johns Hopkins, Tulane, Austin State and York University, as well as at the Miami University Writers' Workshop and at Dartmouth College, New Hampshire. His publications include: *Pathfinder: Black Awakening in the* Arrivants *of Edward Kamau Brathwaite; Calypso and Society in Pre-Independence Trinidad; My Strangled City and Other Essays; The Shape of That Hurt and Other Essays; A Scuffling of Islands: Essays on Calypso; Voiceprint: An Anthology of Oral and Related Poetry from the Caribbean* and *Transgression, Transition, Transformation: Essays in Caribbean Culture.* His most recent work is a collection of essays published by Peepal Tree—*Perfected Fables Now: A Bookman Signs off on Seven Decades.*

Mgr. Zuzana Kršková is Assistant Professor at the Department of English Language and Literature, Faculty of Education, Masaryk University in Brno, the Czech Republic. She graduated from Masaryk University with a degree in English Language and Literature and gained her PhD in Literatures in English. She specialises in postcolonial literature and her current research interests focus on West Indian literature. Part of her dissertation research was conducted during her stay at the University of Bristol. She has presented research at several international conferences and is a member of the Cultural Difference and Social Solidarity Network. She has published articles in the literary journal *Proudy*—in the volume Language, Literature and Culture in a Changing Transatlantic World II. She has also published in *Anglica Wratislaviensia* and in *Ostrava Journal of English Philology.* A book chapter entitled "The Social Function of Postcolonial Literary Theories" was published in the volume *Cultural Difference and Social Solidarity: Solidarities and Social Function* edited by Scott H. Boyd and Mary Ann Walter in 2014. Apart from her research in postcolonial studies with emphasis on the work of Wilson Harris, her current courses focus on the art of critical reading, British literature, presentation skills and rhetoric.

Aaron Eastley is Associate Professor of Literatures in English at Brigham Young University in Utah, USA. He works in the areas of transnational literatures in English, British Modernism, planetary modernisms and diaspora and globalisation studies. Recent publications have appeared in *ARIEL, Conradiana, Research in African Literatures* and *Caribbean Quarterly.* He is currently collaborating with Kenneth Ramchand and Brinsley Samaroo on a collection of the journalism and short fiction of Seepersad Naipaul and writing a biography of Welsh poet Leslie Norris.

John Thieme is Senior Fellow at the University of East Anglia. He previously held chairs at the University of Hull and London South Bank University and has also taught at the Universities of Guyana and North London. His books include *The Web of Tradition: Uses of Allusion in V. S. Naipaul's Fiction*; *Postcolonial Con-Texts: Writing Back to the Canon*; *Postcolonial Literary Geographies: Out of Place*; *The Arnold Anthology of Post-Colonial Literatures in English*; *Paco's Atlas and Other Poems* and studies of V. S. Naipaul, Derek Walcott and R. K. Narayan. He was the editor of *The Journal of Commonwealth Literature* from 1992 to 2011 and is the general editor of the Manchester University Press Contemporary World Writers Series.

Mahesh Hapugoda is Senior Lecturer in English at the Department of Languages, Sabaragamuwa University of Sri Lanka. With twenty years of experience in the field of tertiary education, Dr Hapugoda has authored several books and has published extensively. His research interests include reading politics, philosophy and literature, and writing reviews on contemporary issues and matters of political interest. Dr Hapugoda is also a modern music and film critic.

Sanjay Krishnan is Associate Professor of English at Boston University. He is the author of a recent critical study on V. S. Naipaul, *V. S. Naipaul's Journeys: From Periphery to Center* (2020). He has also written *Reading the Global: Troubling Perspectives of Britain's Empire in Asia* (2007). He recently contributed a chapter on Naipaul to the *Wiley-Blackwell Companion to World Literature* (2020) (edited by Ken Seigneurie et al.). His essays on Naipaul and related topics have appeared in such journals as *Representations*; *NOVEL: A Forum on Fiction*; *Modern Fiction Studies*; *New Literary History*; *Modern Language Quarterly*; *boundary 2*; and *Victorian Studies*.

Robert J. Balfour is Professor and Deputy Vice Chancellor Teaching-Learning at North-West University where he was also Dean of Education Sciences. He is Honorary Professor of Education at the University of KwaZulu-Natal. He was formerly Registrar at St Augustine College of South Africa, has held fellowships at the Institute of Commonwealth Studies and Clare Hall (Cambridge), and taught Creative Writing, Language Education and Literature whilst at Natal, UKZN, St Augustine and NWU respectively. He holds degrees from the University of Rhodes, Natal and Cambridge respectively, and is a published poet, writer of short fiction and an exhibited painter.

INDEX

H

I

J

K

L

M